## STATE RESPONSIBILITY IN THE INTERNATIONAL LEGAL ORDER

State responsibility in international law is considered one of the cornerstones of the field. For a long time it remained the exclusive responsibility system due to the primacy of states as subjects of international law. Its unique position has nonetheless been challenged by several developments both within and outside the international legal order, such as the rise of alternative responsibility ideas and practices, as well as globalization and its consequences.

This book adopts a critical and holistic approach to the law of state responsibility and analyzes the functionality of the general rules of state responsibility in a changed international landscape characterized by the fragmentation of responsibility. It is argued that state responsibility is not equally relevant across the broad spectrum of international obligations, and that alternative constructions of responsibility, namely international criminal law and international liability, have increased in standing.

Dr Katja Creutz is a Senior Research Fellow at the Finnish Institute of International Affairs and an Affiliated Research Fellow at the Erik Castrén Institute of International Law and Human Rights at the Faculty of Law, University of Helsinki. She is a former Executive Editor of the Finnish Yearbook of International Law.

# State Responsibility in the International Legal Order

A CRITICAL APPRAISAL

**KATJA CREUTZ**
Finnish Institute of International Affairs

CAMBRIDGE
UNIVERSITY PRESS

**CAMBRIDGE**
**UNIVERSITY PRESS**

University Printing House, Cambridge CB2 8BS, United Kingdom

One Liberty Plaza, 20th Floor, New York, NY 10006, USA

477 Williamstown Road, Port Melbourne, VIC 3207, Australia

314–321, 3rd Floor, Plot 3, Splendor Forum, Jasola District Centre, New Delhi – 110025, India

79 Anson Road, #06-04/06, Singapore 079906

Cambridge University Press is part of the University of Cambridge.

It furthers the University's mission by disseminating knowledge in the pursuit of education, learning, and research at the highest international levels of excellence.

www.cambridge.org
Information on this title: www.cambridge.org/9781108494298
DOI: 10.1017/9781108637367



First published 2020

*A catalogue record for this publication is available from the British Library.*

*Library of Congress Cataloging-in-Publication Data*
Names: Creutz, Katja, 1973- author.
Title: State responsibility in the international legal order / Katja Creutz, Finnish Institute of International Affairs.
Description: Cambridge, United Kingdom ; New York, NY, USA : Cambridge University Press, 2020. | Based on author's thesis (doctoral - Helsingin yliopisto, 2015) issued under title: State responsibility in international law : from paradigm to periphery. | Includes bibliographical references and index.
Identifiers: LCCN 2019053306 | ISBN 9781108494298 (hardback) | ISBN 9781108736930 (ebook)
Subjects: LCSH: Government liability (International law) | Liability for human rights violations
Classification: LCC KZ4080 .C74 2020 | DDC 341.26--dc23
LC record available at https://lccn.loc.gov/2019053306

ISBN 978-1-108-49429-8 Hardback

# Contents

# Foreword

Like many international lawyers of my generation, I experienced the 1970s as the decade of the rise of international environmental law. The Stockholm Conference on the Human Environment (1972) led to the establishment of the United Nations Environment Programme (UNEP) and triggered an intensive push towards new treaties and all kinds of soft law instruments designed to combat the massive pollution of the atmosphere and the seas. Issues such as offshore mining and drilling, land-based marine pollution, and protection of shared natural resources engaged not only myself but many other international lawyers in an effort to rethink how the old rules could be applied to new problems. At the heart of the early instruments, and in the consciousness of the lawyers working with them, were Principles 21 and 22 of the Stockholm Declaration which dealt with responsibility and liability for damage caused by transfrontier pollution. According to Principle 21, 'States have, in accordance with the Charter of the United Nations and the principles of international law, the sovereign right to exploit their own resources pursuant to their own environmental and developmental policies, and the responsibility to ensure that activities within their jurisdiction or control do not cause damage to the environment of other States or of areas beyond the limits of national jurisdiction.' Under Principle 22, the participating states promised to develop appropriate systems of liability and compensation to implement that responsibility.

It was no accident that it was these two provisions that drew the attention of lawyers and that the text of Principle 21 – and the idea of responsibility for transfrontier pollution – was repeated in countless environmental instruments and declarations in the course of the subsequent years. The idea and concept of 'responsibility' lies at the heart of juristic thinking, connoting somewhat ambiguously both the duty of carrying out one's obligations ('you are responsible for keeping the environment clean') and the consequences of the breach of that obligation ('you must make good the damage you have caused'). But it is generally this second sense that has been predominant. When it was felt necessary to apply legal thinking to the protection of the human environment, international lawyers almost automatically grasped at the vocabulary of state responsibility. It was necessary to establish adequate obligations in that respect. But it was at least as important (and no doubt, many felt even more important) that those duties be accompanied by responsibility for breaches. Lawyers are famously people who are always looking to the dark side of human behaviour. They do this even when things move on correctly, as if obsessed by the prospect of a future breach – trying to imagine violations when they have not taken place. They do this by allocating blame and either seeking to punish those that they understand as 'guilty' or at least obliging them to compensate fully the damage they have caused. It is good to remember that this is not because law (or the lawyers) actually *wants* to punish. The deeper idea is that the presence of responsibility and liability would prevent the causing of damage by deterring people from engaging in the kinds of behaviour that the legislator has deemed harmful.

For lawyers, the substance of Stockholm Principles 21 and 22 contained the hard core of emerging international environmental law, the measure of its seriousness. Everyone can declare their good intentions. Such declarations provide, as the saying goes, photo opportunities for politicians and governments wishing to portray themselves as environment-friendly. They are easy to make. But taking action to avoid damage is hard and costly. The burdens of environmental measures fall differently upon different states and different human groups. It was therefore no surprise that efforts to give substance to environmental responsibility in the traditional legal way – as punishment and compensation – never really moved anywhere. After all, the principal sources of pollution emerged, as they still do, from activities that are not only lawful but often beneficial to communities where they originate. The idea that responsibility should *deter* could not therefore be meaningfully applied. The kinds of industrial or economic activities that created environmental harm could not – with few exceptions – be simply prohibited.

What about liability, then? The painful efforts to create a system of 'liability for the injurious consequences of acts not prohibited by international law' under the International Law Commission (that had its source in Stockholm Principle 22) led finally to rethinking the topic in an altogether new way as 'Principles on the Allocation of Loss in the Case of Transboundary Harm Arising Out of Hazardous Activities' (YbILC 2006, II/2). Comparing the documents from Stockholm 1972 with the ILC (Draft) declaration on 'allocation of loss' over thirty years later, one discovers that the international environmental problem is now thought of primarily in economic rather than legal terms. Perhaps this was to be expected for a project which mostly took place in a time of neoliberal ascendancy. The system of buying and selling emission permits under the Climate Change treaty (Kyoto Protocol) is the most famous example. It is useful to note, however, that economics was there from the outset. In the 1970s, the Organisation for Economic Co-operation and Development (OECD) had declared the 'polluter pays principle' was not really a principle of legal responsibility but one having to do with the sharing of the costs of measures to protect the environment and to repair the damage. It was a cost-internalization technique intended to ensure that the bill for preventing or repairing harm would fall on those who also profited from the activity causing it – an understandable intention that created the massive challenges of how to both calculate 'costs' to the environment and find the appropriate causal chains within an increasingly global network of production and consumer preferences. In such debates, the vocabularies of breach, responsibility, and compensation began to appear hopelessly crude and old-fashioned – unable to take into account the varying interests and needs of human groups across the globe. Issues of development and historical justice were concerned.

State responsibility is a blunt tool. It has been impossible to apply it in a globally uniform way. This is why in practice, state responsibility has been taken over by special – often geographically limited – regimes. These seek to identify relevant actors and economic structures involved in operations with actual or potential harmfulness and then determine how possible liability might be calculated. Oil, nuclear energy, ozone-depleting substances, and climate change have each received their specific regimes of prevention, liability, and cost-sharing. Each regime has received a responsibility system tailored to its needs. This fragmentation has diffused the larger theme of responsibility. The Draft Articles on State Responsibility prepared by the ILC in 2001 do lay out general principles with regard to breach and accountability. But its general provisions have been largely replaced by specific regimes that usually talk about various kinds of preventive measures – about scientific and technical cooperation, information exchange, and measurement. Sometimes they also include economic arrangements to help our weaker actors or to coordinate preventive or restorative measures. The themes of breach and accountability – indeed the very issue of blameworthiness – are rarely broached, and even more rarely developed into any tangible system of reactions resembling domestic responsibility. The Draft Guidelines adopted in first reading by the ILC on the protection of the atmosphere (A/CN4/L.909 [6 June 2018]) discreetly but expressly set aside questions about 'common but differentiated responsibilities' and 'the liability of states and their nationals'. The story that began in Stockholm 1972 has come to an end.

This is the development that is meticulously charted in this wonderful work by Katja Creutz, and not only in the environmental field. *State Responsibility in the International Legal Order* provides a welcome in-depth survey of the 'life and times' of one technical legal doctrine as well as provides tools for the assessment of the wider transformations of international law and the global institutional system in the past half-century. The work's subtitle – *A Critical Appraisal* – is particularly pertinent. The results of international cooperation in the past decades, especially cooperation at a global scale, have not been impressive, although the final assessment depends upon where one looks: environment, development, trade, human rights, war and peace, equality, and discrimination. The UN's sustainable development goals – Agenda 2030 – provide a mixed message. But the legal principle of 'state responsibility' has not played a visible role in any of the seventeen action areas covered by that programme nor in the formation of the many multilateral legal regimes that have arisen in the regulation of trade, environment, human rights, humanitarian law, the prevention of international crime, and so on.

In this work, Dr Creutz lays out many of the difficulties that lie in the way of operationalizing state responsibility as a regulatory instrument. Problems regarding causality and proof, identifying the actors, and finding the right threshold of breach are some of those difficulties. The connotation of blameworthiness may not be appropriate in finely tuned diplomatic contexts. The adversarial nature of responsibility and its formal, on/off quality are likewise difficult to apply at a global scale. As Dr Creutz points out, international lawyers still use the domestic analogy to think about the operation of global law. But as a regulatory context, the 'global' is quite different from the 'domestic'. Situations vary to the extent that uniform rules are in most cases impossible to establish – they will either be excessively indeterminate, and therefore without regulatory effect, or their application will seem unjust in some part of the world. One of the great merits of this work is that it takes a close look at the actual functions that state responsibility has, or could have, in the international world. Can it be employed to regulate and control the activities of states? What about its role as a device signalling shared values or uniting actors behind joint projects? These are the kinds of question that international lawyers too often fail to ask, perhaps owing to our predilection of thinking about international rules in the image of domestic ones, and assuming both are beneficial in the same way. The rise of special regimes should remind us of the much greater heterogeneity of the international world as well as of the fact that there is no single project out there but rather many ambitious actors with different and often conflicting agendas. Dr Creutz's analysis of the development of state responsibility provides an insightful orientation into understanding why global progress is so difficult to achieve and why a formal doctrine such as state responsibility may never be quite adequate in grasping the complexity of world's injustices.

Martti Koskenniemi, FBA
*Professor of International Law*
*Helsinki*

# Preface

This book represents an addition to the growing scholarship on the law of state responsibility within international law. It seeks to assess this body of law in a comprehensive and critical manner because such efforts have so far been relatively few. While the issues regulated by international law have expanded and diversified, as has the range of actors, state responsibility has remained a central institution of international law. These developments nevertheless motivate taking a fresh look at the law of state responsibility in order to ponder whether international lawyers need to adjust their thinking in this area.

My interest in state responsibility awakened in the aftermath of the abuses in the Abu Ghraib prison in 2004. International legal scholars tended to have different ideas about what state responsibility was supposed to achieve in this particular case and by what means. At times, remedying concrete wrongs appeared to be juxtaposed with the larger concerns for legality in the international legal order. Moreover, different opinions seemed to exist with regard to whether or not state responsibility had materialized with respect to the Abu Ghraib abuses. Around the same time, the International Criminal Court (ICC) became operative and promised a different approach to the most serious violations of international law. International responsibility expanded to encompass various practices and ideas of responsibility; yet, a comprehensive understanding of the developments occurring within responsibility in international law seemed to be missing.

This book strives to fill that gap by situating state responsibility within the broader framework of international responsibility. Hence, its focus lies on the big picture. By means of assessing the functionality of the general law of state responsibility separately, as well as against the background of alternative responsibility thinking grounded in international liability and international criminal law, this books seeks to highlight for discussion the fragmentation of responsibility and its consequences for the viability of the general rules of state responsibility. Needless to say, all errors in this effort are my own.

# Acknowledgements

This book is grounded in my doctoral dissertation, which I defended in August 2015 at the Faculty of Law, University of Helsinki. I am indebted to my academic home, the Erik Castrén Institute of International Law and Human Rights, whose creative working atmosphere I was able to enjoy for nearly a decade, and where I wrote the dissertation. Professors Martti Koskenniemi and Jan Klabbers have been crucial in both the writing of the dissertation and the process of turning it into a book. Without their relentless support, this book would not have materialized.

I also wish to extend my gratitude to another inspiring working environment, the Finnish Institute of International Affairs. My position as a Senior Research Fellow at the Institute has enabled me to work on the book with the full support of the leadership, colleagues, and the administrative personnel. I especially wish to thank the former Director Teija Tiilikainen, Director Mika Aaltola, and all my colleagues at the Institute, especially those in the Global Security Programme. Research Assistant Anu Ruokamo's help has been invaluable, as has that of the Institute's librarian Johanna Meltti.

Over the years numerous colleagues and acquaintances from different research environments have provided me with guidance and support. It would be impossible to name them all, but I am especially grateful to Pekka Niemelä, Jarna Petman, Pamela Slotte, and Sanna Villikka for having supported me continuously. I am thankful to Grant White, PhD, for language editing. My gratitude also extends to Tom Randall, Gemma Smith, and others at Cambridge University Press for all their assistance, as well as the reviewers for providing both intrinsic and detailed comments that I greatly benefited from.

Besides the aforementioned institutional and collegiate backing, I am grateful to my parents Märta and Erkki for the support of my academic endeavours throughout the years. The same applies to my parents-in-law. Those who have made this book possible are nevertheless my husband and my children, who have given me the time needed to write this book – whether in the evenings, at weekends, or in the summer holidays. They have shown enormous patience and never complained about my book project. There are no words to thank them. This book is dedicated to you, Henrik, Amanda, and Alexander.

# Table of Cases

ARBITRAL AWARDS

L. F. H. Neer and Pauline Neer (USA) *v.* United Mexican States, in United Nations, *Reports of International Arbitral Awards*, Vol. IV, 60–66, Mexico/USA General Claims Commission, 15 October 1926

Opinion in the "Lusitania" Cases, in United Nations, *Reports of International Arbitral Awards*, Vol. VII, 17–32, Germany/USA Mixed Claims Commission, 1 November 1923

North American Dredging Company of Texas (USA) *v.* United Mexican States, in United Nations, *Reports of International Arbitral Awards*, Vol. IV, 26–35, Mexico/USA General Claims Commission, 31 March 1926

Trail Smelter Case (United States of America *v.* Canada), in United Nations, *Reports of International Arbitral Awards*, Vol. III, 1905–82, USA/Canada Arbitration, 16 April 1938 and 11 March 1941

PCIJ

Factory at Chorzów (Claim for Indemnity) (Jurisdiction) (Germany *v.* Poland) PCIJ, Series A, No. 9 (1927)

Factory at Chorzów (Claim for Indemnity) (The Merits) (Germany *v.* Poland), PCIJ, Series A, No. 17 (1928)

German Settlers in Poland (Advisory Opinion), PCIJ, Series B, No. 6 (1923)

Mavrommatis Palestine Concessions (Greece *v.* United Kingdom), PCIJ, Series A, No. 2 (1924)

Panevezys-Saldutiskis Railway (Estonia *v.* Lithuania), PCIJ, Series A/B, Nos 75 and 76 (1938 and 1939)

Phosphates in Morocco (Preliminary Objections) (Italy *v.* France), PCIJ, Series A/B, No. 74 (1938)
S. S. "Wimbledon", PCIJ Series A, No. 1 (1923)

ICJ

Ahmadou Sadio Diallo (Republic of Guinea *v.* Democratic Republic of the Congo) Compensation, Judgment, ICJ Reports 2012, p. 324
Ahmadou Sadio Diallo (Republic of Guinea *v.* Democratic Republic of the Congo) Merits, Judgment, ICJ Reports 2010, p. 639
Application of the Convention on the Prevention and Punishment of the Crime of Genocide (Bosnia and Herzegovina *v.* Federal Republic of Yugoslavia), Reply of the Government of Bosnia and Herzegovina (23 April 1998)
Application of the Convention on the Prevention and Punishment of the Crime of Genocide (Bosnia and Herzegovina *v.* Yugoslavia) Preliminary Objections, Judgment, ICJ Reports 1996, p. 595
Application of the Convention on the Prevention and Punishment of the Crime of Genocide (Bosnia and Herzegovina *v.* Serbia and Montenegro), Judgment, ICJ Reports 2007, p. 43
Application of the International Convention on the Elimination of All Forms of Racial Discrimination (Georgia *v.* Russian Federation) Application Instituting Proceedings, ICJ Reports 2008, p. 4
Application of the Convention on the Prevention and Punishment of the Crime of Genocide (The Gambia *v.* Myanmar), Order (23 January 2020).
Armed Activities on the Territory of the Congo (Democratic Republic of the Congo *v.* Uganda), Judgment, ICJ Reports 2005, p. 168
Avena and Other Mexican Nationals (Mexico *v.* USA), Judgment, ICJ Reports 2004, p. 12
Barcelona Traction, Power, and Light Company, Limited (Belgium *v.* Spain), Second Phase, Judgment, ICJ Reports 1970, p. 3
Certain Activities Carried Out by Nicaragua in the Border Area (Costa Rica *v.* Nicaragua), Judgment, ICJ Reports 2015, p. 665
Certain Phosphate Lands in Nauru (Nauru *v.* Australia), Preliminary Objections, Judgment, ICJ Reports 1992, p. 240
Construction of a Road in Costa Rica along the San Juan River (Nicaragua *v.* Costa Rica), Judgment, ICJ Reports 2015, p. 665
Corfu Channel case, Judgment of April 9th, 1949 (United Kingdom of Great Britain and Northern Ireland *v.* Albania), Merits, Judgment, ICJ Reports 1949, p. 4

Corfu Channel case, Judgment of December 15th, 1949 (United Kingdom of Great Britain and Northern Ireland *v.* Albania), Judgment, ICJ Reports, 1949, p. 244

Gabčíkovo-Nagymaros Project (Hungary *v.* Slovakia), Merits, Judgment, ICJ Reports 1997, p. 7

LaGrand Case (Germany *v.* USA), Judgment, ICJ Reports 2001, p. 466

Legal Consequences of the Construction of a Wall in the Occupied Palestinian Territory, Advisory Opinion, ICJ Reports 2004, p. 136

Legality of the Threat or Use of Nuclear Weapons, Advisory Opinion, ICJ Reports 1996, p. 226

Military and Paramilitary Activities in and against Nicaragua (Nicaragua *v.* USA), Merits, Judgment, ICJ Reports 1986, p. 14

Obligations concerning Negotiations relating to Cessation of the Nuclear Arms Race and to Nuclear Disarmament (Marshall Islands *v.* United Kingdom), Preliminary Objections, Judgment, ICJ Reports 2016, p. 833

Passage through the Great Belt (Finland *v.* Denmark), Application Instituting Proceedings, 17 May 1991, ICJ Reports 1991, p. 16

Pulp Mills on the River Uruguay (Argentina *v.* Uruguay), Judgment, ICJ Reports 2010, p. 14

South West Africa Cases (Ethiopia *v.* South Africa, Liberia *v.* South Africa), Second Phase, Judgment, ICJ Reports 1966, p. 6

Vienna Convention on Consular Relations (Paraguay *v.* USA), Provisional Measures, Order of 9 April 1998, ICJ Reports 1998, p. 248

## NATIONAL COURTS

Attorney-General *v.* Karl Adolf Eichmann, District Court of Jerusalem, Criminal Case No. 40/61, Judgment

Abbasi and Anor. *v.* Secretary of State for Foreign and Commonwealth Affairs & Secretary of State for the Home Department, England and Wales Court of Appeal (Civil Division) Decisions [2002] EWCA Civ 1598 (Eng.)

Samuel Kaunda et al. *v.* President of the Republic of South Africa before the Constitutional Court of South Africa, CCT 23/04; reproduced in *International Legal Materials*, 44 (2005), 173

## IMT

France and Ors *v.* Göring (Hermann) and Ors, Judgment and Sentence, [1946] 22 IMT 203, 1 October 1946; reproduced in *American Journal of International Law*, 41 (1946), 172

Trial of Alfred Felix Alwyn Krupp von Bohlen und Halbach and Eleven Others, United States Military Tribunal, Nuremberg, 17 November 1947–30 June 1948, *Law Reports of Trials of War Criminals* (UNWCC), Vol. X, p. 84

Trial of Carl Krauch and Twenty-Two Others (I. G. Farben Trial), United States Military Tribunal, Nuremberg, 14 August 1947–29 July 1948, *Law Reports of Trials of War Criminals* (UNWCC), Vol. X, p. 52

Trial of Friedrich Flick and Five Others, United States Military Tribunal, Nuremberg, 20 April–22 December 1947, *Law Reports of Trials of War Criminals* (UNWCC), Vol. IX, p. 1

## ICTY

Prosecutor *v.* Drazen Erdemović, IT-96-22-T, Sentencing Judgment (29 November 1996)

Prosecutor *v.* Duško Tadić, IT-94-1-A, ICTY Appeals Chamber, Judgment (15 July 1999)

Prosecutor *v.* Milomir Stakić, IT-97-24-T, Trial Chamber II, Judgment (31 July 2003)

Prosecutor *v.* Milošević, IT-02-54-T, Trial Chamber, Order inviting Designation of Amicus Curiae, Trial Chamber (30 August 2001)

Prosecutor *v.* Milošević, IT-02-54-T, Prosecution Opening Statement (12 February 2002)

Prosecutor *v.* Zlatko Aleksovski, IT-95-14/1-A (24 March 2000)

## ICTR

Prosecutor *v.* Jean Kambanda, ICTR-97-23-S, Judgment and Sentence (4 September 1998)

## ICC

Le Procureur *v.* Germain Katanga, ICC-01/04-01/07, Jugement rendu en application de l'article 74 du statut (7 March 2014)

Prosecutor *v.* Jean-Pierre Bemba Gombo, Aimé Kilolo Musamba, Jean-Jacques Mangenda Kabongo, Fidèle Babala Wandu and Narcisse Arido, Trial Chamber VII, Decision on Sentence, ICC-01/05-01/13 (22 March 2017)

Prosecutor *v.* Omar Hassan Ahmad Al-Bashir, Judgment in the Jordan Referral re Al-Bashir Appeal, ICC-02/05-01/09 OA (6 May 2019)

Prosecutor *v.* Thomas Lubanga Dyilo, ICC-01/04-01/06, Trial Chamber I, Judgment pursuant to Article 74 of the Statute (14 March 2012)

Prosecutor *v.* Uhuru Muigai Kenyatta, ICC-01/09-02/11, Trial Chamber, Status Conference (5 February 2014)

Prosecutor *v.* Uhuru Muigai Kenyatta, ICC-01/09-02/11, Trial Chamber V (B), Decision on Non-compliance (31 March 2014)

Prosecutor *v.* Uhuru Muigai Kenyatta, ICC-01/09-02/11, Notice of withdrawal of the charges against Uhuru Muigai Kenyatta (5 December 2014)

Situation in Darfur, Sudan, ICC-02/05, Prosecutor's Response to Arbour's Observations of the United Nations High Commissioner for Human Rights Invited in Application of Rule 103 of the Rules of Procedure and Evidence (19 October 2006)

Situation in the Democratic Republic of Congo, ICC-01/04, Appeals Chamber, Judgment on the Prosecutor's Appeal Against the Decision of Pre-Trial Chamber I Entitled 'Decision on the Prosecutor's Application for Warrants of Arrest, Article 58' (13 July 2006)

Situation in the Democratic Republic of Congo in the Case of the Prosecutor *v.* Germain Katanga, ICC-01/04-01/07, Order for Reparations pursuant to Article 75 of the Statute (24 March 2017)

Situation in the Democratic Republic of Congo in the Case of the Prosecutor *v.* Thomas Lubanga Dyilo, ICC-01/04-01/06, Decision Establishing the Principles and Procedures to be Applied to Reparations (7 August 2012)

Situation in the Democratic Republic of Congo in the Case of the Prosecutor *v.* Callixte Mbarushimana, ICC-01/04-01/10, Pre-Trial Chamber I, Decision on the Confirmation of Charges (16 December 2011)

## ECCC

Kaing Guek Eav, alias Duch, Case No. 001/18-07-2007/ECCC/TC, Trial Chamber, Judgment (26 July 2010)

## ECtHR

Behrami and Behrami *v.* France and Saramati *v.* France, Germany and Norway, Application Nos 71412/01 and 78166/01, Grand Chamber Decision (2 May 2007)

Christine Goodwin *v.* United Kingdom, Application No. 28957/95, ECtHR Grand Chamber Judgment (11 July 2002)

Saddam Hussein *v.* Albania and Others, Application No. 23276/04, ECtHR, Decision as to Admissibility (14 March 2006)

Sejdovic *v.* Italy, Application No. 56581/00, Judgment (1 March 2006)

### IACtHR

Case of Montero-Aranguren et al. (Detention Centre of Catia) *v.* Venezuela, Judgment (5 July 2006)

### WTO DSB

Appellate Body Report, United States – Import Prohibition of Certain Shrimp and Shrimp Products, WT/DS58/AB/R (adopted 6 November 1998)

### ICSID

CMS Gas Transmission Company *v.* Argentine Republic, ICSID Case No. ARB/01/8, Award (12 May 2005)

LG & E Energy Corp. and others *v.* Argentine Republic, ICSID Case No. ARB/02/1, Decision on Liability (3 October 2006)

### ITLOS

Responsibilities and Obligations of States Sponsoring Persons and Entities with Respect to Activities in the Area, Case No. 17, International Tribunal of the Law of the Sea, The Seabed Disputes Chamber, Advisory Opinion (1 February 2011)

# Abbreviations

| | |
|---|---|
| ADP | Articles on Diplomatic Protection |
| ARIO | Articles on the Responsibility of International Organizations |
| ASR | Articles on State Responsibility |
| CIA | Central Intelligence Agency |
| CTBT | Comprehensive Test Ban Treaty |
| ECCC | Extraordinary Chamber in the Courts of Cambodia |
| ECHR | European Convention for the Protection of Human Rights and Fundamental Freedoms |
| ECJ | Court of Justice of the European Union |
| ECtHR | European Court of Human Rights |
| EEZ | Exclusive Economic Zone |
| EU | European Union |
| FAO | World Food and Agriculture Organization |
| GA | General Assembly |
| GAL | Global Administrative Law |
| IACtHR | Inter-American Court of Human Rights |
| IAEA | International Atomic Energy Agency |
| ICC | International Criminal Court |
| ICESCR | International Covenant on Economic, Social and Cultural Rights |
| ICJ | International Court of Justice |
| ICRC | International Committee of the Red Cross |
| ICSID | International Centre for Settlement of Investment Disputes |
| ICTR | International Criminal Tribunal for Rwanda |
| ICTY | International Criminal Tribunal for former Yugoslavia |
| ILC | International Law Commission |
| IMO | International Maritime Organization |
| IMT | International Military Tribunal |

| | |
|---|---|
| IMTFE | International Military Tribunal for the Far East |
| ITLOS | International Tribunal for the Law of the Sea |
| JCE | joint criminal enterprise |
| LMO | living modified organism |
| NATO | North Atlantic Treaty Organization |
| NGO | non-governmental organization |
| OECD | Organization for Economic Cooperation and Development |
| OTP | Office of the Prosecutor at the International Criminal Court |
| P&I | Protection and Indemnity |
| PCIJ | Permanent Court of International Justice |
| PMSC | Private Military and Security Company |
| PPP | polluter pays principle |
| PTBT | Partial Test Ban Treaty |
| SC | Security Council |
| SDR | special drawing rights |
| UN | United Nations |
| UNCC | United Nations Compensation Commission |
| UNCLOS | United Nations Convention on the Law of the Sea |
| UNFCCC | United Nations Framework Convention for Climate Change |
| VCLT | Vienna Convention on the Law of Treaties |
| WHO | World Health Organization |
| WTO | World Trade Organization |

# Introduction

## STATE RESPONSIBILITY ISSUES ON THE RISE

State responsibility has for long been at the core of the international legal order with roots in state practice, legal theorizing, and judicial pronouncements. The Permanent Court of International Justice (PCIJ) affirmed in its very first case, that of the *SS Wimbledon*, the duty of the responsible state to compensate for wrongful acts occasioned by it.[1] Almost a century later, the central role played by state responsibility for international law is practically taken for granted. It is considered important whether international lawyers in international judicial institutions, foreign ministries, or universities ponder how to respond to illegal fishing of straddling fish stocks, or how to react to armed aggression. State responsibility – or any other responsibility system for that matter – 'comes across as the final island of certainty in an ocean of doubt'.[2]

The generality of state responsibility law has guaranteed steadfast scholarly interest in the topic, which peaked with the adoption of the International Law Commission's Articles on the Responsibility of States for Internationally Wrongful Acts of 2001 (ASR, the ILC Articles).[3] Analyses of the ILC

[1] *S.S. Wimbledon*, 1923, PCIJ Series A. No.1, p. 15, at p. 30.

[2] Jan Klabbers, 'Responsibility of States and International Organisations in the Context of Cyber Activities with Special Reference to NATO', in Katharina Ziolkowski (ed.), *Peacetime Regime for State Activities in Cyberspace: International Law, International Relations and Diplomacy* (Tallinn: NATO Cooperative Cyber Defence Centre of Excellence, 2013), pp. 485–506 at 505.

[3] Report of the International Law Commission (ILC) on the Work of Its Fifty-third Session, UN Doc. A/56/10 (2001), p. 29. The General Assembly took note of the ASR in UNGA Res. 56/83, 12 December 2001.

codification end-result mushroomed.[4] Around the same time, much attention was also paid to high-profile international incidents involving issues of state responsibility law. Among others, these incidents included: the Kosovo crisis and the bombing of Yugoslavia in 1999, the United States' attack upon Afghanistan in 2001 following the 9/11 terrorist attacks, the Coalition of the Willing invading Iraq in 2003 and the concomitant abuses of prisoners at Abu Ghraib.

These cases enabled international lawyers to apply the newly codified ASR to concrete situations and gave them the opportunity to raise several questions about the law that seemed indecisive or undealt with by the ILC Articles. These questions included: aiding and abetting, how to apportion responsibility among multiple state actors,[5] collective countermeasures,[6] as well as the appropriate level of control needed for attribution of responsibility to the state in the case of non-state actors, such as private military and security companies (PMSCs) or terrorist networks.[7] Unsurprisingly, despite extensive legal codification and development on the matter of state responsibility, not all issues had been solved once and for all.[8]

In some cases, it seemed that the law of state responsibility not only was uncertain, but also that the entire body of law had a lesser role – or no role to play – in spite of its comprehensive scope. For example, two judges of the International Court of Justice (ICJ) held in the *Bosnian Genocide* case that

4 See the 'Symposium on the ILC's State Responsibility Articles' (2002) 96 *American Journal of International Law* 773–890; James Crawford, *The International Law Commission's Articles on State Responsibility* (Cambridge: Cambridge University Press, 2002); René Provost (ed.), *State Responsibility in International Law* (Dartmouth: Ashgate, 2002).

5 For general analysis on coalitions of the willing and responsibility, see Matteo Tondini, 'Coalitions of the Willing', in André Nollkaemper and Ilias Plakokefalos (eds.), *The Practice of Shared Responsibility in International Law* (Cambridge: Cambridge University Press, 2017), pp. 701–732.

6 Martti Koskenniemi, 'Solidarity Measures: State Responsibility as a New International Order?' (2001) 72 *British Yearbook of International Law* 337–356.

7 Derek Jinks, 'State Responsibility for the Acts of Private Armed Groups' (2003) 4 *Chicago Journal of International Law* 83–95; Tal Becker, *Terrorism and the State: Rethinking the Rules of the Law of State Responsibility* (Oxford and Portland, OR: Hart Publishing, 2005); Kimberley Trapp, *State Responsibility for International Terrorism: Problems and Prospects* (Oxford: Oxford University Press, 2011); Katja Nieminen, 'The Rules of Attribution and the Private Military Contractors at Abu Ghraib: Private Acts or Public Wrongs?' (2006) XV *Finnish Yearbook of International Law* 289–319; Marie-Louise Togas, 'La responsabilité internationale d'État pour le fait d'entreprises militaires privées' (2008) 45 *Annuaire Canadien de droit international* 97–130.

8 Guy S. Goodwin-Gill, 'State Responsibility and the "Good Faith" Obligation in International Law', in Malgosia Fitzmaurice and Dan Sarooshi (eds.), *Issues of State Responsibility before International Judicial Institutions* (Oxford and Portland, OR: Bloomsbury, 2004), pp. 75–104 at 75.

international criminal law appeared to be more suitable for dealing with allegations of genocide than the law of state responsibility.[9] The same was argued by many commentators with respect to the torture at Abu Ghraib,[10] particularly after the minor role played by the law of state responsibility. And lately, the limited relevance of state responsibility law to some emerging global problems has become visible. For example, the normative solution provided by state responsibility for handling claims of climate change and cybercrimes, seems thinner and less meaningful than with respect to classic interstate issues. All in all, the predominantly binary, interstate setting of the law of state responsibility seems increasingly ill-fitted to deal with the complexity of actors and issues that characterize the transnational relations of the changing global order.

These developments were naturally reflected in the international legal literature regarding state responsibility. First, following the initial analyses of the ILC Articles, an increasing number of studies sought to analyze state responsibility in conjunction with other responsibility regimes in international law, such as that of the responsibility of international organizations or international criminal law.[11] Such efforts were thus focused on the broader field of international responsibility. However, the past decade has also witnessed the growth of corrective or critical assessments of the law of state responsibility, which suggests that the initial exhilaration over the ILC Articles is fading. Although criticism has been directed towards state responsibility law before,[12] several researchers have now started to pay increasing attention to the lacunae

9 *Application of the Convention on the Prevention and Punishment of the Crime of Genocide (Bosnia and Herzegovina v. Yugoslavia)(Preliminary Objections)*, ICJ Reports 1996, p. 595, Joint Declaration of Judges Shi and Vereschetin, p. 632.

10 Alette Smeulers and Sander van Niekerk, 'Abu Ghraib and the War on Terror – A Case against Donald Rumsfeld?' (2009) 51 *Crime, Law and Social Change* 327–349; Chia Lehnardt, 'Individual Liability of Private Military Personnel under International Criminal Law' (2008) 19 *European Journal of International Law* 1015–1034.

11 Maurizio Ragazzi (ed.), *International Responsibility Today: Essays in Memory of Oscar Schachter* (Leiden and Boston: Martinus Nijhoff Publishers, 2005); Marja Lehto, *Indirect Responsibility for Terrorist Acts: Redefinition of the Concept of Terrorism Beyond Violent Acts* (Leiden and Boston: Martinus Nijhoff Publishers, 2010); Beatrice I. Bonafè, *The Relationship Between State and Individual Responsibility for International Crimes* (Leiden, Boston: Martinus Nijhoff Publishers, 2009); Rafaëlle Maison, *La responsabilité individuelle pour crime d'État en droit international public* (Bruxelles: Bruylant, 2004).

12 See e.g., Philip Allott, 'State Responsibility and the Unmaking of International Law' (1988) 29 *Harvard International Law Journal* 1–26; Christine Chinkin, 'A Critique of the Public/Private Dimension' (1999) 10 *European Journal of International Law* 387–395; Koskenniemi, 'Solidarity Measures'.

and shortcomings of the doctrine.[13] Specific problematic aspects have been explored in greater detail, such as: complicity or shared responsibility,[14] third-party countermeasures,[15] as well as the law's non-institutionalized nature.[16] Recent literature has also focused on the question of how well state responsibility fares with respect to particular issues or wrongdoings such as transnational terrorism and global security.[17] This noticeable shift in interest towards critiques of state responsibility is to be welcomed, particularly since the adoption of the ASR has mostly been seen as a successful endeavour. This study seeks to combine both of the above-mentioned trends in the state responsibility literature by linking the more recent critical approach with analysis of the broader picture of international responsibility,[18] with the aim to unmask in a comprehensive manner uncertainties that characterize the law.

## THE PURPOSES OF STATE RESPONSIBILITY

The law of state responsibility is usually analyzed from the perspective of its elements: that is, issues pertaining to the existence of an internationally wrongful act, as well as the content and implementation of responsibility. However, the aims of state responsibility are rarely spelled out and the social element of state responsibility is often lacking.[19] Yet, what objectives one assigns to a responsibility regime will have implications for how well it is seen to fare in overall terms, as well as for what solutions are envisaged for solving potential problems.

[13] See e.g., Tzvika Alan Nissel, *A History of State Responsibility: The Struggle for International Standards* (1870–1960) (Helsinki: University of Helsinki, 2016); Becker, *Terrorism and the State*.

[14] Vladyslav Lanovoy, *Complicity and Its Limits in the Law of International Responsibility* (Oxford and Portland, OR: Bloomsbury, 2016); Helmut Philipp Aust, *Complicity and the Law of State Responsibility* (Cambridge: Cambridge University Press, 2011); André Nollkaemper and Dov Jacobs (eds.), *Distribution of Responsibilities in International Law* (Cambridge: Cambridge University Press, 2015); Georg Nolte and Helmut Philipp Aust, 'Equivocal Helpers – Complicit States, Mixed Messages and International Law' (2009) 58 *International and Comparative Law Quarterly* 1–30.

[15] Martin Dawidowicz, *Third-Party Countermeasures in International Law* (Cambridge: Cambridge University Press, 2017).

[16] Vincent-Joël Proulx, *Institutionalizing State Responsibility: Global Security and UN Organs* (Oxford: Oxford University Press, 2016); Dawidowicz, *Third-Party Countermeasures*.

[17] Proulx, *Institutionalizing*; Vincent-Joël Proulx, *Transnational Terrorism and State Accountability: A New Theory of Prevention* (Oxford and Portland, OR: Hart Publishing, 2012); Becker, *Terrorism and the State*.

[18] One study which also combines critique with a broad approach to international responsibility is James Crawford, Alain Pellet and Simon Olleson (eds.), *The Law of International Responsibility* (Oxford: Oxford University Press, 2010).

[19] Jan Klabbers, 'Book Review on André Nollkaemper and Dov Jacobs (eds.), *Distribution of Responsibilities in International Law*' (2016) 27 *European Journal of International Law* 541–551 at 541.

But how is one to understand the purposes of state responsibility, whose nature is famously claimed as being neither civil nor criminal, but sui generis? It is not easy to spell out its purposes definitively. Positive sources provide little direction,[20] as much of the general law is of a customary nature. For example, the first point of reference, the ASR, do not explicitly state any goal(s) to be achieved akin to what is to be found in the Statute of the International Criminal Court (ICC).[21] Whereas the latter names punishment and prevention as the objectives to be reached through this particular institution of international criminal law, the general commentary to the ASR presents no explicit goals. However, the content of state responsibility lays bare that the immediate objectives are cessation of the wrongful act as well as reparation for injury. Also prevention of the occurrence of breaches is mentioned.[22]

Therefore, in a manner similar to domestic responsibility systems, there are several aims that can be ascribed to state responsibility. This holds particularly true if one explores the international legal literature, which mentions inter alia the following goals of state responsibility: 'preservation of peace', 'reparation of harm', 'deterrence', 'loss allocation', 'administrative efficiency', and 'securing international cooperation'.[23] The civil aims of state responsibility stand out in listings of purposes of state responsibility, and many scholars take the law's non-punitive nature at face value.[24] However, there are allegedly penal aspects to state responsibility, too, although they may be less apparent with respect to ordinary harms. According to Special Rapporteur Gaetano Arangio-Ruiz, responsibility in itself should be considered a sanction with a penal connotation.[25] Yet, manifestly missing in discourses on the purposes of state responsibility are any expressive goals that are commonly connected to criminal law, whether national or international.

The views on the purposes of state responsibility have varied over time as scholars have attempted to frame the law over the course of several centuries. Moreover, those who have enforced it as adjudicators may have a different take on the purposes of state responsibility. Despite the controversies surrounding

[20] Nissel, *A History of State Responsibility*, p. 16.

[21] Rome Statute of the International Criminal Court, Rome, 17 July 1998, in force 1 July 2002, 2187 *United Nations Treaty Series* 3, preamble.

[22] See Commentary to Art. 30 of the ASR.

[23] Anne van Aaken, 'Shared Responsibility in International Law: A Political Economy Analysis', in André Nollkaemper and Dov Jacobs (eds.), *Distribution of Responsibilities in International Law* (Cambridge: Cambridge University Press, 2015), pp. 153–191 at 159–160.

[24] Trapp, *State Responsibility*, p. 11; Robert Kolb, *The International Law of State Responsibility: An Introduction* (Cheltenham: Edward Elgar, 2017), p. 153.

[25] Fifth report of Arangio Ruiz, ILC Yearbook 1993, vol. II(1), 1, para. 256.

the purposes of state responsibility,[26] broadly speaking it shares some common aims with other responsibility systems: legal and material restoration with both backward- and forward-looking connotations.[27] There is both a relational function, which seeks to restore the relations between the wrongdoing and injured states, and a systemic function, to uphold the international legal order.[28] With regard to both aspects, the aim can be seen as guaranteeing stability and certainty in international relations,[29] an aim which is inherently more forward-looking in nature. To that effect, the aim of deterrence or prevention is important. It contributes to the overarching goal of maintaining peaceful relations between states, the original motivation for codification of state responsibility in the first place.[30]

The existence of several objectives for state responsibility, or any other responsibility system for that matter, is not problem-free: it may be difficult to achieve multiple goals at the same time.[31] The multiplicity of aims also opens the door for a case-by-case selection of the nature and purposes of state responsibility on the part of each commentator or adjudicator.[32] The incidence of multiple objectives may also complicate assessments of how these goals are to be reached, especially since there might be tensions among the different aims. At the same time, a multivalued responsibility system should not be seen as a misfortune. Social objectives can never be 'single or simple',[33] and the interaction between different purposes may also be positive.

## APPROACH AND ARGUMENT OF THE BOOK

This book is a critical study of the general law of state responsibility and its shifting role within the international legal order. It situates state responsibility law within the larger framework of international responsibility and

[26] Nissel, *A History of State Responsibility*, p. 16.

[27] André Nollkaemper and Dov Jacobs, 'Introduction: Mapping the Normative Framework', in André Nollkaemper and Dov Jacobs (eds.), *Distribution of Responsibilities in International Law* (Cambridge: Cambridge University Press, 2015), pp. 1–35 at 16–19.

[28] Brigitte Bollecker-Stern, *Le préjudice dans la théorie de la responsabilité internationale* (Paris: Editions A. Pedone, 1973), p. 10; Pierre-Marie Dupuy, 'Dionisio Anzilotti and the Law of the International Responsibility of States' (1992) 3 *European Journal of International Law* 139–148 at 146.

[29] Comments by the United Kingdom in 1998 on the second reading of the ILC draft articles. ILC Yearbook, 1998, vol. II, part one, p. 99, para. 3.

[30] UNGA Res. 799 (VIII), 7 December 1953.

[31] van Aaken, 'Shared Responsibility', 160.

[32] Nissel, *A History of State Responsibility*, p. 16.

[33] Henry M. Hart Jr., 'The Aims of the Criminal Law' (1958) 23 *Law and Contemporary Problems* 401–441 at 401.

analyzes the law from the perspective of its functionality as well as against the background of alternative responsibility thinking. By adopting this holistic technique, the aim is to encourage more frank discussions regarding state responsibility as a normative solution for the globalized world with its ever-expanding agenda and plethora of actors. Building on the nascent critical turn that has been discernible in the international legal literature on state responsibility in recent years, the objective is to raise awareness of the complexities and difficulties that permeate the law of state responsibility. However, this study attempts to see the forest for the trees rather than exploring a particular doctrine or aspect of state responsibility. Its aim is to contribute to discussions which, in the long run, can lead to improved ideas and practices regarding responsibility.

In doing so, this study moves beyond traditional questions of interpretation and application such as: what entities constitute state organs, what are the limits of necessity, or whether declaratory judgments constitute appropriate means of redress. Although there is nothing wrong with these questions per se, this book seeks to address more profound questions by pursuing a comprehensive assessment of state responsibility, as well as the issue of how the law is affected by the burgeoning of other responsibility regimes in international law. It will focus not only upon the question of whether the present models of state responsibility are sufficient, but also that of whether they are indeed preferable to begin with. The questions this study raises include: Does state responsibility constitute an appropriate solution to all internationally wrongful acts? Can it respond sufficiently to new phenomena and actors in the international arena? Can the law of state responsibility affect the conduct of actors? Can it differentiate between international obligations that are of heightened importance, and those that do not play a major role in the international community? And, ultimately: are there worthy alternatives to the rules of state responsibility within international responsibility?

The argument set forth in the book is twofold. It first focuses on the general law of state responsibility and argues that the law in question enjoys a higher normative value than what may be merited on the basis of the relevance of state responsibility to the operation of different legal branches. The argument will suggest that the practical weight of state responsibility across the whole spectrum of international legal obligations is not equally strong. While state responsibility remains important in some fields of international law such as international investment law, this claim does not hold true for all issue areas, for instance as demonstrated by cyberspace law. Thus, a discrepancy exists between the aspirations imbued in the law of state responsibility and its actual importance. This mixed significance, in broad terms, of state responsibility is partly the consequence of globalization, which has changed significantly the international setting both in terms of actors and issues. As a result, state responsibility law is more and more difficult to apply to the infinite variety of situations calling for responsibility. Other contributing factors to the uneven relevance of the law include the shortcomings of state responsibility law itself. These problems are foremost issues pertaining to the basis of the internationally wrongful act as well as to the law's implementation.

The second part of my argument purports to show how, in international practice, alternative constructions of responsibility have come to challenge state responsibility. This part of the book's argument suggests that there now exist in international law several responsibility systems that in many branches of international law have set aside or at least called into question the exclusive role previously played by the law of state responsibility. International criminal law and international liability, which can be viewed as theoretical alternatives to or even partly as offshoots from state responsibility,[34] can deal with certain problems differently – and often more efficiently – than can the general law of state responsibility. In other words, they may display greater functionality in terms of the requirements laid down in this book. Therefore, in the doctrine they should not merely be perceived as gap-fillers or complements to the rules of state responsibility. Rather, they have reduced the sphere of issues to which state responsibility remains pertinent.

It is important to spell out what this study is not about. In assessing the position and aptness of state responsibility law, this study cannot be a work in legal dogma – understood as the study of the content of rules. While the rules are significant, the main focus of this study is the overall picture of state responsibility and the functions of the law of state responsibility. Neither is the aim of this exercise to undermine the importance of responsibility as an idea and practice in international law. Quite to the contrary, state responsibility is such a well-grounded institution of international law that it also merits critical reflection. Therefore, this study highlights the general value of responsibility because its underlying presumption is the existential importance of sanctions for international law. Finally, despite the fact that this study assesses the functionality of state responsibility law against other responsibility regimes, it does not constitute a full comparative analysis of state responsibility, international criminal law, and international liability. It focuses first and foremost upon state responsibility, with the aim of complementing the book's analysis of state responsibility with insights from different responsibility constructions.

34 Pierre-Marie Dupuy, 'International Law of State Responsibility: Revolution or Evolution?' (1989) 11 *Michigan Journal of International Law* 105–128, referring more generally to international criminal responsibility and international liability.

In spite of much development within the field, a critical approach to state responsibility is needed. Responsibility issues lie at the heart of international law, and as noted by Jules Basdevant in 1930, the practical value of a legal order depends to a large extent upon the effectiveness and scope of its rules on responsibility.[35] There are also more concrete reasons for why the law of state responsibility should be analytically explored. First, the law of state responsibility may be subjected to re-evaluation: the future status of the general law of state responsibility is still being contemplated before the Sixth Committee of the UN with an increasing number of states preferring to turn customary state responsibility law into a convention.[36] It is important that scholars analyze the ILC Articles as a number of the rules have been considered controversial or unclear by states as well as scholars. Such rules pertain mostly to the constitutive elements of the internationally wrongful act itself as well as implementation, rather than to issues of the content of state responsibility. Particularly debated are the rules on attribution, shared responsibility, and countermeasures.[37] Second, a critical assignment is meaningful based on the fact that new responsibility systems have been built upon on older systems such as the responsibility of international organizations, which is largely structured along the lines of state responsibility. Moreover, since the framework of international responsibility remains to some extent underdeveloped,[38] discussions may arise with respect to developing responsibility frameworks for new actors such as transnational corporations or sub-national territorial units like cities.

Throughout the scholarly discussion of responsibility, it has often been maintained that the problems with international responsibility are not so much that of responsibility, but rather that they derive from the vagueness or insufficiency of international legal obligations.[39] Many commentators assert

35 Jules Basdevant, 'Actes de la Conférence SDN', 1930, Vol. 7, cited in Jean-Pierre Quéneudec, *La responsabilité internationale de l'État pour les fautes personelles de ses agents* (Paris: Pichon et Durand-Auzias, 1966), p. 5.

36 Federica Paddeu, 'To Convene or Not to Convene? The Future Status of the Articles on State Responsibility: Recent Developments' (2018) 21 *Max Planck Yearbook of United Nations Law* 83–123.

37 See e.g., Paddeu, 'To Convene'; André Nollkaemper and Ilias Plakokefalos (eds.), *The Practice of Shared Responsibility in International Law* (Cambridge: Cambridge University Press, 2017).

38 Kristen E. Boon, 'Are Control Tests Fit for Future: The Slippage Problem in Attribution Doctrines' (2014) 15 *Melbourne Journal of International Law* 330–377 at 331, 376.

39 Clyde Eagleton, *The Responsibility of States in International Law* (New York: The New York University Press, 1928), p. 218; Ilias Plakokefalos commenting on the use of force by non-state actors, 'The Use of Force by Non-State Actors and the Limits of Attribution of Conduct: A Reply to Vladyslav Lanovoy' (2017) 28 *European Journal of International Law* 587–593 at 593. Christina Voigt holds the same with respect to environmental regulation, 'State Responsibility for Climate Change Damages' (2008) 77 *Nordic Journal of International Law* 1–22 at 22.

that states generally want to follow the rules, but that in many instances they disagree as to their content. In other words, lawmakers ought to draft clearer rules. The difficulty of achieving such rules that would leave no room for interpretation seems to be ignored, as well as the indeterminacy of rules. As noted by Martti Koskenniemi, '[m]odern international law is an elaborate framework for deferring substantive resolution elsewhere: into further procedure, interpretation, equity, context, and so on.'[40] The same seems to apply to the law of state responsibility. While the value of clear legal rules should not be underestimated, this study proceeds from the understanding that primary rules do not end the political debate once and for all.[41] International lawyers must also be able to analyze those institutions that are portrayed as 'innocent victims' of the broader structural problems of international law.

The structure of this study is as follows: The first chapter sets the scene for the book by devoting attention to the role played by state responsibility law in the international legal order, as well as discussing contemporary challenges. In addition, this chapter dwells upon various analytical perspectives, and concludes by proposing *functionality* as the most suitable appraisal standard for the present study (Chapter 1). From there, the study moves to explore the historical evolution of state responsibility law from a law of arbitrations to the status of being the generally accepted primary system of responsibility in international law. An important component of this chapter is also its presentation of the ASR and their regulatory approaches, as these rules represent the best available statement on customary law of state responsibility (Chapter 2). Following this presentation of the general rules of state responsibility, the study will problematize the regulatory choices made by the ILC by way of conducting a functional analysis of the separate parts of the law: the basis for state responsibility, its content, and its implementation (Chapter 3). The final substantive chapter will introduce international criminal law and international liability into the picture by conducting a narrower thematic analysis of their respective capabilities for responding to functionality (Chapter 4). Finally, the study will discuss the shifting role of the law of state responsibility in international law (Conclusions).

## CONCEPTUAL CLARIFICATIONS

From the perspective of this study, it is important to note that there are two distinct ways of using the concept of responsibility in international law, only one of which is relevant for the present undertaking. First, *responsibility* may

[40] Martti Koskenniemi, 'The Politics of International Law' (1990) 1 *European Journal of International Law* 4–32 at 28.

[41] Jan Klabbers, *International law* (Cambridge: Cambridge University Press, 2013), p. 14.

be used synonymously with 'duty' or 'obligation', to denote obligations arising from a legally binding rule. While this meaning used to be standard,[42] there is a second and increasingly prevalent understanding of the term, a view which refers to obligations that follow due to the breach of a binding rule.[43] Indeed, with the ILC work on state responsibility, the term responsibility has increasingly come to signify the consequences flowing from a breach of an international legal obligation.[44]

This latter approach chosen by the ILC seems to take the term 'responsibility' back to its origins, despite claims of 'terminological confusion'.[45] For example, Alan Norrie has claimed that in its very core, elementary meaning, responsibility consists of the elements of being '"called to respond" (answerability) and being "found responsible" (culpability)'.[46] In similar terms, James Crawford and Jeremy Watkins have noted that responsibility consists of both 'answerability' and 'liability'; the former signifying that somebody is called to account for his or her behaviour, and the latter indicating that 'a person has violated their obligations and become liable to some negative response such as punishment, censure, or enforced compensation'.[47]

For the purposes of this study, the meaning and usage of 'responsibility' will follow the practice of the ILC. The term 'responsibility' will thus be used to indicate the legal consequences arising from the breach of an international obligation. However, the practice of associating the term with a

42 M. A. Fitzmaurice, 'International Environmental Law as a Special Field', in L. A. N. M. Barnhoorn and K. C. Wellens (eds.), *Diversity in Secondary Rules and the Unity of International Law* (The Hague: Martinus Nijhoff Publishers, 1995), pp. 181–226 at 203–204. Similarly, Alan Boyle, 'State Responsibility and International Liability for Injurious Consequences of Acts Not Prohibited by International Law: A Necessary Distinction?' (1990) 39 *International and Comparative Law Quarterly* 1–26 at 8–9.

43 Fitzmaurice, 'International Environmental Law', 203–4.

44 Ibid.; Francisco V. García Amador, *First Report on International Responsibility*, UN Doc. A/CN.4/96 (20 January 1956), p. 180, para. 35; Gerhard Hafner, 'Accountability of International Organizations' (2003) 97 *American Society of International Law Proceedings* 236–237 at 236.

45 Fitzmaurice, 'International Environmental Law', 204. She claims that the term 'liability' would have been a more appropriate term for the legal consequences of a breach of an international obligation. For a similar argument, see Peter Cane, *Responsibility in Law and Morality* (Oxford and Portland, OR: Hart Publishing, 2002), pp. 1–2.

46 Alan Norrie, '"Simulacra of Morality"? Beyond the Ideal/Actual Antinomies of Criminal Justice', in Antony Duff (ed.), *Philosophy and the Criminal Law: Principle and Critique* (Cambridge: Cambridge University Press, 1998), pp. 101–155 at 114.

47 James Crawford and Jeremy Watkins, 'International Responsibility', in Samantha Besson and John Tasioulas (eds.), *The Philosophy of International Law* (Oxford: Oxford University Press, 2010), pp. 283–298 at 283–284.

particular form of legal accountability – namely that of state responsibility – calls for caution. The Commission noted from the outset that the term 'responsibility' covered both civil and criminal forms of responsibility, depending on the character of the obligation in question that was breached.[48] In factual terms, international responsibility nevertheless consisted mainly of state responsibility law at the time when the ILC began its codification work.

But much has changed since the early days of ILC codification. While state responsibility is still accepted by most scholars as the main responsibility system in international law, many different understandings and practices of responsibility are on the rise. Individual and collective forms of responsibility find themselves entangled with retrospective and prospective responsibilities; civil, criminal, or international responsibilities; fault-based or objective responsibilities; and so forth.[49] The fragmentation of responsibility is a fact; hence, assertions of a lost conceptual harmony must be taken seriously.[50] As a result, the existence of several responsibility regimes have spurred a broader understanding of the term *international responsibility* in recent international legal literature.[51] Thus, the concept includes state responsibility, individual criminal responsibility, the responsibility of international organizations, and international liability, all of which take place at the international level. As James Crawford, Alain Pellet and Simon Olleson have noted: '[t]o speak of international responsibility is to speak of all such relations.'[52] In line with this, the term 'international responsibility' will be used in this study to denote the whole spectrum of responsibility regimes that currently exist, unless a different meaning is expressly stated.

In this study, the strategy of following the ILC's path with respect to terminology will also be adopted with regard to a third concept bringing confusion to the terminology relevant to the legal consequences of breaches of

48 García Amador, *First Report*, p. 180, para. 35.

49 Scott Veitch, *Law and Irresponsibility: On the Legitimation of Human Suffering* (Oxon: Routledge-Cavendish, 2007), p. 37.

50 Alain Pellet, 'The Definition of Responsibility in International Law', in James Crawford, Alain Pellet, and Simon Olleson (eds.), *The Law of International Responsibility* (Oxford: Oxford University Press, 2010), pp. 3–16 at 6, 12.

51 Crawford, Pellet, and Olleson (eds.), *The Law of International Responsibility*; André Nollkaemper and Harmen van der Wilt, 'Preface', in André Nollkaemper and Harmen van der Wilt (eds.), *System Criminality in International Law* (Cambridge: Cambridge University Press, 2009), pp. vii–viii at vii; Kolb, *The International Law*, p. 15.

52 James Crawford, Alain Pellet and Simon Olleson, 'Preface', in James Crawford, Alain Pellet, and Simon Olleson (eds.), *The Law of International Responsibility* (Oxford: Oxford University Press, 2010), pp. x–xv at v.

international law: that of *liability*. The terms 'responsibility' and 'liability' are often used interchangeably or inconsistently by international lawyers.[53] The distinction between responsibility and liability had already been subject to discussion in the ILC before the introduction of the liability topic to the ILC's agenda. In 1973 the Commission adopted a proposal, according to which: 'the term "responsibility" should be used only in connexion with internationally wrongful acts and that, with reference to possible injurious consequences arising out of the performance of certain *lawful* activities, the more suitable term "liability" should be used.'[54] According to the ILC, then, liability is based upon lawful activities which still give rise to reparation. Nevertheless, the Commission tried, unsuccessfully perhaps, to clarify the term by stating that 'the term "liability" is used … without nuance and in a sense very close to its ordinary meaning': that is, as a generic reference to the consequences of any legal obligation.[55]

While the ILC position has received criticism,[56] for the sake of consistency this study will follow the ILC approach of using 'liability' when referring to harm arising out of lawful activities. It is important to note, however, that the term 'liability' may refer to diversified models of compensation. From the start, liability was attached objectively to the state, but international practices have broadened the notion to include civil liability conventions on oil pollution and nuclear damages, for example. Even though these civil liability conventions can be seen as undertakings of a private law character rather than belonging to the domain of public international law,[57] the present study will include all different arrangements aiming at remedying harm arising out of hazardous activities under the notion of international liability. Such an approach is called for because states are still the driving forces behind

53 Martti Koskenniemi, 'International Liability for Transfrontier Pollution Damage' (1990) 2 *International Environmental Affairs: A Journal for Research and Policy* 309–316 at 310.

54 Summary Records, ILC Yearbook 1973, vol. I, p. 211, para. 37 (emphasis added).

55 Robert B. Quentin-Baxter, Preliminary Report on International Liability for Injurious Consequences Arising out of Acts Not Prohibited by International Law, UN Doc. A/CN.4/334 and Add.1 & Corr.1 and Add.2 (24 and 27 June and 4 July 1980), paras. 11, 12.

56 Boyle, 'State Responsibility', 9.

57 For example, Pierre-Marie Dupuy and Jiménez de Aréchaga have adopted the view that civil liability conventions are private law arrangements that do not give rise to liability obligations on the international plane. See Pierre-Marie Dupuy, *Droit International Public* (5th ed., Paris: Dalloz, 2000), p. 444, and Jiménez de Aréchaga, 'International Law in the Past Third of A Century' (1978) 159 *Collected Courses of the Hague Academy of International Law* 1–343 at 273, both cited in Julio Barboza, *The Environment, Risk and Liability in International Law* (Leiden and Boston: Martinus Nijhoff Publishers, 2011), p. 41. Similarly, Alexandre Kiss, 'State Responsibility and Liability for Nuclear Damage' (2006) 35 *Denver Journal of International Law and Policy* 67–83.

such regulation. They are fiduciaries of these international conventions in the sense that they negotiate, conclude, legislate, implement, and oversee that the undertakings are conformed to.[58] Moreover, states are often guarantors of compensation for such harm, even though they might not be the primary parties upon whom liability is imposed. All in all, it can reasonably be maintained that states have some degree of liability internationally, and that civil liability conventions concern public international law.

58 Barboza, *The Environment*, pp. 41–42.

# 1

# Contemporary Challenges to State Responsibility

Recent profound changes in international relations have had implications for the role and purview of the law of state responsibility. Globalization has empowered non-state actors, the power of individual states has been in decline, and new transnational issues of varying importance have emerged. Besides these external challenges, there have been legal developments affecting the position of state responsibility within the wider international legal order. In addition, different perceptions of what 'responsibility' really means have appeared and gained prominence in the international arena. While state responsibility was once the exclusive responsibility regime to be considered in international law due to the dominant position of states in international affairs, it now exists as part of an international legal order which features both complementary and competing ideas and constructs of responsibility. This fragmentation of responsibility has resulted in the coexistence of multiple responsibility regimes in international law. These developments challenge the position of state responsibility as the primary responsibility system. In this study, the law of state responsibility will be tested against the framework of functionality in order to analyze how well the regime and its rules correspond to the changing international social and legal settings. This study will argue that theoretical significance must be accompanied by meeting the demands of international social reality.

## 1.1 THE ROLE OF STATE RESPONSIBILITY IN INTERNATIONAL LAW

### *1.1.1 Sectoral Overview*

The general rules of state responsibility are prima facie relevant to all fields of international law irrespective of substance or source. This is acknowledged in Article 2 of the Articles of State Responsibility (ASR), which notes that the second element of an internationally wrongful act is the breach of an international obligation irrespective of the nature of the obligation. As aptly put by Jan Klabbers, 'the rules on responsibility, be they of States or international organisations ... are like the rules of the road, applicable to all vehicles without prejudice to the possibility of specific rules applying to specific vehicles.'[1] Despite the generality of the ASR, their practical relevance is a matter of degree. For some international legal issues, the general rules of state responsibility are highly pertinent, but for others they appear to be less applicable. At times, the general rules have been complemented by – or even replaced with – special rules of state responsibility as allowed for by Article 55 of the ASR. In addition, legal branches exist that have moved away altogether from a focus on state responsibility, thus contributing to its shrinking sphere of application. Finally, there are some issues of international law to which state responsibility appears unconnected. Such issues concern, for example, 'allocation of powers and relationships'.[2] Cases of territorial claims or delimitations are usually not formulated in terms of breaches of international obligations involving claims of state responsibility.[3] The following will provide a cursory overview of a number of selected branches of international law from the point of view of the relevance of general and special rules of state responsibility, as well as from the perspective of which elements of the general law of state responsibility have been actively debated.

*International security law* is one of the classic branches of international law pertaining to the use of force against traditional and new security threats, including collective security measures undertaken by the UN Security Council. In conventional terms, this area concerns the protection of states from external military threat; that is, aggression. Since the Iraqi aggression against Kuwait in 1990–91, the number of interstate conflicts has been in decline, and other legal avenues have emerged that also seek to respond to aggression. Aggression is today an international crime under the ICC Statute, although the primary response – for example, to Russia's violations of Ukraine's territorial integrity in 2014 – has been the adoption of targeted

[1] Klabbers, 'Responsibility of States and International Organisations', 485.

[2] Ian Brownlie, 'State Responsibility and the International Court of Justice', in Malgosia Fitzmaurice and Dan Sarooshi (eds.), *Issues of State Responsibility before International Judicial Institutions* (Oxford and Portland, OR: Bloomsbury, 2004), pp. 11–18 at 13.

[3] Rosalyn Higgins, 'Issues of State Responsibility before the International Court of Justice', in Malgosia Fitzmaurice and Dan Sarooshi (eds.), *Issues of State Responsibility, before International Judicial Institutions* (Oxford and Portland, OR: Bloomsbury, 2004), pp. 1–9 at 5.

sanctions, a process which moves more in the direction of civil individual responsibility.[4]

When it comes to new security threats like terrorism, the law of state responsibility has its shortcomings, which have generated not only theories and practices stressing preventive aspects, but also attempts to reformulate the law.[5] In particular, the rules of attribution have been discussed and retheorized since they are viewed as poorly reflecting the use of force by non-state actors.[6] Much attention has been paid by scholars, practitioners, and international judicial institutions upon the correct standard of control applicable to the attribution of conduct of non-state actors under the law of state responsibility. Whereas scholars have noted that the high threshold of the 'effective control' test may not correspond to reality with the changing role of the state in exercising governmental authority,[7] states and courts have arguably not been ready to accept lower thresholds of attribution.[8]

When considering *international human rights law*, the law of state responsibility continues to be utilized, both in terms of the general rules and a vast number of specialized rules. Several human rights treaties include so many specialized rules on responsibility that international human rights law is frequently listed as a self-contained regime to which the applicability of general rules is limited.[9] Regional human rights courts and bodies have ensured that there are enforcement mechanisms available for addressing human rights violations. Findings on state responsibility before bodies such as the European Court of Human Rights (ECtHR) and the Inter-American Court of Human Rights (IACtHR) are frequent. In addition, there are quasi-judicial and other human rights bodies whose findings have also contributed to 'considerable cross-fertilization between these two fields of international law'.[10] The various bodies of international

4 For a discussion on international civil responsibility, see Vincent-Joël Proulx, 'International Civil Individual Responsibility and the Security Council: Building the Foundations of a General Regime' (2019) 40 *Michigan Journal of International Law* 215–287.

5 Becker, *Terrorism and the State*; Proulx, *Transnational Terrorism*; Proulx, *Institutionalizing*.

6 Vladyslav Lanovoy, 'The Use of Force by Non-state Actors and the Limits of Attribution of Conduct' (2017) 28 *European Journal of International Law* 563–585 at 566.

7 Boon, 'Are Control Tests', 340.

8 Ilias Plakokefalos, 'The Use of Force by Non-state Actors and the Limits of Attribution of Conduct: A Reply to Vladyslav Lanovoy' (2017) 28 *European Journal of International Law* 587–593.

9 Bruno Simma and Dirk Pulkowski, 'Of Planets and the Universe: Self-Contained Regimes in International Law' (2006) 17 *European Journal of International Law* 483–529.

10 Theodor Meron, 'State Responsibility for Violations of Human Rights' 1989 (83) *American Society of International Law Proceedings* 372–385 at 372.

human rights law often refer to the International Law Commission (ILC) Articles, in particular to the general rules of attribution, but also to other parts, such as the rules pertaining to the existence of a breach of an international obligation.[11] However, the special rules tend to compete with the ILC Articles concerning the issue of invocation and the applicable sphere of remedies.[12]

Yet, human rights law, which concerns the relations between a government and its citizens, seems difficult a priori to fit into the standard state responsibility model historically grounded in state-to-state relations.[13] Other states are hardly ever injured by human rights violations. In addition, states seem uninterested in pursuing interstate claims, thus leaving a large part of the general rules of state responsibility inapplicable.[14] In fact, it has been claimed that human rights law should not be considered as falling under the province of state responsibility in the first place.[15]

An area in which the law of state responsibility has had less influence is that of *international environmental law*. It is broadly, but by no means unanimously, held that state responsibility is ill-suited overall to environmental problems.[16] This is particularly true for the special issue of climate change,[17] one of the most recent additions to the list of problems of global significance. As Christian Tomuschat notes, '[g]lobal warming ... does not fit into the traditional intellectual framework established for the reparation of tort committed at the

[11] UN Doc. A/71/80/Add.1. Malcolm Evans has claimed that the rules of attribution have been applied in conflict with the ILC Articles. See Malcolm Evans, 'State Responsibility and the European Convention on Human Rights: Role and Realm', in Malgosia Fitzmaurice and Dan Sarooshi (eds.), *Issues of State Responsibility before International Judicial Institutions* (Oxford and Portland, OR: Bloomsbury, 2004), pp. 139–160 at 157.

[12] Simma and Pulkowski, 'Of Planets and the Universe', 525.

[13] Annie Bird, 'Third State Responsibility for Human Rights Violations' (2011) 21 *European Journal of International Law* 883–900 at 884; Dinah Shelton, *Remedies in International Human Rights Law* (2nd ed., Oxford: Oxford University Press, 2005), p. 98.

[14] Rachael Lorna Johnstone, 'State Responsibility: A Concerto for Court, Council and Committee' (2008) 37 *Denver Journal of International Law & Policy* 63–118 at 109.

[15] Evans, 'State Responsibility and the European', 139, 148, 155.

[16] Catherine Redgwell, 'The Wrong Trousers: State Responsibility and International Environmental Law', in Malcolm Evans and Panos Koutrakos (eds.), *The International Responsibility of the European Union: European and International Perspectives* (Oxford and Portland, OR: Hart Publishing, 2013), pp. 257–274; Patricia W. Birnie and Alan E. Boyle, *International Law & the Environment* (2nd ed., Oxford: Oxford University Press, 2002), p. 178; Proulx, *Institutionalizing*, p. 53.

[17] Voigt, 'State Responsibility'; Christian Tomuschat, 'Global Warming and State Responsibility', in Holger Hestermeyer, Nele Matz-Lück, Anja Seibert-Fohr and Silja Vöneky (eds.), *Law of the Sea in Dialogue* (Heidelberg: Springer, 2011), pp. 3–30.

international level.'[18] As a result, states have failed to rely on the rules of state responsibility in response to many environmental problems.[19] What is more, existing special rules often deviate from the overall conception of state responsibility by stressing compliance-enhancing mechanisms instead of utilizing an adversarial logic.

There are several reasons for the difficulty of applying state responsibility thinking and rules to environmental issues and climate change: vague primary obligations and the lack of sufficient special rules on state responsibility, the multitude of involved parties, issues of causation and proof, the difficulty of establishing the threshold for the wrongful act, and the difficulties relating to redress.[20] First, the rules of attribution may need further development in order to properly analyze causation, since multiple states (if not all states) are involved in causing climate change. In some circumstances, the content of state responsibility may also be problematic for climate change claims. The range of victims can be countless, and restitution may seem impossible.[21] Moreover, full reparation appears to exceed the capacities of single states. This situation has elicited suggestions that in the context of climate change, reparations should be limited to 'partial compensation and symbolic measures of satisfaction'.[22] Broadly speaking, instead of reparation of harm, state responsibility would need to be about measures 'incentivizing climate change mitigation'.[23] Moreover, it seems that state responsibility law fails to share the goals of climate change extenuation: '[j]ustice, fairness ... and human security'.[24] It is also paradoxical that all states are at the same time both the author and victim of climate change, even if to varying degrees.[25] The absolute character of the obligation of cessation of the wrongful act is also inapt for dealing with the question of harmful emissions.[26]

Another domain which is generally deemed challenging from the point of state responsibility thinking is *international cyber law*. The special characteristics of cyberspace – as well as the highly fragmented regulation of it – have led to difficulties in applying the general law of state responsibility

[18] Tomuschat, 'Global Warming', 5.

[19] Phoebe Okowa, *State Responsibility for Transboundary Air Pollution in International Law* (Oxford and New York: Oxford University Press, 2000), p. 257; Voigt, 'State Responsibility'.

[20] Proulx, *Institutionalizing*, pp. 53–54; Voigt, 'State Responsibility', 3.

[21] Voigt, 'State Responsibility', 18, 21.

[22] Benoit Mayer, 'Climate Change Reparations and the Law and Practice of State Responsibility' (2017) 7 *Asian Journal of International Law* 185–216 at 185.

[23] Ibid.

[24] Voigt, 'State Responsibility', 1.

[25] Tomuschat, 'Global Warming', 7.

[26] Voigt, 'State Responsibility', 18.

to situations where breaches of international law occur in cyberspace. Simultaneously, there is a lack of specialized rules of responsibility for cybercrimes, although it appears some *lex specialis* (law governing a specific subject matter) is evolving.[27] Yet, it is clear that the general customary rules on state responsibility are applicable to cyberspace.[28] The main problematic issues pertain to attribution – specifically, what level of control is required for attributing non-state actors' attacks to states – and the issue of countermeasures.

One reason for the difficulties involved in the application of the principle of state responsibility is the fact that states rarely use their ordinary governmental agencies when engaged in wrongful conduct in the cyber domain. A variety of actors may be behind cyberattacks.[29] What is more, identifying the origin of the cyberattack is technically extremely difficult.[30] The Tallinn Manual 2.0, however, recognizes the application of several general rules of attribution, while noting that states are responsible for the acts of non-state actors under the 'effective control' test.[31] But there are also dissenting views that hold that the relatively fixed rules of attribution do not function well in this legal field, arguing that 'it is highly unlikely that a state will ever be held publicly accountable under the existing legal framework'.[32] As a result, attribution issues have received much scholarly attention,[33] with some scholars claiming that state practice since 2014 has applied attribution based on criteria different than the 'effective control' test enunciated by the International Court of Justice (ICJ);

27 Peter Z. Stockburger, 'Control and Capabilities Test: Toward a New *Lex Specialis* Governing State Responsibility for Third Party Cyber Incidents', in Henry Roigas, Raik Jakschis, Lauri Lindström and Tomáš Minárik (eds.), *Defending the Core, 9th International Conference on Cyber Conflict* (Tallinn: NATO CCD COE Publications, 2017), pp. 149–162.

28 Michael N. Schmitt (ed.), *Tallinn Manual 2.0 on the International Law Applicable to Cyber Operations* (Cambridge and New York: Cambridge University Press, 2017), p. 80 *et seq.*

29 Martha Finnemore and Duncan B. Hollis, 'Constructing Norms for Global Cybersecurity' (2016) 110 *American Journal of International Law* 425–479 at 431.

30 One recent example showing the difficulty in identifying the actors behind cyber operations is provided from Finland, where the investigations into an extensive case of cyber espionage against the Ministry for Foreign Affairs were terminated because no individual actors behind it could be identified for prosecution.

31 Schmitt, *Tallinn Manual 2.0*, p. 79 *et seq.*

32 Christian Payne, 'International Law Cannot Keep Up with Cyber-Criminals', *World Economic Forum*, 25 February 2019, www.weforum.org/agenda/2019/02/why-international-law-is-failing-to-keep-pace-with-technology-in-preventing-cyber-attacks/ (accessed 20 May 2019).

33 See, e.g., Zhxiong Huang, 'The Attribution Rules in the ILC Articles on State Responsibility: A Preliminary Assessment on Their Application in Cyber Operation' (2014) 14 *Baltic Yearbook of International Law* 41–54; Michael N. Schmitt and Liis Vihul, 'Proxy Wars in Cyberspace: The Evolving International Law of Attribution' (2014) 1 *Fletcher Security Review* 53–72.

that is, the so-called 'control and capabilities' test.[34] However, the lack of clear pronouncements of responsibility by states in the cyber context has contributed to a certain extent to keeping the law unclear,[35] although factually states often are held to be behind cyberattacks.

*International investment law* is closely connected to the law of state responsibility and its development,[36] although this branch of international law relates to the dealings between states and private investors. The traditional law of state responsibility concerned the protection of aliens and their property, an approach that the ILC first sought to codify in the 1950s. But the proximity of the two spheres of international law has remained, even after the ILC shifted its work to laying down the general rules of state responsibility. International arbitration tribunals have extensively referred to a broad range of the ASR, reportedly in more than sixty cases.[37] In particular, the rules on attribution have featured in decisions on international investment law.[38] However, there have been instances in which the rules on attribution have been employed inappropriately; that is, beyond their purpose of deciding matters concerning the responsibility of the state.[39] The rules on circumstances precluding wrongfulness are another part of the general law of state responsibility relevant to international investment law, not systemically so, but in particular cases.[40] All in all, there have been numerous references to the general law of state responsibility in investment treaty arbitration. But as noted by James Crawford, the qualitative side of these references is ambiguous: the usage of the ILC Articles has been more about 'signposting' than about incorporating the ideas explicated in the ASR into arbitration awards.[41] A large part of the general rules of state responsibility also falls outside the scope of the parts of the ASR that relate to invocation of state responsibility and to the consequences of state responsibility, as they pertain only to interstate relations.

34 Stockburger, 'Control and Capabilities Test'.

35 Schmitt and Vihul, 'Proxy Wars', 58.

36 James Crawford, 'Investment Arbitration and the ILC Articles on State Responsibility' (2010) 25 *ICSID Review-Foreign Investment Law Journal* 127–199 at 127.

37 Crawford, 'Investment Arbitration', 128.

38 Ibid., 131–132; Simon Olleson, 'Attribution in Investment Treaty Arbitration' (2016) 31 *ICSID Review* 457–483.

39 Olleson, 'Attribution in Investment', 464.

40 Martins Paparinskis, 'Circumstances Precluding Wrongfulness in International Investment Law' (2016) 31 *ICSID Review* 484–503.

41 Crawford, 'Investment Arbitration', 132.

### 1.1.2 Systemic Importance

The means for assigning responsibility in international law have traditionally been few, with state responsibility at the heart of such efforts.[42] Its significance is recognized by scholars and states alike, many of which assert that state responsibility not only is important, but actually forms one of the cornerstones of the international legal order.[43] This suggests that state responsibility similarly to other foundational parts of international law enjoys a 'sense of immutability',[44] and hence should be left intact.

There are several reasons for the elevated importance of state responsibility. First, the general significance of responsibility to the law cannot be underestimated. Already John Austin highlighted the necessity of sanctions for any legal order. The element of sanctioning – that is, of imposing harm in cases of disobedience – is thus considered a necessary component of the law.[45] This holds especially true for international law, which frequently faces charges of enforcement deficit. Hence, as James Crawford and Simon Olleson have put it, 'responsibility is the necessary corollary of obligation: every breach by a subject of international law of its international obligations entails its international responsibility'.[46] The ILC has also noted that '[t]here is not a single judgment of the Permanent Court of International Justice or of the International Court of Justice, or a single international arbitral award, that recognizes either explicitly or implicitly the existence of international obligations the breach of which would not be a wrongful act and would not

[42] Aust, *Complicity*, p. 5; James Crawford, *State Responsibility: The General Part* (Cambridge: Cambridge University Press, 2014), p. 52.

[43] Dupuy, 'Revolution or Evolution?', 108, describing state responsibility as a 'fundamental institution of the international legal system'; Gilles Cottereau, '*Système juridique et notion de responsabilité*', in *Société Francaise pour le Droit International*, La responsabilité dans le système international: colloque de Mans (Paris: Éditions A. Pedone, 1991), pp. 3–90 at 3; the Nordic countries have described state responsibility as a 'major building block of the international legal order', see Comments and Observations Received from Governments, UN Doc. A/CN.4/515 and Add.1–3, statement by Denmark on behalf of the Nordic countries, p. 42.

[44] See Christian J. Tams generally on the so-called cornerstone image, 'The Use of Force against Terrorists' (2009) 20 *European Journal of International Law* 359–397 at 359–360; Vincent-Joël Proulx calls state responsibility the '*sacred cow*' of international law. See Proulx, *Institutionalizing*, p. 3.

[45] John Austin, *The Province of Jurisprudence Determined and the Uses of the Study of Jurisprudence* (1st published 1832, London: Weidenfeld and Nicolson, 1954), pp. 14–16.

[46] James Crawford and Simon Olleson, 'The Nature and Forms of International Responsibility', in Malcolm D. Evans (ed.), *International Law* (2nd ed., Oxford: Oxford University Press, 2006), pp. 451–477 at 451.

entail international responsibility.[47] Moreover, practice with respect to other responsibility systems is scarce in comparison to that of state responsibility. From this it follows that state responsibility for internationally wrongful acts is one of the most ingrained principles in the doctrine of international law.[48] Thus, responsibility both testifies to the legal character of international law and indicates the international legal order's effectiveness.[49]

Second, state responsibility in particular is significant because states have been the most important actors in international affairs: they are the primary bearers of international obligations. This primacy of states has also allowed the law of state responsibility to become 'the most fully-developed branch of responsibility' in international law.[50] For a long time, state responsibility was the only responsibility system of the international legal order. As such, it constituted one of the manifestations of 'the closed inter-state system of international law'.[51] It merely concerned bilateral or interstate relations; that is, the responsibility of one state to another. In this sense the law resembled classic civil or private law. However, in several respects, the law of state responsibility has distanced itself from this bilateral, interstate approach. Today, the sui generis nature of state responsibility is widely accepted.[52] State responsibility thus forms 'a single system, without any precise comparator in national legal systems'.[53] The source of the breached obligation is irrelevant in the law of state responsibility, which does not make a distinction between different types or degrees of responsibility.[54]

Third, another important feature of state responsibility is its all-encompassing character. There are no material limitations to the law of state responsibility; it applies horizontally across the range of subject matters regulated by international law. It features in different sectors ranging from human rights

47 Report of the International Law Commission on the Work of Its Twenty-eighth Session, UN Doc. A/31/10 (1976), p. 96. See also, Christian J. Tams, 'Law-making in Complex Processes: The World Court and the Modern Law of State Responsibility', in Christine Chinkin and Freya Baetens (eds.), *Sovereignty, Statehood and State Responsibility: Essays in Honour of James Crawford* (Cambridge: Cambridge University Press, 2015), pp. 287–306.

48 Roberto Ago, *Third Report on State Responsibility*, UN Doc. A/CN.4/246 and Add.1–3, p. 205, para. 30.

49 Pellet, 'The Definition of Responsibility', 3.

50 Crawford and Olleson, 'The Nature and Forms', 451.

51 James Crawford, 'International Law as an Open System', in James Crawford, *International Law as an Open System: Selected Essays* (London: Cameron May, 2002), pp. 17–38 at 29.

52 Pellet, 'The Definition of Responsibility', 12–13.

53 James Crawford, 'The System of International Responsibility', in James Crawford, Alain Pellet and Simon Olleson (eds.), *The Law of International Responsibility* (Oxford: Oxford University Press, 2010), pp. 17–25 at 21.

54 Crawford and Olleson, 'The Nature and Forms', 456.

to trade law, and a priori no field of international law exists to which it would not apply. State responsibility is thus premised on the generality of concepts and elements that underlie the system. Irrespective of the substantive obligation, one can find commonality in the rules on attribution, breach, excuses, and consequences.[55] The broad and general scope of state responsibility has caused it to recur frequently in international disputes and scholarly writings, a feature which also has differentiated it from other codified topics in international law.[56]

Several states stressed the systemic significance of state responsibility in their commentaries to the ILC during the long codification process. State responsibility was considered to 'secure legal stability and predictability in international relations'[57] and to play an indisputably important role in 'the smooth functioning of the international order'.[58] The Nordic states, for example, have considered state responsibility 'the last major building block of the international legal order to be placed alongside the law of treaties and the law of the peaceful settlement of disputes'.[59] Indeed, both states and international legal scholars have highlighted the ideological importance of state responsibility[60] as strengthening the international legal system, thus making international law more like 'real law'. Indeed, the perception of international law as a unified whole is largely dependent upon the rules of state responsibility.[61] It has been hailed as a 'metalanguage' of the international legal order,[62] or as the 'glue' that keeps international law together.[63]

55 Ibid., 455.

56 Roberto Ago, *Second Report on State Responsibility*, UN Doc. A/CN.4/233 (1970), p. 179, para. 11.

57 Comments and Observations Received from Governments, UN Doc. A/CN.4/515 and Add.1–3, statement by Japan, p. 43.

58 Ibid., statement by Spain, p. 44.

59 *Comments and Observations Received from Governments*, UN Doc. A/CN.4/515 and Add.1–3 (2001), statement by Denmark on behalf of the Nordic countries, p. 42, para. 1.

60 For a discussion of the centrality of state responsibility to, among other things, the international rule of law and peace, see Helmut Philipp Aust, 'The Normative Environment for Peace – On the Contribution of the ILC's Articles on State Responsibility', in Georg Nolte (ed.), *Peace through International Law: The Role of the International Law Commission* (Dordrecht: Springer, 2009), pp. 13–46.

61 Aust, *Complicity*, p. 86.

62 Thomas Kleinlein, 'The Language of Public International Law', in Société Française pour le droit international (ed.), *Droit international et diversité des cultures juridiques* (Paris: Pedone, 2008), pp. 199–208 at 201, cited in Aust, *Complicity*, p. 86. See also, Aust, 'The Normative Environment', 27.

63 Kristen E. Boon, 'The Law of Responsibility: A Response to Fragmentation' (2012) 25 *Global Business & Development Law Journal* 395–407 at 406.

The systemic importance of state responsibility has been highlighted not only in current times of fragmentation where international law has developed into several subregimes,[64] but also early on in the codification process.[65] As noted by Outi Korhonen and Toni Selkälä, '[t]he concept and the project have had a major significance in steering international law through the many storms of the twentieth century and beyond – not least, the challenges of "fragmentation" and the "fall of international law".'[66] Whereas in the 1960s state responsibility was considered by Special Rapporteur Roberto Ago to have a direct impact on the character of international law as law, lately the importance of state responsibility has shifted to an emphasis on its role as a bridge connecting different subregimes.[67] Irrespective of some discernable changes in the systemic role played by state responsibility, many scholars are still prepared to assign it a quasi-constitutional role, because it 'provides the foundation of the law of treaties and constitutes the most basic part of general international law'.[68] For example, Rosalyn Higgins describes state responsibility as 'an area of major importance, and a central element in the whole theoretical structure of international law'.[69] Paul Reuter has even gone one step further by stating: '*la responsabilité constitue une partie essentielle de ce quel'on pourrait considérer comme la constitution de la communauté internationale*' (responsibility constitutes an essential part of the so-called constitution of the international community).[70]

The perception of state responsibility as an important and unifying part of the international legal order reached its peak in the 1960s with the 'Roberto Ago revolution'. Despite the firm commitment to state responsibility even as a quasi-constitutional doctrine of international law, the bedrock of the classic

64 Simma and Pulkowksi, 'Of Planets and the Universe', 64.

65 Special Rapporteur Roberto Ago, for example, held in 1963 that there was a lack of 'general studies of the international responsibility of the State assigning to each element its true place in a systematic whole'. See Report by Roberto Ago, Chairman of the Sub-Committee on State Responsibility, UN Doc. A/CN.4/152 (1963), p. 252.

66 Outi Korhonen and Toni Selkälä, 'Theorizing Responsibility', in Anne Orford and Florian Hoffmann (eds.), *The Oxford Handbook on the Theory of International Law* (Oxford: Oxford University Press, 2016), pp. 844–861 at 848.

67 Boon, 'The Law of Responsibility', 405.

68 Brownlie, 'State Responsibility and the International Court', 12.

69 Rosalyn Higgins, *Problems & Progress: International Law and How We Use It* (Oxford: Clarendon Press, 1994), p. 146.

70 Paul Reuter, 'Trois observations sur le codification de la responsabilité international des Etats pour fait illicite' (1991) *Le droit international au service de la paix, de la justice et du développement. Etudes dédiées à la mémoire de Michel Virally* 389–398 at 390. Other scholars noting the 'constitutionalist component' of state responsibility are, e.g., Nissel, *A History of State Responsibility*, p. 18.

theory of state responsibility began to unravel in the second half of the 1960s when attempts were made to extract from state responsibility that part which was not grounded in an internationally wrongful act.[71] Indeed, the ILC itself separated the question of liability for lawful acts from the state responsibility project. Another crack in state responsibility law appeared with the turn to state criminality in the codification work of the ILC,[72] which sought to establish a penalizing regime for serious violations of the most important norms of the international community. Despite the failure of the Draft Article 19 project in the ILC, the manifestation of international criminal law in the 1990s further eroded the significance of state responsibility. By the time the ILC managed to conclude its codification work, the sphere of application of the law of state responsibility had been substantially reduced. This fragmentation left it being less important than was originally construed, while it still allegedly enjoyed the status of the paradigmatic form of responsibility in international law.[73] Section 1.2 will discuss developments – both internal and external to the international legal order – that have come to challenge state responsibility.

## 1.2 INTERNAL CHALLENGES: DOMESTIC ANALOGY AND FRAGMENTATION

There are no predetermined truths regarding how one should think about the matter of responsibility in law.[74] Legal responsibility means different things to different people, both conceptually and with regard to purposes and practices. This plurality of understanding strongly influences thinking about responsibility in international law, which traditionally has had only one single system to address a wide range of needs. Thus, the law of state responsibility must continually confront the manifold existing views on the subject of responsibility. The sui generis character of state responsibility in international law makes it vulnerable to competing responsibility ideas that derive their weightiness from the different responsibility branches in national legal systems.

71 Dupuy, 'Revolution or Evolution?', 106.

72 Ibid., 107.

73 On the question of state responsibility as the primary form of responsibility, see Crawford, 'The System of International Responsibility', 17; Jutta Brunnée 'International Legal Accountability through the Lens of the Law of State Responsibility' (2005) XXXVI *Netherlands Yearbook of International Law* 21–55; James Crawford and Jeremy Watkins, 'International Responsibility', in Samantha Besson and John Tasioulas (eds.), *The Philosophy of International Law* (Oxford: Oxford University Press, 2010), pp. 283–298.

74 See, e.g., Cane, *Responsibility in Law and Morality*, pp. 279–283.

### 1.2.1 *Conceptual Diversity*

General legal discourse on responsibility often takes criminal responsibility as a starting point for discussion[75] – a responsibility system that features concepts such as 'guilt' and 'punishment'. These notions have traditionally played only a minor role in international responsibility and as such are foreign to the law of state responsibility. However, the domestic analogy has provided international legal scholars addressing responsibility issues with not only one model of responsibility, but with three basic models that differ from one another: criminal law, private law, and public law. All these models have featured to some extent in discourses on state responsibility.

Besides the criminal law model, which is an 'agent-focused account' built around the concepts of guilt and punishment,[76] there are the private law and public law models of responsibility. The private law model of responsibility is based on the idea of two equals that strive to restore equilibrium to their relationship.[77] In this sense, responsibility is a remedy for undoing harm so that the actors can move on as if no harm had taken place. Therefore, the actor who has committed the wrong is obliged to repair the harm, but no element of punishment is relevant for the private law model. The victim, rather than the agent, is central.[78] The public law model is concerned with the performance of public functions, usually with respect to governmental bodies. Public law models of responsibility are also highly relational: in this case, not between two equals but between a government and its citizens. The aim of responsibility understood in this way is controlling the exercise of public power. Thus, group interests and a concern for the 'consequences of conduct' are essential to a public law model of responsibility.[79]

Another angle from which diversity is brought into the responsibility discourse is that of the separation between individual and collective forms of responsibility. Collective responsibility has represented the traditional form of responsibility in international law and can be defined as '[holding] individuals … responsible for a delict, not because they have committed it but because they belong to the group – family, tribe, or state – to which the delinquent belongs'.[80] The situation is thus reversed from domestic law,

75 Ibid., p. 29.
76 Ibid., pp. 49, 56.
77 Pellet, 'The Definition of Responsibility', pp. 12–13.
78 Cane, *Responsibility in Law and Morality*, pp. 49–53.
79 Ibid.
80 Hans Kelsen, *Principles of International Law* (3rd printing, Clark, NJ: the Lawbook Exchange Ltd, 1959), p. 10.

in which responsibility is primarily naturalistic – that is, attached to individual human beings.[81] However, the precise nature of state responsibility continues to be debated. Whereas some scholars have stressed its collective nature,[82] others maintain that state responsibility constitutes a form of individual responsibility. For example, James Crawford and Jeremy Watkins have claimed that one should not equate the artificial legal entity of the state as being the same as 'any "collectivity" of natural persons'.[83] According to this position, states are viewed as 'kinds of individuals, legal persons … at the international level'.[84] Yet, this study will understand state responsibility as a collective responsibility system on the grounds that the consequences of state responsibility are collectivized. As recognized by Antonio Cassese, 'collective responsibility means both that the whole State community is liable for any breach of international law committed by any State official and that the whole State community may suffer from the consequences of the wrongful act.'[85]

However, changes in international responsibility have taken place that have brought the conversation about responsibility in the international sphere closer to its domestic counterpart. A move from collective responsibility to individual responsibility has occurred, although development within collective forms has also taken place. International law now embraces both individual and collective forms of responsibility: the former exemplified by individual criminal responsibility, the latter mainly by state responsibility but also by the responsibility of international organizations, the responsibility of armed groups, and even by tentative efforts for corporate social or criminal responsibility.

Although international law remains formally neutral as to any preference for individual or collective responsibility, the two forms are often juxtaposed. Collective responsibility is seen as a trademark of a primitive legal system; therefore it has increasingly begun to suffer from a bad reputation. It is even portrayed as dangerous, if one is to believe the International Criminal Tribunal for Former Yugoslavia (ICTY), which described collective responsibility in terms of *fiat justitia et pereat mundus* (let justice be done, even if the world were to perish). According to the Tribunal, collective responsibility endangers

[81] Cane, *Responsibility in Law and Morality*, pp. 42–43.

[82] See, e.g., Shane Darcy, *Collective Responsibility and Accountability under International Law* (Leiden: Brill, 2007), p. xvi.

[83] See Crawford and Watkins, 'International Responsibility', 289.

[84] John R. Morss, *International Law as the Law of Collectives* (Farnham: Ashgate Publishing Limited, 2013), p. 1.

[85] Antonio Cassese, *International Law* (Oxford and New York: Oxford University Press, 2001), p. 7.

peace and security for generations, while individual criminal responsibility ultimately brings lasting peace.[86]

Overall, many developments have affected and characterized international responsibility during the past decades. The collective foundation of state responsibility has been questioned in favour of approaches utilizing a more individual focus. At the same time, the individualization of responsibility has brought with it the criminalization of responsibility in international law, with practices and purposes vastly different from the goals of state responsibility. State responsibility, usually portrayed as a civil system, is no longer uncritically accepted as the evident – or even correct – mechanism for distributing responsibility when it comes to certain transgressions. Responsibility in international law is thus torn between its individual and collective forms, between criminal, civil, and public law interpretations of responsibility and between the interests those different forms of responsibility signify.

### 1.2.2 *Normative Fragmentation*

This diversity of ideas and practices has resulted in the broadening of international responsibility, both in terms of legal subjects and types of regimes. On the one hand, the state responsibility model has spurred the creation of similar responsibility regimes for other subjects of international law such as international organizations and armed groups. On the other hand, there has been a divergence into *qualitatively* different responsibility regimes with the emergence of international liability and international criminal law.

The fragmentation of international responsibility into qualitatively diverse responsibility regimes – with different rules and rationales – raises questions about the relationship between these regimes in terms of specialization, systematization, and substance. A first point to be discussed with respect to the proliferation of responsibility regimes is the unfolding of the distinction between general and special law. The traditional view holds that state responsibility is the only general responsibility regime in international law;

[86] In 1994, the ICTY stated regarding the threats of collective responsibility: 'eventually whole groups will be held guilty of massacres, torture, rape, ethnic cleansing, the wanton destruction of cities and villages. The history of the [Yugoslav] region clearly shows that clinging to feelings of "collective responsibility" easily degenerates into resentment, hatred and frustration and inevitably leads to further violence and new crime'. See UNGA, *Report of the International Tribunal for the Prosecutions of Persons Responsible for Serious Violations of International Humanitarian Law Committed in the Territory of the Former Yugoslavia since 1991*, UN Doc. A/49/342 (29 August 1994), para. 16.

there are no material limitations to state responsibility,[87] and the rules of state responsibility are of general and secondary character. This is acknowledged by Article 55 of the ASR in that *lex specialis* establishes that the rules of state responsibility do not apply 'where and to the extent that the conditions for the existence of an internationally wrongful act or the content or implementation of international responsibility of a State are governed by special rules of international law'.[88]

Having laid down that the rules of state responsibility are general law still leaves open the question of the precise nature of the international liability and international criminal law regimes.[89] It could easily be assumed due to the general character of state responsibility that both international liability and international criminal law are specialized law. But the separate nature of state responsibility from these regimes makes it difficult to describe them as special law. Indeed, the ILC Study Group on Fragmentation of International Law has aptly expressed that 'it is often hard to distinguish what is "general" and what is "particular"'.[90] Nevertheless, describing international criminal law and international liability as particular or special international law is beyond doubt, since particular law regulates matters more precisely and 'to the point'[91] than can be accomplished using general legal rules. On the other hand, the fact that both international criminal law and international liability have distinct foundations leaves their exact relationship to state responsibility unclear; that is, what is general and what is particular becomes obscure.

The discussion around the degree of specificity with which the different responsibility regimes set down rules is intrinsically linked to their mutual relations, a further contentious issue following from the coexistence of multiple responsibility regimes. It is noteworthy, however, that scholars generally do not discuss all three responsibility regimes at the same time; the relations between state responsibility, international criminal law, and international liability as a whole are rarely dealt with on a theoretical level, nor from the perspective

87 This is evident from Art. 2 (b) of the ASR, which holds that the second element of an internationally wrongful act of a state consists of an action or an omission which 'constitutes a breach of an international obligation of the State'. See, Report of the International Law Commission on the Work of Its Fifty-third Session, UN Doc. A/56/10 (2001), Chapter IV.

88 Ibid., Chapter IV.

89 In this respect, James Crawford has held that 'it is doubtful whether any *general* regime of responsibility' has developed to cover other subjects of international law outside of states. See Crawford, 'The System of International Responsibility', 18 (emphasis in original).

90 Martti Koskenniemi, *Fragmentation of International Law: Difficulties Arising from the Diversification and Expansion of International Law. Report of the Study Group of the International Law Commission*, UN Doc. A/CN.4/L.682 (13 April 2006), para. 58.

91 Ibid., para. 60.

of specific problems.[92] This is due at least in part to the remote connection between harmful but lawful acts, and the most egregious breaches that are punishable under international criminal law.

The relations between state responsibility and international criminal law have been well explored. Three different approaches can be discerned. First, there are scholars that hold these two responsibility regimes to be connected to such an extent that they form one coherent system. Second, there are those scholars who insist on their distinctiveness. A third approach is intermediary; it focuses on the points of contact between the two regimes. To begin with, scholars maintaining the unity of the different responsibility ideas and regimes consider individual criminal responsibility to be a part of state responsibility; it is perceived as constituting one consequence of state responsibility, rather than as forming a system of its own. It is explicitly the special nature of individual criminal responsibility – in contrast to the general character of state responsibility – which leads some to understand the former as a function of the latter.[93]

Another justification for perceiving the two responsibility regimes as a coherent system is that individual criminal responsibility is most often attached to state officials.[94] Thus, punishing the individual means that the state is indirectly punished.[95] Support for a unitary understanding in addition to the collective character of international crimes is found in the ILC's commentary to Article 37 of the Articles on State Responsibility, which enlists 'penal action against the individuals whose conduct caused the internationally wrongful act' as a form of satisfaction.[96]

Nevertheless, for the most part the position that state responsibility and individual criminal responsibility form one unitary system has been rejected.[97]

92 An important exception in this regard is Dupuy, 'Revolution or Evolution?', although he discusses international criminal responsibility, not international criminal law.

93 Maison, *La responsabilité individuelle*, p. 1.

94 Nina H. B. Jørgensen, *The Responsibility of States for International Crimes* (Oxford: Oxford University Press, 2000), p. 154.

95 Bonafè, *The Relationship*, pp. 65–66.

96 Commentary to Art. 37 of the ASR, para. 5.

97 See Christian Dominicé, 'La question de la double responsabilité de l'Etat et de son agent', in Emile Yakpo and Tahar Boumedra (eds.), *Liber Amicorum Mohammed Bedjaoui* (The Hague, London and Boston: Kluwer Law International, 1999), pp. 143–157 at 147; Andrea Bianchi, 'State Responsibility and Criminal Liability of Individuals', in Antonio Cassese (ed.), *The Oxford Companion to International Criminal Justice* (Oxford: Oxford University Press, 2009), pp. 16–24 at 16; Pierre-Marie Dupuy, 'International Criminal Responsibility of the Individual and International Responsibility of the State', in Antonio Cassese, Paolo Gaeta and John R. W. D. Jones (eds.), *The Rome Statute of the International Criminal Court: A Commentary (Volume II)* (Oxford: Oxford University Press, 2002), pp. 1085–1099.

It has been held that individual responsibility is not to be seen 'merely as a form of reparation to be used in case of state crimes'.[98] State responsibility and individual criminal responsibility respectively have their own legal basis, their own subjects, different legal standards, and separate functions to fulfil. As a result, both the substantive law and its enforcement are different.[99] Moreover, the ILC has always advanced the idea that state and individual responsibility are separate regimes.[100] During the codification of 'A Code of Crimes against Peace and Security of Mankind', the ILC noted that '[t]he régime of the criminal responsibility of individuals for offences against the peace and security of mankind thus stands apart from the general régime of responsibility for internationally wrongful acts.'[101] It has also held that the same applies to those rules of state responsibility that concern serious breaches.[102] The ILC has further pointed out that the very fact that the General Assembly had separately requested the codification of international crimes and internationally wrongful acts, proved them to be two different systems.[103]

A number of studies on the relationship between state and individual responsibility have endorsed an intermediary approach to the coexistence of the regimes. Many point out the existence of so-called bridges (or links) between the two regimes, thus claiming that although they are in principle separate, 'it seems impossible to see them as perfectly isolated fields of international law'.[104] To be more precise, it has been suggested that 'aggravated state responsibility and individual criminal liability are to be seen under a unitary legal framework'.[105] However, a cautious position towards linking the two responsibility systems more generally should be adopted, since the conditions for such attempts are still unclear.[106] This might change, however, if the ICC chooses to exercise

98 Andrea Bianchi, 'State Responsibility', 17.

99 Bonafè, *The Relationship*, p. 237; Dupuy, 'International Criminal Responsibility', 1094–1099.

100 Giorgio Conetti, 'State's Crime and Individuals' Crimes: What Relationship?', in Mauro Politi and Giuseppe Nesi (eds.), *The Rome Statute of the ICC: A Challenge to Impunity* (Dartmouth, Aldershot: Ashgate, 2001), pp. 131–133 at 131.

101 Report of the ILC on the Work of Its Thirty-fifth Session, UN Doc. A/38/10 (1983), p. 15, para. 60.

102 Report of the ILC on the Work of Its Twenty-eighth Session, UN Doc. A/31/10 (1976), p. 119.

103 Report of the ILC on the Work of Its Thirty-fifth Session, UN Doc. A/38/10 (1983), p. 15, para. 60.

104 Bonafè, *The Relationship*, p. 253. On the discussion of the links between the regimes, see Natalie L. Reid, 'Bridging the Conceptual Chasm: Superior Responsibility as the Missing Link between State and Individual Responsibility in International Law' (2005) 18 *Leiden Journal of International Law* 795–828.

105 Bonafè, *The Relationship*, p. 253. Such a perception, however, dismisses the consequences it would have on the unity of state responsibility.

106 Dupuy, 'International Criminal Responsibility', 1098.

its jurisdiction with respect to the crime of aggression which – according to the Kampala definition of aggression – requires a 'determination of state responsibility as a prerequisite for the finding of individual criminal responsibility for the commission of the crime'.[107] The discussion of the relationship between state responsibility and individual criminal responsibility would hence gain new momentum with the entry into force of the Kampala definition.[108]

However, the independent standing of international liability is not as straightforward as that of the unique character of international criminal law. Still, the difference in kind – not in degree – between state responsibility and issues of liability was explicitly recognized by the ILC: 'Because of the entirely different basis of the liability for risk and the different nature of the rules governing it, as well as its content and the forms it may assume, a joint examination of the two subjects could only make both of them more difficult to grasp.'[109] In spite of the ILC's recognition of liability as a type of responsibility differing from state responsibility, some scholars have refused to embrace their distinctiveness. The motivation for this refusal seems both principled and pragmatic. It has been held that 'a global distinction between lawful and unlawful activities is useless' because it is the content of the primary rule which is important.[110] The assumption by the ILC that wrongfulness entails prohibition has thus been described as a misconception.[111] Moreover, Alan Boyle has pointed out that uncoupling liability from state responsibility would also have deleterious consequences, since international efforts to agree upon 'effective principles of international environmental law' would be undermined.[112]

Despite criticism of the ILC decision to separate the topic of liability from state responsibility, it is important to note that the obligation to make good for harm caused by hazardous activities truly forms a separate legal regime from rules relating to the commission of an internationally wrongful act. State responsibility and international liability 'are two different legal species';[113] the latter represents not a slight technical diversion from the former, but rather a completely new way of approaching international problems that are a fact – perhaps even a desirable fact – of life.

107 Dapo Akande and Antonios Tzanakopoulos, 'The Crime of Aggression in the ICC and State Responsibility' (2017) 58 *Harvard International Law Online Journal* 33–36 at 34.
108 See Frédéric Mégret, 'State Responsibility for Aggression: A Human Rights Approach' (2017) 58 *Harvard International Law Online Journal* 62–65; Leila Nadya Sadat (ed.), *Seeking Accountability for the Unlawful Use of Force* (Cambridge: Cambridge University Press, 2018).
109 Report of the ILC (1976), p. 70, para. 65.
110 Brownlie, *State Responsibility: Part I*, p. 50.
111 Ibid.; Boyle, 'State Responsibility', 14.
112 Boyle, 'State Responsibility', 1.
113 Barboza, *The Environment*, p. 28.

To sum up, the point to be made with respect to the discussions on the general/special distinction and the mutual relations between the three responsibility regimes is indeed that international criminal law and international liability are meant to serve as alternatives to state responsibility. Irrespective of numerous efforts to construe these alternative constructions of responsibility as elements of state responsibility, either by way of calling them specialized law or by claiming that they form part of a systemic whole, their distinctiveness should be recognized. International liability and criminal law, as any other new rules or regimes, are the means of expressing 'the differing pursuits and preferences that actors in a pluralistic (global) society have'.[114] They represent new types of thinking about responsibility on the international plane, precisely aimed at deviating from the general law of state responsibility.

### 1.2.3 *Overlaps*

Regardless of how one chooses to theoretically construct the coexistence of qualitatively different responsibility regimes, the fact is that situations arise which may trigger responses under both state responsibility and international criminal law. However, no violations of international law exist that would potentially fall under all three responsibility regimes. Lawful acts that trigger a duty to compensation and international crimes that are punishable are simply each other's opposite. The former seeks to achieve compensation, whereas the latter is grounded in reproach. Nor do international liability and state responsibility cover the same acts; liability represents acts not prohibited by international law, in contrast to the wrongfulness of acts covered by state responsibility. Admittedly, a harmful event can be construed both as lawful and wrongful, but not with respect to the same actor. Thus, for example, a nuclear power plant operator may not be at fault for a radiation accident, but still be under an obligation to compensate for the harm caused. At the same time, such an accident can be the result of bad oversight by state authorities, thus leading to the responsibility of the state. Nevertheless, the two responsibilities are not based on the same act: the duty of the operator to compensate stems from the harm itself, and the responsibility of the state results from a failure to exercise due diligence.[115]

114 Koskenniemi, *Fragmentation Report*, paras. 15–16.

115 The ILC Principles on Loss Allocation note the close connection to issues of state responsibility by stating that '[s]tates are responsible for infringements of their obligations of prevention under international law.' See the Draft Principles on the Allocation of Loss in the Case of Transboundary Harm arising out of Hazardous Activities (hereafter Loss Allocation Principles), Report of the ILC on the Work of Its Fifty-eighth Session, UN Doc. A/61/10 (2006), Chapter V, preamble, p. 107.

But a number of acts constituting violations of international law open the door for dual responsibility under the regimes of state responsibility and individual criminal responsibility. Whereas state responsibility can be attached for all sorts of violations of international law regardless of the substance of international obligations, international criminal law has a different, more limited nature. It concerns only a small number of violations categorized either as treaty-based crimes or crimes under international law. The possibility of choosing between two different legal remedies thus concerns only a limited number of violations of international law relating to gross breaches upon human dignity and life. These breaches include 'planning, preparing, or ordering wars of aggression, genocide, crimes against humanity, killings of protected persons in armed conflicts, terrorism, and torture'.[116] Thus, for example, the same act constituting the crime of genocide can be perpetrated both by a state and an individual.

The concurrence of the state and individual responsibility regimes has rarely been viewed as problematic.[117] Their respective evolution into two different systems is marked by ample acceptance of the separate and independent existence of the two regimes. On the subject of individual responsibility, Article 58 of the ASR states: '[t]hese articles [on state responsibility] are without prejudice to any question of the individual responsibility under international law of any person acting on behalf of a State'.[118] A similar provision is found in Article 25 (4) of the 1998 ICC Statute: 'No provision in this Statute relating to individual criminal responsibility shall affect the responsibility of States under international law.'[119] Beyond this mutual recognition of the existence and independence of state responsibility and individual criminal responsibility, no other regulation regarding their relationship is found in international law.

116 André Nollkaemper, 'Concurrence between Individual Responsibility and State Responsibility in International Law' (2003) 52 *International and Comparative Law Quarterly* 615–640 at 618–619.

117 For opposite views, see Héctor Gros Espiell, 'International Responsibility of the State and Individual Criminal Responsibility in the International Protection of Human Rights', in Maurizio Ragazzi (ed.), *International Responsibility Today: Essays in Memory of Oscar Schachter* (Leiden: Martinus Nijhoff Publishers, 2005), pp. 151–160; Gerry Simpson, *Law, War & Crime: War Crimes Trials and the Reinvention of International Law* (Cambridge: Polity Press, 2007), p. 58; Thomas Franck, 'Individual Criminal Liability and Collective Civil Responsibility: Do They Reinforce or Contradict One Another?' (2007) 6 *Washington University Global Studies Law Review* 567–573; Katja Creutz, 'International Responsibility and Problematic Law-making', in Rain Liivoja and Jarna Petman (eds.), *International Law-making: Essays in Honour of Jan Klabbers* (Oxon: Routledge, 2014), pp. 171–189.

118 Report of the ILC on the Work of Its Fifty-third Session, UN Doc. A/56/10 (2001), Chapter IV.

119 Rome Statute of the International Criminal Court, Rome, 17 July 1998, in force 1 July 2002, 2187 *United Nations Treaty Series* 3.

These saving clauses function as 'dividing walls between the different systems'.[120] Their aim is to ensure that any findings relating to state responsibility do not ipso facto equal decisions on individual responsibility, or vice versa. It was thought important enough to separately point this out, because many international crimes are committed by individuals acting as state officials. The ILC Commentary expands upon this connection by further stating that the state cannot escape its international responsibility by prosecuting and punishing the state officials who committed the wrongful act.[121] To state the reverse, state officials cannot 'hide behind the State in respect of their own responsibility for conduct of theirs which is contrary to the rules of international law which are applicable to them'.[122]

International judicial practice supports the separation and peaceful coexistence of the responsibility regimes, although some recent criticism has been made against too high a dependence of state responsibility upon individual criminal responsibility in the ICJ's reasoning and findings on genocide.[123] The World Court has confirmed the duality of responsibilities while simultaneously maintaining their distinctiveness in its case law on genocide, namely in the *Bosnian Genocide* case and the *Croatian Genocide* case. In the former case, the Court noted that the 'duality of responsibility continues to be a constant feature of international law'.[124] In the more recent case between Croatia and Serbia, the ICJ adhered to the same conceptual scheme in holding that '[s]tate responsibility and individual criminal responsibility are governed by different legal régimes and pursue different aims.'[125] International criminal law institutions have also maintained the separation between state responsibility and individual criminal responsibility. Chief Prosecutor of the ICTY Carla del Ponte opened the case of the international community versus Slobodan Miloševic´ in 2002 with the following words: 'The accused in this case, as in all cases before the Tribunal, is charged as an individual. He is prosecuted on

120 Daniel Bodansky and John R. Crook, 'Symposium: the ILC's State Responsibility Articles. Introduction and Overview' (2002) 96 *American Journal of International Law* 773–791 at 788.

121 Report of the ILC on the Work of Its Fifty-third Session, UN Doc. A/56/10 (2001), Chapter IV, Commentary to Art. 58 of the ASR, para. 3.

122 Ibid.

123 Beatrice I. Bonafè, 'Reassessing Dual Responsibility for International Crimes' (2016) 73 *Seqüênica (Florianópolis)* 19–36 at 35–36.

124 Case Concerning Application of the Convention on Prevention and Punishment of the Crime of Genocide (*Bosnia and Herzegovina* v. *Serbia and Montenegro*) Judgment, ICJ Reports 2007, p. 43, para. 173.

125 *Application of the Convention on the Prevention and Punishment of the Crime of Genocide* (*Croatia* v. *Serbia*) Judgment, ICJ Reports 2015, p. 3, para. 129.

the basis of his individual criminal responsibility. No state or organization is on trial here today.'[126]

It is not an accident that multiple legal avenues are available concerning a limited number of wrongs. When it comes to genocide, for example, the drafters of the Genocide Convention clearly intended there to be both individual criminal responsibility and state responsibility for the same crime. This is evident from Article IV, which provides that '[p]ersons committing genocide or any of the other acts ... shall be punished, whether they are constitutionally responsible rulers, public officials or private individuals'.[127] The responsibility of states is again expressed in Article IX, which stipulates that '[d]isputes between the Contracting Parties ... including those relating to the responsibility of a State for genocide' shall be settled by the ICJ.

Another motivation behind the emergence of these new and alternative responsibility regimes is that they can be viewed as filling voids or gaps that exist in the law of state responsibility. For example, Jutta Brunnée has noted: '[o]ne way to read these developments is that they help fill the accountability gaps left by the law of state responsibility and serve to channel accountability to the appropriate actor.'[128] Hence, overlaps between state responsibility and international criminal law may be both intended and incidental; responsibility constructions outside of state responsibility help to solve outstanding issues because they have a different underlying philosophy and rely on different principles than does state responsibility.[129] For that reason, the real questions to be asked with respect to state responsibility have to do with both how the law is affected by the evolution of alternative responsibility regimes and whether it is still considered to be relevant, despite facing not only internal challenges, but also external ones – specifically globalization.

## 1.3 THE EXTERNAL CHALLENGE OF GLOBALIZATION

It is often taken for granted that the state is the basis for international law and concomitantly is the foundation for arranging legal responsibility within this particular normative order. However, globalization has challenged this presumption: '[t]o speak of globalization is inevitably to raise interrogations about

[126] *Prosecutor* v. *Milošević*, Case No. IT-02-54-T, Prosecution Opening Statement (12 February 2002), p. 4.

[127] Convention on the Prevention and Punishment of the Crime of Genocide, New York, 9 December 1948 by UNGA Res. 260(III)A, in force 12 January 1951, 78 *United Nations Treaty Series* 277.

[128] Brunnée, 'International Legal Accountability', 54.

[129] Koskenniemi, *Fragmentation Report*, paras. 15–16.

the fate of the State.'[130] Globalization has affected the distribution of power in international relations: the centrality of states is generally thought to have diminished because of deterritorialization, which largely results from the increased movements of people, goods, and ideas across the globe.[131] The world has become more interdependent at all governance levels,[132] which also affects the tenets of international law. Indeed, 'the basic conceptual framework of international law as a primarily inter-State matter' is increasingly under pressure.[133]

Although the question is still open regarding how and to what extent globalization will eventually affect the nation-state, tendencies fortifying the effects of globalization are also occurring internally within states. Many states have embarked upon the road of privatization and outsourcing, but this trend has also been accelerated by the liberalization of global trade and an 'ideological predilection for privatization in a number of Western countries'.[134] Functions that used to belong to the governmental sphere have increasingly been taken over by private actors; private companies are more and more engaged in water services, the provision of security, prison management, participation in hostilities, and even training in the exercise of the rule of law. It is clear that the intrinsic nature of the state is changing, thus affecting its position as the most important subject of international law.[135] Another factor contributing to the lessened importance of states is their breakdown, which is characterized by the lack of an efficient government capable of performing traditional state functions.[136] Many of the poorest states in the world have faced the collapse of functioning state institutions – meaning that within these states no governmental authorities remain to uphold international legal obligations or to blame for failure to abide by them.

At the same time, non-state entities such as international organizations, individuals, transnational corporations, and non-governmental organizations (NGOs) have gained in prominence.[137] They act as the social forces of

[130] Frédéric Mégret, 'Globalization', in Rüdiger Wolfrum (ed.), *Max Planck Encyclopedia of Public International Law* (Oxford: Oxford University Press, 2009), para. 12.

[131] Stephan Hobe, 'The Era of Globalisation as a Challenge to International Law' (2001–2002) 40 *Duquesne University Law Review* 655–665 at 662; Frédéric Mégret, 'Globalization', paras. 31, 33; Becker, *Terrorism and the State*, p. 362.

[132] Dinah Shelton, 'Protecting Human Rights in a Globalized World' (2002) 25 *Boston College International and Comparative Law Review* 273–322 at 275.

[133] Vaughan Lowe, 'The Iraq Crisis: What Now?' (2003) 52 *International and Comparative Law Quarterly* 859–871 at 859.

[134] Andrew Clapham, *Human Rights Obligations of Non-State Actors* (Oxford: Oxford University Press, 2006), p. 8.

[135] Boon, 'Are Control Tests', 332.

[136] Clapham, *Human Rights Obligations*, pp. 12–15.

[137] Arguably, international organizations can also be seen as manifestations of traditional state power.

globalization, often outside the control of states. For example, the conclusion of the Ottawa Treaty prohibiting landmines and the creation of the ICC have been viewed as manifestations of the increased significance of NGOs and an international civil society.[138] Indeed, some scholars have even claimed that the state may no longer be the 'primary source of regulation'.[139] But non-state actors are involved not only in positive and constructive international activities. The most notorious actors in today's world are non-statal – one only needs to think about threats posed to international peace and security by Al Qaeda, Islamic State militants, or Boko Haram. Transnational criminality is also implicated in many current international problems; cyberattacks upon Georgia in 2008 were at least in part orchestrated by Russian criminal organizations.[140]

But globalization has not only challenged the traditional understanding of actors in international law. A concurrent development is seen in the expansion of subject matters covered by international law, in particular the rise of global issues affecting the entire world.[141] International law is now concerned with a broad spectrum of issues ranging from protecting oceans to the prohibition of chemical weapons. Issues like artificial intelligence, autonomous weapons systems, climate change, and the loss of biodiversity have arisen that threaten the very survival of humankind. Increasingly, these problems require global efforts; the individual state is no longer considered the appropriate unit for handling the global market, the protection of the earth, or the protection of the human beings.[142] These 'public goods' or 'global commons' have redefined the logic of issue areas in international law.[143] There has been an awakening to the fact that not all subject matters regulated by international law can be dealt with equally. Some norms are of greater significance for the international community than others. The perception that there are common fundamental norms for the international community as a whole has increasingly gained ground, despite the contentiousness of the claim.

138 For assessments of the importance of non-governmental organizations (NGOs) in these law-making processes, see Nicola Short, 'The Role of NGOs in the Ottawa Process to Ban Landmines' (1999) 4 *International Negotiation* 481–500, and Kenneth Anderson, 'The Ottawa Convention Banning Landmines, the Role of International Non-governmental Organizations and the Idea of International Civil Society' (2000) 11 *European Journal of International Law* 91–120.

139 Boon, 'Are Control Tests', 332–333.

140 Andreas Krieg and Jean-Marc Rickli, *Surrogate Warfare: The Transformation of War in the Twenty-first Century* (Washington, DC: Georgetown University Press, 2019), p. 99.

141 Mégret, 'Globalization', para. 26.

142 Ibid., paras. 26–30.

143 Ibid.

A communitarian approach emphasizing international solidarity has also developed regarding obligations that purport to regulate state conduct with respect to hazardous activities.[144]

## 1.4 MEETING THE CHALLENGES: IS STATE RESPONSIBILITY LAW USEFUL?

To a varying extent, the challenges explored in this chapter have affected the general rules of state responsibility: the state increasingly finds itself operating alongside a broad range of non-state actors, thereby diminishing the exclusive power of states, in addition to which the range of issues regulated and protected by international law is ever-expanding. Moreover, alternative constructions of responsibility have emerged that serve specific objectives, in contrast to the general and broad nature of state responsibility. Understandably, in light of these developments, there has been growing discussion about the relevance of the law of state responsibility in the context of the changing international setting and the increasing diversity of thought with respect to international responsibility.

### 1.4.1 *Diverse Scholarly Opinions*

Among international legal scholars, different discernible standpoints exist on the question of how well the law of state responsibility can adapt to the changed international social and normative reality. First, there are those who support the traditional approach towards state responsibility. They see the claims of the demise of the state as the central actor in the international context as premature.[145] The rules of state responsibility are taken to apply only in those cases where the state truly is behind the wrong committed, and the rules are generally held to be sufficient for resolving these situations. Such an understanding is supported by the practice of the ICJ,[146] but scholars as well maintain the relevance of state responsibility as the standard system.[147]

[144] Pellet, 'The Definition of Responsibility', 15.

[145] Clapham, *Human Rights Obligations*, p. 7.

[146] Andrea Bianchi has more broadly claimed that the ICJ adheres to 'the state-centered system of international law'. Andrea Bianchi, 'Choice and (the Awareness of) Its Consequences: The ICJ's "Structural Bias" Strikes Again in the *Marshall Islands* Case' (2017) 111 *American Journal of International Law Unbound* 81–87 at 85.

[147] Crawford, 'The System of Responsibility', 17; Brunnée, 'International Legal Accountability', 23. James Crawford, for example, maintains that the 'foundations [of international law] do not appear to have changed'. See Crawford, 'International Law as an Open System', 17.

In part, such a normative approach also finds support from those scholars who seek to uphold state responsibility through a process of changing its rules internally. Thus, by way of interpretation or adapting the substantive and procedural rules, the law can be accommodated to the challenges posed by globalization.[148] For example, as a reaction to the 9/11 terrorist attacks on the United States, many scholars adhered to the state responsibility framework while they attempted to remodel rules to better suit terrorist actors and activities. There have been claims that as a result of the 9/11 terrorist attacks, the threshold of attribution has been substantially lowered.[149] Some scholars argued that the imputation of responsibility was no longer dependent on the 'effective control' test but instead that the concept of 'harbouring' became the ruling principle.[150] Other scholars argued for the abandonment of the agency model in state responsibility, so that causation would become the guiding principle in determining state responsibility.[151]

Expansion of the rules of state responsibility has not only been a scholarly endeavour. The United Nations Compensation Commission (UNCC), which handled claims relating to Iraq's responsibility for its invasion of Kuwait in 1990, has applied the rules of state responsibility in an expansive manner, coming closer to causation than the agency paradigm. For example, the UNCC has held that damage caused by 'hooligans' looting in Iraq and Kuwait is attributable to Iraq irrespective of nationality, because of these persons being 'broadly speaking, de facto Iraqi "agents"'.[152] In addition, the UNCC has also held that, in certain situations, damage caused by traffic accidents due to the overall breakdown of civil order as a result of Iraq's invasion can fall under Iraq's duty to compensate.[153] Special methods of deviating from the rules on diplomatic protection have also been adopted to ensure that all victims – even those that are stateless – are able to present reparation claims.[154]

148 See Proulx, *Institutionalizing*, p. 21.

149 At least Derek Jinks and Luigi Condorelli seem open to such a view. See Jinks, 'State Responsibility', and Luigi Condorelli, '*Les attentats du 11 septembre et leurs suites: où va le droit?*' (2001) 105 *Revue Générale de Droit International Public* 829–848 at 839.

150 Jinks, 'State Responsibility', 88.

151 Becker, *Terrorism and the State*, pp. 315–317.

152 See personal communication reported in Gregory Townsend, 'State Responsibility for Acts of De Facto Agents' (1997) 14 *Arizona Journal of International and Comparative Law* 635–678 at 660.

153 Becker, *Terrorism and the State*.

154 Maria Jose Recalde Vela, 'Statelessness at the United Nations Compensation Commission', *Institute on Statelessness and Inclusion*, Statelessness Working Paper Series No. 2015/03, December 2015.

At the other end of the spectrum, there are international legal scholars who consider the law of state responsibility to be outdated due to the current multitude of actors. For them, globalization has changed political and social realities, thus reorganizing the realm of actors. A dichotomized setting in international law in which the public entity of the state is held responsible, and private entities are not, is no longer tenable. Instead, scholars critical of state responsibility consider power and responsibility to be fragmented, straddling the divide between public and private. As put by Jan Arno Hessbruegge, '[t]he law cannot indefinitely set off the relocation of functions to the non-state sector by burdening weak states with increased duties of due diligence and an ever-increasing ambit of state responsibility.'[155] For some scholars, it thus appears necessary to go beyond a mere redefinition of the state responsibility rules. They call for a fundamental reconceptualization of the norms and institutions of international legal responsibility. New international legal norms and new institutional arrangements that take account of all actors and participants in the international legal process are needed.[156] One such example is the proposed World Court of Human Rights, which would be designed to be competent to try both public and private actors for their transgressions.[157]

But there is also another pragmatic way of meeting the criticism directed against state responsibility. Instead of calling for a complete revision of international responsibility, one can analyze the practical fragmentation of responsibility in international law and highlight the fact that state responsibility has already been challenged by other responsibility regimes.[158] The goal, then, is to raise for discussion that international responsibility is highly fragmented and that several responsibility regimes now purport to ensure that harmful or wrongful events are redressed. State responsibility has been partly decentred by competing responsibility ideas, which in fact benefits the international legal system. It is within this framework that the present study falls.

[155] Jan Arno Hessbruegge, 'The Historical Development of the Doctrines of Attribution and Due Diligence in International Law' (2004) 36 *New York University Journal of International Law & Politics* 265–306 at 306.

[156] Claudio Grossman and Daniel D. Bradlow, 'Are We Being Propelled Towards a People-Centered Transnational Legal Order' (1993–1994) 9 *American University Journal of International Law and Policy* 1–26 at 23–24.

[157] Julia Kozma, Manfred Nowak and Martin Scheinin, *A World Court of Human Rights: Consolidated Statute and Commentary* (Vienna, Graz: Neuer Wissenschaftlicher Verlag, 2010).

[158] Dupuy, 'Revolution or Evolution', 108.

### 1.4.2 *Assessing the Law of State Responsibility*

The challenging developments to which state responsibility law is increasingly applied to make an evaluation of the law especially timely. However, there are many standards against which state responsibility law can be judged. An appropriate framework of appraisal needs to take into account both the sui generis nature of state responsibility and those concerns presented against it. The setting of standard(s) is also important for the discussion of how the alternative constructions of responsibility actually fare in replacing parts of state responsibility. Therefore, the second part of my argument, that other responsibility regimes have reduced the relevance of state responsibility, depends on the appraisal framework that will be discussed in Section 1.4.2.1.

#### 1.4.2.1 Exploring Different Standards of Assessment

The international legal literature on state responsibility provides little guidance on how to best assess the law of state responsibility. In other branches of international law, specific standards stand out as obvious candidates – fairness, for example, in international environmental law. However, this is not the case with state responsibility. One reason is that comprehensive assessments of state responsibility are rare, with the bases of assessment infrequently spelled out in explicit terms.

An obvious starting point in the search for an appropriate basis of assessment for issues of responsibility and liability is the nature of the *responsibility model* in question – in particular its aims and main features. Such an approach builds upon the domestic analogy and the three basic models of responsibility within national legal systems – criminal law, private law, and public law.[159] For example, some scholars have attempted to evaluate international criminal law from the perspective of due process,[160] a standard drawn from national criminal law.

A second and more contemporary way of evaluating a particular regime in international law is to assess it in a *rule of law* framework. Indeed, rule of law has commonly constituted a benchmark against which different regimes, including responsibility regimes, are assessed.[161] Using this framework, one

159 Cane, *Responsibility in Law and Morality*, pp. 49–53.

160 Cristian DeFrancia, 'Due Process in International Criminal Courts: Why Procedure Matters' (2001) 87 *Virginia Law Review* 1381–1489.

161 See Jeremy Farrall, *United Nations Sanctions and the Rule of Law* (Cambridge: Cambridge University Press, 2009); Robert Cryer, *Prosecuting International Crimes. Selectivity and the International Criminal Law Regime* (Cambridge: Cambridge University Press, 2005); Aust, *Complicity*.

can claim that a responsibility system should treat similar cases in the same way and that these processes should be characterized by due process. It has been claimed that the rule of law approach 'seems particularly suited for investigating a legal regime',[162] because it is an 'important virtue which legal systems should possess'.[163] The rule of law approach can thus be justified in almost any discourse on legal phenomena simply because a matter is juridical.

Arguably, the connection between the rule of law and the law of state responsibility is also intimate. It has been stressed that the law of state responsibility enhances a 'climate of legality' in international law from two perspectives: it ensures that laws are being enforced and it provides a means of dealing with community interests.[164] The importance of state responsibility to the international rule of law is also recognized by the United Nations, whose former Secretary-General Kofi Annan noted in 2004 that 'accountability to the law' is central to the concept of international rule of law.[165] In a similar vein, in 2010 the president of the ICJ noted: 'While every part of the [United Nations] Organization has a role to play in the promotion of the rule of law, the Court, as the principal judicial organ of the United Nations, is expected to play a central role in this area.'[166] Despite the vague content of the term, 'rule of law' is generally understood and used to denote the material completeness of the international legal system; there is a presumption that international legal norms are capable of answering 'practical questions from an informed and principled standpoint'.[167] One can also choose to extract concrete principles from an overarching concept, such as transparency, which forms part of rule of law considerations.[168]

*Fairness* is another standard featured in analyses of different branches of international law. It has been used to examine international environmental law and climate change law, international trade and investment law, as well

[162] Cryer, *Prosecuting International Crimes*, p. 191.

[163] Joseph Raz, 'The Rule of Law and Its Virtue', in Joseph Raz (ed.), *The Authority of Law: Essays on Law and Morality* (Oxford: Clarendon Press, 1970), pp. 210–229 at 211.

[164] Aust, *Complicity*, p. 86 *et seq.*

[165] Report of the Secretary-General, *The Rule of Law and Transitional Justice in Conflict and Post-conflict Societies*, UN Doc. S/2004/616, 23 August 2004, at para. 6.

[166] ICJ, Press Release No. 2010/35, 29 October 2010.

[167] Aust, *Complicity*, p. 423.

[168] Transparency has been used to assess international law in general, but also international investment law in particular.

as international arbitration.[169] Fairness is also applicable to state responsibility in international law as well as responsibility of international organizations.[170] Thomas Franck famously posed the question of international law's fairness by exploring two sides of the concept: distributive justice and procedural fairness.[171] Despite his efforts to pinpoint the constituent elements of fairness, it remains an elusive concept closely tied to equity and justice.[172]

Indeed, analyses of the just or unjust character of international law are prevalent. One perception of justice particularly suitable for present purposes is that of corrective justice, considering that the basic functions and aims of state responsibility relate to correcting wrongs. In its classic formulation, *corrective justice* entails a duty to repair, an obligation embodied in the rules of state responsibility.[173] Corrective justice 'involves adding back what has been taken away, or subtracted from someone'[174] and is often connected to issues of compensation. Since reparation of wrongs is at the heart of state responsibility, corrective justice in its classic formulation seems to be relevant to assessments of state responsibility.

However, in my assessment of the general law of state responsibility and the two alternative constructions of responsibility, none of the approaches mentioned earlier will be followed in a clear-cut fashion. It follows from the rudimentary character of state responsibility that it cannot be analyzed in a meaningful way based upon a predetermined responsibility model or against a rule of law framework. To begin with, the responsibility models that are discussed in the literature are usually derived from national legal systems. This means that they cannot be directly transposed into the international

169 See Elli Louka, *International Environmental Law: Fairness, Effectiveness, and World Order* (New York: Cambridge University Press, 2006); Friedrich Soltau, *Fairness in International Climate Change Law and Policy* (New York: Cambridge University Press, 2009); Zeray Yihdego and Alistair Rieu-Clarke, 'An Exploration of Fairness in International Law through the Blue Nile and GERD' (2016) 41 *Water International* 528–549; Diane A. Desierto, 'Rawlsian Fairness and International Arbitration' (2015) 36 *University of Pennsylvania Journal of International Law* 939–993.

170 Samantha Besson, 'State and Individual Secondary Liability in Case of International Organizations' Responsibility: The Challenge of Unfairness Unveiled' (2017) 1 *Rivista di filosofia del diritto* 51–78.

171 Thomas Franck, *Fairness in International Law and Institutions* (Oxford: Clarendon Press, 1995), esp. p. 7.

172 Yihdego and Rieu-Clarke, 'An Exploration', 529; Soltau, *Fairness*, p. 152.

173 Gabriella Blum and Natalie J. Lockwood, 'Earthquakes and Wars', in Larry May and Elisabeth Edenberg (eds.), *Jus Post Bellum and Transitional Justice* (New York: Cambridge University Press, 2013), pp. 178–216 at 199.

174 Tarcísio Hardman Reis, *Compensation for Environmental Damages under International Law: The Role of the International Judge* (Alphen aan den Rijn: Wolters Kluwer, 2011), p. 117.

legal system. State responsibility is famously considered to be 'neither civil nor criminal',[175] but 'simply "international"'.[176] Comparing the civil and penal elements of state responsibility with those of national legal systems has been considered both risky and questionable because of the sui generis nature of state responsibility.[177] However, that same unique nature of state responsibility means that no single responsibility model can provide a sufficient basis for assessment of state responsibility law, as that law is considered a mix of elements from all three basic responsibility models.

Neither is the rule of law framework workable for present purposes. The unclear meaning of the concept makes it difficult to discern clear standards. One could opt for a minimalist understanding of the rule of law such as 'the state of affairs that obtains when a legal system exists and functions',[178] but such vagueness provides no answers regarding how well the system functions. Apart from this, the inherent attraction to rule of law,[179] can be questioned in relation to state responsibility. 'Rule of law' has been described as a 'way of living; a way of organizing society'.[180] The concept seems an antidote to discretion,[181] but the law of state responsibility is filled with manoeuvring room for states. State responsibility operates between law and politics, a quality which should not be automatically perceived as a disadvantage. Moreover, rule of law often approaches law through the prism of formal lawmaking procedure,[182] which in the case of state responsibility seems to miss the point.

175 Hans Kelsen, 'Théorie du droit international public' (1953–III) 84 *Recueil des cours* 1–204, p. 87.

176 Alain Pellet, 'Can a State Commit a Crime? Definitely, Yes!' (1999) 10 *European Journal of International Law* 425–434 at 433.

177 Pellet, 'The Definition of Responsibility', 13.

178 Matthew H. Kramer, 'On the Moral Status of the Rule of Law' (2004) 63 *Cambridge Law Journal* 65–97 at 65.

179 See James Farrall, who notes that the desirability of rule of law is often taken for granted. Farrall, *United Nations Sanctions*, p. 24.

180 Lowe, 'The Iraq Crisis', 863.

181 Aust, *Complicity*, p. 424.

182 Matthew H. Kramer has summarized as follows Lon Fuller's classic definition of the rule of law, which stresses the formal elements of law: '(1) a system of governance operates through general norms, and all or most of the norms partake of the following properties; (2) they are promulgated to the people who are required to comply with them; (3) they are prospective rather than retrospective; (4) they are understandable rather than hopelessly unintelligible; (5) they do not contradict one other and do not impose duties that conflict; (6) they do not impose requirements that cannot possibly be fulfilled; (7) they persist over substantial periods of time, instead of being changed with disorienting frequency; and (8) they are generally given effect in accordance with their terms, so that there is congruence between the norms as formulated and the norms as implemented.' See Lon Fuller, *The Morality of Law* (New Haven and London: Yale University Press, 1964), chapter 3, as summarized in Kramer, 'On the Moral Status', 65.

One can certainly agree with the argument that state responsibility can contribute to a climate of legality through its mere existence as a 'metalanguage', but concretizing the rule of law into workable standards when it comes to state responsibility seems futile. Admittedly, state responsibility can be discussed in terms of transparency, universality, objectivity, and consistency. Nevertheless, it seems more accurate to employ such standards in the case of legal systems or regimes in which institutions are the rule and not the exception in enforcing the law. Indeed, it would be too much to expect and demand 'the law of state responsibility to guarantee the universal application and enforcement of international law'.[183] Evaluating state responsibility against a rule of law framework would thus skew the point of departure of the evaluation.

Neither is fairness unproblematic as an evaluation standard, as many difficulties abound in the application of the concept to international responsibility, particularly state responsibility. To begin with, there exists no single interpretation of fairness; it is a concept involving both substantive and procedural considerations that are hard to deal with separately.[184] Moreover, it appears that the secondary and general rules of state responsibility, which do not relate to substance, do not generally comport with an analysis of the substantial side of fairness, distributive fairness, or justice.[185] To be sure, some aspects of state responsibility can be subject to fairness assessments, such as its form as a non-distributional responsibility system.[186] Assessment on the basis of procedural fairness is also workable, to the extent that one discusses due process concerns of the general law. But the law of state responsibility contains no explicit mention of fairness or fair treatment which would explicitly motivate an analysis from the perspective of fairness. Moreover, both distributional and procedural fairness tend to overlook the functions or aims of responsibility, which are central to this book, as well as the broader question of whether the legal rules and principles are capable of attaining their goals. The same applies to corrective justice; it would constitute too narrow an approach to the function(s) of state responsibility, while simultaneously leaving unaddressed the question of the operationality of rules.

183 Aust, *Complicity*, p. 84.
184 Yihdego and Rieu-Clarke, 'An Exploration', 545.
185 Admittedly, fairness could work better in considering international criminal law and international liability. However, since this book's main interest is state responsibility, fairness will not be chosen as the general appraisal standard.
186 Besson, 'State and Individual', 58.

#### 1.4.2.2 Functionality in Focus

An examination of the relevance of state responsibility necessarily orients the research towards the functions of responsibility. To adopt a functional approach is an 'accepted device of acknowledged utility' in international law[187] and its specific subsystems. This holds particularly true when it comes to responsibility. It has been argued that functionalist approaches are the most suitable for dealing with responsibility in the international legal order.[188] This book will accordingly adopt a functional approach to the analysis of state responsibility. In other words, the purposes or functions of a legal regime will be explored alongside the issue of whether the operation of the rules is successful in achieving the goals. Put differently, the aim of this book is to assess whether state responsibility is capable of serving its purposes well. This means that there should be more to state responsibility than only theoretical importance.[189] Such an approach is not unique, as several scholars hint towards or highlight similar requirements upon the law of state responsibility: Vladyslav Lanovoy analyzes the 'utility and effectiveness' of the rules on complicity in the law of state responsibility;[190] Lauri Mälksoo discusses the 'workability' of state responsibility;[191] and Rachael Lorna Johnstone alludes to the 'usefulness' of state responsibility.[192] Still, these innuendos of the need for a quality of state responsibility akin to practical usefulness are rarely opened up or further developed.

The underlying argument of this book is that state responsibility can stand the test of time and meet the challenges of globalization and normative fragmentation only if the system itself is functional. The core of a functional analysis is often understood to be a study of the functions – or purposes – of a legal regime. Thus, any study analyzing the concept of responsibility on a more principled level should take into account the main functions of legal rules and principles of responsibility. Studying responsibility independently

[187] Michael Barkun, 'International Law from a Functional Perspective' (1970) 1 *Georgia Journal of International and Comparative Law* 19–28 at 19.

[188] Cane, *Responsibility in Law and Morality*, p. 43. See also Bonafè, *The Relationship*, pp. 224–237, who adopts a functional approach to state responsibility and international criminal law.

[189] Jan Klabbers, for instance, notes that 'the idea that states can be held responsible for acts attributable to them is generally regarded… as a useful legal fiction'. See Klabbers, *International Law*, p. 126.

[190] Lanovoy, *Complicity and Its Limits*, p. 10 (emphases omitted).

[191] See Lauri Mälksoo, 'State Responsibility and the Challenge of the Realist Paradigm: The Demand of Baltic Victims of Soviet Mass Repressions for Compensation from Russia' (2003) 3 *Baltic Yearbook of International Law* 57–76 at 61.

[192] Johnstone, 'State Responsibility: A Concerto', 117.

from the purposes it intends to serve would leave the picture incomplete.[193] It is important to note, however, that the purposes of the law of state responsibility are less clear in comparison to domestic legal regimes on responsibility and even to the alternative forms of responsibility explored later in this book. In fact, state responsibility is understood as serving several goals at the same time. The fact that state responsibility encompasses elements of both civil and criminal law, as well as public law, makes it reasonable to claim that state responsibility is multifunctional. It traditionally encompasses the reparative function, while the element of sanctioning entered it during the codification process. The common denominator of these different purposes lies in the ability of the regime to ensure stability and predictability in the international legal order by providing consequences for breaches of international law.

But there is more to functionality than function(s).[194] Ulf Linderfalk, for example, separates function and functionality; the former equals effect, while the latter indicates 'what the uttering of the term *potentially* does to the beliefs, attitudes, or behaviour of participants of that same discourse'.[195] Although the concept of functionalism is difficult to define in general terms,[196] at a minimum it must entail that a regime is able to utilize its means to such an extent that it achieves its purposes; there is a fit between the rules and the environment they aim to influence. For Hans Morgenthau, functionalism implies that the means are suitable to the problems which they are intended to solve. In other words, the rules must 'come closer to the reality'.[197] Douglas Johnston similarly argues that functionality entails diversified solutions rather than normative development on an abstract and general level.[198] The focus should be on 'problem-solving specificity' instead of 'doctrinal generality'.[199] Thus, two separate dimensions of functionality can be discerned: first, the fit between the content of the rules and the functions they are supposed to perform, and

193 Cane, *Responsibility in Law and Morality*, p. 281.
194 In scholarly literature, the terms *function, functionalism* and *functionality* are sometimes used interchangeably; at other times they are given different meanings.
195 Ulf Linderfalk, 'The Functionality of Conceptual Terms in International Law and International Legal Discourse' (2013/2014) 6 *European Journal of Legal Studies* 27–50 at 33 (emphasis added).
196 Douglas M. Johnston, 'Functionalism in the Theory of International Law' (1988) 26 *Canadian Yearbook of International Law* 3–60 at 19.
197 Hans Morgenthau, 'Positivism, Functionalism, and International Law' (1940) 34 *American Journal of International Law* 260–284 at 273.
198 Johnston, 'Functionalism', 39.
199 Ibid., 39, note 123.

second, whether or not these functions are 'realised in practice'.[200] To sum up, this book will discuss functionality in terms of the question of 'whether a given legal system [state responsibility] operating in a particular environment at a specified point in time is performing all the functions of which it is capable'.[201]

Although there are many challenges that a general responsibility regime – like that of state responsibility – should be able to handle, the mindset of a functional approach entails a focus upon basic standards. Even in a minimalist understanding, a functioning responsibility system should be concrete, possess the necessary tools to deal with both the proliferation and fluidity of actors, and allow the expansion of international law to new and complex societal phenomena. In other words, state responsibility should make a difference by being sensitive to a variety of both actors and issues alike.

Hence, the functional analysis of this book will address, among other things, the following questions when it comes to the usefulness of the general rules: Does state responsibility contribute to concrete problem-solving in issues of responsibility? Is state responsibility apt to reach the actors that violate international law? Is state responsibility flexible enough to adapt to varying behaviours? Can state responsibility achieve its functions? Does it ensure or contribute to legal stability through the prevention of lawbreaking in the first place? Can it respond to the expansion of subject matters regulated by international law and the complexity of contemporary problems by providing differentiated responses? Does the law provide the means to deal with the most fundamental obligations of the international legal system?

This broad analysis of state responsibility's functionality will be followed by a more condensed functionality assessment of the two alternative forms of responsibility discussed in this book: international liability and international criminal law. It is important to note, however, that the aim of this book is not to provide a full comparative analysis of the three responsibility regimes. Instead, the aim of this secondary and supplementary assessment is to shed further light on how alternative constructions of responsibility have responded to the respective problems. The results of this assessment will assist in drawing the book's final conclusions about the functionality of state responsibility. Consequently, the findings of the study will be brought together in order that a conclusive and comprehensive picture will emerge about the current place and position of state responsibility in the international legal order.

[200] Cane, *Responsibility in Law and Morality*, p. 283. Cane calls this operational approach an analogy to the functional approach.

[201] Barkun, 'A Functional Perspective', 26.

Due to limitations of space, the examination of international liability and international criminal law will be thematic, featuring three selected elements from the broader functionality analysis to which state responsibility law is subjected to in the book. These elements are important goals or requirements for all three responsibility regimes under scrutiny. These are (1) social control, (2) collectivity, and (3) signalling effect. Although by no means are they exclusive standards for a well-functioning responsibility regime, they are most certainly important for any system aiming to assign responsibility upon actors on the international plane.

First, social control is a common denominator for different types of responsibility regimes; responsibilities premised on both private law and criminal law seek to prevent or deter actors from breaking the law in the first place. Although it may not be the primary or the most obvious function of a responsibility system in international law, minimizing deviant behaviour is nonetheless a goal that is shared by state responsibility, international liability, and international criminal law.[202] Some scholars have even claimed that the function of discouraging states from violating international law 'might well be the most important function of the law of state responsibility'.[203]

Second, a well-functioning responsibility regime must be capable of addressing the range of actors that may have bearing upon the compliance with international obligations. Although it is to be noted that the individual has come to be increasingly empowered internationally both in political and legal terms, various organized collective formations seem to be those at the centre of the changing actor landscape.[204] Thus, in order for a responsibility regime to be useful, it must be able to deal with collectives beyond and below the state level. Social and legal structures are based on group identification, as many rights and obligations under international law are characteristics of groups.[205] Collectives are important to international law at large, as international law deals with 'populations distributed across geographical territories and between states, across affiliations, and between affinities'.[206]

Third, an important part of the state responsibility project relates to 'the qualitative distinction' between different violations of international law.[207]

202 See e.g., Bonafè, *The Relationship*, p. 225; Jan Willisch, *State Responsibility for Technological Damage in International Law* (Berlin: Duncker and Humblot, 1987), p. 27.

203 Willisch, *State Responsibility*, p. 27.

204 Hessbruegge, 'The Historical Development', 306.

205 Morss, *International Law as the Law of Collectives*, p. viii.

206 Ibid., p. 2.

207 Commentary to Part Two, Chapter III, para. 2 of the ASR.

Although no division into state 'crimes' and 'delicts' entered the final articles, Articles 40 and 41 of the ASR recognize the existence of a category of serious breaches of obligations arising under peremptory norms of general international law. Furthermore, special consequences follow from violations of this kind. Indeed, it is more and more commonplace for international lawyers to hold that some wrongs committed are more serious than others.[208] Hence, we are motivated to discuss this issue also with respect to international criminal law and international liability. The analyses will explore, among other things, how the responsibility systems deal with the distinctiveness of breaches; how they recognize the sliding scale of normativity; and how they express these value statements to the members of the international community. This signalling effect thus explores whether a responsibility system contains mechanisms for articulating that certain fundamental international legal norms are to be specially protected,[209] while others are not to enjoy such special protection.

[208] ILC Yearbook 1976, vol. II(2), p. 117, para. 53; Christian J. Tams and Alessandra Asteriti, 'Erga Omnes, Jus Cogens and Their Impact on the Law of Responsibility', in Malcolm Evans and Panos Koutrakos (eds.), *International Responsibility of the European Union: European and International Perspectives* (Oxford and Portland, OR: Hart Publishing, 2013), pp. 163–188 at 178, who note that 'it seems difficult not to accept that breaches of fundamental interest obligations protecting core values should trigger particular consequences: an act of genocide is different from the violation of a bilateral trade agreement, and the rules on responsibility should be seen to reflect that difference'. Similarly, Alain Pellet, 'Responsibility of States in Cases of Human-rights or Humanitarian-law Violations', in James Crawford, Abdul B. Koroma, Said Mahmoudi and Alain Pellet (eds.), *The International Legal Order: Current Needs and Possible Responses – Essays in Honour of Djamchid Momtaz* (Leiden and Boston: Brill Nijhoff, 2017), pp. 230–251 at 234.

[209] Lisa Yarwood, *State Accountability under International Law: Holding States Accountable for a Breach of Jus Cogens Norms* (London and New York: Routledge, 2012), p. 61.

# 2

# The Evolution of State Responsibility

In order to better understand the current formulation and standing of state responsibility in international law, it is necessary to study a sketch of its main stages of evolution. The purpose is to trace the development of state responsibility from an underlying principle into a separate legal branch, and further into its becoming the main system of responsibility in international law. This narrative will place state responsibility – as a concept, practice, and as an institution – within the larger framework of international law by way of chronological systematization.

This excursion into the evolution of state responsibility will disclose the contentious character of the law. There is nothing self-evident about the way the law stands today, which is illustrated by the different responsibility models that have been discussed and proposed by international legal scholars over the centuries. State responsibility has varied over time, and doctrine and international practice have not always coincided with the evolution of state responsibility law. While state responsibility has developed in conjunction with the broader international law project, doctrinal debates reveal the influence of the domestic analogy upon the design of state responsibility, perhaps to a larger extent than in many other legal categories of international law. Although its foundation lies in bilateral state relations and the remedying of concrete wrongs, the analysis will show that state responsibility was developed with broader considerations in mind, such as that of legality and rule of international law. Still today, some elements remain in dispute, and it has been claimed that competing versions of state responsibility still coexist.

Besides these broader and more principled matters, technical, or procedural issues will also be discussed to a limited extent, but only insofar they relate to or in some way illustrate the larger developments. Most notably, the ASR – which codified and developed existing customary law in the field – will be presented as they represent the best available statements on customary law of state responsibility. Thus, by way of exploring different sources of international law – such as customary law, scholarly writings, case law, and state practice – this chapter will journey from ancient times to the finalization of the ILC Articles. The goal of this process is to clarify what state responsibility means, what its consequences are, and how it has been implemented at different stages in the development of international law. It is nevertheless important to realize that the ASR do not constitute the end point in the development of the law of state responsibility. Therefore, the narrative will conclude by investigating recent claims regarding the constitutional function of state responsibility.

A few caveats are necessary, however. First, we must appreciate that international legal scholars have turned to analyzing history in recent years, also when it comes to the law of state responsibility.[1] But, the aim here is not to provide a comprehensive and in-depth historical analysis of state responsibility. The objective is rather to present a brief overview beyond the modern era, which sheds light not only upon the functions of state responsibility but also on the historical development of its rules. Although some scholars warn against '"[t]racing the origins" of legal concepts',[2] a historical outlook is necessary in order to gain a better understanding of the reasons for the present design of the law, as well as its current limitations. Admittedly, this task may not be easy, due to the implicit nature of state responsibility in the early days of international law.[3] However, this testifies to a different function in historical times than is observed today, and this is valuable information in itself.

Second, it needs to be acknowledged that an analysis into state responsibility will necessarily be an academic exercise since it is detached from the primary obligations; as a rule, governments do not discuss state responsibility as such. Instead, they are concerned with such things as fighting oil pollution or trade barriers, protecting the rights of their citizens, or seeking to ensure that unlawful weapons are not used in armed conflicts. Thus, although the primary task of the law of state responsibility is to protect the rights of each and every state by ensuring that obligations are kept – an essential feature of any legal system – one needs to be aware of the fact that responsibility is generally

[1] Nissel, *A History of State Responsibility*; Crawford, *State Responsibility. The General Part*, Ch. 1; James Crawford, Thomas Grant and Francesco Messineo, 'Towards an International Law of Responsibility: Early Doctrine', in Laurence Boisson de Chazournes and Marcelo Kohen (eds.), *International Law and the Quest for Its Implementation:* Liber Amicorum *Vera Gowlland-Debbas* (Leiden: Martinus Nijhoff Publishers, 2010), pp. 377–402.

[2] Brownlie, *State Responsibility: Part I*, p. 1.

[3] Ibid., p. 2.

contextualized to specific situations. From this, it follows that there are inherent limits to purely academic discussion. However, jurisprudence can help to disclose inherent problems that are common to the practical cases in which the law of state responsibility operates. It is precisely to this that I will turn after telling the story of state responsibility as it has unfolded in the general context of international law.

## 2.1 RESPONSIBILITY AS AN IMPLICIT DOCTRINE

In the early doctrine of international law the concept of responsibility was latent, discussed only incidentally in connection with substantive obligations on the law of war, law of the sea, law of diplomatic relations, or law on the treatment of foreigners.[4] Responsibility did not exist as a separate legal topic; rather, it was thought of as a conflation of religious and legal arguments.[5] Private law notions – most notably the 'Roman law of delicts' and the 'law of actions' – contributed to the first fragments of responsibility in international law.[6] Nevertheless, the development of a clear and distinct idea of responsibility was hindered by the rudimentary character of the principles of Roman law, as well as the lack of international procedures and institutions capable of dealing clearly and in a non-abusive manner with non-performance as well as its excuses and its consequences.[7] The different existing practices in international law – such as reprisals or the concept of a "just war" – gave impetus to the idea of responsibility,[8] but still tended to create more problems than they solved.[9]

Doctrinal efforts to secularize responsibility can be traced to the Italian scholars Pierino Belli and Alberto Gentili, who both discussed the responsibility of citizens to their sovereign.[10] Yet, neither of them saw responsibility as a distinct legal category because they were unable to rid themselves completely of religion.[11] Change came about, however, with Hugo Grotius in the

4 Ibid.; See also Clyde Eagleton, 'The Responsibility of the State for the Protection of Foreign Officials' (1925) 19 *American Journal of International Law* 293–314 at 293.
5 See Borzu Sabahi, *Compensation and Restitution in Investor-State Arbitration: Principles and Practice* (New York: Oxford University Press, 2011), pp. 23–27; Crawford, Grant and Messineo, 'Early Doctrine', 379–382.
6 Sabahi, *Compensation and Restitution*, pp. 8, 41.
7 Crawford, Grant and Messineo, 'Early Doctrine', 384.
8 Brownlie, *State Responsibility: Part I*, p. 2; Sabahi, *Compensation and Restitution*, p. 8.
9 Crawford, Grant and Messineo, 'Early Doctrine', 384.
10 Crawford, *State Responsibility: The General Part*, p. 7.
11 Ibid.

seventeenth century. Although Grotius did not deal distinctly with responsibility in international law,[12] his thoughts on civil liability – based upon fault in domestic law – came to influence attitudes towards wrongs committed internationally as well.[13] For Grotius and his contemporaries, the implicit discussion of international responsibility was nevertheless limited to the issue of when – and under what circumstances – the acts of private individuals gave rise to the responsibility of the sovereign.[14]

The development of a responsibility doctrine was also affected by the Peace of Westphalia and the birth of a state-centred system.[15] The new principles of sovereignty and equality helped to form ideas and institutions of responsibility in the future.[16] General rules pertaining to responsibility began to emerge not only with regard to issues of imputation but also concerning means of redress. Yet, the familiar modern vocabulary of state responsibility did not appear in scholarly writings before the 1850s with August Heffter's *Faits Illicit* in his treatise *Le Droit International Public de L'Europe*.[17]

### 2.1.1 *The Scope of Responsibility*

From the start, theories of imputation dominated scholarly discussion.[18] The question of whose actions actually triggered responsibility – and on what grounds – were widely discussed. In the beginning these theories were sovereign-centred. Responsibility was directly connected to the sovereign and

[12] Two works of Grotius deal with responsibility, namely *Introduction to the Laws of Holland* and *The Law of War and Peace*, the latter which encompasses the ideas set forth in the former work. See Hugo Grotius, *De Jure Belli Ac Pacis Libri Tres* (1625) (trans. Francis W. Kelsey, Oxford: Clarendon Press, 1925).

[13] Crawford, *State Responsibility: The General Part*, p. 10; Sabahi, *Compensation and Restitution*, pp. 28–29.

[14] Dionisio Anzilotti, *Teoria generale della responsabilità dello stato nel diritto internazionale* (Florence: F. Lumachi Libraio-editore, 1902), pp. 10, 14, 17.

[15] Peter Malanczuk, *Akehurst's Modern Introduction to International Law* (7th revised ed., London and New York: Routledge, 1997), p. 10.

[16] Ian Brownlie observes that the parallel of historic institutions, such as that of reprisals, 'with modern ideas of state responsibility is not direct and patent, these old institutions were part of the lines drawn in the construction of the figure of responsibility of states whilst not forming part of the finished figure'. Brownlie, *State Responsibility: Part I*, pp. 4–5.

[17] Crawford, *State Responsibility: The General Part*, p. 21. See, August Wilhelm Heffter, *Le Droit International Public de L'Europe* (transl. Jules Bergson, Paris: Cotillon, 1857), Book I, Chapter III, Section II on *Faits Illicites*.

[18] Anzilotti, *Teoria generale*, p. 10.

his or her representatives.[19] Despite the absolute powers of the sovereign, the sovereign's responsibility was considered to be anything but comprehensive; the sovereign was considered unable to control all the actions that his subjects engaged in. The uncontrollability of subjects was repeatedly pointed out, for example, by Grotius, who held that 'we could not avoid utilizing the services of wicked men, that otherwise an army cannot be collected'.[20] Thus, for Grotius responsibility was fault-based; unless the sovereign had personally contributed to the wrong no state responsibility existed.

The first causes of action involving claims of reparation in the seventeenth century and onwards also related to the sovereignty of states and representatives of this sovereignty.[21] As explicated by Georg Friedrich von Martens: '*c'était une violation des immunités qui servit presque toujours de raison ou fournit un prétext de brouillerie entre des gouvernemens qui avaient vécu jusqu'alors en bonne intelligence*' (It was a violation of immunities, which almost always served as a reason or a pretext for a dispute between governments, which had previously lived in harmony).[22] Von Martens enumerated several cases in which ambassadors, ministers, or other representatives of the sovereign state had suffered wrongs committed by other states: for example, the attack upon the Russian ambassador Mathweof in London 1709, which was settled by the satisfaction rendered by Queen Anne of England in the form of punishing the perpetrators.[23] Other grounds of wrongfulness in international relations at that time were the toleration or favouring of conspiracies by one state against another state.[24] For example, the relations between France and Spain became strained in 1718 when the Spanish ambassador – Antonio del Giudice, Prince de Cellamare – was involved in a conspiracy against the French regent Philippe D'Orléans.[25]

The idea that in terms of responsibility a state is something more than its sovereign was introduced in the eighteenth century by both Christian Wolff and Emmerich de Vattel. Wolff expanded a state's responsibility from Grotius'

19 Fredrick S. Dunn, *The Protection of Nationals: A Study in the Application of International Law* (New York: The Johns Hopkins Press, 1932), p. 47. Similarly, Jan Arno Hessbruegge notes that 'Grotius and his successors were writing at the height of absolutism', which also came to affect responsibility ideas. The state and the sovereign were one and the same. See Hessbruegge, 'The Historical Development', 285–286.

20 Grotius, *De Jure Belli*, Book II, Chapter XVII, pp. 436–437.

21 Anzilotti, *Teoria generale*, p. 6; Similarly, Georg Friedrich von Martens, *Causes célèbres du droit des gens. Tome Premier* (Leipzig: F. A. Brockhaus and Paris: Ponthieu, 1827), p. xiii.

22 von Martens, *Causes célèbres*, p. xiii.

23 Ibid., pp. 47–74.

24 Anzilotti, *Teoria generale*, p. 6.

25 von Martens, *Causes célèbres*, pp. 139–173.

understanding by way of imputation. Yet, Wolff rejected a general imputation of acts of private individuals to the sovereign. However, he made clear that in certain special situations of ratification or acceptance, the state would be responsible for the acts of private individuals or citizens.[26] In addition to this attribution of acts to the state, Wolff introduced the idea of imputing the acts of state agents to the state. He noted a further exception to the differentiation between private and public acts: '[t]he situation is different if he acts by order of the ruler of the state, whom he obeys as a superior.'[27]

Wolff's contemporary, Emmerich de Vattel, also accepted the attribution of private acts through adoption,[28] and even broadened the range of private acts that fell under the state's responsibility. According to Vattel, acts that were conducted in circumstances 'when, by its manners, and by the maxims of its government, it accustoms and authorizes its citizens indiscriminately to plunder and maltreat foreigners…' should be considered acts of the state.[29] Although Vattel recognized state responsibility under some specific circumstances, he expressly rejected a system under which every fault committed by a citizen would be imputed to the sovereign.[30]

A shift towards thinking about responsibility in terms of the territorial state is visible from the mid-nineteenth century onwards.[31] Robert Phillimore advanced the idea that the state was to control not only its citizens but all acts committed from its territory.[32] Similar arguments were presented in 1884 by William Edward Hall, who claimed that 'a state is of course responsible for all acts or omissions taking place within its territory by which another state or the subjects of the latter are injuriously affected'.[33] Hall also developed

[26] Christian Wolff, *Jus Gentium Methodo Scientifica Pertractatum* 1764 (1st published 1750, trans. Joseph H. Drake, Oxford: Clarendon Press, 1934), p. 160, para. 314.

[27] Wolff, *Jus Gentium*, p. 161, para. 315. This passage can be understood either as incurring responsibility on the basis of an agency relation or, due to perceiving the act conducted by an individual as an act of the ruler himself since the individual acted based on an order. However, Hessbruegge maintains that a contextual reading of Wolff makes clear that he speaks for 'a general order-obedience relationship'. See Hessbruegge, 'The Historical Development', 289.

[28] Emmerich de Vattel, *The Law of Nations; or Principles of the Law of Nature, Applied to the Conduct and Affairs of Nations and Sovereigns* (1st published in 1758, trans. Joseph Chitty, Philadelphia: T. and J. W. Johnson, 1839), Book II, Chapter VI, p. 162, para. 74.

[29] Ibid., p. 163, para. 78.

[30] Ibid., p. 161, para. 73.

[31] Hessbruegge, 'The Historical Development', 292.

[32] Robert Phillimore, *Commentaries upon International Law* (3rd ed., London: Butterworths, 1879), vol. I, pp. 316–317.

[33] William Edward Hall, *A Treatise on International Law* (8th ed., Oxford: Clarendon Press, 1924), p. 268.

doctrines of attribution based on agency. According to his writings, the acts of state officials – whether administrative or military – were carried out under governmental orders and were thus authorized by the state. Hence, 'the state may fairly be supposed to have identified itself with them [the acts]'.[34] State responsibility for the acts of private individuals was due to a loose organizational connection formulated only in terms of due diligence. The state could only be responsible for such acts that 'it may reasonably be expected to have knowledge of and to prevent'.[35]

### 2.1.2 *Means of Redress*

Besides rules on attribution and the grounds for responsibility, other general and analytical rules on wrongdoing and its consequences slowly began to emerge as well. In the mid-eighteenth century, it was noted that the equality of states guaranteed that all nations are free to act as they choose, 'so long as they do not affect the proper and perfect rights of any other nation … If she makes an ill use of her liberty, she is guilty of a breach of a duty.'[36] A prohibition against injuring other nations was thought to exist. This prohibition nevertheless related to the obligations of the natural law not to impede the perfection and progress of other nations, rather than to consensual obligations adopted by states. However, the prohibition as expressed by Vattel explicitly covered acts that were aimed at 'any evil manoeuvres tending to create disturbance in another state, to foment disorder, to corrupt its citizens, to alienate its allies, to raise enemies against it, to tarnish its glory, and to deprive it of its natural advantages'.[37]

The concept of reparation was also developed in the direction of a more juridical form.[38] According to Vattel, a nation was obliged to address justified complaints against its behaviour: either it shall 'repair any damage that she herself may have caused, or any injury she may have done' or 'to give adequate satisfaction for such injuries as cannot be repaired'.[39] As a means of redress, the injured state could still declare war in the pursuit of correcting an injustice. Accordingly, an injury suffered or a threatened injury were just causes for war. Nevertheless, as a general idea the right of resort to war belonged only to the

34 Ibid.
35 Ibid., p. 269.
36 de Vattel, *The Law of Nations*, Book I, Preliminaries, p. lxiii, para. 20.
37 Ibid., Book II, Chapter I, p. 142 (emphasis omitted).
38 Brownlie, *State Responsibility: Part I*, p. 5.
39 de Vattel, *The Law of Nations*, Book II, Chapter XVIII, p. 274, para. 324.

injured nation. However, Vattel also extraordinarily admitted a right to wage war for all states whenever community interests were at stake: 'All nations have therefore a right to resort to forcible means for the purpose of repressing any one particular nation who openly violates the laws of the society which Nature has established between them, or who directly attacks the welfare and safety of that society.'[40]

Despite the acceptance of forcible means to redress wrongs, ample development also took place with respect to other, peaceful means of redress. Parties to conflicts were recommended to solve their dispute by peaceful means or 'the gentlest methods of terminating their differences'.[41] Since one major cause of international disputes was precisely that a state had suffered injuries, Vattel spoke for amicable settlements, such as compromise or arbitration. Such redresses were to be resorted to only with regard to rights of an inferior nature. If essential rights of a nation were at stake, such as its very existence, all methods could be used.[42] Nevertheless, the important development was that the right to wage war as a means of redress was no longer considered automatic. With arbitration, peaceful means of settling disputes emerged as a viable alternative and even as the primary option, not only in theory, but little by little in practice as well. Indisputably, the idea of peaceful settlement of disputes and the possibility of making use of arbitration came to affect thinking about state responsibility.[43] With the turn to peaceful means of settling international disputes, the handling of wrongs became more 'technical and analytical',[44] allowing specific rules pertaining to state responsibility to develop. The foundation for an explicit doctrine of state responsibility could thus be established.

## 2.2 TRADITIONAL STATE RESPONSIBILITY: INJURIES TO ALIENS

The shift in emphasis from war to peaceful settlement of international disputes was strengthened by the proliferation of arbitration in interstate relations in the nineteenth and early twentieth centuries. During this period, approximately sixty special tribunals or mixed claims commissions were established in order to settle claims presented by states on behalf of their nationals for injuries that had occurred in other states.[45] Most of these

[40] Ibid., Book I, Preliminaries, p. lxiv.
[41] Ibid., Book II, Chapter XVIII, pp. 275–276.
[42] Ibid., Book II, Chapter XVIII, p. 279.
[43] Brownlie, *State Responsibility: Part I*, p. 5.
[44] Ibid.
[45] Manley O. Hudson, *International Tribunals: Past and Future* (Washington, DC: Carnegie Endowment for International Peace & Brookings Institute, 1944), p. 196, paras. 18–19.

arbitrary bodies dealt with large numbers of claims in the aftermath of war, internal strife, or revolution.[46] For example, the 1868 Mexico/United States General Claims Commission was confronted with over 2,000 claims,[47] whereas the German/Polish Mixed Arbitral Tribunal following World War I had before it 30,000 claims.[48]

The question of responsibility was not limited solely to situations of commotion, however. The political and social changes that took place after the First World War led to the adoption of new ideologies with respect to private ownership, and private property rights in particular. The governmental policies of a number of states that restricted or confiscated private property brought the issue of responsibility of a state for injuries to aliens to the forefront of the international legal agenda.[49] For example, the Bolsheviks' Soviet Union extensively confiscated alien property, as did the nationalization programme of Mexico, both of which roiled international relations.[50] Indeed, as García Amador notes, 'the responsibility of States for damage done in their territory to the person or property of foreigners' formed the core of state responsibility in traditional international law.[51] Thus, the scope of what has been called traditional responsibility,[52] which developed in the nineteenth and early twentieth centuries, was formed through international case law. In fact, in 1946 the responsibility of states for injuries to aliens was considered to be 'one of the most highly developed branches' of international law.[53]

46 Daniel Müller, 'The Work of García Amador on State Responsibility for Injury Caused to Aliens', in James Crawford, Alain Pellet and Simon Olleson (eds.), *The Law of International Responsibility* (Oxford: Oxford University Press, 2010), pp. 69–74 at 70.

47 Hudson, *International Tribunals*, p. 4. For a general overview of Mexican Claims Commissions, see, e.g., Abraham H. Feller, 'The Mexican Claims Commissions' (1933–1934) 19 *Iowa Law Review* 225–230.

48 Hudson, *International Tribunals*, p. 9. The German/Polish Mixed Arbitral Tribunal was established by virtue of Article 304 of the Treaty of Versailles and was terminated following a bilateral agreement in 1931. See *League of Nations Treaty Series* (1933) No. 3272, p. 317.

49 Frederick S. Dunn, 'International Law and Private Property Rights' (1928) 28 *Columbia Law Review* 166–180 at 166.

50 Ibid.; Philip C. Jessup, 'Responsibility of States for Injuries to Individuals' (1946) 46 *Columbia Law Review* 903–928 at 906.

51 García Amador, *First Report*, p. 199, para. 134.

52 Several scholars have termed the early decades of state responsibility for injuries to aliens as the 'traditional' law of state responsibility. See, e.g., Richard R. Baxter, 'Reflections on Codification in Light of the International Law of State Responsibility for Injuries to Aliens' (1964–1965) 16 *Syracuse Law Review* 745–761 at 746; Yoshiro Matsui, 'The Transformation of the Law of State Responsibility', in René Provost (ed.), *State Responsibility in International Law* (Dartmouth: Ashgate, 2002), pp. 3–63.

53 Jessup, 'Responsibility of States', 904.

### 2.2.1 Substantive and Procedural Law

Responsibility for injury to aliens was based on a so-called international or minimum standard of justice thought to be common to all states of the civilized world.[54] Nevertheless, its precise content remained somewhat unclear. It covered a variety of state actions in different fields ranging from standards for the operation of tribunals to the acts of armed forces in the suppression of riots. The basic idea was still to protect foreign persons and properties by way of guaranteeing the standards of civilized nations. Elihu Root's description of the minimum standard of justice is often taken as a definitional starting point:

> There is a standard of justice very simple, very fundamental, and of such general acceptance by all civilized countries as to form a part of the international law of the world. The condition upon which any country is entitled to measure the justice due from it to an alien by the justice which it accords to its own citizens is that its system of law and administration shall conform to this general standard.[55]

Failure by a state to live up to this international standard of justice resulted in international responsibility. Fredrick S. Dunn noted in 1928 with regard to the law:

> In fact there is almost unanimous agreement among the authorities that a nation which, in the exercise of its territorial sovereignty, does not observe the standard of justice of civilized states in its treatment of foreigners incurs responsibility to the governments of the countries to which those foreigners belong for any injury which they may sustain.[56]

The general view of this minimum standard was that it was universally accepted, but this failed to reflect the whole truth for many reasons. First, the precise content of the standard remained vague and devoid of universal content. Despite many definitional attempts, the meaning of *justice* remained relative to particular times and places; there was no 'absolute standard of justice'.[57] Instead, the standards for the protection of the 'security of the person from injury or restraint, and the preservation of private property rights, not only against the actions of other individuals but against the government as well' mirrored European values only.[58] The lack of general agreement on the

54 Elihu Root, 'The Basis of Protection to Citizens Residing Abroad' (1910) 4 *American Journal of International Law* 517–528 at 521–522.

55 Ibid.

56 Dunn, 'Private Property Rights', 175.

57 Ibid.

58 Ibid., pp. 175–176.

minimum standard of justice was obvious in arbitration commission reports. The Mexico/United States General Claims Commission recognized in the *Neer* case 'the difficulty of devising a general formula for determining the boundary between an international delinquency of this type and an unsatisfactory use of power included in national sovereignty'.[59] The Commission did, however, go a bit further in its analysis on the meaning of 'denial of justice'. It noted: 'the treatment of an alien, in order to constitute an international delinquency, should amount to an outrage, to bad faith, to wilful neglect of duty, or to an insufficiency of governmental action so far short of international standards that every reasonable and impartial man would readily recognize its insufficiency'.[60] Another factor militating against the universality of the minimum standard was that states outside the nucleus of the international community resisted this minimum standard of justice. Their resistance was based on a number of arguments. It was held that when a state interfered on behalf of a national who had assumed the risk of moving to another country, this action constituted a violation of the latter state's national sovereignty. In fact, comparison of any domestic justice system against 'an external yardstick' was considered inappropriate, whether or not it reached the level of the minimum standard.[61] The minimum standard of justice was understood as paving the way towards a theory of absolute responsibility for injuries to aliens, something conceived to be an impossibility in countries undergoing constant turmoil, such as those in Latin America.[62]

Another argument used to deny the validity of the minimum standard of justice was the claim that it generated situations of inequality between nationals and aliens. The different levels of protection afforded to nationals and aliens would only serve to widen the gap between the two, and thus complicate the 'free intercourse among peoples of different states'.[63] Thus, many Latin American, Asian, and East European states advocated instead for the principle of 'equality of treatment between nationals and foreigners'.[64] This principle governed the protection of aliens in Latin America.[65] According to

[59] *L. F. H. Neer and Pauline Neer (United States* v. *United Mexican States)*, IV Reports of International Arbitral Awards (1926), p. 60, para. 4.

[60] Ibid.

[61] S. N. Guha Roy, 'Is the Law of Responsibility of States for Injuries to Aliens A Part of Universal International Law?' (1961) 55 *American Journal of International Law* 863–891 at 889.

[62] Julius Goebel Jr., 'The International Responsibility of States for Injuries Sustained by Aliens on Account of Mob Violence, Insurrections and Civil Wars' (1914) 8 *American Journal of International Law* 802–852 at 831.

[63] Guha Roy, 'Is the Law', 889.

[64] Matsui, 'The Transformation', 5.

[65] García Amador, *First Report*, p. 201, para. 144.

the principle of equality of nationals and aliens, 'the foreigner who voluntarily moves to a country ... in search of a personal benefit, accepts in advance, together with the advantages which he is going to enjoy, the risks to which he may find himself exposed'.[66] The so-called Calvo Doctrine was developed in order to advance the equal treatment of nationals and aliens.[67] Carlos Calvo, an Argentine jurist, held that '[a]liens who establish themselves in a country are certainly entitled to the same rights of protection as nationals, but they cannot claim any greater measure of protection.'[68] The practical result of the Calvo Doctrine was the so-called Calvo Clause. This contractual clause set forth that any dispute between a foreign national and a government 'be settled solely by local remedies excluding the right of diplomatic protection of the foreigner's State'.[69]

Although the criticism embodied in the Calvo Doctrine against the minimum standards of justice gained acceptance in Latin America, it was generally repudiated by other states. The repudiation was based on the grounds that the right to diplomatic protection of aliens resided with the state, and not the individual. The Mexico/United States General Claims Commission commented on the Calvo Clause in the case of *North American Dredging Company*,[70] that an alien 'can not deprive the government of his nation of its undoubted right of applying international remedies to violations of international law committed to his damage'.[71] According to the Commission, the state of nationality of an alien has a larger interest in ensuring compliance to international legal norms which exceeds the state's interest in 'recovering damage for one of its citizens in a particular case'.[72] Hence, an individual could not give up the right to diplomatic protection.[73]

Indeed, diplomatic protection constituted the gist of the procedural aspect of the responsibility of a state for injury to aliens. With regard to the diplomatic protection of nationals, Emmerich de Vattel stated in 1758:

[66] This statement was rendered by the Mexican Minister of Foreign Affairs in a note of 3 August 1938 to the United States concerning the deprivation of land of an American national residing in Mexico. The correspondence is cited in Edwin Borchard, 'The "Minimum" Standard of the Treatment of Aliens' (1939) 33 *Proceedings of the American Society of International Law at Its Annual Meeting* 51–63.

[67] See, Matsui, 'The Transformation', 21.

[68] García Amador, *First Report*, p. 201, para. 145.

[69] Matsui, 'The Transformation', 21.

[70] *North American Dredging Company of Texas (United States of America* v. *United Mexican States)*, IV Reports of International Arbitral Awards (1926), p. 26, para. 11.

[71] Ibid.

[72] Ibid.

[73] Matsui, 'The Transformation', 20.

> Whoever uses a citizen ill, indirectly offends the state, which is bound to protect this citizen; and the sovereign of the latter should avenge his wrongs, punish the aggressor, and, if possible, oblige him to make full reparation; since otherwise the citizen would not obtain the great end of civil association, which is, safety.[74]

The right of states to exercise diplomatic protection was also explicitly recognized by the Permanent Court of International Justice (PCIJ) in the *Mavrommatis Palestine Concessions* case of 1924 when the Court held that:

> [i]t is an elementary principle of international law that a State is entitled to protect its subjects, when injured by acts contrary to international law committed by another State, from whom they have been unable to obtain satisfaction through ordinary channels. By taking up the case of one of its subjects and by resorting to diplomatic action or international judicial proceedings on his behalf, a State is in reality asserting its own rights – its right to ensure, in the person of its subjects, respect for the rules of international law.[75]

Thus, by subsuming the claim, a state came to be in charge of the entire process of settlement. The individual was no longer in control of negotiations, settlement of the claim, or any compensation that followed from the claim. This state absorption of claims in the name of diplomatic protection was heavily critiqued. It was considered to be an institutional pretext for external intervention by one state into the affairs of another state.[76] A common view was that the practice of diplomatic protection was resorted to only by strong states 'against weaker countries, and never against each other'.[77]

### 2.2.2 *The Economic Rationale*

The traditional law of state responsibility, namely, the responsibility of a state for injury to aliens, received much criticism in the immediate aftermath of the active years of arbitration when codification work was initiated. The criticism covered various aspects of the law of responsibility of states for injury to aliens, including its customary basis, the importance of the theory of diplomatic protection, the unequal status between aliens and citizens with respect to the enjoyment of rights, and finally what was considered the essential purpose of the whole branch: namely the protection and advancement of the

74 de Vattel, *The Law of Nations*, Book II, Chapter VI, p. 161, para. 71.

75 *The Mavrommatis Palestine Concessions* (*Greece* v. *Great Britain*), 1924 PCIJ Series A, No. 2 at p. 12.

76 Matsui, 'The Transformation', 19.

77 Dunn, *The Protection of Nationals*, p. 55.

economic and political interests of Western states. As Richard Baxter noted, the topic 'gave every indication of being ideologically controversial'.[78] It was widely argued that the doctrine of responsibility of a state for injury to aliens represented a means of Western imperialism and colonialism. Thus, the main objectors to this branch of law came from Latin America and Asia, particularly from new states that had emerged after the Second World War.

Joining in this criticism, the Indian High Court Judge Guha Roy described the history of the responsibility of states for injuries to aliens as an institutional tool 'for the mastery of the politically and economically undeveloped regions of the globe'.[79] Thus, arguably, the law of responsibility was born out of the desire by some states to politically influence others with a view towards markets and raw materials.[80] Frederick S. Dunn explicated the purpose of traditional responsibility as follows: '[it is] ultimately concerned with the possibility of maintaining a unified economic and social order for the conduct of international trade and intercourse among independent political units of diverse cultures and stages of civilization, different legal and economic systems, and varying degrees of physical power and prestige.'[81] Thus, the law of responsibility of a state for injuries to aliens represents nothing more than 'a handmaid of power in the preservation of its spoils'.[82]

The reasons for perceiving traditional state responsibility as a means to further Western economic interests were manifold. First, most of the international intercourse that had taken place since the middle of the nineteenth century was concerned 'not with high politics, alliances, armaments, and balance of power, but with the difficulties and clashes of interest arising out of the tremendous flow of people and goods across the borders of nations'.[83] States that had benefited from this flow of people and goods had sought to invest their extra monies in foreign locations for the benefit of their 'ranchers, bankers, mining engineers, railroad builders, constructors of ports', and so forth.[84] Thus the economic power of a state was dependent on both its people and its properties abroad. Dunn notes that 'a vast number holding membership in that group [of individuals composing the United States] are scattered all over the world, and an equally vast amount of their property, both real and personal, is situated in foreign jurisdictions'.[85]

[78] Baxter, 'Reflections on Codification', 746.
[79] Guha Roy, 'Is the Law', 865.
[80] Ibid., 885.
[81] Dunn, *The Protection of Nationals*, p. 1.
[82] Guha Roy, 'Is the Law', 866.
[83] Dunn, 'Private Property Rights', 170.
[84] Jessup, 'Responsibility of States', 905.
[85] Dunn, 'Private Property Rights', 170.

Second, despite the significance of economic issues in international relations, critics conceived of the entire international legal system as an invention of a few 'Christian states of Europe'.[86] In the view of critics, due to the instrumental value of state responsibility, these states attempted to impose this system as general international law upon states that had not accepted it.[87] In a similar vein, Dunn held that the entire body of international law was formulated to 'keep up with the enlarging economic activities of man'.[88] As a logical corollary, the specific rules on responsibility were also perceived as guaranteeing interaction and trade.

## 2.3 RESPONSIBILITY AT THE CROSSROADS

The arbitration practices involved in settling injuries caused to aliens and their property during the second half of the nineteenth century and first decades of the twentieth century, contributed to bringing the issue of responsibility to the forefront of the international legal system. Along with increased scholarly interest in the topic,[89] codification initiatives on state responsibility mushroomed, particularly in the 1920s. Between 1890–1965, eighteen initiatives on the topic were drawn up in instruments ranging from recommendations and resolutions to draft conventions.[90] Many of these codification drafts were undertaken by private persons and bodies, but regional and universal organizations were material in the process as well.

Three main approaches were discernible among these codification initiatives: (1) 'the obligations approach'; (2) 'the delicts approach'; and (3) 'the

86 Guha Roy, 'Is the Law', 866.

87 Ibid., 867.

88 Dunn, 'Private Property Rights', 170.

89 Among works on state responsibility drawing attention to its importance are: Anzilotti, *Teoria generale*; Dionisio Anzilotti, 'La responsabilité internationale des États à raison des dommages soufferts par des étrangers' (1906) 13 *Revue générale de droit international public* 5–29; Paul Schoen, 'Die völkerrechtliche Haftung der Staaten aus unerlaubten Handlungen' (1917–1918) 10 *Zeitschrift für Völkerrecht*; Karl Strupp, *Das völkerrechtliche Delikt* (Stuttgart: W. Karlhammer, 1920); Charles Visscher, *La Responsabilité des États* (Leiden, Lugduni Batavorum: Brill, 1924); Eagleton, 'Protection of Foreign Officials'; Eagleton, *The Responsibility of States*; Edwin M. Borchard, 'Theoretical Aspects of the International Responsibility of States' (1929) *Max-Planck-Institut für ausländisches öffentliches Recht und Völkerrecht* 223–250.

90 All codification efforts were listed by Special Rapporteur Roberto Ago in his *First Report on State Responsibility*, UN Doc. A/CN.4/217 and Add.1 (1969), pp. 125–126. The calculation used here excludes codification efforts undertaken under the ILC mandate.

principles approach'.[91] The 'obligations approach' meant that the international obligations the breach of which gave rise to legal responsibility were identified (a duty to maintain order, a duty to afford aliens with redress); the 'delicts approach' focused on the particular breaches that generate responsibility (denial of justice, state-sponsored personal injury); and finally, the 'principles approach' purported to define general principles applicable to all sorts of wrongful acts.[92]

A common denominator of many codification initiatives was that they approached the topic of state responsibility from the perspective of specific rules that had developed into customary law through the practice of numerous arbitration bodies. The reach of these initiatives was consequently often limited to that of responsibility for injuries to aliens. The 1925 project of the American Institute of International Law on diplomatic protection dealt with procedural aspects of responsibility; in 1926 the Japanese International Law Association prepared a code on international law containing a chapter on responsibility for injuries to aliens, as did the Institute of International Law in 1927. Finally, two draft conventions on the rights of aliens were drafted, one by the Harvard Law School in 1929 (later revised in 1961), and another by the German International Law Society in 1930. In recent years, the Harvard draft convention has been appreciated as the most valuable of these codification efforts, based on the level of its comprehensiveness.[93]

However, more general approaches to the law of state responsibility also emerged. In 1902, the Italian scholar Dionisio Anzilotti had developed a general theory of state responsibility. His approach was followed by a number of German professors: first by Schoen, and later by Strupp and Roth, who each developed their own respective draft conventions on state responsibility in 1927 and 1932 respectively. Their aim was to set forth 'the rules governing State responsibility in general, regardless of the content of the obligations violated,

[91] Allott, 'State Responsibility and the Unmaking', 4. The obligations approach can further be divided into initiatives attempting to lay down the responsibilities of governments (e.g., 'Responsibility of Governments' prepared by the American Institute of International Law in 1925) and those efforts setting forth the rights of aliens (e.g., 'Convention relative to the Rights of Aliens' prepared by the Second International Conference of American States, 1902). Examples of obligations exemplifying the two categories are, for example, the obligation of the government 'to maintain on its own territory the internal order and governmental stability' (Responsibility of Governments, Article 1), and '[a]liens shall enjoy all civil rights pertaining to citizens' (Rights of Aliens).

[92] Ibid., 4.

[93] Lucie Laithier, 'Private Codification Efforts', in James Crawford, Alain Pellet, and Simon Olleson (eds.), *The Law of International Responsibility* (Oxford: Oxford University Press, 2010), pp. 53–59 at 55.

instead of confining themselves to failure by a State to observe its obligations relating to treatment of aliens'.[94]

Although many of the codification efforts were generated by and targeted at the League of Nations General Codification Conference in 1930, no breakthrough was achieved at the conference with respect to the topic of 'Responsibility of States for Damage done in their Territory to the Person or Property of Foreigners'.[95] Several factors hampered the codification work: the time afforded to the work was too short, the delegates were swamped with work, and the governmental backing of the whole project was insufficient.[96] In addition, 'the theoretical foundations of the topic were not prepared enough'.[97] The broadening of responsibility to new issue areas had given rise to two distinct strategies with respect to state responsibility codification. While some scholars highlighted the influence on state responsibility of private law from the domestic setting, others pursued the strategy of creating a regime of objective responsibility freed from private law analogies. In other words, the domestic analogy played an important role in state responsibility thinking, leaving it unclear how the law was to be construed.

### 2.3.1 *The Relevance of the Domestic Analogy*

The domestic analogy has been among one of the most debated issues in international law,[98] although the international legal system lacks institutions similar to those in the domestic sphere, namely, 'compulsory adjudication, legislation, and enforcement'.[99] The domestic analogy is built on the idea that

94 Ago, *First Report*, reproduced in ILC Yearbook (1969), vol. II, p. 128, para. 14.

95 The League of Nations Assembly had decided in 1927 to place the topic on the codification agenda. See League of Nations Resolution of 27 September 1927, reproduced in *American Journal of International Law* (1928) 22 *Special Supplement* 1–233 at 231.

96 Shabtai Rosenne (ed.), 1 *League of Nations Conference for the Codification of International Law (1930)* (1975), pp. xli–xlii, cited in Brownlie, *State Responsibility: Part I*, p. 12. See also, Crawford, *State Responsibility: The General Part*, pp. 30–32.

97 Shabtai Rosenne (ed.), 1 *League of Nations Conference for the Codification of International Law (1930)* (1975), at xli, cited in Brownlie, *State Responsibility: Part I*, p. 13.

98 Hidemi Suganami, *The Domestic Analogy and World Order Proposals* (Cambridge: Cambridge University Press, 1989); Martti Koskenniemi, *From Apology to Utopia: The Structure of International Legal Argument* (reissue with new epilogue, Cambridge: Cambridge University Press, 2005), p. 22. For an overview of the domestic analogy and classic writers on international law, see Edwin DeWitt Dickinson, 'The Analogy between Natural Persons and International Persons in the Law of Nations' (1917) 26 *The Yale Law Journal* 564–591.

99 Koskenniemi, 'Solidarity Measures', 337.

interstate relations are comparable to the relations between individuals.[100] The domestic analogy thus portrays the international world as an equivalent to the national setting. Thus, experiences from the domestic sphere are capable of being transferred to the international sphere.[101]

A consensus on this vague definition of the domestic analogy prevails. A deeper examination of the concept quickly reveals that it encompasses a variety of understandings, perceptions, and proposals. No commonly agreed definition of the term exists. For some, it entails the building of unity in international law; for others, it means the importation of national rules into the international legal system but only up to a certain point. Thus, there appear to be intermediate positions between the two main views with respect to the domestic analogy. The first view emphasizes the special character of international law and thus rejects the analogy. The second understanding embraces the fact that international law can develop towards a unified system similar to that of the national system, and that tools for achieving this development can be found in national law. The variation in type and extent of the domestic analogy is more aptly described as a continuum between those accepting and those rejecting its use.

The relevance of the domestic analogy for the law of state responsibility has been clear since the days of arbitration. The widespread practice of resolving disputes through the courts, arbitrations, and their judges bore resemblance to dispute settlement in domestic settings. In addition, arbitration judges often resorted to national rules in contradiction to existing international rules while settling claims.[102] In fact, Hersch Lauterpacht sought to show that most of the law of responsibility actually derived from private law. The domestic analogy thus came to play a decisive role in the formative years of the law of responsibility, and it served as the preferred external benchmark against which state responsibility's level of development was measured. For example, in 1939 Roberto Ago held that the theory of state responsibility was much less developed than its counterparts of criminal law and tort law in domestic legal systems.[103]

[100] Thomas Erskine Holland famously held in 1898 that '[t]he Law of Nations is but private law "writ large". It is an application to political communities of those legal ideas which were originally applied to the relations of individuals'. *Studies in International Law* (Oxford: Clarendon Press, 1898), p. 152.

[101] Andreas L. Paulus, 'From Territoriality to Functionality? Towards a Legal Methodology of Globalization', in Ige F. Dekker and Wouter G. Werner (eds.), *Governance and International Legal Theory* (Leiden: Martinus Nijhoff, 2004), pp. 59–96 at 62.

[102] See e.g., Hersch Lauterpacht, *Private Law Sources and Analogies of International Law* (1st published by Longmans, Green and Co. Ltd, 1927, North Haven: Archon Books, 1970) at 147–151.

[103] Roberto Ago, 'Le délit international' (1939–II) 68 *Collected Courses of the Hague Academy Lecture of International Law* 415–554 at 420–421.

Not all scholars were fond of the domestic analogy, however. In 1912, Dionisio Anzilotti held that international responsibility was different from responsibility in the domestic legal orders due to its cooperative character.[104] The rift between scholars on the relevance of the domestic analogy for state responsibility widened in the 1920s and 1930s, with some scholars highlighting the importance of private law in the field of international responsibility, and others pursuing a path in which they sought to construct international responsibility on the basis of its own premises. Roughly speaking, they either built upon Grotius' principle of fault, or they advanced the theory of objective responsibility.[105]

The role played by the domestic analogy is different in these two main strands of responsibility in legal thinking. Yet, it is arguably present in both. The former attempts to complete international legal rules with rules derived from national law, while the latter tries to build a unified system similar to any national legal system. The commonality between both schools of thought is still the idea of a natural progress towards the unity of international law. Few scholars actually manage – or desire – to approach the topic of responsibility from a pragmatic viewpoint. Yet, there were also scholars who accepted the incompleteness of the law of responsibility as it stood in the early decades of the twentieth century.[106]

### 2.3.2 *The Role of Fault*

One central element in the private law analogy of state responsibility has been the principle of fault and its relevance to the different understandings of how state responsibility ought to be formed.[107] Should responsibility follow only from situations in which there was intent to violate international law, is it the result of blameworthy negligence, or should it simply be an automatic consequence of the violation of another state's interests? At one end of the spectrum, there are those arguing for a fault-based responsibility and at the other end those advancing objective responsibility.[108] Between these two extreme

[104] Dionisio Anzilotti, *Corso di Diritto Internazionale* (Rome: Atheneum, 1912), pp. 239–240.
[105] Eagleton, *The Responsibility of States*, p. 208.
[106] Ibid., p. 208.
[107] Lauterpacht, *Private Law Sources*, p. 135.
[108] While most authors would view the objective responsibility theory as being opposed to the fault-based school, some go even further and advocate that absolute responsibility or so-called strict liability constitutes the other end of the spectrum. However, both the fault-based and objective responsibility schools build on the necessity of an internationally wrongful act, which is not a necessary element of absolute responsibility. Since wrongfulness is an essential part of contemporary state responsibility and consequently in the analysis here, it suffices to acknowledge that absolute responsibility disregards both the elements of fault and wrongfulness.

positions a variety of views are to be found. Despite the eventual move away from fault-based responsibility, the concept of fault has not become obsolete in the law of state responsibility. It continues to raise debate and it plays a role in the determination of the consequences of responsibility.

The importance of the principle of fault in determining responsibility stems from the work of Hugo Grotius, who introduced this concept of Roman law into international law.[109] According to the principle of fault, a person is responsible for an injury committed to another person when the act has been perpetrated intentionally or negligently in breach of the legal rule in question. Or, to put it the other way around, no responsibility exists without fault for the occasioned fact, which consequently means that there is no obligation to pay damages.[110] This principle, which is 'the foundation of the doctrine of liability in modern systems of private law',[111] was transferred to the realm of international legal relations by Grotius, who accordingly conceived of responsibility as a consequence only of situations of subjective fault on the part of the state.[112] For such an understanding, the state of mind is decisive. Thus, his exploration of the liability of the sovereign for the acts of soldiers and sailors acting on the basis of letters of reprisals excludes responsibility in which the sovereign was not the cause of the wrongdoing, had no share in the wrong, or had taken precautionary measures to keep his subjects in order.[113] As concerns private subjects, Grotius claimed that '[a] community, or its rulers, may be held responsible for the crime of a subject if they know of it and do not prevent it when they could and should prevent it.'[114]

Understanding fault as a subjective state of mind means that one perceives fault as 'the *mens rea* of the state organ'.[115] Fault seen this way entails an act by a state which is blameworthy or in which the state failed to act diligently.[116] Establishing the psychological element of the state might, however, prove difficult. Consequently, fault-based responsibility is often connected to situations

[109] F. V. García Amador, Louis B. Sohn and Richard R. Baxter, *Recent Codification of the Law of State Responsibility for Injuries to Aliens* (Dobbs Ferry, NY: Oceana Publications, 1974), p. 14.

[110] Dionisio Anzilotti cites von Jhering's *Das Schuldmoment im römischen Privatrecht* by stating: '*senza colpa nessuna responsabilità pel fatto accaduto, cioè nessun obbligo al risarcimento del danno*', *Teoria generale*, p. 14.

[111] Lauterpacht, *Private Law Sources*, p. 136.

[112] Mohammed Bedjaoui, 'Responsibility of States: Fault and Strict Liability', in Rudolf Bernhardt (ed.), *Encyclopedia of International Law*, vol. IV (Amsterdam: North Holland, 1984), pp. 212–216 at 213.

[113] Grotius, *De Jure Belli*, Book II, Chapter XVII, para. XX.

[114] Ibid., Book II, Chapter XXI, section II.

[115] Bonafè, *The Relationship*, p. 121.

[116] Antoine Favre, 'Fault as an Element of the Illicit Act' (1963–1964) 52 *Georgetown Law Journal* 555–570 at 555.

in which the state as a legal and physical person is one and the same. State-based fault becomes possible when there is 'perfect identity between the legal person (the state) and the physical person (the monarch)'.[117] Indeed, fault 'was normally conceived of as resulting from a complicity between the king and the perpetrator of the act'.[118] However, according to many commentators, the complexities of a modern state make fault-based responsibility utterly difficult if not impossible.[119] Not only would it generally be problematic to prove fault, but it is often problematic even to recognize the precise state agents who committed the wrong in the first place: multiple persons and acts might be involved.[120]

As an alternative to basing responsibility on subjective fault – that is, a subjective state of mind including malicious intent or negligence – some proponents of the fault-based responsibility school advance the idea of objective fault. The exact content of objective fault remains nevertheless unclear. On the one hand it is asserted that this construction of fault understands the mere violation of an international legal obligation as 'fault' and consequently denies the necessity of establishing subjective fault as a general principle.[121] On the other hand, objective fault is defined as 'a violation of the standard norm of diligency'.[122] Both perceptions nevertheless leave the difference to the objective school of responsibility unexplained.

Those promoting objective responsibility dismiss the principle of fault altogether as a general rule; 'responsibility of a State flows "objectively" from the breach of an international obligation caused by an action or omission attributable to that State'.[123] Thus, responsibility is autonomous from any fault on the part of state agents.[124] Although in this theory the actor's subjective state of mind does not play a role, the theory of objective responsibility is generally

[117] Bonafè, *The Relationship*, p. 121.

[118] Favre, 'Fault as an Element', 555.

[119] Oscar Schachter, *International Law in Theory and Practice* (Dordrecht: Martinus Nijhoff Publishers, 1991), p. 203; Favre, 'Fault as an Element', 555; Bonafè, *The Relationship*, esp. p. 125.

[120] Schachter, *Theory and Practice*, p. 203; Favre, 'Fault as an Element', 555.

[121] Ian Brownlie notices that 'both writers and tribunals may use the words *faute* or fault to mean a breach of a legal duty, an unlawful act'. See Brownlie, *Principles of International Law* (6th ed., Oxford: Oxford University Press, 2003), pp. 424–425. Similarly, Mohammed Bedjaoui explains objective fault as 'close in meaning to the non-observance of an international duty'. See Bedjaoui, 'Responsibility of States', 213.

[122] Favre, 'Fault as an Element', 570.

[123] Bedjaoui, 'Responsibility of States', 213. Bedjaoui also notes that some writers have called objective responsibility with the term causal responsibility, since the essence of the determination of responsibility lies in attributing a wrongful act to the state (Ibid.).

[124] Favre, 'Fault as an Element', 560.

held to better correspond to the necessities of maintaining good international relations as it safeguards reparation.[125]

### 2.3.3 *Different Approaches to the Domestic Analogy and State Responsibility*

#### 2.3.3.1 Continental Institutionalization of Responsibility

The first international legal scholar to explore in-depth the subject of state responsibility was the Italian Dionisio Anzilotti, who developed a general theory of state responsibility.[126] The wish for a general theory derived from Anzilotti's view that the only real law was positive law.[127] For him, responsibility was an element of all legal systems, including international law.[128] In his *Teoria generale della responsabilità dello Stato nel diritto internazionale* of 1902, Anzilotti – the 'positivist and dualist' that he was[129] – advanced the separation between the legal spheres of domestic law and international law. The international legal system, which was considered to be economically oriented and of a lower status, had a special character different from private law.[130] Hence, Anzilotti's efforts were largely focused on making international law, including the law of international responsibility, autonomous and free from private law arguments.[131] This is especially so with regard to the most notable private law analogy, that of *culpa*, the principle of fault.[132] He favoured an approach whereby the source of responsibility stems from the mere fact that an international obligation has been violated. Anzilotti argued: 'It is not fault (*culpa*), but a fact contrary to international law, which creates responsibility.'[133] He promoted

125 See Brownlie, *Principles*, p. 425.

126 His main works include titles such as *Teoria generale della responsabilità dello Stato nel diritto internazionale* (1902), and 'La responsabilité internationale des États a raison des dommages soufferts par des étrangers'. The meaning of a general theory can be understood as something else than abstract rules. During the work of the ILC, a member of the Committee, Mr. Yasseen, described a general theory as 'the idea of a systematic and consolidated body of generally applicable rules'. See ILC, Report by Mr. R. Ago, Chairman of the Sub-Committee on State responsibility, UN Doc. A/CN.4/152 (1963), p. 233.

127 Anzilotti states: '*Cela dit, comme le droit international positif, c'est-à-dire le veritable droit international, ne dérive que de la volonté des États, qui se manifest, expressément, dans les traités générateurs de règles obligatoires de leur conduit, ou implicitement, dans les faits qui engendrent la coutume*', see 'La responsabilité', 16.

128 Anzilotti, 'La responsabilité', 13.

129 Giorgio Gaja, 'Positivism and Dualism in Dionisio Anzilotti' (1992) 3 *European Journal of International Law* 123–138 at 123.

130 Lauterpacht, *Private Law Sources*, p. ix; Anzilotti, 'La responsabilité', 7–8.

131 Dupuy, 'Dionisio Anzilotti', 140–141.

132 Ibid., 140.

133 Anzilotti, cited in Lauterpacht, *Private Law Sources*, p. 138.

a theory of objective responsibility according to which the state was responsible for all acts of its agents, 'because it had issued a legal guarantee that other states would not be injured by acts emanating from its sphere of activity'.[134]

Anzilotti no doubt has had a seminal influence upon the law of state responsibility, particularly because much of the ILC's approach towards codifying this branch of law has its roots in Anzilotti's theory.[135] This 'father of the modern law of responsibility',[136] was also the first to articulate a 'theoretical framework for the law of state responsibility'.[137] Thus, he responded to an emerging need for the systematization of state responsibility law.[138] In particular, continental legal scholarship favoured Anzilotti's general theory due to the fact that it was 'positive, formal and systematic law'.[139] Especially, German jurists had a predilection for developing 'sophisticated theories' on various aspects of international law.[140] This was the case as well when it came to the responsibility of states.

Anzilotti's theory of state responsibility was carried further by the scholarship of the German jurists Schoen, Strupp, and Roth. Karl Strupp demonstrated a clear desire to theorize the law of state responsibility. In 1920 he authored *Das völkerrechtliche Delikt*, which included draft articles on state responsibility. In 1927, Strupp enumerated different approaches to responsibility. He wrote:

Théories:

1. La théorie dominante: *Toute responsabilité internationale suppose une culpabilité de l'Etat* (Currently dominant theory: Any international responsibility presupposes guilt by the state).
2. Théorie de M. Anzilotti: Toute *violation d'une norme international engage la responsabilité des Etats auteurs de ladite violation* (Mr. Anzilotti's theory: All violations of an international norm engages the responsibility of the state committing the violation).
3. *Théorie* Strupp: *L'Etat est responsable, abstraction faite de toute culpabilité, s'il s'agit de faits positifs (ou de commission,* delicta commissiva).

[134] Hessbruegge, 'The Historical Development', 299.

[135] Dupuy, 'Dionisio Anzilotti', 140, 143.

[136] Pierre-Marie Dupuy, 'A General Stocktaking of the Connections between the Multilateral Dimension of Obligations and Codification of the Law of Responsibility' (2002) 13 *European Journal of International Law* 1053–1081 at 1056.

[137] Georg Nolte, 'From Dionisio Anzilotti to Roberto Ago: The Classical International Law of State Responsibility and the Traditional Primacy of a Bilateral Conception of Inter-state Relations' (2002) 13 *European Journal of International Law* 1033–1098 at 1088.

[138] Ibid.

[139] Ibid.

[140] Martti Koskenniemi, *The Gentle Civilizer of Nations: The Rise and Fall of International Law 1870–1960* (Cambridge: Cambridge University Press, 2002), p. 181.

> *Au contraire, en cas de faits négatifs (délits d'omission), sa responsabilité n'est engagée que s'il y a faute de sa part (manque de diligence usuelle)* (Strupp's theory: The state is responsible regardless of any guilt, if it is a question of positive facts [or commission, delicta commissiva]. On the contrary, in the event of negative facts [offences of omission], its responsibility is engaged only if there is fault on its part [usual lack of diligence]).[141]

Thus, Strupp distanced himself from bringing private law analogies into the law of responsibility. He discarded the dominant theory, which always required fault as a condition for responsibility. Instead, Strupp constructed his own theory upon Anzilotti's objective theory while, contrary to Anzilotti, accepting fault in cases of indirect responsibility. Strupp did not shy away from stating that his theory finds support among many jurists, allegedly among them Edwin Borchard.[142] However, his ideas failed to make their way to the 1930 General Codification Conference in The Hague. To Strupp's disappointment, the codification project was unsuccessful; state responsibility remained outside the structures of legal formalism.[143]

The aim of the 'objective responsibility' school was to distance the international law of responsibility from the domestic analogy. As Eagleton noted, the purpose was to guarantee that other states would never suffer injustice from the international system, which gave each state the right to rule how it pleased.[144] It can nevertheless be questioned whether the proponents of objective responsibility truly managed to abandon the domestic analogy, or if in fact they simply contemplated another version of it. It could be argued that in constructing the responsibility of states as an institution of international law they tried to imbue the international legal order with the same coherence that domestic legal systems possessed.

[141] Karl Strupp, *Éléments du droit international public universel, européen et americain* (2nd ed., Paris: Les Éditions Internationales, 1930), p. 330.

[142] Strupp, *Éléments*, p. 330. Interestingly, however, Borchard expressly rejected Strupp's theory in 1929. Borchard seems to side with Anzilotti rather than Strupp when he states: 'One conclusion that it seems possible to draw from the practice is that apart from "political crimes", some wrongful invasion of the rights of an alien by an agency of the State seems to be required, a conclusion which would seem to support Anzilotti's theory.... Whether we can go further still and support in practice the Strupp distinction between acts of commission, which require no fault, and acts of omission, which do require fault, is open to question.... The wrongful act of the state in enacting and enforcing the law suffices to impose responsibility. No different is the case with omissions'. See Borchard, 'Theoretical Aspects', 225–226.

[143] Koskenniemi, *The Gentle Civilizer*, p. 265.

[144] Eagleton, *The Responsibility of States*, p. 211.

### 2.3.3.2 Responsibility of States as Tort Law

The claims of the special character of international law and the law of responsibility in particular failed to convince all scholars. Hersch Lauterpacht was one scholar who explicitly accepted the domestic analogy. For him, the use of private law arguments for the development of international law could both be proved and approved of. The development of international law was not only furthered by but also was necessitated on the premise of recourse to domestic law.[145] Formal, but not material, completeness thus characterized international law. Here 'formal completeness' means that the international legal system should be perceived as containing solutions to any problem, even though substantive rules on each particular issue are lacking.[146] A complete legal system, such as the international legal system, can resort to other means besides positive law. Available techniques include: general principles of law, judicial balancing, social purposes, or, for example, resort to domestic tort law.[147] Tort law was considered the 'twin' to state responsibility;[148] similar to the horizontal relationship between states, tort law regulated wrongs between two consociates in the domestic sphere. Just as tort law, state responsibility is understood to protect 'the subjective rights of any state against acts of another state'.[149] Hence, according to Lauterpacht international law should neither be considered 'special' nor 'primitive'. Instead, the domestic analogy could be used to create unity in international law, a scientific construction inherent in any system of law.[150]

With respect to the law of responsibility, Lauterpacht repudiated Anzilotti's ideas of the unitary and absolute character of responsibility. Instead, he set out to demonstrate that state responsibility is filled with private law elements and

145 Lauterpacht, *Private Law Sources*, p. viii. Lauterpracht draws his primary proof of the significance of private law from international arbitration, which applies private law in its decisions. Ibid., pp. 38–42.

146 Lauterpacht states: 'The completeness of the rule of law – as distinguished from the completeness of individual branches of statutory or customary law – is an *a priori* assumption of every system of law, not a prescription of positive law. [...] There may be gaps in a statute or in the statutory law as a whole; there may be gaps in the various manifestations of customary law. There are no gaps in the legal system taken as a whole'. See Hersch Lauterpacht, *The Function of Law in the International Community* (Oxford: Clarendon Press, 1933), p. 64. Lauterpacht emphasizes, however, the necessity of each legal order also to strive towards material completeness. Ibid., p. 86.

147 Koskenniemi, *The Gentle Civilizer*, p. 363; Lauterpacht, *The Function*, p. 134.

148 Randall Lesaffer, 'Argument from Roman Law in Current International Law' (2005) 16 *European Journal of International Law* 25–58 at 27.

149 André Nollkaemper, 'Towards Public Responsibility in International Law', conference presentation at Global Constitutionalism: Process and Substance, Kandersteg, 17–19 January 2008, p. 2.

150 Koskenniemi, *The Gentle Civilizer*, pp. 363–364. See Lauterpacht, *The Function of Law*, p. 64.

needs to rely on these components in order to develop.[151] For Lauterpacht, the principle of fault was the central issue which ultimately demonstrated the relevance of the domestic analogy. Lauterpacht contended that by virtue of the adoption of the Roman law concept of fault, Grotius had 'dealt a death-blow to the doctrine of collective responsibility'.[152]

According to Lauterpacht, state practice had remained loyal to Grotius 'orthodox theory', and hence Anzilotti's theory of responsibility was detached from reality and state practice.[153] Moreover, accepting the theory of absolute responsibility would ultimately mean the separation of law and morality. Lauterpacht argued that at the end of the day, even those promoting the special character of international law and following Anzilotti's lead on absolute responsibility have, to a certain extent, come to accept the principle of fault.[154] Ultimately, Schoen and Strupp restrictively and reluctantly accepted recourse to private law arguments in some instances. Strupp explicitly recognized the application of the principle of fault in the case of state omissions with respect to the acts of private individuals which gave rise to injuries.[155] And since Lauterpacht held that most cases of state responsibility related to omissions rather than commissions, the principle of fault arguably reigned over the theory of absolute responsibility.[156]

#### 2.3.3.3 Anglo-Saxon Pragmatism

In the 1920s, international legal scholarship was not merely divided into groups of those rejecting and those embracing the domestic analogy in the law of responsibility. There also existed intermediate positions emphasizing pragmatic solutions. One such scholar devoted to the law of state responsibility in the 1920s was Clyde Eagleton. In his monograph *The Responsibility of States in International Law*, Eagleton approached the topic from existing international practice, from which he derived substantive and procedural rules in a systematic manner.[157] By deriving his rules from case law Eagleton, similarly to Lauterpacht, sought to show to his home audience of Anglo-Saxon tradition that the international legal order was proper law which could be read through cases.[158] Eagleton's stance on state responsibility was in part opposite to that of

[151] Lauterpacht, *Private Law Sources*, p. 134 .
[152] Ibid., p. 136.
[153] Ibid., pp. 134, 137.
[154] Ibid., p. 141.
[155] Lauterpacht, *Private Law Sources*, pp. 141–142.
[156] Ibid., pp. 141–143.
[157] Eagleton, *The Responsibility*, preface.
[158] Martti Koskenniemi, 'Hersch Lauterpacht and the Development of International Criminal Law' (2004) 2 *Journal of International Criminal Justice* 810–825 at 815; Eagleton, *The Responsibility of States*, p. 22.

Anzilotti, but Eagleton also distanced himself from Lauterpacht. He rejected both the importation of private law arguments into the law of responsibility and the construction of responsibility theories.[159] First, Eagleton contended that the tools of enforcement in international law are 'essentially different from that for private law'.[160] Consequently, he held that 'it is the employment of such private law concepts as this [the principle of fault] which has produced so much confusion as to responsibility in international law'.[161] Second, he dismissed the role of responsibility theories as unimportant in deciding actual cases.[162] It thus appears that Eagleton occupied an intermediate position to that of Anzilotti's tacit and Lauterpacht's explicit adherence to the domestic analogy.

However, Eagleton had no intention of belittling the topic of responsibility in international law. He admitted to its importance by embracing the efforts of other scholars to raise the concept of responsibility to the level of an institution of international law. According to Eagleton, the fact that responsibility was discussed as a topic in its own right and not as a corollary to other topics would be advantageous for the entire international legal system.[163] After all, he noted: '[t]he primary sanction behind this law – for law it is, observed and enforced by state action – is the moral sense of responsibility; and this, translated into terms of law, becomes an institute of international law, and indeed the very cornerstone of it.'[164] In Eagleton's opinion then, responsibility was necessary for demonstrating the legal character of international rules, a belief which he shared with many contemporary international lawyers. The importance Eagleton attached to the law of responsibility was built on pragmatism: the rules of law should be the focus, not the theories behind them.[165] Eagleton argued that one cannot simply deduce any particular theory of state responsibility from practical cases.[166] In his opinion, the reason for the increased significance of the law of responsibility lies not in an increased tendency by states

159 Eagleton, *The Responsibility of States*, p. 213.

160 Ibid., p. 5.

161 Ibid., p. 213.

162 Ibid. Eagleton also notes that the measurement of damages is one example of inconsistency between theory and practice in the law of responsibility. See Clyde Eagleton, 'Measure of Damages in International Law' (1929–1930) 39 *Yale Law Journal* 52–75 at 55.

163 Eagleton, 'Protection of Foreign Officials', 293.

164 Ibid., 293–294.

165 Frederick S. Dunn appears to hold a similar position as he notes that the analysis on state responsibility should move beyond a mere juristic analysis to embrace 'the practice of diplomatic protection as a man-made institution designed for particular social ends'. See Dunn, *The Protection of Nationals*, pp. 1–3.

166 Eagleton, 'Measure of Damages', 58.

to disregard international obligations, but instead with the fact that international obligations are imprecise.[167] What serves responsibility best is clearer international legal rules.[168]

For Eagleton, the decisive criterion giving rise to the responsibility of states is always 'whether, in a given set of circumstances, the state has itself violated or failed to meet an obligation placed upon it by international law. Once this appears, responsibility is established, whether the next step be resort to local courts, or diplomatic interposition.'[169] From the perspective of responsibility, then, it is of the essence to have an effective apparatus capable of its interpretation, administration and enforcement.[170] Therefore, according to Eagleton, advancement of the responsibility of states would require 'better organs of the community of nations'.[171]

Eagleton's position resembles that of another Anglo-Saxon scholar, Edwin Borchard. Similar to Eagleton, Borchard saw the wrongful act as the underlying basis of responsibility. Building his analysis on case law from international tribunals and the work of Foreign Offices, Borchard rejected unnecessary theorizing about responsibility, such as considerations of '*culpa* or *dolus*', as 'sophistry'.[172] Further, Borchard argued, 'While it is possible that any or all of these theories can be supported by abstract reasoning, they apparently play little or no part in the determinations of international tribunals or in the work of Foreign Offices, which are not concerned with the distinction between responsibility for risk or for fault.'[173] For Borchard, the element of fault has neither an independent meaning nor is it widely utilized in international practice. Thus the concept of fault only served to introduce unnecessary confusion into the topic of international responsibility. Indeed, Borchard noted, '[t]he subject of state responsibility is intimately identified with … broad terms which have a meaning only in their application to a concrete case'.[174]

Contrary to the views of many other contemporary scholars, Borchard held international responsibility law to be weak.[175] In his opinion, the reason for the feeble character of responsibility was the enforcement system, which rested on 'a qualified system of self-help'.[176] According to him, '[e]very claim should, if

[167] Eagleton, *The Responsibility of States*, p. 218.
[168] Ibid.
[169] Ibid., p. 214.
[170] Ibid., p. 229.
[171] Ibid., p. 219.
[172] Borchard, 'Theoretical Aspects', 226.
[173] Ibid., 225.
[174] Ibid., 248.
[175] Ibid., 247.
[176] Ibid.

not easily settled diplomatically, be submitted by convention, as automatically as possible, to an international court.'[177] He thus proposed the depoliticization of disputes and – in much the same way as Eagleton – highlighted the importance of international courts.

## 2.4 RESPONSIBILITY AS A SYSTEM BUILDER

### 2.4.1 *ILC and the Difficulty of Finding a Suitable Approach*

The varying approaches to the topic of state responsibility which had been set forth after the consolidation of the law to the responsibility of the state for injuries to aliens, left a gap between the approach of theorists and the law as it had formed in actual state practice. All codification efforts had failed to materialize, and there was no clear understanding of how such a codification should be undertaken. In his 1939 Hague Academy lectures on the topic of state responsibility, Roberto Ago held that, despite vast research, there was still the need for a systematic treatment of the subject: '*Et surtout l'existence de tant d'analyses portant sur des points particuliers fait sentir plus vivement encore la nécessité d'une synthèse, d'une vue d'ensemble complète, qui donne à chaque élément sa place réelle dans un seul cadre systématique.*' (And especially the existence of so many analyses on specific points makes the need for a synthesis even more vivid, for a complete overview, which gives each element its real place in a single systematic framework.)[178]

Despite the unclear status of state responsibility, the UN General Assembly placed the topic on the codification agenda of the ILC immediately following its establishment.[179] It was held by the ILC members themselves, although not unanimously, that codification of the topic was necessary in spite of the failure of the League of Nations General Codification Conference.[180] It was further noted that since 1930 specific developments with respect to state responsibility had occurred – such as the establishment of penal responsibility for both states and individuals – which motivated placement of the topic on the agenda

[177] Ibid., 249.

[178] Ago, 'Le délit', 420.

[179] *Survey of International Law in Relation to the Work of Codification of the International Law Commission*, UN Doc. A/CN.4/1/Rev.1 (1949), pp. 56–57. The work was resumed in 1953 when the UNGA re-introduced the topic on the agenda with the express task of 'the codification of the principles of international law governing state responsibility', UNGA 799 (VIII) 1953, 7 December 1953.

[180] Summary Records of the First Session, ILC Yearbook 1949, pp. 49–50, paras. 27–32.

of the ILC.[181] An approach beyond the traditional law of state responsibility for injuries to aliens was consequently envisaged.[182] In 1955, Francisco García Amador was appointed the first Special Rapporteur of the topic, and under his mandate six reports, including an entire set of draft articles, were produced and presented.

To start with, the Special Rapporteur noted the uncertainty and complexity of the topic, which he ascribed to the discrepancy between 'traditional doctrine and practice'.[183] Moreover, the two World Wars had spurred developments within international law which were bound to affect the codification of the law of state responsibility. The role of the individual – and potentially also that of international organizations – as subjects of international law had come to challenge the traditional law of state responsibility, as had the development of the idea of community interests in international law.[184] Despite these new international legal developments, García Amador remained within the confines of traditional law as it had developed in state practice. State responsibility for injuries to aliens was back as a subject of focus, along with the work of numerous arbitration commissions and mixed tribunals. The approach chosen by Special Rapporteur García Amador came under heavy criticism for relying on case law, which meant privileging the law imposed on Latin American states by their more powerful neighbours to the North. Eventually his work turned out to be unacceptable both to states and the ILC members themselves.[185] Thus, the ILC decided not to proceed with the work on the basis of García Amador's approach, but instead to start afresh.

In order to move ahead, the ILC established a subcommittee – under the leadership of the Italian Roberto Ago – to examine alternative approaches. When Roberto Ago became García Amador's successor as the Special Rapporteur on the topic in 1963, he advocated and undertook a complete shift in focus regarding the law of responsibility. In what has been described as 'the Ago revolution',[186] Ago turned the previous approach upside down: no longer were the rights of man and injuries to them (obligations and delicts

[181] Ibid., p. 49, para. 27.
[182] Ibid., pp. 49–50, paras. 27 and 28.
[183] As García Amador notes, 'the subject of responsibility has always been one of the most vast and complex of international law; it would be difficult to find a topic beset with greater confusion and uncertainty'. See García Amador, *First Report*, p. 175, para. 6.
[184] Ibid., p. 175, para. 8.
[185] See e.g., Ago, *First Report*, p. 134, para. 55; and Müller, 'The Work of García Amador', 70–72.
[186] Alain Pellet, 'The ILC's Articles on State Responsibility for Internationally Wrongful Acts and Related Texts', in James Crawford, Alain Pellet and Simon Olleson (eds.), *The Law of International Responsibility* (Oxford: Oxford University Press, 2010), pp. 75–94 at 76.

approaches) the prime focus as had been developed under international case law. Instead, the 'definition of the general rules governing the international responsibility of States' were now to be determined.[187] According to the ILC, a shift in the doctrine of responsibility had occurred which made the reliance on analogies to private law – the predominant position from the inter-war and League of Nations period – lose its prominence. Unlike private law, the law of state responsibility included both reparations and the institution of sanctions.[188] Thus, the responsibility of states was now considered to be broader than liability under private law.[189] It appeared clear that Special Rapporteur Ago would not pursue the path of domestic analogy, despite the opinion of some members of the Committee that '[i]nternational law was not a totally different technique from private law and it was impossible to regard it as an island by itself.'[190]

The approach adopted by Ago resembles the position of another Italian scholar, Dionisio Anzilotti, who also attempted to portray the law of responsibility as a system of international law. Both Anzilotti and Ago advanced the idea that responsibility can be generalized. Thus, Ago's approach to state responsibility was broader than the traditional law of state responsibility, which related to injuries to aliens. At the same time, it was narrower: issues ranging from the primary obligations of states to diplomatic protection characteristic of the traditional law had been replaced by secondary rules only.[191] The main feature of both Anzilotti's and Ago's general approaches was the idea that a mere breach of an international obligation generated responsibility. There was no need for fault or injury; responsibility had a different function to fulfil: to guarantee the observance of rules in the international legal system.[192]

Thus instead of material injury, Anzilotti stressed legal harm, which he defined as a non-material component,[193] a view shared by Special Rapporteur Ago. Responsibility was more than simply the consequences upon an injury; responsibility existed irrespective of whether injury had taken place or not. Such a seemingly narrow change, however, was based on a fundamental claim. Instead of a sovereignty-based state system, which aimed to protect the interests of particular states, responsibility now characterized a community of

187 Ago, *First Report*, p. 139, para. 90.
188 Roberto Ago, Chairman of the Sub-Committee on State Responsibility, *Report*, UN Doc. A/CN.4/152 (1963), reproduced in ILC Yearbook 1963, vol. II, p. 233.
189 Ibid.
190 Ibid., p. 234.
191 Daniel Bodansky and John R. Crook, 'Symposium: The ILC's State Responsibility Articles. Introduction and Overview' (2002) 96 *American Journal of International Law* 773–791 at 776.
192 Dupuy, 'Dionisio Anzilotti', 145.
193 Ibid.

states as a whole which uphold a system of international law rather than the consortium of 'inter-subjective norms'.[194]

The law of state responsibility now contained a social idea beyond mere reparation; it was a necessary building block of the system of international law. In fact, it was alleged by some commentators that the secondary and general approach aimed at constructing a 'system of multilateral public order' rather than merely laying down the rules of state responsibility.[195] Irrespective of its function, this general and secondary approach set forth by Special Rapporteur Ago and adopted by the ILC – which in effect detached responsibility from the consequences of a breach[196] – nevertheless meant that the work on codification of the law of responsibility could continue without any major opposition.

### 2.4.2 *The 2001 ILC Articles on State Responsibility*

#### 2.4.2.1 General Remarks on the ASR

The Articles on State Responsibility were finalized in 2001,[197] after nearly five decades of work under the guidance of five different Special Rapporteurs.[198] The articles were adopted by the General Assembly without a vote in December 2001, and are annexed to General Assembly Resolution 56/83 under the title 'Responsibility of States for internationally wrongful acts'.[199] With this resolution the General Assembly took note of the articles and called them to the attention of all states, leaving open the possibility that a more formal instrument, such as a convention, could be adopted at a later stage.

194 Pellet, 'The ILC's Articles', 78.

195 Report of the ILC on the Work of Its Fifty-second Session, UN Doc. A/55/10 (2000), p. 60, para. 365.

196 In his 1939 Hague Academy lectures, Roberto Ago had already distinguished between the wrongful act itself and its consequences. Concerning the delimitation of his topic he noted: '*Pour délimiter plus clairement encore la tâche actuelle, on laissera rigouresement de côté tout ce qui regarde les conséquences du délit plutôt que le délit lui-même*' (To delimit the current task even more clearly, we will rigorously set aside all that concerns the consequences of the offence rather than the offence itself), Ago, 'Le délit', 421.

197 Draft Articles on the Responsibility of States for Internationally Wrongful Acts, in Report of the International Law Commission on the Work of Its Fifty-third Session, UN Doc. A/56/10 (2001), Chapter IV, p. 29. For the text of the articles with commentaries, see p. 59 *et seqq.* All references in this chapter to single articles of the ASR and to their commentaries will refer to this document.

198 The five Special Rapporteurs were: F. V. García Amador (1955–1961), Roberto Ago (1963–1979), Willem Riphagen (1979–1986), Gaetano Arangio-Ruiz (1987–1996), and James Crawford (1997–2001).

199 UNGA Res. 56/83, 12 December 2001.

The entirety of the 59 articles was adopted in two readings; the articles were provisionally adopted in 1996 on a first reading by the ILC. During 1997–2001, the ILC still had to address some unresolved issues as well as complete the coordination of the articles. Thus the final articles were adopted on a second reading on 9 August 2001.[200] Taking into consideration that the topic of state responsibility had become one of the most laborious ever undertaken by the ILC, it comes as no surprise that many legally relevant questions were excluded from the articles. The responsibility of other subjects of international law (i.e., individuals and international organizations) was left outside the scope of the articles, as well as responsibility for certain lawful acts, such as activities in space and activities having to do with nuclear energy. The question of the criminal responsibility of states was also eventually left out of the articles. Nor do the ASR deal directly with the responsibility of states to other international actors. Moreover, elements of responsibility such as fault and injury were not to be decided under the aegis of the ILC Articles, but instead under the specific terms of the international obligation in question.[201]

Indeed, one technique through which the work on state responsibility became manageable for the ILC was restricting discussion solely to secondary rules of state responsibility: the general conditions under international law for the state to be considered responsible for wrongful acts, and the legal consequences thereof. Thus, the articles do not attempt to define the content of specific international obligations, since that function is the purpose of primary rules. These general rules apply to all substantive obligations except 'where and to the extent that the conditions for the existence of an internationally wrongful act or the content or implementation of the international responsibility of a State are governed by special rules of international law'.[202] From this follows that the rules laid down in the ASR have a residual character. That is, where some matter otherwise dealt with in the articles is governed by a special rule of international law, the latter will prevail to the extent of any inconsistency that exists. Thus, the *lex specialis* rule lays down that, if states in the primary obligations between themselves have included provisions for determining whether a breach exists and what the legal consequences are, the secondary rules are set aside.

200 Although several small changes were made, the core of Part One as formulated by Special Rapporteur Ago was retained essentially in unchanged form. Crawford, *The International Law Commission's*, p. 27.

201 Bodansky and Crook, 'Symposium', 790.

202 Art. 55 of the ASR.

#### 2.4.2.2 The Basis of State Responsibility: An Internationally Wrongful Act

The ASR begin with the fundamental rule that a state bears responsibility for its wrongful acts. According to the ILC, this principle is 'one of the principles most strongly upheld by State practice and judicial decisions and most deeply rooted in the doctrine of international law.'[203] The ILC sets forth this basic principle in Article 1 of the ASR, which reads: 'Every internationally wrongful act of a State entails the international responsibility of that State'.[204]

In order to define what constitutes an internationally wrongful act and consequently engages international responsibility, the ILC identifies two prerequisites: attribution and breach of obligation. The conditions for an internationally wrongful act are to be found in Article 2 of the ILC Articles: 'There is an internationally wrongful act of a State when conduct consisting of an action or omission:

(a) is attributable to the State under international law; and
(b) constitutes a breach of an international obligation of the State.'[205]

2.4.2.2.1 THE SUBJECTIVE ELEMENT: ATTRIBUTION TO THE STATE. The first element of an internationally wrongful act is that the conduct must be attributable to the state, meaning that the state must be identified as the one performing the conduct breaching the international obligation. However, the state is merely an abstraction and consequently it can act only through 'a human being or group'.[206] The task then becomes to identify which specific acts or omissions by individuals can be classified as belonging to the state. Thus, the state is not responsible for the acts of all entities within the scope of its territory or jurisdiction. The rationale behind this limitation is apparent; it is considered both impractical and undesirable for the state to be responsible for the private acts of its citizens or even all persons or entities within its jurisdiction.

[203] Report of the ILC on the Work of Its Twenty-fifth Session, UN Doc. A/9010/Rev.1 (1973), p. 173. The principle has been applied since the early days of the PCIJ, e.g., in the case of *Phospates in Morocco* where it was observed that when a state commits an internationally wrongful act against another state, international responsibility is established immediately between the two states. See *Phosphates in Morocco*, Preliminary Objections, PCIJ Series A/B, No. 74 (1938), p. 28.

[204] Art. 1 of the ASR.

[205] Art. 2 of the ASR.

[206] Commentary to Art. 2 of the ASR, para. 5. The PCIJ observed in *German Settlers in Poland*: 'States can only act by and through their agents and representatives'. See *German Settlers in Poland*, PCIJ Series B, No. 6 (1923), p. 22.

A point of departure in the process of attribution is the primacy of international law. The attribution to the state as a subject of international law can take place only on the basis of international law itself.[207] This notwithstanding, for its own purposes, international law may take into account situations as they exist under municipal law. However, the question of responsibility in international law specifically concerns the state as a legal person under international law and should not be confused with the notion of the state as a person under municipal law.[208] Consequently, the consideration of certain acts as acts of state in international law may be based on criteria that are both wider and more limited than the corresponding criteria in municipal law.

The ASR contain eight rules on attribution of conduct to a state.[209] The starting point for attribution is the attachment of the conduct of state organs (i.e., departments or organizations that perform a specified function) to the state concerned.[210] This basic rule, which appears uncontested,[211] specifies that acts or omissions of persons who form part of the internal organization of the state (i.e., are organs according to the state's internal law) are to be considered an act of state under international law. The ILC Articles do not strictly define what constitutes an 'organ' as states are free to organize their machinery as they please. In this case, international law relies on facts provided by internal law; as a consequence, there is a presumption of attribution for actors that are de jure part of the state. The rule embodies the principle of unity of the state by positing that acts and omissions of *all* its organs are to be viewed

[207] Commentary to Part One, Chapter II, para. 4.

[208] David D. Caron, 'The Basis of Responsibility: Attribution and Other Trans-Substantive Rules', in Richard B. Lillich and Daniel Barstow Magraw (eds.), *The Iran-United States Claims Tribunal: Its Contribution to the Law of State Responsibility* (New York: Transnational Publishers, Inc., 1998), pp. 109–184.

[209] The rules of attribution are: Conduct of organs of a State (Art. 4), Conduct of persons or entities exercising elements of governmental authority (Art. 5), Conduct of organs placed at the disposal of a State by another State (Art. 6), Excess of authority or contravention of instructions (Art. 7), Conduct directed or controlled by a State (Art. 8), Conduct carried out in the absence or default of the official authorities (Art. 9), Conduct of an insurrectional or other movement (Art. 10), and Conduct acknowledged and adopted by a State as its own (Art. 11).

[210] Art. 4 reads: '1. The conduct of any State organ shall be considered an act of that State under international law, whether the organ exercises legislative, executive, judicial or any other functions, whatever position it holds in the organization of the State, and whatever its character as an organ of the central government or of a territorial unit of the State. 2. An organ includes any person or entity which has that status in accordance with the internal law of the State.'

[211] Already in 1871 in the *Moses case*, the Mixed Claims Commission Mexico/United States of America acknowledged that '[a]n officer or person in authority represents *pro tanto* his government, which in an international sense is the aggregate of all officers and men in authority.' Reproduced in Commentary to Art. 4, para. 3.

as acts of state. For the purposes of attribution, it notes the irrelevance of the branch and rank of the organ, as well as the level of government the organ possesses in the state organization. It is noteworthy, however, that the classification of organs may be broader than what is stipulated under internal law.

However, the basic rule of attribution to the relevant state of the acts or omissions of state organs is neither absolute nor exclusive. It can be extended to cases where an organ, acting in an official capacity but nonetheless in an abusive way, exceeds its competence. Thus it is commonly accepted that 'the State must recognize that it acts whenever persons or groups of persons whom it has instructed to act in its name in a given area of activity appear to be acting effectively in its name.'[212] This rule is a logical sequel of the need for stability and guarantees in international relations. Otherwise, a state could attempt to escape international responsibility by hiding behind the notion of ultra vires – that the act or omission was beyond the powers intended to be granted. Thus, a state cannot take refuge behind provisions of its internal law or to instructions given to its organs. The notion of appearance emerges as the governing principle when determining whether the state is to be held responsible for acts in contravention of its internal law or its orders. Instead of real competence, international law emphasizes apparent competence as a criterion for responsibility of acts ultra vires.[213] Nevertheless, limitations to the basic rule also exist. The physical person possessing the status of an organ is at the same time also an individual, capable of acting on his or her own behalf. Therefore, in every case the application of the rule must include an examination of whether the person in question acted under cover of his or her status as an organ, or as a physical person distinct from the state.[214] Thus, the presumption attributing to the state the conduct of its organs may be rebutted by evidence showing that 'the officials' acts relate to their private lives and that they do not have a connection with the machinery of the State.'[215]

Nevertheless, state responsibility does not arise solely from organs which form part of the official state structure. The emerging trend of privatization and decentralization in the 1970s did not go unnoticed by the ILC, which recognized that new entities were in part taking over public functions traditionally performed by the state. Consequently, in order to complete the picture the rules on attribution also had to deal with the conduct of bodies which were

[212] Report of the ILC on the Work of Its Twenty-seventh Session, UN Doc. A/10010/Rev. 1 (1975), p. 67.

[213] Commentary to Art. 7, paras. 7–8.

[214] Roberto Ago, *Third Report on State Responsibility*, UN Doc. A/CN.4/246 and Add. 1–3 (1971), p. 241, para. 129.

[215] Caron, 'The Basis of Responsibility', 136.

not organs stricto sensu, but nevertheless were authorized to exercise governmental authority. The ultimate motivation behind this rule is the desire to treat all states equally. As the ILC states: 'If the same public function were performed in one State by organs of the State proper and in another by para-state institutions, it would indeed be absurd if the international responsibility of the State were engaged in one case and not in the other.'[216] Therefore, responsibility can arise from a wide variety of bodies which, though not state organs, may be empowered by the law of a state to exercise elements of governmental power. This category includes, for example, 'public corporations, semi-public entities, public agencies of various kinds and even, in special cases, private companies'.[217] The ASR do not provide a precise meaning or scope of what is meant by 'governmental authority'. Instead, it notes that 'what is regarded as "governmental" depends on the particular society, its history and traditions'.[218]

Many situations involve not only actors that, presumptively, do have a connection to the state, but others as well. Still, these situations can give rise to state responsibility based on the functional link between the state as a principal and any other entity actually acting on behalf of the state. The first kind of situation addressed in the ILC Articles is that in which another state places its organs at the disposal of another state.[219] It is set forth that the receiving state bears responsibility for the acts or omissions of the sending state's organ when the organ placed at their disposal – the loaned organ – actually exercises elements of governmental authority 'with the consent, under the authority of and for the purposes of the receiving State'.[220] Other entities are also acknowledged to form part of the effective – albeit not formal – structure of a state. The principles of unity and effectiveness in international law further require that the conduct of persons or groups of persons 'in fact acting on the instructions of, or under the direction or control of' a state also be considered,[221] especially in situations of armed conflicts.[222] Special Rapporteur Ago had already acknowledged the need to differentiate between 'acts of organs of certain entities which, although separate from the State, had powers, under the internal legal order of the State, which involved the exercise of a portion of public power', and on the other hand, 'attribution to the State of acts of persons or groups of persons who were

[216] Summary Records, ILC Yearbook 1974, vol. I, p. 8, para. 17.

[217] Commentary to Art. 5, para. 2.

[218] Ibid., para. 6.

[219] Art. 6 of the ASR.

[220] Commentary to Art. 6 of the ASR, para. 2.

[221] Art. 8 of the ASR.

[222] Claus Kress, 'L'organe de facto en droit international public, réflexions sur l'imputation à l'État de l'acte d'un particulier à la lumière des développements récents' (2001) 105 *Revue Générale de Droit International Public* 93–144 at 96.

not in any way part of the machinery of the State' but still in special circumstances, in reality performed state functions.[223] The latter may often take place when states complement their own action and that of their underlings by the action of private persons or groups. He recognized the existence of situations where private natural or legal persons – while definitely remaining such – are entrusted by the public authorities with the performance of a specific task, such as that of private persons or groups used as auxiliaries in the armed forces.[224]

Responsibility can also be triggered by exceptional circumstances in which the functional link between the state and the private actor is established not beforehand but ex post facto. The rules of attribution recognize that in some situations private persons or groups may also act without any authorization to do so, in the absence of official authorities.[225] Thus, people may exercise governmental authority out of necessity, for example in situations such as of self-defence in the absence of regular forces 'during revolution, armed conflict or foreign occupation'.[226] Another rare case of attribution may take place when an insurrectional movement becomes the new government of a state and its previous conduct is attributed to the (new) state. Thus, the purpose is to guarantee 'continuity between the movement and the eventual Government'.[227] A final basis for attribution is provided in the ILC Articles for conduct which the state 'acknowledges and adopts … as its own'.[228]

2.4.2.2.2 THE OBJECTIVE ELEMENT: BREACH OF AN INTERNATIONAL OBLIGATION. The second element of an internationally wrongful act is the existence of a breach of an international obligation. In contrast to the first element of attribution, which allows a certain generalization, the question of whether a breach has occurred will require examination of the primary obligation in question on a case-by-case basis.[229] As the ILC points out: '[t]here is no such thing as a breach of an international obligation in the abstract'.[230] Conduct amounts to a

[223] ILC Yearbook 1974, vol. I, p. 32, para. 2.

[224] Report of the ILC on the Work of Its Twenty-sixth Session, UN Doc. A/9610/Rev.1 (1974), p. 283. The most well-known case with regard to attribution of conduct of de facto organs in the jurisprudence of the ICJ is the case of *Military and Paramilitary Activities in and against Nicaragua (Nicaragua v. United States of America)*, Merits, Judgment, ICJ Reports 1986, p. 14.

[225] Art. 9 of the ASR.

[226] Commentary to Art. 9 of the ASR, para, 1.

[227] Commentary to Art. 10 of the ASR, para 4.

[228] Art. 11 of the ASR.

[229] Claire de Than and Edwin Shorts, *International Criminal Law and Human Rights* (London: Sweet and Maxwell, 2003), p. 21.

[230] Commentary to Part One, Chapter III, para. 2.

breach of an obligation when it 'is not in conformity with what is required of it by that obligation, regardless of its origin or character'.[231] Nevertheless, the determination of non-conformity is guided by 'the precise terms of the obligation, its interpretation and application, taking into account its object and purpose and the facts of the case'.[232] A breach may therefore consist of a range of conduct from omissions (such as failure to pass legislation) to prohibited state acts (such as torture). The conduct referred to in Article 2 can thus have either a positive or a negative character. It is positive when a state commits an affirmative act that violates its international obligation. Negative conduct again signifies that a state has omitted to perform an act required of it under international law. The ILC notes that 'the cases in which the international responsibility of a State has been invoked on the basis of an omission are perhaps more numerous than those based on action taken by a State'.[233]

Another defining criterion in the determination of the existence of a breach is the irrelevance of the origin of the obligation in question. Whether an obligation stems from treaty law or general international law makes no difference when considering an act as unlawful. Any separation between contractual or tortious responsibility is consequently rejected, as is the division of responsibility into criminal and civil.[234] Similar to the irrelevance of the origin of the obligation, no distinct role is played by the obligation's character. A breach may ensue from bilateral or multilateral obligations, and even from obligations owed to the international community as a whole. A breach of an international obligation is thus a flexible and comprehensive concept covering all subject matters irrespective of the gravity of the breach. As the ILC notes in its commentary, '[i]t can involve relatively minor infringements as well as the most serious breaches of obligations under peremptory norms of general international law.'[235]

In contrast to the general scope of the rule laying down the existence of a breach, it is specifically required that the state must be 'bound by the obligation in question at the time the act occurs'.[236] Although this principle is well-established and appears clear, other temporal questions may arise in connection with the determination of a breach: when is the breach considered to begin, and for how long does it continue? The importance of the issue lies in the fact that

[231] Art. 12. of the ASR.

[232] Commentary to Art. 12, para. 1.

[233] Roberto Ago, *Second Report on State Responsibility*, UN Doc. A/CN.4/233 (1970), p. 188, para. 35.

[234] Commentary to Art. 12 of the ASR, para. 5.

[235] Ibid., para. 6.

[236] Art. 13 of the ASR.

'[i]nternationally wrongful acts usually take some time to happen'.[237] Two kinds of breaches can be discerned: continuous and non-continuous (or completed) acts, although their distinction remains relative.[238] The former category is exemplified by foreign occupation or unlawful detention, whereas the latter is illustrated by the violation of a state's airspace. The temporal dimension of a breach is important from the perspective of the content of state responsibility; cessation and restitution remain dependent upon this dimension. Another aspect of continuous breaches is the fact that composite acts may amount to one breach. Here, a series of acts or omissions 'defined in aggregate as wrongful' may constitute a single breach.[239] Genocide, for example, is defined as a composite act, as are many other of the most serious wrongful acts in international law.[240]

But the ILC Articles recognize that there are situations in which responsibility does not follow from the breach of an international obligation. Six different circumstances that preclude wrongfulness are identified, namely: consent, self-defence, countermeasures, force majeure, distress, and necessity.[241] The reasons for the circumstances precluding wrongfulness vary; sometimes they relate to behaviour in situations of compulsion or the previous conduct of the injured state, but wrongfulness may also be precluded due to an 'irreconcilable conflict' of interests.[242] Situations in which these excuses or justifications are pleaded to must be exceptional,[243] and they do not 'annul or terminate the obligation in question'.[244] More importantly, circumstances precluding wrongfulness are not applicable in the situation of the peremptory norms of international law.[245] The ILC Articles also admit that in some situations, irrespective of the shield against responsibility, there may still be a duty to compensate for material loss.[246]

#### 2.4.2.3 Consequences of an Internationally Wrongful Act

The general legal consequences of an internationally wrongful act require the responsible state to cease from the wrongful conduct and give assurances that

[237] Commentary to Art. 14 of the ASR, para. 2.
[238] Ibid., para. 5.
[239] Art. 15 of the ASR.
[240] Commentary to Art. 15 of the ASR, para. 2.
[241] The articles on circumstances precluding wrongfulness are: Consent (Art. 20); Self-defence (Art. 21); Countermeasures in respect of an internationally wrongful act (Art. 22); *Force majeure* (Art. 23); Distress (Art. 24); and Necessity (Art. 25).
[242] Commentary to Art. 25 of the ASR, para. 2.
[243] *Gabčíkovo-Nagymaros Project (Hungary* v. *Slovakia)*, Judgment, 25 September 1997, ICJ Reports (1997), p. 40, para. 51.
[244] Commentary to Chapter V of the ASR, para. 2.
[245] Art. 26 of the ASR.
[246] Art. 27 of the ASR.

it will not repeat the conduct, as well as to make full reparation for any injury caused by the act in question.[247] To begin with, it needs to be pointed out that the commission of an internationally wrongful act by a state gives rise to a new legal relationship between the state committing the wrongful act and the state(s) to which the original obligation was owed. These new legal relations do not affect the old legal setting; the responsible state still has a duty to fulfil the primary obligation which it breached in the first place.[248] To strengthen this obligation, the ILC Articles stipulate that the responsible state must cease from the wrongful act, and if necessary offer 'guarantees of non-repetition'.[249] The importance of cessation is highlighted by the fact that many internationally wrongful acts are continuous in character; for example, the practice of the Security Council often primarily entails a call for cessation of hostilities.[250] The primary aim consequently becomes ensuring the 'continuing validity and effectiveness of the underlying primary rule',[251] rather than to focus on issues of reparation. Similarly, guarantees of non-repetition relate to the 'reinforcement of a continuing legal relationship', the focus of which is 'on the future, not the past'.[252]

Another general consequence of an internationally wrongful act is the responsible state's obligation to make full reparation.[253] This principle is firmly rooted in the law of state responsibility.[254] The purpose of the reparation is to 'wipe out all the consequences of the illegal act and re-establish the situation which would, in all probability, have existed if that act had not been committed'.[255] In other words, the injured party is to 'be made whole' again.[256] The ILC has clarified that reparation relates to all sorts of injury, whether material

[247] Art. 30 (Cessation and Non-Repetition) and Art. 31 (Reparation) of the ASR.

[248] Art. 29 of the ASR.

[249] Art. 30 of the ASR.

[250] For example, UNSC Res. 1973 (2011), 17 March 2011 with respect to Libya, states that the Security Council demands 'a complete end to violence, and all attacks against, and abuses of, civilians', para. 1.

[251] Commentary to Art. 30 of the ASR, para. 5.

[252] Commentary to Art. 30 of the ASR, para 11.

[253] Art. 31 of the ASR reads:

> '1. The responsible State is under an obligation to make full reparation for the injury caused by the internationally wrongful act.
> 2. Injury includes any damage, whether material or moral, caused by the internationally wrongful act of a State.'

[254] The PCIJ stated in the *Chorzów Factory* case with regard to reparation: 'It is a principle of international law that the breach of an engagement involves an obligation to make reparation in an adequate form'. *Case Concerning the Factory at Chorzów (Claim for Indemnity) (Jurisdiction) (Germany* v. *Poland)*, PCIJ, Ser. A., No. 9 (1927), p. 21.

[255] *Case Concerning the Factory at Chorzów (Germany* v. *Poland) (Claim for Indemnity) (Merits)*, PCIJ, Ser. A., No. 17 (1928) p. 47.

[256] *Lusitania cases*, VII Reports of International Arbitral Awards (1923), p. 39.

or non-material. Both assessable damage, such as destruction of property, and moral damage, such as 'individual pain and suffering', are to be repaired by the responsible state.[257]

The forms of reparation set forth by the ASR include 'restitution, compensation and satisfaction', or any combination thereof.[258] The primary form of reparation available to a state that has committed an internationally wrongful act is restitution.[259] This means that the situation that existed before the wrongful act was committed should be re-established if possible. The broad meaning of restitution entails that 'any action that needs to be taken by the responsible State to restore the situation' falls under the scope of restitution.[260] Depending on the specific circumstances, seized property or persons should be returned, or juridical acts repealed.[261] The impossibility of restitution in some situations is recognized, however. Restitution may be disproportionate or a sheer impossibility if the 'object in question has been destroyed'.[262] In instances in which restitution is meaningless, other forms of reparation are introduced.

Compensation entails that 'financially assessable damage including loss of profits' is compensated.[263] The ILC notes that '[o]f the various forms of reparation, compensation is perhaps the most commonly sought in international practice.'[264] Monetary compensation thus addresses the actual losses, material and/or moral, stemming from an internationally wrongful act whether the losses relate to the state itself or its nationals. The aim of monetary compensation is not to punish the wrongdoer in any way.[265] In addition to restitution and compensation, satisfaction is a third form of reparation available to the responsible state. This form of reparation is rarely used, since most internationally wrongful acts can be repaired through restitution or compensation. Indeed, satisfaction is to be resorted to only in instances in which the two other forms of reparation have not fully repaired the situation. Satisfaction remedies

[257] Commentary to Art. 31 of the ASR, para. 5.

[258] Art. 34 of the ASR.

[259] This was confirmed by the PCIJ in the *Chorzów Factory* case when it stated that the responsible state is under 'the obligation to restore the undertaking and, if this be not possible, to pay its value at the time of the indemnification, which value is designed to take the place of restitution which has become impossible'. See *The Factory at Chorzów (Merits)*, p. 48, para. 126.

[260] Commentary to Art. 35, para. 5.

[261] Ibid.

[262] Ibid., para. 9.

[263] Art. 36 of the ASR.

[264] Commentary to Art. 36 of the ASR, para. 2. Indeed, many permanent and ad hoc bodies have dealt with issues of compensation. International bodies exemplifying the latter category are, e.g., the United Nations Compensation Commission addressing claims related to the Gulf war; the Eritrea/Ethiopia Claims Commission, and the Iran/US Claims Tribunal.

[265] Commentary to Art. 36 of the ASR, para. 4.

non-financially assessable damage, usually of a symbolic nature.[266] It may consist of, inter alia, an apology or an 'expression of regret'.[267] As with respect to the other forms of reparation, the ILC highlighted that 'satisfaction is not intended to be punitive in character, nor does it include punitive damages'.[268]

2.4.2.3.1 THE SERIOUS BREACHES REGIME. During its work on state responsibility, the ILC had repeatedly been confronted with the problem of whether to acknowledge – and how to deal with – the issue of gradation of norms; that is, that some norms are more important than others. From the outset, the ILC struggled with a division of internationally wrongful acts into 'international delicts' and 'international crimes of states' as embodied in Draft Article 19. The 2001 final articles nevertheless rejected this categorization and instead specified special consequences for breaches of peremptory international norms committed in a serious manner. The main difference in the ILC's approach to breaches of peremptory norms of international law lay in the non-recognition of penal consequences. Whereas Draft Article 19 adhered to the idea of punitive damages, the serious breaches regime fails to cover penal consequences. Thus, the ILC has stated that 'the award of punitive damages is not recognised in international law even in relation to serious breaches of obligations arising under peremptory norms'.[269]

The ILC Articles recognize two breach criteria that generate special consequences: (1) the obligation violated must arise under a jus cogens norm of international law, and (2) it must reach the level of 'gross or systematic failure'.[270] As examples of peremptory norms of international law, the ILC mentions the following: prohibition of aggression, prohibition of torture, prohibition of slavery and the slave trade, prohibition of genocide, prohibition of racial discrimination and apartheid, along with the right to self-determination.[271] Moreover, violation of these norms must be considered either relatively grave or systematic in order for them to be considered serious breaches. Thus, as the ILC notes, 'a violation would have to be carried out in an organised and deliberate way' and it would

266 Commentary to Art. 37 of the ASR, para. 3.
267 Art. 37 of the ASR.
268 Commentary to Art. 37 of the ASR, para. 8.
269 Commentary to Chapter III of the ASR, para. 5.
270 Article 40 of the ASR reads:

'1. This Chapter applies to the international responsibility which is entailed by a serious breach by a State of an obligation arising under a peremptory norm of general international law'.
2. A breach of such an obligation is serious if it involves a gross or systematic failure by the responsible State to fulfil the obligation.'

271 Commentary to Art. 40 of the ASR, paras. 4–5.

need to attack the very 'values protected by the rule'.[272] Despite the heightened importance of the norms in question, the ILC Articles do not create any institutional procedures for dealing with the determination of whether a serious breach of a peremptory norms has been committed or not. Instead, the ILC expressly states that these issues will generally be dealt with by 'competent international organizations including the Security Council and the General Assembly'.[273]

The particular consequences prescribed by the ASR following a serious breach entail that '[s]tates shall cooperate to bring to an end through lawful means any serious breach' and that '[n]o State shall recognize as lawful a situation created by a serious breach.'[274] In addition, states are obliged not to assist or aid in the maintenance of a serious breach. Thus all states should take efforts in concert to remove the serious breach irrespective of whether they have been affected by the breach or not. The modalities through which this may be done are left open. Although the ILC recognizes the importance of institutionalized means, especially cooperation within the framework of the United Nations, the 'possibility of non-institutionalised cooperation' is also stressed.[275] The Iraqi aggression against Kuwait in 1990 serves as an example of a serious breach: states did not recognize the illegal annexation of Kuwait, and meanwhile they cooperated within the United Nations to bring an end to the invasion. Beyond the particular consequences mentioned in the ASR, the ILC acknowledges that 'further consequences of a serious breach [...] may be provided for by international law'.[276] By this token the ILC admits that 'the legal regime of serious breaches is itself in a state of development'.[277]

#### 2.4.2.4 Implementation of State Responsibility

The *mise-en-oeuvre* of state responsibility is an integral part of the entire regime despite the fact that state responsibility is automatic in the sense that it arises 'independently of its invocation by another State'.[278] Still, without rules on invocation of responsibility and measures that can be resorted to in order to ensure compliance, the concept and practice of state responsibility would be in vain. The prospects of states policing themselves are remote, even though the ILC Articles define 'the consequences of internationally wrongful acts in the field of responsibility as *obligations* of the responsible State, not as rights

[272] Ibid., para. 8.
[273] Ibid., para. 9.
[274] Art. 41 of the ASR.
[275] Commentary to Art. 41 of the ASR, para. 2.
[276] Ibid., para. 14.
[277] Ibid.
[278] Commentary to Part Three of the ASR.

of any other State, person or entity'.[279] Nevertheless, the ILC also admits that 'in practice it is necessary for an injured State and/or other interested State(s) to respond, if they wish to seek cessation or reparation'.[280]

The starting point for the implementation of state responsibility is the invocation of responsibility by the affected state(s); that is, the injured state(s). The ASR define the notion of 'injured state' narrowly, so that only the state(s) affected by the internationally wrongful act has a right to invoke the responsibility of another state unless the legal interest of the international community as a whole is affected. A state is considered injured if the obligation which was violated was owed to it individually. Thus, for example, one party to a bilateral treaty has the right to invoke the responsibility of the other state if the latter breaches the treaty. However, bilateral treaty relations may also be established under a multilateral convention. In such cases, the obligation of performance is owed to a particular state instead of all parties to the convention.[281]

The act of invocation is defined as 'taking measures of a relatively formal character, for example, the raising or presentation of a claim against another State or the commencement of proceedings before an international court or tribunal.'[282] Mere criticism, protests, or calls for obedience do not count as invocation of responsibility.[283] The form of the invocation is left to the freedom of the injured state. The ILC notes that '[i]n practice claims of responsibility are raised at different levels of government, depending on their seriousness and on the general relations between the States concerned.'[284] Although the injured state is free to express its wishes with regard to the form of reparation, and can thus in general choose between different forms of reparation, the responsible state is not obliged to follow the specification given by the injured state. The main idea is that the dispute is brought to a resolution in one way or another. Other aspects affect the admissibility of claims as well. First, the claim must be brought in accordance with the rules on the nationality of claims, and second, all local remedies must have been exhausted.[285] With respect to the nationality of claims, the ASR merely point out that 'the responsibility of a State may not be invoked other than in accordance with any applicable rule relating to the nationality of claims'.[286] In other words, a state is entitled to

279 Commentary to Part Three, Chapter I of the ASR, para. 1 (emphasis added).
280 Commentary to Art. 43 of the ASR, para. 2.
281 One example is the Vienna Convention on Diplomatic Relations, Vienna, 18 April 1961, in force 24 April 1964, 596 *United Nations Treaty Series* 261.
282 Commentary to Art. 42 of the ASR, para. 2.
283 Ibid.
284 Commentary to Art. 43, para. 4.
285 Art. 44 of the ASR.
286 Commentary to Art. 44, para. 2.

protect its own, and only its own, subjects when they have been injured by the acts of another state. A further criterion for admissibility of a claim is the requirement that effective local remedy has been exhausted. Since it is also possible for a state to lose its right to invoke responsibility, it must be affirmed that the injured state has not 'validly waived' its right to invocation of responsibility or acquiesced to the loss of the right in question.[287]

2.4.2.4.1 COUNTERMEASURES. The implementation of state responsibility is primarily dependent on the will of the responsible state to return to conduct in line with its obligations. However, it is generally accepted in international practice and jurisprudence that occasionally states must be 'induced' to comply with their international obligations. Such acts undertaken to induce or compel a responsible state to behavioural change are called *countermeasures*. The ILC defines countermeasures as 'measures which would otherwise be contrary to the international obligations of the injured State vis-à-vis the responsible State'.[288] The purpose of the rules on countermeasures in the ASR is to create an acceptable system of self-help with checks and balances in place to keep countermeasures 'within generally acceptable bounds'.[289]

The resort to countermeasures is limited in terms of substance, form and procedure. First, the ILC Articles stipulate that countermeasures can only be undertaken by an injured state against the state having committed the wrongful act.[290] Countermeasures may thus only be used against the responsible state on a temporary basis. As soon as the objective of compliance has been achieved, countermeasures should be terminated.[291] Their usage is not 'intended as a form of punishment for wrongful conduct'.[292] Second, countermeasures are also limited with respect to their subject matter. The ASR explicitly exclude countermeasures that relate to the threat or use of force, fundamental human rights, humanitarian obligations or other jus cogens obligations.[293] Further substantive limitations are provided by the obligation of the state taking countermeasures to comply with relevant dispute settlement procedures and the 'inviolability of diplomatic or consular agents, premises, archives and documents'.[294] Proportionality is another constraining factor in the taking of countermeasures. Thus, '[c]ountermeasures must

[287] Art. 45 of the ASR.
[288] Commentary to Part Three, Chapter II of the ASR, para. 1.
[289] Ibid., para. 2.
[290] Art. 49 of the ASR.
[291] Art. 53 of the ASR.
[292] Commentary to Art. 49 of the ASR, para. 1.
[293] Art. 50 of the ASR.
[294] Art. 50 (2) of the ASR.

be commensurate with the injury suffered' and not result in an unbalanced legal situation.[295] Third, procedural conditions lay down the requirements for resorting to countermeasures. The injured state must both urge the responsible state to live up to its obligations and notify the same state of its intention to use countermeasures. In addition, the door to negotiations must be kept open. Urgent countermeasures may be adopted only if they are necessary for the preservation of the rights of the injured state. If the responsible state ceases the internationally wrongful act or engages in dispute settlement capable of issuing binding decisions upon the parties, the injured state must abstain from or suspend initiated countermeasures.[296]

The ILC Articles regulate only the adoption of countermeasures by an injured state. However, the ASR do not prejudice the right of other states to invoke responsibility. States with a vested legal interest in the commission of an internationally wrongful act may also take measures to induce compliance. This right belongs to any state when it comes to the breach of an international obligation owed to the international community as a whole, or to any state member of a group 'in the case of other obligations established for the protection of the collective interest of the group'.[297] In these cases, the states in question may take lawful measures to make sure that the wrongdoing ends and that reparation is provided. Although international practice shows the existence of some instances in which collective countermeasures have been taken, the ILC claims that 'the current state of international law on countermeasures taken in the general or collective interest is uncertain'.[298] For example, collective measures resorted to against Iraq in 1990 and Yugoslavia in 1998 do not constitute unambiguous evidence of the extent and nature of this rule. The Commission held international practice to be scarce and that such practice involves only a limited number of states.[299] Thus, an explicit right of states other than the injured state to adopt countermeasures is left outside the scope of the ILC Articles.

#### 2.4.2.5 Form and Legal Effect of the ASR

With regard to many seminal topics and in accordance with its statute, the ILC has usually recommended to the UN General Assembly that it call for an international conference with the aim of concluding an international

[295] Art. 51 of the ASR.
[296] Art. 52 of the ASR.
[297] Commentary to Art. 54 of the ASR, para. 1.
[298] Ibid., para. 6.
[299] Ibid.

agreement on the topic.[300] With respect to state responsibility, another route was chosen, despite decades of work and the perceived importance of the topic. On the basis of the ILC's proposal, the UN General Assembly *took note* of the ASR in its resolution 56/83, whereby it commended them 'to the attention of Governments without prejudice to the question of their future adoption or other appropriate action'.[301] The ILC recommendation for such modest action was accompanied by a further recommendation to the General Assembly to possibly convene an international diplomatic conference at a later stage, tasked with concluding an international convention on the topic.[302]

From the outset, the work of the ILC on state responsibility seems to have been geared towards the conclusion of an international convention. The treaty-like form of the ASR testifies to this. As David Caron states: 'the draft had the look and feel of a treaty'.[303] Indeed, as pointed out by the final Special Rapporteur on state responsibility, 'the traditional mode of adoption of Commission texts has involved a diplomatic conference and a convention',[304] a form which would give both 'durability and authority' to the articles.[305] The question of the form of the articles was nonetheless explicitly deferred to the end of the work.[306]

However, at the time of the finalization of the articles the members of the Commission were split between recommending an international convention and the mere adoption of the articles.[307] James Crawford has taken the stance

[300] This happened, for example, with respect to the law of treaties and Consular and diplomatic relations. See Art. 23 of the Statute of the International Law Commission, adopted in UNGA Resolution 174(II) of 21 November 1947.

[301] UNGA Res. 56/83, 12 December 2001, para. 3. David D. Caron has interpreted the act of 'taking note' as meaning that the General Assembly 'takes a position neither in agreement nor in opposition to the articles'. See Caron, 'The ILC Articles', 865.

[302] Report of the ILC on the Work of Its Fifty-third Session, UN Doc. A/56/10 (2001), paras. 72–73. Robert Rosenstock has praised the adopted solution as a 'sensible approach' See 'The ILC and State Responsibility' (2002) 96 *American Journal of International Law* 792–797 at 796. According to David D. Caron the chosen form could nevertheless be considered 'startling' after four decades of work. See Caron, 'The ILC Articles', 865.

[303] Ibid., 862.

[304] Caron, 'The ILC Articles', 862. Nevertheless, the ILC has departed from this approach somewhat in recent years, which has triggered analyses claiming this new trend to be 'codification light'. See Santiago Villalpando, 'Codification Light: A New Trend in the Codification of International Law at the United Nations' (2013) 8 *Anuário Brasileiro de Direito Internacional* 117–156.

[305] Crawford, *The International Law Commission's*, p. 58.

[306] In his first report in 1998, the final Special Rapporteur on the topic, James Crawford, stated that the '[d]iscussion of the eventual form of the draft articles is premature, at a time when their scope and content have not been finally determined.' James Crawford, *First Report on State Responsibility*, UN Doc. A/CN.4/490 (1998), para. 41.

[307] Report of the ILC (2001), Chapter IV, para. 61.

that 'probably the dominant view was to prefer the process and form of a law-making convention'.[308] The idealists (or legalists, if you will) sought to conclude an international convention due to the importance of the topic, which was expressly seen by them as 'one of the fundamental pillars of public international law'.[309] Further arguments for a convention can be found in the ILC's tradition of subjecting major topics to conventional form, as well as in the general desire to consolidate the law of state responsibility. The pragmatists, however, viewed a non-binding form as more suitable. They based their cautious position on the inherent difficulties in creating international conventions; the prospect of a long process in conjunction with an uncertain outcome was seen as a threat to the balance of the articles. Thus, 'reversed codification' was seen as a danger to the entire topic, and hence a soft-law form appeared preferable.[310] It was further recognized that the draft articles had 'already been frequently cited and have had a strong formative effect even as drafts'.[311]

Couching the rules in a set of articles which were taken note of has left the question of their legal force unclear. The perception held by many that the articles needed to mature through a 'continued process of legal development',[312] clarifies little as to their legal status. This consideration period, which was thought necessary by both the ILC and the UN General Assembly in order to see how the articles were welcomed by states, has not yet come to any specific outcome. The future of the ILC Articles has been regularly discussed in the UNGA, states have given their comments on the ASR as well as on their potential future form, and the UN has compiled information on references to the ASR from international case law.[313] Still, almost twenty years after the adoption of the ASR, no international diplomatic conference has been convened tasked with turning the articles into a binding international convention. Disagreement over whether to proceed to an international convention on state responsibility still prevails. Some states appear willing to 'take no further action on the draft articles, leaving the draft articles to exert a growing

[308] Crawford, *The International Law Commission's*, p. 59.

[309] Report of the ILC (2001), Chapter IV, para. 62.

[310] Ibid., paras. 61–71.

[311] James Crawford, *Fourth Report on State Responsibility*, UN Doc. A/CN.4/517 and Add.1 (2001), p. 7, para 25.

[312] Crawford, *The International Law Commission's*, p. 58.

[313] In 2004 the UNGA took a step forward regarding the ASR when in UNGA Res. 59/35 (2 December 2004), it requested the Secretary-General to invite governments to comment upon the ASR, as well as requested the Secretary-General to compile references to the articles in international judicial practice.

influence through State practice and jurisprudence',[314] while some claim that 'the time is ripe for making a decision on the future action regarding the articles'.[315] However, recent discussions before the UNGA Sixth Committee show that the position favouring negotiating a treaty on state responsibility is in the ascendant, with Latin American and Caribbean states being the foremost proponents of that position.[316]

Nevertheless, the divergent views as to the future status of the ASR have not rendered the articles useless. On the contrary, their legal effect and authority have perhaps been greater than thought: or even too influential, as some scholars have suggested. Even before their finalization, the ICJ referred to the provisionally adopted articles on state responsibility, inter alia, in the *Gabčíkovo-Nagymaros* case.[317] During the period from 2001 to 2016, the ILC Articles were referred to by courts, tribunals or comparable bodies in 163 different cases (392 times in total).[318] In addition, state parties to disputes and opinions of judges have frequently made reference to the rules. The authority of the ASR seems to be steadily increasing with the passage of time.

As one of the critics of the form chosen for the ILC Articles, David Caron has argued that they will 'inappropriately and essentially [be] accorded the authority of a formal source of law'.[319] Indeed, he argues that every reference to the ASR as 'articles' instead of 'a study on' or a 'restatement of' state responsibility further builds on the illusion of legal authority.[320] Furthermore, he argues that the chosen form of 'articles' falsely implies that the expressed rules are simple, rather than complex and abstract. As Caron recognizes, the articles will have great effect, '[b]ut they should have effect because of their integrity and value, not because they emerged from the ILC in a form that looks like a treaty'.[321] It appears that the ILC itself was aware of the fact that undue authority could be attributed to the articles. As the final Special Rapporteur James Crawford stated in 2002, '[t]he articles will have to prove themselves in practice.'[322]

[314] Report of the Secretary-General, *Responsibility of States for Internationally Wrongful Acts: Comments and Information Received from Governments*, UN Doc. A/62/63 (2007), p. 7, para. 9.
[315] Ibid., p. 5, para. 13.
[316] Paddeu, 'To Convene or Not to Convene?' 87.
[317] *Gabčíkovo-Nagymaros Project (Hungary/Slovakia)*, Judgment, ICJ Report 1997, p. 7, at 38, para. 47.
[318] Report of the Secretary-General, *Responsibility of States for Internationally Wrongful Acts. Compilation of Decisions of International Courts, Tribunals and Other Bodies*, UN Doc. A/71/80/Add.1 (20 June 2017), para. 5.
[319] Caron, 'The ILC Articles', 861.
[320] Ibid., 867 (emphasis added).
[321] Ibid., 872–873.
[322] James Crawford, 'The ILC's Articles on Responsibility of States for Internationally Wrongful Acts: A Retrospect' (2002) 96 *American Journal of International Law* 874–890 at 889.

Their form notwithstanding, the 2007 description of the ASR by the Nordic countries seems accurate: '[t]he draft articles have in a few years since their adoption become the most authoritative statement available on questions of State responsibility.'[323] Two main reasons stand out for why the ILC Articles have been afforded legal weight. First, the ASR have been considered as important due to their systematic nature. As has been pointed out, they 'show the value of an expert body which can give systematic shape to legal principles of quite fundamental importance to the character and scope of contemporary international law'.[324]

Additional significance has been given to them because they embody customary law. To a large extent, the ASR reflect customary law in the matter of state responsibility, which accredits them with legal authority. Accordingly, '[t]he ILC articles represent (at best) a restatement of customary international law of the secondary principles of state responsibility.'[325] Indeed, the question of the extent to which they reflect customary law is of utmost importance as long as no international convention on the topic has yet materialized. It is noteworthy, however, that it could be hard to identify which article represents what, since the articles often are a combination of both customary law and progressive development.[326] Whereas most rules in the ASR are based on case law, which in itself forms a means of developing customary rules, they may themselves paradoxically help to validate a rule whose existence has been in doubt; as with, for example, the general excuse of necessity.[327] In addition, concerning the ASR the ILC acknowledged that certain rules represent a more progressive development than codification of customary law.[328] Hence, whether a specific rule represents codification of customary international law or progressive development of international law becomes

323 *Comments and Information Received from Governments* 2007, p. 3, para. 2.

324 Alan Boyle and Christine Chinkin, *The Making of International Law* (Oxford: Oxford University Press, 2007), p. 185.

325 Caron, 'The ILC Articles', 872.

326 Ibid., 873.

327 For a general overview of the problems surrounding the principle of necessity, and especially the dilemma of institutional circularity, see Robert D. Sloane, 'On the Use and Abuse of Necessity in the Law of State Responsibility' (2012) 106 *American Journal of International Law* 447–508 at 452–453.

328 The ILC states in its general commentary on the Articles that '[t]hese articles seek to formulate, by way of codification and *progressive development*, the basic rules of international law concerning the responsibility of States for their internationally wrongful acts' (General Commentary, para. 1 (emphasis added)). With respect to single articles representing progressive development, the ILC states, for example, concerning the obligation of States to cooperate in cases involving the breach of a *jus cogens* obligation in Art. 41 that '[i]t may be open to question whether general international law at present prescribes a positive duty of cooperation, and paragraph 1 in that respect may reflect the progressive development of international law'. See Commentary to Art. 41 of the ASR, para. 3.

clear only after studying its commentary or drafting history, if even then. The quality of the commentaries also varies, which creates situations in which 'the commentaries may convey a deceptive degree of clarity and authority' where none exists.[329] Pierre-Marie Dupuy has aptly noted that 'a codification text once drafted takes on a life of its own, escaping from the custody of its authors, whose wisdom will not necessarily be shared by the later users of the text.'[330] Thus, although the ASR clearly have legal authority, they should be treated as neither self-explanatory nor contextualized. The articles 'remain soft law, whose legal significance will derive only from whatever authority they possess as evidence of customary law'.[331]

### 2.4.3 *State Responsibility, Public Law and Constitutionalization*

The formation of the law of state responsibility, including the ILC Articles, is largely based upon the conventional bilateral and consensual basis of international law[332] or, as James Crawford has characterized it, by 'civilian modes of thought'.[333] Yet, the ASR are not void of public law elements.[334] International law has begun 'to display more and more features which do not fit into the "civilist", bilateralist structure of the traditional law. In other words, it is on its way to being a true *public* international law.'[335] This tendency is also discernible

329 Bodansky and Crook, 'Symposium', 789.

330 Dupuy, 'A General Stocktaking', 1074.

331 Boyle and Chinkin, *The Making*, p. 184.

332 Andrea Gattini, 'A Return Ticket to Communitarisme, Please' (2002) 13 *European Journal of International Law* 1181–1199 at 1181; Dupuy, 'A General Stocktaking', 1053.

333 James Crawford, 'Responsibility to the International Community as a Whole' (2001) 8 *Indiana Journal of Global Legal Studies* 303–322 at 304.

334 What 'public' refers to can be debated, but in general it seems to imply the protection of the interest of 'the polity as a whole, rather than only the interests of individual states'. See André Nollkaemper, 'Constitutionalization and the Unity of the Law of International Responsibility' (2009) 16 *Indiana Journal of Global Legal Studies* 535–563 at 540. Benedict Kingsbury and Megan Donaldson have found that 'public law' can mean (a) 'an international law which is "inter-public" law, being made by and for a set of entities (primarily States) that are not merely "actors"... but public entities operating under public law'; (b) 'a quality of publicness in law'. According to the authors, these two meanings are separate but overlapping. See Benedict Kingsbury and Megan Donaldson, 'From Bilateralism to Publicness in International Law', in Ulrich Fastenrath, Rudolf Geiger and Daniel-Erasmus Khan et al. (eds.), *From Bilateralism to Community Interests: Essays in Honour of Judge Bruno Simma* (Oxford: Oxford University Press, 2011), pp. 79–89 at 80.

335 Bruno Simma, 'Universality of International Law from the Perspective of a Practitioner' (2009) 20 *European Journal of International Law* (2009) 265–297 at 268 (emphasis in original). Norms relating to 'public interest' or 'community interest' are, for example, international human rights norms, *erga omnes* and *jus cogens* norms (see for example Nollkaemper, 'Constitutionalization', 540). According to Bruno Simma, community interests rise above

in the law of state responsibility. In 2000, James Crawford noted that the ASR include elements 'which are closely analogous to public law interests in other legal systems'.[336] Concordant views are set forth by André Nollkaemper, who holds that different attempts to 'make the law of international responsibility relevant to public order and perhaps to constitutional order' are visible.[337] In fact, he takes his claim about the public elements in the ASR a step further by stating that it appears justified to hold that there is not only a public law dimension to international responsibility,[338] but that '[t]he modern international law of responsibility has constitutional ambitions that go beyond the traditional, tort-like system of international responsibility.'[339]

There are different aspects of the law of state responsibility which can be said to either directly or indirectly possess a public law function. First, one can generally claim that the traditional bilateral approach to state responsibility in itself seeks to advance public law goals by upholding the integrity of the international legal system.[340] This may be called a 'public or constitutional function, in the guise of a private law model'.[341] The approach chosen by the ILC with respect to the ASR, which embraced Anzilotti's construction of an objective responsibility, further strengthens the overall public law function of state responsibility. Responsibility is not contingent upon injury;[342] as a consequence, the law seeks to protect from violations not only the injured parties, but the international legal system as well. This basis for responsibility symbolizes a turn towards a 'public law—oriented law of responsibility'.[343]

the interests of states and 'correspond to the needs, hopes and fears of all human beings, and attempt to cope with problems the solution of which may be decisive for the survival of the entire humankind'. See Bruno Simma, 'From Bilateralism to Community Interest in International Law' (1994) 250 *Receuil des Cours de l'Académie de Droit International* 217–384 at 244, cited in Kingsbury and Donaldson, 'From Bilateralism', 81. The following categories exemplify community interests: preservation of international peace and security, environmental protection, human rights, minimal economic solidarity, (ibid).

336 Crawford, 'Responsibility to the International', 322.

337 Nollkaemper, 'Towards Public Responsibility', 3.

338 See André Nollkaemper and Dov Jacobs, 'Shared Responsibility in International Law: A Conceptual Framework' (2012–2013) 34 *Michigan Journal of International Law* 359–438 at 401.

339 Nollkaemper, 'Constitutionalization', 545. André Nollkaemper understands constitutionalization within this framework as something different from its meaning within domestic law; it 'rather is shorthand for referring to certain organizational principles of international law' (Ibid., 541).

340 Nollkaemper, 'Towards Public Responsibility', 3.

341 Ibid.

342 Nollkaemper, 'Constitutionalization', 545.

343 Nollkaemper and Jacobs, 'Shared Responsibility', 403.

Thus, safeguarding legality can be separated from the reparative function of the law of state responsibility. Certainly, this variety in function did not come about by mistake. It appears clear that the intention behind various components of the ASR was indeed to show 'the existence of an international public order'.[344] A number of rules in the ASR attempt to ensure the protection of the international legal order itself: the obligation of cessation, the obligation to provide guarantees of non-repetition, the recognition of the right to invoke responsibility of third states, and the obligations of third states with respect to serious violations of peremptory norms of international law.

A segment of the ASR which clearly is motivated by constitutional thinking pertains to the rules regarding serious breaches of peremptory norms.[345] Having depenalized the ASR – that is, discarded the separation of violations into 'crimes' and 'delicts' – the ILC still sought to recognize that extra consequences follow upon all states in the case of breaches of international obligations of a peremptory nature. The additional obligations set forth by the ILC Articles establish that all states are under an obligation to cooperate in bringing the serious breach to an end, in addition to which they are not allowed to recognize as lawful the situation created under the breach.[346] The obligations placed upon all states when it comes to serious breaches of peremptory norms thus aim to 'induce and secure a return to legality'.[347] Nevertheless, since the ASR expressly reject punitive damages,[348] there are no additional consequences placed upon the wrongdoer for the violation of serious breaches.[349] Thus, one can argue that the public law element is not fully embraced with respect to serious breaches of peremptory norms.[350]

The other aspect of constitutional value with respect to serious violations of peremptory norms of international law relates to the right of third states to invoke the responsibility of the wrongdoer. This prerogative is confirmed in Article 48 of the ILC Articles, which identifies the right of third states to invoke responsibility when it comes to obligations owed to the international community as a whole. Consequently, although the subjective rights of a state have not been injured, it can invoke responsibility in the name of community

[344] *Comments and Observations Received by Governments*, UN Doc. A/CN.4/488 (1998), reproduced in ILC Yearbook 1998, vol. II, part 1, p. 96, para. 6 (France).
[345] Nollkaemper, 'Constitutionalization', 548.
[346] Art. 41 of the ASR.
[347] Nollkaemper, 'Constitutionalization', 549.
[348] Commentary to Part Two, Chapter III, para. 5.
[349] For an evaluation and criticism of the lack of specific consequences for the wrongdoer, see Dupuy, 'A General Stocktaking'.
[350] Gattini, 'A Return Ticket', 1199.

interest. In order for this rule to have a true public law function, one would be entitled to expect that the rights of the injured state would be different from those rights pertinent to states pursuing legal interest. Otherwise, the rule would simply fall back upon private law, in which every party is treated similarly.[351] Whereas the draft article did not distinguish between different categories of right-holders, the final article does so. Thus, third states acting on behalf of the international community as a whole do not have a general right to seek restitution, but only cessation and non-repetition. Restitution can only be sought on behalf of the injured state or its beneficiaries. Thereby, the 'primacy of the interests of the actual victims' is considered paramount.[352]

A third component of the ASR must also be mentioned in this connection: the institution of countermeasures and the possibility for third states to make use of such measures. Indeed, international practice shows that third states with a legal interest in ascertaining responsibility have resorted to countermeasures.[353] However, since these situations have mostly been limited to third states acting 'at the request and on behalf of' the injured state, the law remains arguably unclear as to whether a legal interest gives third states the right to resort to countermeasures.[354] The existence of such a right would obviously contribute to strengthening the public law function of state responsibility, as the concept of collective countermeasures is based on 'the idea of decentralized enforcement on behalf of the international community'.[355]

Although all the above-mentioned elements in the ASR clearly represent efforts to reflect the rise of community interests within international law at large, they are not fully and systematically developed to that effect.[356] For example, the rule on collective countermeasures has been considered 'unduly restrictive' and not reflecting the views of the majority of states.[357] According to Andrea Gattini, 'despite their appearance of *communitarisme*, [the ASR] leave one with a sense of half-heartedness.'[358] Thus, the existence of public law aspects in the ILC Articles does not constitute a coherent and strong representation of community interests.

351 Crawford, 'Responsibility to the International', 320.

352 James Crawford, *Third Report on State Responsibility*, UN Doc. A/CN.4/507 and Add. 1–4 (2000), reproduced in ILC Yearbook 2000, vol. II, part 1, p. 99, para. 376.

353 According to the ILC, such examples are: the collective measures taken against Argentina with respect to the Falkland Islands in 1982, collective measures against Iraq in 1990, and collective measures against Yugoslavia in 1998. See Commentary to Art. 54 of the ASR.

354 Ibid., paras. 5–6.

355 Nollkaemper, 'Towards Public Responsibility', 5.

356 Nollkaemper and Jacobs, 'Shared Responsibility', 406.

357 Christian J. Tams, *Enforcing Obligations* Erga Omnes *in International Law* (Cambridge: Cambridge University Press, 2005), p. 311.

358 Gattini, 'A Return Ticket', 1185 (emphasis in original).

# 3

# Problems in the General Law of State Responsibility

## 3.1 PRELIMINARY OBSERVATIONS

Having traced the development of state responsibility from an implicit doctrine into an essential component of the international legal order, it is time to proceed to analyze the general law of state responsibility from the perspective of functionality. This chapter identifies and discusses problems with the general law of state responsibility ranging from the abstract nature of the law to difficulties with its implementation. The aim is to probe into tensions and shortcomings that characterize the general law of state responsibility and its elements, despite their broad acceptance and frequent prevalence.

### 3.1.1 *Methodological Choices*

The analysis below warrants a few comments on the methodology used in this study as well as on the normative environment in which state responsibility law exists and operates. To begin with, any legal weighing of the law of state responsibility remains susceptible to charges of partiality. What one commentator sees as beneficial, another may construe as a drawback. A value-free assessment of a legal phenomenon is impossible: 'without some form of preference or bias, one would not be able to identify an issue or a situation, let alone pass judgment on it'.[1] The same applies to this book's analysis of the law of state responsibility, the starting point of which is a perception of international legal relations that questions state-centredness and for which the fragmentation of international responsibility is a fact.

[1] Thomas Skouteris, 'The Vocabulary of Progress in Interwar International Law: An Intellectual Portrait of Stelios Seferiades' (2005) 16 *European Journal of International Law* 823–856 at 824.

In the first chapter of this book it was argued that the analysis of state responsibility will be based on the desire to have a well-functioning responsibility regime in international law, a regime able to address the variety of social actors and problems of the contemporary world. It was argued that the position of state responsibility as the foremost responsibility regime can only be supported if the regime is functional. Admittedly, functionality is only one of many possible evaluative approaches against which the law of state responsibility can be judged; furthermore, it is not even the most commonly used.[2] Nonetheless, it is the appraisal framework chosen by the author in order to discuss the gap between doctrine and real-world demands. Two dimensions of functionality will be explored in this chapter: the functions of state responsibility and whether the rules are suited to their realization, and whether these rules have been operationalized to such an extent that state responsibility achieves what it sets out to do.[3]

Another feature of the following analysis is its emphasis on the foundations of state responsibility. Two limitations follow from this. First, the arguments raised in the analysis relate to the challenges confronting the *general* law of state responsibility. Admittedly, it is difficult to discuss state responsibility without resort to special rules, but special rules of state responsibility will only be discussed to the extent that they point to problematic patterns in the general law. A second limitation is that the following analysis leaves out procedural problems; such as what constitutes a notice of claim, issues of immunity, problems in the calculation of reparations, and so forth. Rather, the purpose here is to pay attention to the constitutive principles and structures of the law of state responsibility; that is, issues that play a crucial role in state responsibility's functioning as an efficient remedy in international law.

A third point concerns the organization of the problems selected for analysis. These problems are categorized in accordance with the different parts of the ASR: the internationally wrongful act and its elements, content, and implementation. This systematization is familiar to most international lawyers contemplating issues of state responsibility. It is worth noting, however, that many of the difficulties discussed in this chapter are intertwined and thus defy strict categorization. For example, the interstate character of the law of state responsibility affects not only its viability in a globalized world, but also the means of implementing the law. Also, the insertion of community interests into the ILC's Articles on State Responsibility generates problems both with

[2] See Section 1.4.2, 'Assessing the Law of State Responsibility'.

[3] Ibid. For an in-depth discussion of functionality, see in particular Section 1.4.2.2, 'Functionality in Focus' above.

the unity of the rules and with how these interests are implemented and by whom. Consequently, it has been difficult to avoid overlaps in the evaluation. Nevertheless, the analysis attempts to combine in a comprehensive and systematic way two areas of discussion: the fragments of criticism that have previously been aimed at the law of state responsibility, as well as new problems that have come to the fore with the diversification of the international legal order and the multiplication of actors.

### 3.1.2 *Contextualizing the Critique*

A first step in the analysis of the general law of state responsibility is to recognize that the rules do not exist in a legal vacuum. The criticism directed against the general law of state responsibility must therefore be contextualized, so that one acknowledges the existence of factors that may, in part, mitigate or contribute to the critique. Three such factors are: the implications to the law of state responsibility of the deficiencies in international law writ large, the nature of customary international law, and the prevalence of special rules of state responsibility.

The law of state responsibility suffers from the same limitations as international law in general: the decentralization of both law-making and law enforcement. To a large extent, the lack of both an international legislature and an international enforcement body makes state responsibility non-institutionalized and, similar to the larger international legal system, highly dependent on the will of states. Two observations follow from these conditions that impact the functioning of state responsibility law: first, the imperfect nature of primary obligations; and second, that enforcement in international law is underdeveloped and relies to a substantial degree on outmoded means such as self-help. However, the meagre leverage of institutionalized enforcement in international law makes it even more important to consider the general regime of responsibility in international law, particularly since state responsibility can be understood as discouraging states from violating international law in the first place.[4]

While acknowledging the setting in which state responsibility operates, this book deals with problems that are common to both the international legal order in general and to the law of state responsibility, but only from the perspective of state responsibility. For example, general shortcomings of law enforcement in international law will be treated only with respect to their normative points of contact with the ASR. Thus, the lack of an international police force will

[4] Willisch, *State Responsibility for Technological*, p. 27.

not be addressed, since the law of state responsibility has arranged the matter of enforcement in other terms. What will be discussed are various problems in the law of state responsibility, specific aspects of which may or may not overlap with critique of the international legal order in general.

A second factor considered to influence the usefulness of state responsibility is the fact that state responsibility is governed by customary international law. Customary international law – whose main features are its non-written, unnegotiated, and universal nature[5] – is viewed by some legal scholars as less preferable in comparison to treaty or conventional law. It has been argued that treaty law has become 'the prime source of law',[6] an argument that has triggered claims of the death of custom.[7] Hence, it could be argued that what state responsibility law lacks in detail and precision is due not to the topic itself, but rather to the legal form in which it is entrenched.

Although international law was to a large extent originally customary international law,[8] recent decades have witnessed a clear proliferation of treaty law to the detriment of customary international law.[9] Indeed, it seems that some international legal scholars prefer treaty law over customary law due to the fact that '[a]ny written text provides more certainty and reliability than an unwritten rule'.[10] Customary international law is considered to be 'frequently disorderly and often uncertain',[11] leaving rules highly abstract and malleable. Yet things are rarely black and white. First, not all issues in international law find their way into conventional law. Many basic subject matters in international law are customary international law, and the same applies to topics that are

5 Laurence R. Helfer and Ingrid B. Wuerth, 'Customary International Law: An Instrument Choice Perspective' (2016) 37 *Michigan Journal of International Law* 563–609.

6 H. W. A. Thirlway, *International Customary Law and Codification* (Leiden: A.W Sijthoff, 1972), p. 7; Klabbers, *International Law*, p. 25, noting that 'the treaty has become the dominant source of international law'. For a general discussion of the hierarchy of sources, see Mario Prost, 'Hierarchy and the Sources of International Law: A Critique' (2017) 39 *Houston Journal of International Law* 285–330.

7 Gerald J. Postema, 'Custom in International Law: A Normative Practice Account', in Amanda Perreau-Saussine and James Bernard Murphy (eds.), *The Nature of Customary Law: Legal Historical and Philosophical Perspectives* (Cambridge: Cambridge University Press, 2007), pp. 279–306 at 279; Joel P. Trachtman, 'Reports of the Death of Treaty Are Premature, but Customary International Law May Have Outlived Its Usefulness' (2014) 108 *AJIL Unbound* 36–40.

8 Christian Tomuschat, 'The Complementarity of International Treaty Law, Customary International Law, and Non-Contractual Lawmaking. Comment by Christian Tomuschat', in Rüdiger Wolfrum and Volken Röber (eds.), *Developments of International Law in Treaty Making* (Berlin: Springer, 2005), pp. 401–408 at 404.

9 Thirlway, *International Customary Law*, p. 31.

10 Tomuschat, 'The Complementarity', 402; See also, Trachtman, 'Reports'.

11 Thirlway, *International Customary Law*, p. 144.

closely related to state responsibility, such as the law of diplomatic protection,[12] or state immunity. Moreover, customary law features different levels of precision; admittedly, some are vague and require further development, while other customary norms can be more detailed.

Some legal rules may be more suitable for customary international law than treaty law. Laurence Helfer and Ingrid Wuerth identify three such categories of custom: (1) rules that benefit all states, such as freedom of navigation or the prohibition against piracy; (2) rules that serve the interests of hegemonies, such as jurisdictional claims over the continental shelf beyond territorial waters; and (3) 'normative custom'; that is, rules akin to the prohibition of genocide that serve the whole international legal system, despite potential distributional costs.[13] State responsibility rules must be understood as falling into the first category: custom that benefits all states. Indeed, traditional customary rules are seen as enabling interstate cooperation,[14] as is the case with state responsibility law. They do so in general, by seeking to ensure that all states have recourse to remedies if their rights are violated. But they also do so by explicitly prescribing interstate cooperation in cases of serious breaches of international law.[15] Facilitative rules rather than distributional, are particularly suitable for the abstract level of customary international law.[16] This applies to state responsibility law as well. Further, in these circumstances custom can develop in a more 'detailed and specific' direction.[17]

Instead of viewing the customary form of state responsibility predominantly as an impediment to its efficiency, it must be recognized that customary international law was crucial for the whole development of the law in question, and that state responsibility is a field of international law still largely governed by customary international law.[18] In fact, the international legal system probably would lack a general regime of responsibility were it not for customary international law, which allows for generality, flexibility, and incompleteness. As Thirlway has pointed out: 'the ordered and complete law cannot be

[12] Tomuschat, 'The Complementarity', 402.

[13] Helfer and Wuerth, 'Customary International Law', pp. 580–594.

[14] Anthea Roberts, 'Traditional and Modern Approaches to Customary International Law: Reconciliation' (2001) 95 *American Journal of International Law* 757–791 at 764.

[15] Art. 41 of the ASR.

[16] Helfer and Wuerth, 'Customary International Law', 582.

[17] Laurence R. Helfer and Ingrid Wuerth, *Custom in the Age of Soft Law* (Working Paper), p. 5.

[18] Andrew T. Guzman, 'Saving Customary International Law' (2005) 27 *Michigan Journal of International Law* 115–176 at 116, note 1.

universal'.[19] Moreover, it can be disputed that treaty law is always stronger or more compelling, as treaties allow for reservations and interpretative declarations to be made, as well as withdrawals.[20]

The form of state responsibility law is not decisive to its functionality, although admittedly it might affect some of its aspects. The criticism of the generality of the rules is related to the customary law nature of state responsibility. However, the subject of critical discussion in this chapter is not the details of the rules of state responsibility, but rather the grand scheme of law set forth in the ASR. The discussion in this chapter will focus on the constitutive ideas of state responsibility and how they affect the law's capability to address the contemporary world.

A final topic that needs to be addressed when contextualizing the critique of state responsibility law is Article 55 of the ASR and the prevalence of special rules on state responsibility. Article 55 of the ASR reads: 'these articles [on state responsibility] do not apply where and to the extent that the conditions for the existence of an internationally wrongful act or the content or implementation of the international responsibility of a State are governed by special rules of international law.' To raise such a substantial critique of state responsibility as will be done in this book may seem unfair, given that a substantial body of special rules exists with the precise aim to complement or deviate from general law. Indeed, Article 55 on the primacy of special rules on state responsibility contains one of the most apparent mechanisms, and perhaps also the most important, for dealing with the shortcomings of the general rules as embodied in the ASR. The question is whether the possibility of drafting and using special rules on state responsibility can save the general law from its shortcomings; that is, whether it can compensate for its problems either by complementing the general rules in part, or by setting them aside by virtue of providing for self-contained regimes.

Three separate issues need to be taken into account when considering the degree to which special rules can compensate for deficiencies in the general rules. First, although the ASR state that its rules are residual, it seems possible that the general and the special rules can coexist without interfering with each other. Tzvika Alan Nissel claims that the duality of state responsibility has allowed both a doctrinal and a common law version of it to prevail at

[19] Thirlway, *International Customary Law*, p. 145.

[20] Prost, 'Hierarchy and the Sources', 302; John Tasioulas, 'Customary International Law and the Quest for Global Justice', in Amanda Perreau-Saussine and James Bernard Murphy (eds.), *The Nature of Customary Law: Legal Historical and Philosophical Perspectives* (Cambridge: Cambridge University Press, 2007), pp. 307–335 at 307.

the same time. In his view, the doctrinal law version of state responsibility amounts to general law, while the common law version, on alien protection, amounts to special law.[21] A second point relates to the question of the extent to which states actually agree upon and utilize special rules. Although many branches of international law contain independent rules on issues related to the legal consequences following from an internationally wrongful act, few actually cover the whole range of legal consequences that ensue from the breach of an international obligation.[22] World Trade Organization (WTO) law, human rights law, and European Community law are branches of international law featuring strong special rules,[23] in addition to which the ICJ has cited diplomatic law as being another example of a so-called self-contained regime.[24] Moreover, some issues of state responsibility such as shared responsibility or complicity often are not addressed by special rules, leaving general rules to dominate regulation.[25]

Third, there is also the question of whether states actually are capable of substituting their own rules for the general rules. It has been suggested that this is not always the case, since 'the rules that derogate must have at least the same rank as those they derogate from'.[26] Thus, there are limits to the possibility of states creating special rules. This is the case, for example, when it comes to the operation of the rules governing the aggravated breaches regime: 'serious breaches of obligations under peremptory norms of general international law'.[27] Further, the general rules are often understood to prevail to the degree that the special rule(s) do not regulate the question fully,[28] even though scholars disagree as to their coexistence. The fallback upon the general rules is much debated, particularly when it comes to the use of countermeasures.[29]

[21] Nissel, *A History of State Responsibility*, pp. 369–370.

[22] Simma and Pulkowksi, 'Of Planets and the Universe', 484.

[23] Ibid., 512.

[24] *United States Diplomatic and Consular Staff in Tehran, Judgment*, ICJ Reports 1980, p. 3, at p. 40, para. 86, in which the ICJ states: 'The rules of diplomatic law, in short, constitute a self-contained regime…'.

[25] This is noticeable, for example, with respect to discussions of the practice of shared responsibility in international law. See André Nollkaemper and Ilias Plakokefalos (eds.), *The Practice of Shared Responsibility in International Law* (Cambridge: Cambridge University Press, 2017).

[26] Koskenniemi, *Fragmentation Report*, p. 38, para. 64.

[27] Ibid.

[28] Kate Parlett, 'The Application of the Rules on Countermeasures in Investment Claims. Visions and Realities of International Law as an Open System', in Christine Chinkin and Freya Baetens (eds.), *Sovereignty, Statehood and State Responsibility: Essays in Honour of James Crawford* (Cambridge: Cambridge University Press, 2015), pp. 389–405 at 393.

[29] Simma and Pulkowksi, 'Of Planets and the Universe', 493.

Therefore, it seems difficult to circumvent the general rules and their underlying principles. In fact, the general rules are taken as applying, unless it can be proven that they do not.[30] The general rules also have a role to play in legal reasoning even when special rules exist.[31]

To sum up, irrespective of the existence of special rules in the law of state responsibility, the general rules maintain their doctrinal relevance. In fact, it has been argued that 'many central building blocks of the traditional international legal system, such as the rules on diplomatic protection or state responsibility, have remained remarkably stable'.[32] State responsibility cannot be discussed without resort to the general rules, a situation which is testified to by the literature on state responsibility. Nonetheless, although special rules cannot wholly substitute for the general law, they do express the irrelevance of certain aspects of the general rules as well as contain a seed of discontent with them. For example, there is a discernible trend in special rules on state responsibility to deal with and include non-state actors within the context of the invocation or implementation of state responsibility. One such example is the Statute of the International Tribunal for the Law of the Sea (ITLOS), which opens up the Tribunal 'to entities other than States Parties'.[33] Especially in the field of international environmental law, special rules also frequently set forth softer forms of responsibility emphasizing cooperation and prevention rather than adversarial models of responsibility. The Montreal Protocol on the Ozone Layer is one case in point in which non-compliance procedures have replaced the language of wrongfulness that features in the ILC Articles.[34] Thus, special rules have innovatively created mechanisms and remedies that do not exist under the general law of state responsibility.[35] This situation indicates a starting point for the analysis below: the general law of state responsibility contains tensions and gaps that states wish to circumvent.

30 James Crawford, 'The International Court of Justice and the Law of State Responsibility', in Christian J. Tams and James Sloan (eds.), *The Development of International Law by the International Court of Justice* (Oxford: Oxford University Press, 2013), pp. 71–86 at 82.

31 Silvia Zorzetto, 'The Lex Specialis Principle and Its Uses in Legal Argumentation: An Analytical Inquire' (2012–2013), *Eunomia: Revista en Cultura de la Legalidad* 61–87 at 75.

32 Simma and Pulkowksi, 'Of Planets and the Universe', 484.

33 Art. 20(2) of the Statute of the International Tribunal for the Law of the Sea, Montego Bay, 10 December 1982, in force 16 November 1994, 1833 *United Nations Treaty Series* 561.

34 Art. 8 of the Montreal Protocol on Substances That Deplete the Ozone Layer, Montreal, 16 September 1987, in force 1 January 1989, 1522 *United Nations Treaty Series* 3.

35 Simma and Pulkowksi, 'Of Planets and the Universe', 484.

### 3.2 THE PROBLEMATIC NATURE OF GENERAL AND SECONDARY RULES

The different approaches to state responsibility in its formative years had mostly concerned efforts to codify concrete obligations or breaches rather than laying down general rules. As a consequence, many draft conventions contained rules on primary obligations such as: 'Denial of Access to a Tribunal or an Administrative Authority', 'Denial of a Fair Hearing', or 'Destruction of and Damage to Property'.[36] The codification work of the ILC on state responsibility was initiated by Special Rapporteur García Amador in a similar manner, but his successor Roberto Ago changed the focus of the work to an approach based on general and secondary rules.[37] What had used to be concrete international duties placed upon states now turned into general rules applicable to all kinds of breaches irrespective of source or subject matter.

The reception of the chosen methodology of codification was ambiguous; many applauded the secondary rules approach, whereas others thought the approach had little merit. The advantages of the approach were obvious and pragmatic; the choice to focus on general and secondary rules avoided the pitfall of political contestation. Instead of quarrels over concrete international issues such as expropriation, the conceptualization of state responsibility as 'lawyers' law' served to desensitize the topic.[38] Secondary rules also 'evince neutrality on many disputed or controversial substantive matters'.[39] The general and secondary rules approach thus created a legal environment conducive to the progress of codification of state responsibility. The rapid proliferation of primary international obligations also left the ILC without any optional forms of codification.[40]

However, the general and secondary principles approach is problematic for at least two interrelated reasons: it decouples responsibility from tangible international obligations, and at the same time it is highly abstract. As Scott points out, '[t]his kind of critique has its basis in the premise that a statement

[36] These rules are found in the 1961 revised Harvard Draft Convention on the International Responsibility of States for Injuries to Aliens, Arts. 6, 7, 9 respectively. See Louis B. Sohn and Richard Baxter, 'Responsibility of States for Injuries to the Economic Interests of Aliens' (1961) 55 *American Journal of International Law* 545–584.

[37] See Section 2.4.1, 'ILC and the difficulty of Finding a Suitable Approach'.

[38] Bodansky and Crook, 'Symposium', 778; Boyle and Chinkin, *The Making*, p. 183.

[39] Bodansky and Crook, 'Symposium', 780. Similarly, Sterling Scott notices that the chosen approach 'facilitate[s] international agreement on broad organizing principles rather than specific rules'. See Sterling Scott, 'Codification of State Responsibility in International Law: A Review and Assessment' (1985) 9 *ASILS International Law Journal* 1–36 at 26.

[40] Crawford, *State Responsibility: The General Part*, p. 65.

of the secondary rules of state responsibility have [*sic*] negligible utility to real life conflict resolution either because they restate the obvious or provide inadequate guidance to the resolution or adjudication of specific problems.'[41] In particular, lawyers with a common law background considered the relevance of secondary norms as peripheral. For them, 'the abstract treatment of "responsibility" as such', was strange.[42] This view is explained by the fact that states with a common law system lack a 'general regime of legal responsibility'.[43] As James Crawford has admitted, the ASR 'are inspired by civilian modes of thought, not by the common law.'[44] Against this background, criticism levelled against the secondary rules approach becomes explicable.[45]

Conceptualizing the responsibility of states in the abstract or in terms of primary and secondary obligations will only provide partial solutions to concrete problems; it will leave attempts to understand state responsibility as a doctrine incomplete. This is because no 'truthful' or 'objective' responsibility exists that can be detached from the practices that embody state responsibility. The basis of the international legal order lies in practice, not in theory;[46] without connecting the concepts and functions of state responsibility to their practical realization, our understanding of international law will be imperfect. Thus, 'law should not be viewed as an autonomous universe of discourse or a closed analytical system, but as part of the normative life of a society'.[47] Moreover,

41 Scott, 'Codification of State Responsibility', 27.

42 Bodansky and Crook, 'Symposium', 773–774.

43 Ibid., 780. Bodansky and Crook further describe the arrangements of responsibility in the common law system as follows: 'Substantive rules are classified by their subject matter (e.g., criminal law, tort, contracts, property, family law), each characterized by its own regime of "responsibility" with its own remedies, rules of attribution and invocation, and so forth' (Ibid.). Peter Cane has also pointed out that common law is based on inductive legal reasoning, which deviates from the deductive approach in which general rules are applied to particular cases. See Cane, *Responsibility in Law*, p. 25.

44 James Crawford, 'Responsibility to the International Community as a Whole' (2000–2001) 8 *Indiana Journal of Global Legal Studies* 303–322 at 304.

45 Richard Baxter holds that '[t]he circumstances under which responsibility attaches and the remedies to be provided for violations of the rules of law cannot be divorced from the substantive rules of conduct themselves'. See Baxter, 'Reflections on Codification', 748; Richard Kearney claims that 'abstract responsibility might prove too "metaphysical"'. See Kearney, Summary Records, ILC Yearbook 1970, vol. I, p. 217, para. 32; Richard B. Lillich says that the approach chosen by the ILC offers 'little or no guidance'. See Richard B. Lillich, 'The Current Status of the Law of State Responsibility for Injuries to Aliens', in Richard B. Lillich (ed.), *International Law of State Responsibility for Injuries to Aliens* (Charlottesville: University Press of Virginia, 1983), pp. 1–61 at 21.

46 Koskenniemi, *From Apology to Utopia*, p. 600. See also Peter Cane, who notes that any system of responsibility must be anchored in particular 'social activities and problems'. Cane, *Responsibility in Law*, p. 280.

47 Cane, *Responsibility in Law*, p. 279.

the abstract approach may even have detrimental effects upon the ability of the general law of state responsibility to prevent future violations from taking place: the very fact that responsibility is theorized, instead of portrayed 'concretely in relation to particular obligations',[48] makes it difficult to grasp. More importantly, however, such theorization leaves 'room for argument in every conceivable case of potential responsibility'.[49]

A second concern that arises from the general form of the ASR has to do with the high level of abstraction of the rules, and the sustainability of having such rules. As many scholars have claimed, the value of too-abstract rules diminishes when they become difficult to use.[50] Nonetheless, the widespread practice by international non-judicial and judicial bodies of referring to the ASR indicates that such fears may have been groundless. In their decisions, international bodies ranging from the ICJ to regional human rights courts have included references to a broad range of the rules of the ASR. These rules often relate to the elements of the internationally wrongful act, such as the rules of attribution, but they also frequently refer to rules on restitution and compensation, as well as the rules regarding invocation of responsibility.[51] The authority of the rules codified in the ASR also seems constantly to be rising, as the number of references seems to slowly increase year after year.[52] However, some international legal scholars have pointed out that the practice of referencing is like a 'self-fulfilling prophecy'; that is, international lawyers begin to accept a certain practice or rule the more we articulate it.[53] It has also been suggested that at times referencing the ASR may be more about 'signposting rather than actually integrating the substance of the Articles into the decision'.[54]

48 Allott, 'Unmaking', 12.

49 Allott, 'Unmaking', 12, 14.

50 David D. Caron claims that 'these abstract rules are devilishly difficult to apply'. See, David D. Caron, 'The ILC Articles on State Responsibility' (2002) 96 *American Journal of International Law* 857–873 at 872; Sterling Scott says that the Articles 'do not typically provide satisfactory responses to the meritorious issues of specific conflicts'. See Scott, 'Codification of State Responsibility', 27; Myres S. McDougal, Harold D. Lasswell and Lung-chu Chen hold ILC's work to be 'at such a high level of abstraction as to shed but a dim light upon specific controversies'. See Myres S. McDougal, Harold D. Lasswell and Lung-chu Chen, *Human Rights and World Public Order* (New Haven: Yale University Press, 1980), p. 762, note 92.

51 *Responsibility of States for Internationally Wrongful Acts. Compilation of Decisions of International Courts, Tribunals and Other Bodies*, Report of the Secretary-General, UN Doc. A/71/80/Add.1, 20 June 2017.

52 Ibid., p. 18 *et seq*.

53 See Carlo Focarelli, who claims the same with respect to the practice of third-party countermeasures. 'International Law and Third-party Countermeasures in the Age of Global Instant Communication' (2016) 29 *Questions of International Law* 17–24 at 23; see also Caron, 'The ILC Articles', 867–868.

54 Crawford, 'Investment Arbitration', 132.

The ILC attempted to avoid the inoperability of general rules through the incorporation of the institution of *lex specialis* into the ASR. By the insertion of *lex specialis* into the Articles, the ILC sought to maintain the relevance of general law while at the same time recognizing that different subject matters call for different solutions in terms of responsibility. The ILC clearly intended states to be free to 'develop, apply and to derogate from the general rules of State responsibility by agreements between themselves'.[55] Paradoxically, the general law needs special norms in order to respond to social complexities.[56] On the other hand, special law should not become the rule rather than the exception. Otherwise, the special law can override the general law.

If states repeatedly express (highly) different ideas in special law, it can be argued that such a practice diminishes the credibility of the general rules. They are no longer viewed as representing the current state of affairs: consequently, the general law does not conform to the states' perception of the content and implementation of responsibility. In such a situation, general law becomes meaningless. Therefore, an extensive use of *lex specialis* can pose a threat to a unified set of general rules on state responsibility. This danger of special law making the general law useless within the field of responsibility has been recognized by states themselves. In the course of the ILC work on the Articles on the Responsibility of International Organizations (ARIO), some states hesitated to adopt a strong rule regarding *lex specialis*. Belgium felt that a very broad scope of the *lex specialis* rule would 'render the draft articles entirely pointless'.[57] In a similar vein, Germany acknowledged that 'special rules relating to international responsibility might not only supplement but *replace in full* the more general rules'.[58]

Although few are prepared to declare the general rules of state responsibility to be futile,[59] it is indisputable that, to varying degrees, in several branches of international law the general rules have receded into the background. Dispute settlement bodies within specialized systems of international law commonly solve cases based on 'their' special law rather than on general law of

55 Koskenniemi, *Fragmentation Report*, p. 38, para. 64.

56 Ibid., p. 15, paras. 15–16.

57 *Responsibility of International Organizations. Comments and Observations Received from Governments*, UN Doc. A/CN.4/636 and Add. 1–2 (2011), p. 130.

58 Ibid., p. 131 (emphasis in original).

59 One of the sceptics regarding state responsibility is Martti Koskenniemi, who asks himself: 'How long, for example, can one be committed to a project to [*sic*] state responsibility that commenced in the United Nations in 1949 and is today no more than a set of controversial draft articles with no realistic prospect of being accepted as hard law in the foreseeable future?'. See Martti Koskenniemi, *The Politics of International Law* (Oxford and Portland, OR: Hart Publishing, 2011), p. 276.

responsibility. This particularly holds true with respect to the WTO Appellate Body, European Community law, and international investment arbitrations. These bodies tend to resort to the general law mostly in cases that are unsolvable solely on the grounds of special law, or where decisions require legitimacy.[60] Although it is frequently argued that general law exists in the background in order to provide cohesion to special law, it appears that the 'operational effectiveness' provided by special rules is one reason for the limited practical role of general rules within certain specialized branches of international law.[61]

## 3.3 PROBLEMS RELATED TO THE INTERNATIONALLY WRONGFUL ACT

### 3.3.1 *Identifying the Actor*

One aspect for which the ILC Articles have been criticized relates to the question of what relations the law of state responsibility seeks to govern, as well as how to define who the state is for the purposes of responsibility.[62] Over the course of the several decades during which the ILC codification work on the law of state responsibility took place, 'the essence of the state' changed in numerous ways due to globalization and the concomitant liberalization and privatization that arrived in its wake.[63] While the ILC codified several rules pertaining to attribution that attempt to reflect the broad array of actors whose actions can be imputed to the state, the application of the attribution rules still often testify to '[a] restrictive or outdated view of the state'.[64] Furthermore, the ASR are only applicable to interstate relations, despite the diversification and multiplication of actors that has occurred. The justification for such an approach was understandable at the time when the ILC began working on the topic of state responsibility. However, when the ILC Articles were finalized, the vision had partially changed regarding which relations should be governed by the ASR. For example, in 2002 Edith Brown Weiss criticized the ASR for not satisfactorily addressing state relations to non-state entities.[65] Thus, the work of the ILC appears to be unable to respond to two of globalization's prominent

[60] Bruno Simma and Dirk Pulkowski, 'Leges Speciales and Self-Contained Regimes', in James Crawford, Alain Pellet and Simon Olleson (eds.), *The Law of International Responsibility* (Oxford: Oxford University Press, 2010), pp. 139–163 at 140; Simma and Pulkowksi, 'Of Planets and the Universe', 510–511.

[61] Simma and Pulkowksi, 'Of Planets and the Universe', 510.

[62] Boon, 'Are Control Tests', 331; Johnstone, 'State Responsibility', 64.

[63] Boon, 'Are Control Tests', 332.

[64] Ibid., 333.

[65] Edith Brown Weiss, 'Invoking State Responsibility in the Twenty-First Century' (2002) 96 *American Journal of International Law* 798–816 at 799.

tendencies: (1) the reduced control capacity of states, and (2) the increased ability of non-state entities to exercise power in international affairs.[66] While arguably it may not be the role and place of the law of state responsibility to attain to actors outside the state (after all it is *state* responsibility we are discussing), the underdevelopment of international responsibility concerning several non-state actors – such as transnational corporations or individuals outside the criminal context – has led to the employment of different legal mechanisms that still point responsibility back to the state. These mechanisms include the lowering of the threshold for the attribution of various control tests, as well as shifting focus to the due diligence obligations of the state.

#### 3.3.1.1 Legal Pluralization

The ILC Articles uphold a traditional understanding of the international legal system. According to this system, states were – if not still are – the primary actors of international law. This makes state responsibility one of the doctrines of international law whose core is based upon 'the interests and needs of territorial states'.[67] The rules on state responsibility do not take sufficiently into account the fact that globalization has brought numerous non-state actors alongside the state, while simultaneously challenging the state. It can easily be argued that 'states have progressively lost ground in their competition with other international actors'.[68] Although international law in certain contextualized settings has been forced to deal with a number of non-state actors such as the individual,[69] international organizations,[70] and corporations,[71] all non-state

[66] Hobe, 'The Era of Globalisation', 662; Mégret, 'Globalization', paras. 31, 33; Becker, *Terrorism and the State*, p. 362; Vincent-Joël Proulx, 'An Uneasy Transition? Linkages between the Law of State Responsibility and the Law Governing the Responsibility of International Organizations', in Maurizio Ragazzi (ed.), *Responsibility of International Organizations: Essays in Memory of Sir Ian Brownlie* (Leiden: Martinus Nijhoff Publishers, 2013), pp. 109–120 at 110.

[67] Frank J. Garcia, 'Globalization and the Theory of International Law' (2005) 11 *International Legal Theory* 9–26 at 11.

[68] David J. Bederman, 'Counterintuiting Countermeasures' (2002) 96 *American Journal of International Law* 817–832 at 829.

[69] For example, international law has admitted legal standing to the individual as a beneficiary in international human rights law and as a duty-holder in international criminal law.

[70] For example, in 2011 the ILC finalized its Draft Articles on the Responsibility of International Organizations. See Report of the ILC on the Work of Its Sixty-third Session, UN Doc. A/66/10 (2011), Chapter V, p. 52.

[71] Bilateral investment treaties in international investment law give corporations the right to raise a claim against states before an international arbitration tribunal. For a general overview of international investment law and general international law, see Anne van Aaken, 'Fragmentation of International Law: The Case of International Investment Law' (2006) XVII *Finnish Yearbook of International Law* 91–130.

actors are explicitly or implicitly excluded from the realm of the law of state responsibility. The ASR lay down that international obligations owed to 'any person or entity other than a State' lie outside the scope of the Articles.[72] From this, it follows that nothing is stipulated with regard to the responsibility of states towards individuals, international organizations, non-governmental organizations, transnational corporations, ad hoc transnational groups, or public–private partnerships. These relationships are left to the rules of primary obligations, and not dealt with under the secondary and general rules on state responsibility.[73] Such a traditional and rigid approach lacks vision, and fails to meet the demands for adaptation ensuing from globalization.[74] Admittedly, there may exist customary rules relating to the relations between state and non-state actors in terms of responsibility although they are not codified in the ASR. Any such rules, however, are often overshadowed by the focus on the ILC Articles.

The approach to leave out non-state actors altogether is regrettable for several reasons. First, their increased leverage in global affairs cannot be disputed. These new actors are not merely passive agents. Instead, they actively seek 'new structures and rules (or different rules) to solve problems, change outcomes, and transform international life'.[75] This diffusion of power or 'legal pluralization', as Jan Klabbers puts it, is widely acknowledged.[76] Hence, states are no longer the sole 'politico-legal authority';[77] non-state entities increasingly challenge the law-making powers of states. In other words, they 'do not merely wish to be involved in monitoring international law, as the traditional role

[72] Article 33 (2) of the ASR.

[73] Dinah Shelton argues that the articles 'could, for example, have stated that the rules on state responsibility apply to breaches of obligations toward nonstate actors as well as toward states'. See Dinah Shelton, 'Righting Wrongs: Reparations in the Articles on State Responsibility' (2002) 96 *American Journal of International Law* 833–856 at 837. Alternatively, the increased importance of non-state actors could have been mentioned in the rules.

[74] See Bederman, 'Counterintuiting', 829. Karl Zemanek sums up the insufficiency of state responsibility: 'State responsibility in its present form which, as indicated by the term, applies only to State to State relations, is, under frequently existing present circumstances, inadequate to assure the observance of international law'. See Karl Zemanek, 'Does the Prospect of Incurring Responsibility Improve the Observance of International Law', in Maurizio Ragazzi (ed.), *International Responsibility Today: Essays in Memory of Oscar Schachter* (Leiden: Martinus Nijhoff Publishers, 2005), pp. 125–134 at 132.

[75] Deborah D. Avant, Martha Finnemore and Susan K. Sell, 'Who Governs the Globe?' in Deborah D. Avant, Martha Finnemore and Susan K. Sell (eds.), *Who Governs the Globe?* (Cambridge: Cambridge University Press, 2010), pp. 1–31 at 1.

[76] Jan Klabbers, 'Setting the Scene', in Jan Klabbers, Anne Peters and Geir Ulfstein (eds.), *The Constitutionalization of International Law* (Oxford: Oxford University Press, 2009), pp. 1–44 at 11–13.

[77] Ibid., p. 12.

of NGOs was, or wish to receive benefits created under international law by states; instead they increasingly demand a seat at the table'.[78]

A similar trend is also discernible with respect to issues of responsibility or liability. The involvement of non-state actors in issues of responsibility and liability under international law is steadily on the rise.[79] They appear 'before international courts in a variety of guises, be it as petitioners..., amicus curiae, or stake-holders in proceedings'.[80] Their increasing participation takes both indirect and direct forms. For example, Palestine, the League of Arab States, and the Organization of Islamic Cooperation participated in the Advisory Opinion Proceedings of the ICJ in the *Palestinian Wall* case.[81] Liberty, a Belgium-based (non-governmental organization) NGO promoting transsexual rights, has appeared before the ECtHR on several occasions, in addition to providing the Court with comparative legal studies.[82] Further, individuals have appeared as amicus curiae on behalf of the accused in ICTY proceedings.[83] A host of arrangements that increasingly replace interstate modes of enforcement, such as international human rights courts and bodies and investment tribunals,[84] also provide non-state actors a formal role or standing. To name a few such arrangements, individuals can lodge complaints directly to the ECtHR for violation of their rights under the European Convention for the Protection of Human Rights and Fundamental

78 Ibid., p. 12.

79 For example, Emmanuel Roucounas notes that the 'share of [non-state actors in] international responsibility/liability under international law is growing'. See 'Non-State Actors: Areas of International Responsibility in Need of Further Exploration', in Maurizio Ragazzi (ed.), *International Responsibility Today: Essays in Memory of Oscar Schachter* (Leiden: Martinus Nijhoff Publishers, 2005), pp. 391–404 at 403.

80 Mégret, 'Globalization', para. 33. Similarly, Dinah Shelton notes that an 'increase in international litigation between states and nonstate actors' has taken place. See Shelton, 'Righting Wrongs', 855. One example is the permission afforded to NGOs by the WTO Appellate Body in the *Shrimps Turtle* case to submit *amicus curiae* briefs. See Appellate Body Report, *United States-Import Prohibition of Certain Shrimp Products*, WT/DS58/AB/R, adopted 6 November 1998. For the issue of *Amicus Curiae* in international judicial bodies, see Lance Bartholomeusz, 'The *Amicus Curiae* before International Courts and Tribunals' (2005) 5 *Non-State Actors and International Law* 209–286.

81 *Legal Consequences of the Construction of a Wall in the Occupied Palestinian Territory*, Advisory Opinion, ICJ Reports 2004, p. 136, paras. 4, 6.

82 See Bartholomeusz, 'The *Amicus Curiae*', 237–241. One case in which Liberty intervened as a third party was *Christine Goodwin* v. *United Kingdom*, Application no. 28957/95, European Court of Human Rights, Grand Chamber, Judgment (11 July 2002).

83 Bartholomeusz, 'The *Amicus Curiae*', 248. For example, the ICTY appointed several *amici curiae* to the Milosevic trial, who officially were designated 'not to represent the accused but to assist in the proper determination of the case'. See *Prosecutor* v. *Milošević*, Case no. IT-02-54-T, ICTY Trial Chamber, Order Inviting Designation of Amicus Curiae (30 August 2001).

84 Mégret, 'Globalization', para. 38.

Freedoms (ECHR),[85] and corporations can vindicate their rights before the International Centre for Settlement of Investment Disputes (ICSID). The International Tribunal for the Law of the Sea (ITLOS) is also open to non-state actors subject to approval by all parties, and the Seabed Disputes Chamber under ITLOS possesses the jurisdiction to settle disputes involving private actors such as natural and juridical persons engaged in the exploration or exploitation of the seabed.[86] International environmental law also provides non-state actors with legal rights. Under the Aarhus and Alpine Conventions, NGOs possess a limited right to trigger non-compliance procedures.[87]

When one takes into account this active role played by non-state entities in the contemporary world, one may come to question the limitation of state responsibility to interstate situations only. This is especially so, given that the argument has been made that, since general international law binds different branches of international law together, why then should responsibility issues – which can be categorized as general international law – not cover other actors as well? Thus, the ILC Articles should better have recognized and should have dealt with the core feature of globalization: 'de-territorialization in which production, culture and ultimately politics are decoupled from the space occupied by States'.[88]

A second reason why non-state actors ought to have been afforded a role within the law of state responsibility relates more to the relevance of state responsibility itself within the international legal order. History has shown that international law in general,[89] and so arguably also state responsibility, has managed to evolve and fulfil various functions in different previous phases of globalization. Ignoring the rise of non-state entities surely guarantees that the law of state responsibility remains uncontested; however, this happens at the

85 European Convention for the Protection of Human Rights and Fundamental Freedoms, Rome, 4 November 1950, in force 3 September 1953, 213 *United Nations Treaty Series* 222.

86 See Part XI, Section 3, Art. 153 (2)(b) of the United Nations Convention on the Law of the Sea (UNCLOS), Montego Bay, 10 December 1982, in force 16 November 1994, 1833 *United Nations Treaty Series* 3; see also Arts. 20(2) and 37 of the Statute of the ITLOS, i.e., Annex VI of the UNCLOS, which gives the same actors access to the Seabed Disputes Chamber.

87 On the role of NGOs in non-compliance procedures and more generally, see Cesare Pitea, 'The Legal Status of NGOs in Environmental Non-Compliance Procedures: An Assessment of Law and Practice', in Pierre-Marie Dupuy and Luisa Vierucci (eds.), *NGOs in International Law: Efficiency in Flexibility?* (Cheltenham: Edward Elgar Publishing, 2008), pp. 181–203.

88 Mégret, 'Globalization', para. 11.

89 Mégret claims that '[o]ne of the lessons to be learnt from globalization historically is the remarkably plastic and adaptable nature of international law, as a law less wedded to certain objectives than it is a supple system of regulation designed to make the most of any epoch's priorities'. Mégret, 'Globalization', para. 45. For more on historic phases of globalization, see ibid., paras. 3–7.

cost of its usefulness. With globalization, fewer and fewer situations calling for responsibility fall squarely under the interstate paradigm of the general law of state responsibility. The refusal to recognize this increasing complexity of responsibility situations will contribute to the marginalization of state responsibility law, and arguably even to a diminished role of the whole international legal order.[90] The ILC's decision to preclude non-state actors as a whole from the ASR thus reflects an overcautiousness which ultimately stands in the way of adaptation and reinvention of the law of state responsibility.[91] The capacity of international law to assign responsibility has traditionally separated it from other branches of regulation. If the general law of state responsibility is unable to respond to the challenges of globalization, international law will find itself at risk of losing one of its 'founding strengths'.[92]

### 3.3.1.2 Blurring of the Public and the Private

Even as states still exist, interact, and consequently continue to create bilateral and multilateral state relations, the ASR choose to turn a blind eye to legal pluralization and to the fact that states do not exercise their powers as independently as they once did. As Abram Chayes and Antonia Handler Chayes claimed in the 1990s: 'modern states are bound in a tightly woven fabric of international agreements, organizations, and institutions that shape their relations with each other and penetrate deeply into their internal economics

90 As Frédéric Mégret notes, 'international law may be tempted to retreat to a *domaine réservé* of inter-State interaction where it is relatively unchallenged… [but where it] may condemn itself to irrelevance'. See Mégret, 'Globalization', para. 40. In a similar fashion, Philip Alston warns that international lawyers and their legal order will be sidetracked by non-state actors if they continue to occupy themselves with 'yesterday's issues and concepts'. See Philip Alston, 'The Myopia of the Handmaidens: International Lawyers and Globalization' (1997) 3 *European Journal of International Law* 435–448 at 447; Jann K. Kleffner also notes that non-state actors challenge 'the fabric of international law' because of 'the statist assumption underlying international law as a whole.' See Jann K. Kleffner, 'The Collective Accountability of Organized Armed Groups for System Crimes', in André Nollkaemper and Harmen van der Wilt (eds.), *System Criminality in International Law* (Cambridge: Cambridge University Press, 2009), pp. 238–269 at 269.

91 International lawyers generally tend to agree on the fact that international law must transform itself in response to the challenges of globalization, instead of remaining unchanged despite the minimal and tardy attention that has been paid to globalization and international law. In 1997, Philip Alston urged international lawyers to pay more attention to globalization and its implications upon international law. See Alston, 'The Myopia', 447. Concerning the consensus that international law should somehow be transformed, see Frank J. Garcia, who holds that '[c]ontemporary globalization both requires and permits the re-casting of international law away from a "society of states" model' ((emphasis omitted), Garcia, 'Globalization', 9).

92 Mégret, 'Globalization', para. 46.

and politics … These considerations in turn reflect profound changes in the international system within which states must act and decide.'[93] Indisputably, globalization has blurred the division between public and private actors and between the public and private spheres in international law.[94] We can discern two different ways in which this blurring has taken place. First, many situations involve a multiplicity of actors acting together as a network rather than as separate entities. With respect to contemporary terrorism, for example, it has been argued that 'the State and the private terrorist group are more readily viewed as functioning on the same plane, as capable of operating in some kind of partnership without necessitating a principal-agent relationship'.[95] This dilemma is exemplified by the United States attack on Afghanistan following the 9/11 terrorist attacks, an attack which was justified on the basis of extending the acts of the terrorists to Afghanistan. Although there was clear proof of some governmental support for the terrorists, no evidence suggested that the Afghan government per se was the 'principal' of the attack and hence should be viewed as the main subject of responsibility.

The example of cyberattacks may help to demonstrate the intrinsic link between various actors in today's globalized world and the difficulty of maintaining the public/private distinction. For example, in August 2008 cyberattacks were launched against Georgian governmental websites as part of an armed conflict that broke out between the Russian Federation and Georgia concerning the latter's breakaway region of South Ossetia.[96] When it comes to cyberattacks, proving state responsibility remains exceedingly difficult. Applying the rules of state responsibility by making use of the effective or

[93] Abram Chayes and Antonia Handler Chayes, *The New Sovereignty: Compliance with International Regulatory Agreements* (Cambridge: Harvard University Press, 1995), p. 26.

[94] Edith Brown Weiss, 'The Rise or the Fall of International Law' (2000) 69 *Fordham Law Review* 345–372 at 351. Jan Klabbers also holds that 'the rigid distinction between public and private spheres is no longer generally accepted'. See Jan Klabbers, 'Reflections on Soft International Law in a Privatized World' (2005) XVI *Finnish Yearbook of International Law* 313–328 at 318; Mégret, 'Globalization', para. 31, claims that '[t]he erosion of sovereignty, in turn, has eroded the public/private divide, one upon which much of the international legal edifice relied'.

[95] Becker, *Terrorism and the State*, p. 156. The author names, for example, Hizbollah, Hamas, and Al-Qaeda as examples of terrorist groups which, despite some reliance on state support, still exist independently of the state. Accordingly, it would be a misconception to describe them as mere state auxiliaries (Ibid., p. 249).

[96] Among others, the National Bank of Georgia and the Department of Defence came under attack. For more information on the attack, see Pia Palojärvi, *A Battle in the Bits and Bytes: Computer Network Attacks and the Law of Armed Conflict. The Erik Castrén Institute Research Reports* 27/2009 (Helsinki: The Erik Castrén Institute, 2009), pp. 43–45.

overall control tests appears badly fitted to cyberattacks, in which speed and anonymity renders it hard to distinguish 'among the actions of terrorists, criminals, and nation states'.[97]

A second way of blurring the public/private distinction is related to the first: the emergence of the 'minimalist state' due to privatization and downsizing, in which private actors take over functions previously performed by governmental actors.[98] To name a few examples of the blurring of the public and private: the UN has received billions in donations from private persons or companies while governmental funding debts grow;[99] private military and security companies are hired by legitimate governments to fight off rebels or to provide governments with training in rule of law;[100] water supply systems are taken over by private companies;[101] and international networks deal with outbreaks of pandemics.[102] Or consider the following scenario: Uruguay passes anti-tobacco legislation for the purpose of reducing smoking. Consequently, the Philip Morris Tobacco Company sues the state of Uruguay before an arbitral tribunal appointed under the ICSID arbitration rules. In order to help Uruguay in its fight against smoking and tobacco, the former New York Mayor Michael Bloomberg donates hundreds of thousands of dollars to help Uruguay in its litigation. Michael Bloomberg, today the World Health Organization (WHO) Global Ambassador for Non-Communicable Diseases, is also known for having donated several hundreds of million USD to the WHO, in order to assist low-income countries in the implementation of an anti-smoking programme as

97 The White House, *The National Strategy to Secure Cyberspace*, February 2003, Washington, p. viii, www.us-cert.gov/reading_room/cyberspace_strategy.pdf (accessed 31 July 2019).

98 Alston, 'The Myopia', 442.

99 Philip Alston reports that, in the autumn of 1997, Ted Turner and George Soros made huge donations to the UN while at the same time the US Congress rejected paying back its debt to the UN. See Alston, 'The Myopia', 445.

100 For example, DynCorp International has been awarded projects in rule of law training of the Haitian National Police as an element of the US contingent of the UN Police mission. See: 'Haiti – Justice: Mission of DynCorp international, for the strengthening of rule of law in Haiti', 11 April 2013, available at: www.haitilibre.com/en/news-8315-haiti-justice-mission-of-dyncorp-international-for-the-strengthening-of-the-rule-of-law-in-haiti.html (accessed 31 July 2019).

101 See e.g., Sylvia Cesar, 'Privatization of Water: Evaluating Its Performance in the Developing World' (2019) 90 *Annals of Public and Cooperative Economics* 5–23.

102 One example is the Global Outbreak Alert and Response Network (GOARN), which was one of the main providers of information upon which the WHO and states relied in response to the 2003 SARS outbreak. See Lisa Clarke, 'Global Health Public-Private Partnerships: Better Protecting against Disease but Creating a Gap in Responsibility under International Law' (2009) XX *Finnish Yearbook of International Law* (2009) 349–372, esp. at 354–355.

well as other global efforts against tobacco.[103] Indeed, as Philip Alston argues, the effects of globalization are most noticeable in the relations between public and private power.[104] Whereas the blurring of the public and private is more blatant in specific branches of international law such as international commercial and trade law, the blending of the two categories has occurred as a general phenomenon in international relations.[105]

Regardless of the increasing difficulty in contemporary international relations of separating acts or actors into the categories of public and private, state responsibility – contrary to what one may expect – is resorted to in situations involving non-state actors.[106] One noticeable way of dealing with non-state actors has been to deconstruct the actor into either the public or private category by stretching the rules of attribution.[107] In fact, numerous efforts have been made to prove how, despite its public focus, the law of state responsibility is still relevant to all kind of actors, both public and private.[108] When these private

[103] Donald G. McNeil Jr, 'Billionaires Back Antismoking Effort', *New York Times*, 24 July 2008 www.nytimes.com/2008/07/24/health/24tobacco.html (accessed 29 July 2019); Bloomberg Philanthropies, Press Release 5 December 2016, 'Michael R. Bloomberg Commits $360 Million to Reduce Tobacco Use – Raising Total Giving on Tobacco Control Efforts to Nearly $1 Billion', www.bloomberg.org/press/releases/michael-r-bloomberg-commits-360-million-reduce-tobacco-use-raising-total-giving-tobacco-control-efforts-nearly-1-billion/ (accessed 29 July 2019).

[104] Alston, 'The Myopia', 442.

[105] Brown Weiss, 'The Rise or the Fall', 352–353. On the question of international commercial law and the blurring of the public and private, see Claire Cutler, *Private Power and Global Authority: Transnational Merchant Law in the Global Political Economy* (Cambridge: Cambridge University Press, 2003).

[106] A similar trend is observed by Rüdiger Wolfrum, who notes that '[t]he issue has become of renewed relevance recently since States seem increasingly to entrust functions to private organizations which traditionally have been carried out by public officials (outsourcing)'. See Rüdiger Wolfrum, 'State Responsibility for Private Actors: An Old Problem of Renewed Relevance' in Maurizio Ragazzi (ed.), *International Responsibility Today: Essays in Memory of Oscar Schachter* (Leiden: Martinus Nijhoff Publishers, 2005), pp. 423–434 at 423. One could reasonably argue that reduced responsibility follows from a diminished governmental sphere due to privatization and outsourcing, as did the United Kingdom in its comments on the ILC Articles on State Responsibility. See Chinkin, 'A Critique of the Public', 390.

[107] The rules of attribution most used to cover non-state actors are Articles 5 and 8 of the ASR. Both rules derive from the state; Article 5 requires that the state has handed over governmental authority, whereas Article 8 sets forth the responsibility of the state in situations where it exercises effective control over the non-state actor. Article 5 of the ASR reads: 'The conduct of a person or entity which is not an organ of the State under article 4 but which is empowered by the law of that State to exercise elements of the governmental authority shall be considered an act of the State under international law, provided the person or entity is acting in that capacity in the particular instance'. Art. 8 of the ASR reads: 'The conduct of a person or group of persons shall be considered an act of a State under international law if the person or group of persons is in fact acting on the instructions of, or under the direction or control of, that State in carrying out the conduct'.

[108] See Chia Lehnardt, 'Private Military Companies and State Responsibility', in Simon Chesterman and Chia Lehnardt (eds.), *From Mercenaries to Market* (Oxford: Oxford

actors act as proxies of governments, state responsibility is the correct legal avenue. But state responsibility is also resorted to when issues of responsibility are unclear, and when it is often and quite rightly asserted that gaps in responsibility exist. Indeed, '[t]he repositioning of the state within wider governance networks of non-state actors ... or state surrogates renders the task of identifying and prosecuting the planners and perpetrators of violations particularly difficult.'[109] Despite these problems, a state-centric view prevails, although state-centrism is recognized as the central problem.[110] Paradoxically, non-state actors are hence dealt with in terms of the state instead of as moving away from the state.

The stretching of the rules of attribution in such situations often extends beyond 'that which their existing conceptual frameworks can logically bear'.[111] To maintain such a legal fiction which fails to correspond to the complex reality ultimately results in a distorted calculus of responsibility. There is thus ample room for the argument that '[t]he more significant the international role of private actors, the less any regime of public law responsibility is able to regulate the effects of globalization'.[112] The ICJ has also noted with concern the tendency to stretch the rules of attribution and to lower the threshold for imputing actions committed by private actors to states. It has expressed concern over the effects of the 'overall control' test which, according to the Court,

University Press, 2007), pp. 139–157; Katja Creutz, *Transnational Privatised Security: The Erik Castrén Institute Research Reports 19/2006* (Helsinki: The Erik Castrén Institute, 2006); Charlotte Beaucillon, Julian Fernandez and Hélène Raspail, 'State Responsibility for Conduct of Private Military and Security Companies', in Francesco Francioni and Natalino Ronzitti (eds.), *War by Contract: Human Rights, Humanitarian Law, and Private Contractors* (Oxford: Oxford University Press, 2011), pp. 396–420; Becker, *Terrorism and the State*.

109 Ruth Jamieson and Kieran McEvoy, 'State Crime by Proxy and Juridical Othering' (2005) 45 *British Journal of Criminology* 504–527 at 505.

110 Susan Marks argues that one characteristic of the criticism of state-centrism is that it 'always seems in some sense to re-centre the state' or 'draw[ing] us back to the state'. For an analysis of state-centrism, see Susan Marks, 'State-Centrism, International Law and the Anxieties of Influence' (2006) 19 *Leiden Journal of International Law* 339–347, esp. at 344, 345. Some authors legitimize the continued focus on state responsibility by arguing that states intentionally use non-state actors to escape legal responsibility. For such an argument, see Ruth Jamieson and Kieran McEvoy, who claim that states use a 'range of strategies...to obfuscate their responsibility in state crime', Jamieson and McEvoy, 'State Crime by Proxy', 504.

111 Becker, *Terrorism and the State*, p. 236.

112 Martti Koskenniemi, 'Doctrines of State Responsibility', in James Crawford, Alain Pellet and Simon Olleson (eds.), *The Law of International Responsibility* (Oxford: Oxford University Press, 2010), pp. 45–51 at 51. A similar argument is presented by Jean D'Aspremont, André Nollkaemper, Ilias Plakokefalos and Cedric Ryngaert, 'Sharing Responsibility Between Non-State Actors and States in International Law: Introduction' (2015) 62 *Netherlands International Law Review* 49–67 at 54.

only broadens the scope of state responsibility beyond its real basis. According to the Court:

> [T]he 'overall control' test has the major drawback of broadening the scope of State responsibility well beyond the fundamental principle governing the law of international responsibility: a State is responsible only for its own conduct, that is to say the conduct of persons acting, on whatever basis, on its behalf ... the 'overall control' test is unsuitable, for it stretches too far, almost to breaking point, the connection which must exist between the conduct of a State's organs and its international responsibility.[113]

Yet, the division into public and private acts is rarely questioned.[114] Few international lawyers outside the field of feminist legal scholarship have expressly demanded a re-evaluation of the distinction. Philip Alston holds that 'there is an urgent need to revisit the distinction that is reflected in international law between the public and private domains'.[115] On the specific issue of responsibility, Tal Becker claims that '[a] conception of responsibility founded on a strict public/private dichotomy rests on weak foundations.'[116] Undeniably, one repercussion of globalization is that one must be prepared to reconsider the conceptual straitjacket of the public/private division. In the view of the present author, such a dichotomized setting fails to take account of the mixture of actors, settings, and processes that characterize globalization. Efforts to force actors into a traditional mould through stretching the rules of attribution simply hinder a conceptual shift towards new modes of thinking.

Furthermore, the division of actors into public or private is no longer a simple matter. As argued above, intermediate categories have begun to emerge due to the difficulty of classifying an entity or an actor as purely public or private. One only needs to think of private companies performing 'public or governmental functions', such as guarding prisons or even working alongside national militaries. Thus, '[t]he intermediate entity gets treated "as though" it were public for some purposes, and "as though" it were private for

[113] *Case Concerning Application of the Convention on the Prevention and Punishment of the Crime of Genocide* (*Bosnia and Herzegovina* v. *Serbia and Montenegro*) (Judgment), ICJ Reports 2007, p. 43, para. 406.

[114] Gordon A. Christenson notices that '[t]he central function of international law in determining this separation has remained unquestioned'. See Gordon A. Christenson, 'Attributing Conduct to the State: Is Anything New?' (1990) 84 *ASIL Proceedings* 51–59 at 52, and also, Gordon A. Christenson, 'The Doctrine of Attribution in State Responsibility', in R. B. Lillich (ed.), *International Law of State Responsibility for Injuries to Aliens* (Charlottesville: University of Virginia Press, 1983), pp. 321–360 at 327.

[115] Alston, 'Myopia', 448.

[116] Becker, *Terrorism and the State*, p. 273.

other purposes.'[117] According to Duncan Kennedy, this clearly demonstrates the collapse of a consensus on categorization.[118] The uncertainty in each case about the factual outcome justifies a critical approach towards the existing public/private division. Although the rules of attribution codified by the ILC are generally accepted as *lex lata*, their application is anything but clear when it comes to the acts of private entities performing public functions. According to the law of state responsibility, when it comes to issues of responsibility private entities performing governmental functions should be considered state actors. But what is considered to be 'governmental' is a culturally dependent notion. Moreover, if a state chooses to outsource a function for decades, is the function still considered to be inherently 'governmental'? It appears clear that 'there is no reliable or constant basis for the distinction'.[119]

Confusion is also discernible with respect to the exact level of control required in order for the acts of de facto organs and agents to be attributable to the state. Indeed, it has been claimed that 'control tests may no longer be fit for the future'.[120] International adjudication seems to be torn between the tests of 'complete control', 'effective control', and 'overall control' as standards for attribution. The ICJ has been criticised for its attribution with respect to the *Bosnian Genocide* case,[121] the ECtHR for the *Saramati and Behrami* cases,[122] and the ICTY in the *Tadić* case.[123] This criticism proves that different understandings prevail about what is to be considered public

[117] Duncan Kennedy, 'The Stages of the Decline of the Public/Private Division' (1981–1982) 130 *University of Pennsylvania Law Review* 1349–1357 at 1351.

[118] Ibid.

[119] Chinkin, 'A Critique', 389.

[120] Boon, 'Are Control Tests', 376.

[121] In the *Bosnian Genocide case*, the ICJ applied a complete dependence test with regard to de facto organs under Art. 4. This has spurred some criticism as to whether the correct rule of attribution was applied. See Jörn Griebel and Milan Plücken, 'New Developments Regarding the Rules of Attribution? The International Court of Justice's Decision in *Bosnia* v. *Serbia*' (2008) 21 *Leiden Journal of International Law* 601–622.

[122] See *Behrami and Behrami* v. *France* and *Saramati v. France, Germany and Norway*, Application Nos 71412/01 and 78166/01, Grand Chamber Decision (2 May 2007). The ECtHR used a test of 'ultimate authority and control', which deviates from ICJ case law and is not to be found in the work of the ILC or the Court's own case law. For comments and criticism, see Kjetil Mujezinović Larsen, 'Attribution of Conduct in Peace Operations: The "Ultimate Authority and Control" Test' (2008) 19 *European Journal of International Law* 509–531; Marko Milanović and Tatjana Papić, 'As Bad as It Gets: The European Court of Human Rights's *Behrami* and *Saramati* Decision and General International Law' (2009) 58 *International and Comparative Law Quarterly* 267–297.

[123] It has been argued that the overall control test applied by the ICTY is not applicable when deciding on issues of state responsibility but only in cases relating to individual criminal responsibility. See *Bosnian Genocide Case*, para. 403.

and what private. The varying perceptions of what constitutes a state for the purposes of determining state responsibility call into question one basic dimension of the law of state responsibility.

### 3.3.1.3 Multiple and Multilevel Actors

The increasing interdependence between states on the one hand, and between states and other actors on the other hand, has triggered questions around how to deal with wrongs committed by multiple actors. Governments are increasingly aware that certain more risky cooperative acts may incur possible charges of complicity if the acts progress badly.[124] However, the fact that states and non-state actors can act in many different configurations with a varying degree of participation makes it difficult to grasp and articulate the problems involved in multiple party responsibility. Moreover, some states may prefer to give the impression of acting alone, although they are acting together with other actors.[125]

It has been argued that the current approach of deconstructing non-state actors to fit into the state responsibility paradigm does not resolve issues of responsibility fairly. Placing full responsibility on the state – when in reality the state does not stand alone behind the wrongful act – is not a satisfactory way of handling situations in which various parties have joined together in the commission of a wrongful act. The application of state responsibility becomes increasingly difficult to realize since the blurring of the public and private spheres creates situations in which no principal–agency relationship exists. But multiple party responsibility is problematic not only when it comes to wrongful acts committed by a mixture of private and public actors. Situations involving several states are also challenging to solve on the basis of the general rules of state responsibility. Thus, one can distinguish two scenarios of multiple party responsibility, both of which the law of state responsibility deals with inadequately: cases involving multiple actors where state responsibility

[124] Aust, *Complicity*, p. ix. One example of governmental awareness or fear of responsibility was uttered in 2013 by Finnish Government Minister of the Environment Ville Niinistö, who stated that it would be unwise for the state-owned company Arctia Shipping to be involved in oil drilling in the Arctic due to the great risk of liability for environmental harm that might occur. See Teppo Ovaskainen and Linda Pelkonen, 'Ville Niinistöltä karut haukut: Seikkaillaan maailmalla veronmaksajien rahoilla', *Uusi Suomi*, 14 October 2013, www.uusisuomi.fi/kotimaa/63183-ville-niinistolta-karut-haukut-seikkaillaan-maailmalla-veronmaksajien-rahoilla (accessed 29 June 2019).

[125] James Crawford notes that 'in practice States hunt in packs but like to be seen as hunting alone'. James Crawford, 'Responsibility of States and Non-State Actors', Speech at the Biennial Conference of the Japanese Association of International Law, Tokyo, 14 May 2005, cited in Aust, *Complicity*, p. 2.

is difficult to justify or fails to constitute the logical form of responsibility, and those situations in which state responsibility is appropriate but unclear or unhelpful.

Numerous examples of multiple party responsibility exist. Cyberattacks or terrorist activity reveal the difficulty of applying state responsibility to a network of actors in which no one party holds a principal position, thus rendering state responsibility unsuitable. Ascribing responsibility solely to Afghanistan for the 9/11 terrorist attacks ignores the issue of Al Qaeda's responsibility; therefore, it seems manifestly distorted. The law and its application appear equally unclear on the question of how to share responsibility among multiple states whose cooperation has amounted to an internationally wrongful act. For example, how is responsibility to be shared among several states for failing to protect wide-ranging fish stocks (such as tuna, that straddle territorial waters) against illegal, unreported, and unregulated fishing?[126]

Outstanding questions on how to share responsibility among different actors become even more pressing when it comes to serious violations of international law. In connection to the United States' practice of extraordinary rendition, one may ask whether and to what degree Poland and Romania are responsible for allowing torture to take place in secret Central Intelligence Agency (CIA) prisons on their territory from 2003 to 2005.[127] And what share of responsibility should Sweden bear for the mistreatment during transport (under US custody) and the subsequent torture and false imprisonment in Egypt of two Egyptian citizens extradited by Swedish authorities back to Egypt in 2001?[128] Another oft-mentioned example of multiple party wrongs is the failure of UN peacekeeping troops to stop the Srebrenica genocide. It is unclear which involved parties should be held responsible: should responsibility be shared between the United Nations and the Netherlands, or should the North Atlantic Treaty Organization (NATO) be held responsible for failing to launch air strikes against Bosnian Serbs?

[126] The Seabed Disputes Chamber at the International Tribunal of the Law of the Sea (ITLOS) was confronted with the precise question of joint liability in advisory proceedings, *Responsibilities and Obligations of States Sponsoring Persons and Entities with Respect to Activities in the Area*, Case No. 17, Advisory Opinion (1 February 2011), see esp. paras. 190–192.

[127] Andy Worthington, 'New Evidence about Prisoners Held in Secret CIA Prisons in Poland and Romania', www.andyworthington.co.uk/2010/08/04/new-evidence-about-prisoners-held-in-secret-cia-prisons-in-poland-and-romania/ (accessed 31 July 2019).

[128] Sweden expelled two Egyptians, Mohammad Alzery and Ahmed Agiza, in 2001 to Egypt. They were transported to Egypt by the CIA and after their arrival were tortured and imprisoned. Several years later, the Swedish government paid them 3 million Swedish Crowns each in reparation for its contribution to the abuses. See Karin Airaksinen, Sveriges Radio, 'Miljonskadestånd till avvisad egyptier', 19 September 2008, sverigesradio.se/sida/artikel.aspx?programid=83&artikel=2324275 (accessed 26 June 2019).

The responsibility of multiple (state) actors is not unknown to the law of state responsibility, although the topic remains underdeveloped.[129] The rules of state responsibility recognize the possibility of multiple state involvement in a single wrong, through either concerted or independent action.[130] First, several states can be co-perpetrators of a wrong; thus, all incur responsibility independently. In such situations, all states are under obligation to provide reparation. The ICJ held in 1992 in the case of *Certain Phosphate Lands in Nauru*, that Nauru was entitled to bring a claim against Australia only, in spite of the fact that Australia had shared administrative authority over Nauru under the Trusteeship system together with two other states.[131] A more recent example of concerted action is the illegal invasion of Iraq by the Coalition Forces in 2003. Second, by virtue of different acts multiple states may contribute to one wrong. Such a view was taken in the *Corfu Channel* case in which it was alleged that the United Kingdom suffered injuries in 1946 due to the separate acts of Yugoslavia and Albania. The former was accused for minelaying, whereas the latter was found responsible for not informing about the danger despite having knowledge of the existence of the mines in the strait.[132] The clarity of multiple state responsibility ends, however, with the ascertaining of joint responsibility for cooperative and cumulative acts.[133]

129 For accounts of so-called shared or joint responsibility and of its furtherance in international law, see André Nollkaemper and Dov Jacobs, 'Shared Responsibility in International Law: A Conceptual Framework' (2012–2013) 34 *Michigan Journal of International Law* 359–438; André Nollkaemper, 'Procedural Aspects of Shared Responsibility in International Adjudication: Introduction' (2013) 4 *Journal of International Dispute Settlement* 277–294; John E. Noyes and Brian D. Smith, 'State Responsibility and the Principle of Joint and Several Liability' (1988) 13 *Yale Journal of International Law* 225–267; Christine Chinkin, 'The Continuing Occupation: Issues of Joint and Several Liability and Effective Control', in Phil Shiner and Andrew Williams (eds.), *The Iraqi War and International Law* (Oxford and Portland, OR: Hart Publishing, 2008), pp. 161–183; Stefan Talmon, 'A Plurality of Responsible Actors: International Responsibility for Acts of the Coalition Provisional Authority in Iraq', in Phil Shiner and Andrew Williams (eds.), *The Iraqi War and International Law* (Oxford and Portland, OR: Hart Publishing, 2008), pp. 185–230.

130 Art. 47(1) of the ASR, which states: 'Where several States are responsible for the same internationally wrongful act, the responsibility of each State may be invoked in relation to that act'. For discussion of the ASR and multiple state responsibility, see Christian Dominicé, 'Attribution of Conduct to Multiple States and the Implication of a State in the Act of Another State', in James Crawford, Alain Pellet and Simon Olleson (eds.), *The Law of International Responsibility* (Oxford: Oxford University Press, 2010), pp. 281–289.

131 *Certain Phosphate Lands in Nauru (Nauru* v. *Australia), Preliminary Objections, Judgment*, ICJ Reports 1992, p. 240, at pp. 258–259, para. 48.

132 *Corfu Channel Case* (*United Kingdom* v. *Albania*)(Judgment), ICJ Reports 1949, p. 4, at 36.

133 These terms are used by Nollkaemper and Jacobs to denote, respectively, joint responsibility of co-authored wrongs and for wrongs composed of different breaches. See Nollkaemper and Jacobs, 'Shared Responsibility in International Law', 368–369.

The rules embodied in the ASR are built on the premise that the contribution of each participating state can be separately identified. The basis of state responsibility is the principle of independent responsibility; that is, the responsibility of a state for its *own* acts. Moreover, state responsibility is exclusive, which means that one act can be attributed only to one actor. It is generally acknowledged that '[d]ual attribution is rare.'[134] Hence, multiple state responsibility works only when one wrongful act with many perpetrators can be split into causally established individual responsibilities. But many concerted acts nowadays are indivisible into separately identifiable acts: either because they are in fact truly common in nature, or because it may be difficult to show the connection of each state to the wrong. In such situations, responsibility is shared rather than composed of many independent acts calling for multiple instances of independent responsibility. Nonetheless, the concept of shared responsibility remains underdeveloped within the state responsibility framework.[135] The lack of a conceptual understanding of shared responsibility has also hindered determinations of responsibility and thus has hampered the efforts of injured parties to seek relief. In the *Saddam Hussein* case, the applicant brought a complaint against twenty-one states for the illegal invasion of Iraq and his capture. However, the ECtHR considered the inability of the applicant to connect each respondent state with a specific wrong as preventing any findings of responsibility.[136]

In reality, splitting collective acts into many instances of individual responsibility falls short of the complex nature of concerted action, and may give rise to accountability gaps or a distorted calculus of responsibility. Instead of looking for more nuanced solutions to the issue of shared responsibility, state responsibility is unable to reach multiple actors in a precise way due to its all-or-nothing character: a state is either considered 100 per cent responsible for a wrong, or it is not. For example, such an approach leaves it unclear whether, and to what degree, a state that contributes to an internationally wrongful act perpetrated by another state, without committing a wrong itself, is to be held responsible. To cite one example, Italy made its airports available to fighters involved in the illegal use of force against Iraq in 2003. As a result, is Italy to be held responsible for the illegal invasion? The deconstruction of multifaceted cooperation into a dichotomy of responsible/not responsible seems too simplistic.

134 Nollkaemper and Jacobs, 'Shared Responsibility in International Law', 383.

135 Ibid., 363; Nollkaemper, 'Procedural Aspects of Shared Responsibility', 268. For a critique of the lack of shared responsibility in international law, see also Yossi Dahan, Hanna Lerner and Fain Milman-Sivan, 'Shared Responsibility and the International Labour Organization' (2012–2013) 34 *Michigan Journal of International Law* 675–743.

136 *Saddam Hussein v. Albania and Others*, Application no. 23276/04, European Court of Human Rights, Decision as to Admissibility (14 March 2006).

A potential consequence of such deconstruction is one state being held solely responsible, whereas other states or entities who participated in the wrong act are let off the hook. Contribution to or complicity in an internationally wrongful act committed by another state is dealt with under the ASR, which recognize that a state that aids or assists,[137] directs or controls,[138] or coerces[139] another state in the commission of an internationally wrongful act incurs responsibility for implication in the wrongful act. However, many questions remain unanswered. The question of the normative basis for shared responsibility is left open, and no specific rules exist for how to allocate responsibility and reparations among the various involved states.[140] In addition, international practice regarding shared responsibility is scarce and unclear.

The tendency to construe non-state activity in terms of state responsibility has been challenged by the search for specific responsibility systems for different non-state actors. For a limited number of intentionally criminal acts, individuals can now be held responsible on their own account under international law. In addition, a system is in place for the responsibility of international organizations. This would seemingly make it easier to resolve the question of wrongful acts involving multiple actors or layered actors. If one takes the Srebrenica genocide as an example, the following options for ascribing responsibility are possible: the state of Serbia for failing to prevent genocide, the Netherlands and the United Nations for evicting persons from the UN compound in Srebrenica, and single individuals such as Mlatko Radić for the commission of genocide. Other avenues of accountability outside the international legal order could also be pursued.

Nevertheless, the rules on state responsibility are silent as to its relationship to other avenues of responsibility.[141] Although complementarity in general is assumed,[142] the lack of norms regarding the interaction between different

[137] Art. 16 of the ASR. See Report of the ILC on the Work of Its Fifty-third Session, UN Doc. A/56/10 (2001), Chapter IV, at 29. For the text of the articles with commentaries thereto, see, p. 59 *et seqq*.

[138] Art. 17 of the ASR.

[139] Art. 18 of the ASR.

[140] Nollkaemper and Jacobs, 'Shared Responsibility in International Law', esp. 390–391.

[141] The only rule on the relation of state responsibility to other responsibility regimes is found in Article 58 of the ASR. It reads: 'These articles [on state responsibility] are without prejudice to any question of the individual responsibility under international law of any person acting on behalf of the State'.

[142] For proponents of the complementarity view see, for example, Antônio Augusto Cançado Trindade, 'Complementarity between State Responsibility and Individual Responsibility for Grave Violations of Human Rights: The Crime of State Revisited', in Maurizio Ragazzi (ed.), *International Responsibility Today: Essays in Memory of Oscar Schachter* (Leiden: Martinus Nijhoff Publishers, 2005), pp. 253–269; Bianchi, 'State Responsibility and Criminal Liability', pp. 16–24;

responsibility regimes makes dilution of responsibility not only possible, but also likely.[143] Therefore, it is hardly surprising that actors involved in multi-level breaches have reacted to allegations by denying responsibility and have simply passed the buck. The extension of responsibility to other international legal subjects has nevertheless opened the door to the idea that responsibility can truly be shared and that it follows not only from one's own acts, but also from the acts of others. Article 1 of the Articles on the Responsibility of International Organizations (ARIO) recognizes that an international organization can be held responsible for 'an internationally wrongful act'.[144] Thus, the responsibility of an international organization can stem from wrongful acts of its own and 'conduct other than its own'.[145] Whether or not 'responsibility might flow from conduct that itself need not be wrongful but that triggers responsibility because it contributes to wrongful conduct of another state or organization' remains unclear.[146] Still, further consideration is needed concerning how the law of state responsibility, together with other responsibility and accountability mechanisms, should respond to the increased interdependence and cooperation of the globalized world.[147]

#### 3.3.1.4 The Fragmented State

State responsibility is grounded in the idea of a unitary state. Yet, ascribing responsibility upon the unitary state seems problematic, or even wrong, in cases where the state is fragmented. As a responsibility system that collectivizes the legal consequences following from a breach of an international legal obligation, state responsibility can be described as overinclusive. The so-called fairness complaint is grounded in the fact that state responsibility as a collective responsibility system does not 'limit the group to the aggregate of those

W. Michael Reisman, 'Legal Responses to Genocide and Other Massive Violations of Human Rights' (1996) 59 *Law & Contemporary Problems* 75–80; André Nollkaemper and Harmen van der Wilt, 'Conclusions and Outlook', in André Nollkaemper and Harmen van der Wilt (eds.), *System Criminality in International Law* (Cambridge: Cambridge University Press, 2009), pp. 338–353 at 347.

143 For scholars who do not take complementarity for granted, see Espiell, 'International Responsibility'; Simpson, *Law, War & Crime*; Franck, 'Individual Criminal Liability'; and Creutz, 'International Responsibility'.

144 See Articles on the Responsibility of International Organizations (ARIO), in the Report of the ILC on the Work of Its Sixty-third Session (2011), UN Doc. A/66/10, Chapter V. The General Assembly took note of the Articles in UNGA Res. 66/100, 9 December 2011.

145 Nollkaemper and Jacobs, 'Shared Responsibility in International Law', 383. See also commentary to Art. 1 of the ARIO, para. 4.

146 Nollkaemper and Jacobs, 'Shared Responsibility in International Law', 383.

147 One such example is the elaboration of 'The Guiding Principles on Shared Responsibility in International Law' by the SHARES project.

individuals whose action or inaction culminated in atrocity'.[148] In this sense, it can be described as a 'crude' form of responsibility.[149] All members of a state together bear responsibility, irrespective of whether or not they contributed to the wrongs. Mark Drumbl notes that '[d]amages ultimately pass through to and are borne by all group members, regardless of how bravely they resisted, how servilely they complied, how eagerly they killed, or how much hurt they endured'.[150] Thus, the problem with state responsibility is that it holds each and every citizen responsible, irrespective of a causal connection to the wrongs.

The problem of the overly inclusive nature of state responsibility becomes manifest in situations of internal wrongdoing. Small collectives or groups within the state, which de facto can often be liable for the commission of genocide, do not alone stand responsible for the actions. For example, the Rwandan genocide was perpetrated mainly by Hutus against Tutsis, the ethnic groups constituting the Rwandan people. Still, the law of state responsibility does not differentiate between collectives within the state. Accordingly, if the acts of the Hutus can be ascribed to the Rwandan state, then the state as a whole becomes responsible for the genocide. This means that, for international legal purposes, the ethnic group that actually is the victim of the genocide becomes co-responsible. This clearly testifies to the overinclusive character of state responsibility: people who in no way participated in the wrongdoing are implicated as having partaken in the atrocities. Because the same argument applies in any commission of an internationally wrongful act, the consequences of overinclusiveness become absurd in situations where the wrongful act was targeted against one's own population. Clearly, there are never situations in every citizen of a state participates in the commission of an internationally wrongful act, but when the actual victim is assimilated with the perpetrator, something has gone manifestly wrong. Indeed, it would seem 'deeply inequitable to hold *all* Cambodians, Rwandans, or Sudanese responsible on the basis of citizenship for the crimes the state committed internally'.[151] The law is simply unable to deal effectively with the victims of internal wrongdoings, and in a sense it 'juridically others' them.[152] Victims of internal atrocities are thus removed from the normal application of the law.

148 Mark Drumbl, 'Collective Responsibility and Postconflict Justice', in Tracy Isaacs and Richard Vernon (eds.), *Accountability for Collective Wrongdoing* (New York: Cambridge University Press, 2011), pp. 23–60 at 44. For an in-depth discussion of the fairness complaint, see Crawford and Watkins, 'International Responsibility', and Liam Murphy, 'International Responsibility', in Samantha Besson and John Tasioulas (eds.), *The Philosophy of International Law* (Oxford: Oxford University Press, 2010), pp. 299–315.

149 Drumbl, 'Collective Responsibility', 44.

150 Ibid.

151 Ibid. (emphasis in original).

152 For more on 'juridical othering', see Jamieson and McEvoy, 'State Crime by Proxy'.

The law of state responsibility is thus indifferent towards the fragmented state, to smaller groups or collectives that exist within the state. However, as has been explained above, states are no longer the only actors that can violate international legal obligations, and thus commit internationally wrongful acts. The same holds true on the internal level; wrongful acts can be committed by ethnic groups against other ethnic groups within a single state, as occurred in the Rwandan genocide and during the Yugoslav war. Armed groups such as the Kosovo Liberation Army can commit atrocities within a state, and so forth.[153] Two different situations of a fragmented state can be discerned: either there is a complete absence of governmental power, or various entities compete for governmental authority. In both scenarios, however, state responsibility fails to offer adequate solutions.[154] The lack of a unitary state in control of a territory obscures the potential of state responsibility. When no actor can be identified as holding the executive power over a state's territory, allocating responsibility becomes utterly difficult. Similarly, when rebels manage to take over the daily administration over a territory, '[t]he value of state responsibility as an accountability mechanism is considerably diminished'.[155]

In the case of *Georgia* v. *Russia*,[156] Georgia argued that it had no control over the separatist regions of Abkhazia and South Ossetia. This raises the question of who bears responsibility for human rights violations committed by de facto regimes. Once again, the traditional response of public international law remains state-centred in a situation in which the state is demonstrably weakened. Since in general the international legal system refrains from assigning responsibility to groups, a common approach is to attempt to implicate another state as being responsible for the acts of the rebels. Thus, one tries 'to secure accountability by passing the baton to the so-called sponsoring state'.[157] Indeed, in many situations yet another (third) state might be involved in the activities of rebels or separatists.[158] However, proving such a connection is difficult and paved with ambiguity as to the necessary level of control over the rebels required to incur responsibility. If no sponsorship connection can

[153] For the question of developing a responsibility regime for organized armed groups, see Kleffner, 'The Collective Accountability'.

[154] Phoebe Okowa, 'State and Individual Responsibility in Internal Conflicts: Contours of an Evolving Relationship' (2009) XX *Finnish Yearbook of International Law* 143–188 at 168.

[155] Ibid., 169.

[156] *Application of the International Convention on the Elimination of All Forms of Racial Discrimination (Georgia* v. *Russian Federation)* Application Instituting Proceedings, ICJ Reports 2008, p. 4, at 42, para. 81.

[157] Okowa, 'State and Individual Responsibility', 169.

[158] This is precisely what Georgia claimed. See *Application of the International Convention on the Elimination of All Forms of Racial Discrimination (Georgia* v. *Russian Federation), Application Instituting Proceedings*, ICJ Reports 2008, p. 4, at 42, para. 81.

be found, the question of responsibility is left open. For example, in the case of *Armed Activities on the Territory of the Congo*,[159] the ICJ concluded that the acts of Ugandan rebel groups could not be attributed to the Democratic Republic of Congo.

The ASR recognize and deal with the problem of the fragmented state to a certain extent, which nevertheless is inadequate if one looks at international practice. The rules establish that insurrectional movements can retroactively become responsible for their wrongful acts if they seize power over the state in question at a later stage.[160] Their responsibility is thus dependent upon their post-conflict status rather than on the fact that they have done harm, a line of reasoning which seems difficult to sustain. The ASR further recognize that in situations of 'absence or default' of governmental power, persons or groups may in fact take over the exercise of statal functions.[161] Nevertheless, the responsibility for such acts is still ascribed to the state instead of to those perpetrating the acts; that is, the rebels or other groups acting in the absence of governmental officials. The unresponsiveness of the international legal system as a whole, and state responsibility in particular, towards other entities within the state makes the law of state responsibility irrelevant in many cases. The sheer rise in the number of wrongdoings and atrocities committed within a state has thus triggered the search for and attraction to other forms of responsibility and accountability mechanisms.

### 3.3.2 *Breach Threshold*

#### 3.3.2.1 The Importance of Wrongfulness

The law of the responsibility of states as articulated by the ASR is based upon the existence of an internationally wrongful act. This element is fundamental, irrespective of the role one assigns to fault in the theories of responsibility in

[159] *Armed Activities on the Territory of Congo (Democratic Republic of the Congo v. Uganda) Judgment*, ICJ Reports 2005, p. 168, at 269, para. 304.

[160] Article 10 of the ASR reads:

1. 'The conduct of an insurrectional movement which becomes the new government of a State shall be considered an act of that State under international law.
2. The conduct of a movement, insurrectional or other, which succeeds in establishing a new State in part of the territory of a pre-existing State or in a territory under its administration shall be considered an act of the new State under international law.
3. This article is without prejudice to the attribution to a State of any conduct, however related to that of the movement concerned, which is to be considered an act of that State by virtue of articles 4 to 9.'

[161] Art. 9 of the ASR.

international law. There are, however, several intertwined considerations that make it valid to question the significance of wrongfulness in the law of state responsibility. First, although interstate relations are both portrayed as cooperative and interdependent on the one hand, and as adversarial on the other, the law of state responsibility embodies mainly the latter. Thus there exists a discrepancy between the character of international relations and the way in which international law deals with violations of international legal obligations. Moreover, the effect of an adversarial-based system of state responsibility on compliance can be questioned, since it is frequently maintained that repercussions grounded in reproach fail to increase compliance. A second and connected aspect to be considered is that recent developments have demonstrated a desire by many states to depart from the idea of wrongfulness, or at least to diminish its importance. As a result, less-adversarial avenues have been created in order to achieve increased compliance. Third, even if one accepts wrongfulness as a basis for state responsibility, international legal obligations are not always as clear-cut as they seem. As a result, it is difficult to perceive claims in terms of '"right" versus "wrong"',[162] a dichotomy inherent in the current structure of state responsibility premised on the existence of an internationally wrongful act.

#### 3.3.2.2 Wrongfulness and Its Adversarial Nature

Before proceeding to the arguments against an adversarial system of responsibility in international law, one must start with establishing the basis for the claim that state responsibility – along with its constituent element, the internationally wrongful act – possesses an adversarial or confrontational character. We can trace two different motivations for this perception. First, as has been argued above, state responsibility has a private law foundation in tort law.[163] Accordingly, the system is built upon the situation in which two states are pitted against each other, wherein one accuses the other of a violation of its rights. Although the law of state responsibility admits to other configurations as well, this is nevertheless the archetypal situation, which consequently explains why the law of state responsibility is considered an adversarial system.

A second point relevant to the adversarial character of state responsibility is the suggestion implied in labelling an unlawful act as 'wrongful'. There is a clear implication that the act is more than against the law, it is also to be considered reproachable. Thus, one can argue that, in addition to being unlawful,

[162] Martin Dixon, *Textbook on International Law* (7th ed., Oxford: Oxford University Press, 2013), p. 13.

[163] See Section 2.3, 'Responsibility at the Crossroads'.

the act is morally wrong.[164] Admittedly, the International Law Commission's usage of the term 'internationally *wrongful* act' is not intended to be used to imply this conclusion. According to the Commission, the term 'internationally wrongful act' covers the violation of all kinds of international obligations, irrespective of fault.[165] As a consequence, this term includes both violations that can be perceived as morally reproachable and those that arguably lack such an element altogether. For example, the obligation not to torture contains a moral dimension lacking in the obligation of a state to grant duty-free admission of professional equipment necessary for carrying out business activity,[166] or in the case of an accidental trespassing of an airplane into foreign airspace.[167] Yet, calling all violations 'wrongful' imbues the law of state responsibility with a moral overtone that may or may not be called for.[168] It invests the law of state responsibility with the assumption that one state has behaved immorally, which calls for reproach and response by another state.

Moving on to the discussion on the demerits of the adversarial nature of wrongfulness, one must necessarily start by comparing the character of the international legal system with that of the law of state responsibility. To begin with, it must be noted that the nature of the international community and its legal system is generally not portrayed as 'adversarial'; instead, quite the opposite is the case. International relations may historically have been more antagonistic than cooperative in character, but with the rise of international institutions in the early twentieth century, along with the rise of globalization in the new millennium, this no longer holds true.[169] In other words, cooperation and interdependence mark the contemporary international legal system.

The idea of cooperation cannot be excluded even from the branch of dispute settlement. Some scholars have paradoxically argued that the specific field of international dispute settlement actually is built on the idea of cooperation.[170]

164 Gertrude E. M. Anscombe, 'Modern Moral Philosophy' (1958) 33 *Philosophy* 1–16 at 14–15.

165 See Commentary to Art. 2 of the ASR, para. 10.

166 See North American Free Trade Agreement (NAFTA), adopted 17 December 1992, in force 1 January 1994, 32 *International Legal Materials*, 605 (1993), Article 305 (1)(a).

167 This has been argued also by Alain Pellet, who notes that 'a genocide cannot be compared with a breach of a trade agreement; it is, by its very nature, different in kind'. See Pellet, 'Can a State', 434.

168 Because state responsibility attaches to both ordinary and more serious violations, one can also make the contrary argument that the usage of the term 'wrongful' actually downplays the moral implications connected to serious violations of international law. See discussion in Sections 3.4.1 'Functional Diversity' and 3.4.2.2, 'Marginalization in Serious Violations of International Law'.

169 Martin Dixon, for example, explicitly holds that '[i]nternational law is not an "adversarial" system of law.' See Dixon, *Textbook*, p. 12.

170 Anne Peters, 'International Dispute Settlement: A Network of Cooperational Duties' (2003) 14 *European Journal of International Law* 1–34 at 2, 9.

This cooperative view makes it difficult to justify an adversarial system – such as the state responsibility regime – as the main legal avenue along which to proceed in cases of wrongs. In the international system, wrongfulness may not be the primary interest of states. The focus may lie elsewhere. Mohammed Bedjaoui argues that 'states are above all concerned with the reparation of loss or injury, and much less with what is in this context the secondary point as to whether the State causing the damage acted in a legitimate or a wrongful way, or exercised reasonable care in carrying on its activities'.[171] International practice testifies to the truth of this statement, notwithstanding the proliferation of international courts and tribunals in recent decades. Despite the rising trend of legal adjudication, it is still frequently claimed that states are reluctant to invoke state responsibility by formal means, and that as a consequence the settlement of disputes operates to a large extent behind the scenes.[172] Thus, in order to avoid the embarrassment of shaming judicial arenas and international adjudication, states resolve their legal disputes and claims through politico–diplomatic means. As Anne Peters admits, '[w]estphalian elements persist in the form of mere horizontal, interstate cooperation in political dispute settlement'.[173] Claims for reparation of loss and injuries often override the desire to seek declaratory judgments on wrongfulness. Even disputes subjected to international adjudication may eventually be resolved through other means. For example, Finland did not pursue the *Great Belt* case before the International Court of Justice in order to receive the court's judgment on whether Denmark was in violation of its obligations.[174] Instead, what mattered in the case was that the dispute was settled by means of compensation for the Finnish losses.

Wrongfulness not only goes against the character of the international system, but its ability to maintain or augment compliance can also be questioned. This, despite the fact that the public might be drawn to configurations where the

[171] Bedjaoui, 'Responsibility of States', 214. A similar point is also made by Geir Ulfstein, who claims that 'states are not likely to take each other to an international court'. See Geir Ulfstein, 'Reflections on Institutional Design – Especially Treaty Bodies', in Jan Klabbers and Åsa Wallendahl (eds.), *Research Handbook on the Law of International Organizations* (Cheltenham: Edward Elgar Publishing, Cheltenham, 2011), pp. 431–447 at 440.

[172] Tullio Scovazzi argues that the reluctance to lodge formal claims of responsibility may also have to do with concerns about creating precedents that 'could play against them in future cases'. He argues that this holds true, for example, with respect to claims of transboundary harm. See Tullio Scovazzi, 'Some Remarks on International Responsibility in the Field of Environmental Protection', in Maurizio Ragazzi (ed.), *International Responsibility Today: Essays in Memory of Oscar Schachter* (Leiden: Martinus Nijhoff Publishers, 2005), pp. 209–222 at 215.

[173] Peters, 'International Dispute Settlement', 33.

[174] *Passage through the Great Belt (Finland* v. *Denmark), Application Instituting Proceedings*, 17 May 1991, ICJ Reports 1990–1991, p. 16.

wrongdoer is publicly exposed for having committed international violations.[175] In order to make implementation of obligations more effective, many international institutions have created procedures that are based on cooperative forms of dealing with non-conformity other than an adversarial procedure.[176] This holds true especially within the branches of international environmental law, human rights and arms control.[177] Already in 1995, Abram Chayes and Antonia Handler Chayes drew attention to the need to replace coercive sanctions with 'managerial model[s]' of compliance which are based on 'a cooperative, problem-solving approach instead of a coercive one'.[178] The preference for mechanisms of so-called soft responsibility increasingly finds support in the 'focus on a return to full compliance, with assistance if necessary'.[179] Non-compliance procedures have become commonplace, especially in multilateral environmental treaties, because they are non-confrontational and focus on 'prevention rather than reparation'.[180] An example of the successful functioning of a non-compliance procedure can be found in the case of Russia's agreeing to comply with the Montreal Protocol on the Ozone Layer in exchange for financial assistance.[181]

175 For example, Steve Charnovitz argues that the WTO Dispute Settlement bodies 'should convene a public hearing where the government would be asked to explain its delay, and other governments and concerned private economic and social actors could respond to those excuses. The public likes this sort of adversarial theatre, and the ensuing embarrassment could elicit compliance'. See an updated version www.worldtradelaw.net/articles/charnovitzlastresort.pdf (accessed 31 July 2019) to Steve Charnovitz, 'The WTO's Problematic "Last Resort" against Noncompliance' (2002) 57 *The Swiss Review of International Economic Relations* 409–440.

176 For example, Jessica Templeton and Pia Kohler note with respect to MEAs that '[p]unitive measures have fallen out of favour in recent years'. See Jessica Templeton and Pia Kohler, 'Implementation and Compliance under the Minamata Convention on Mercury' (2014) 23 *Review of European Community & International Environmental Law* 211–220 at 214.

177 Ulfstein, 'Reflections on Institutional Design', 440; Shelton, 'Righting Wrongs', 855; Chayes and Handler Chayes, *The New Sovereignty*, p. 3.

178 Chayes and Handler Chayes, *The New Sovereignty*, p. 3.

179 Kirsten Schmalenbach, 'Dispute Settlement', in Jan Klabbers and Åsa Wallendahl (eds.), *Research Handbook on the Law of International Organizations* (Cheltenham: Edward Elgar Publishing, 2011), pp. 251–284 at 259.

180 Geir Ulfstein, Thilo Marauhn and Andreas Zimmerman, 'Introduction', in Geir Ulfstein, Thilo Marauhn and Andreas Zimmerman (eds.), *Making Treaties Work: Human Rights, Environment and Arms Control* (Cambridge: Cambridge University Press, 2007), pp. 3–12 at 9–10. Similarly, Dinah Shelton acknowledges the trend towards compliance procedures. According to Shelton, '[i]nterstate issues of compliance and breach are increasingly handled through nonconfrontational procedures within international organizations and treaty bodies'. See Shelton, 'Righting Wrongs', 854.

181 See Jacob Werksman, 'Compliance and Transition: Russia's Non-Compliance Tests the Ozone Regime' (1996) 56 *Zeitschrift für ausländisches öffentliches Recht und Völkerrecht* 750–773. The Montreal Protocol on Substances that Deplete the Ozone Layer, Montreal, 16 September 1987, in force 1 January 1989, 1522 *United Nations Treaty Series* 3.

It appears to be widely accepted by various actors that non-adversarial means of settling disputes generate win-win situations that are preferable to end results in which one party triumphs and the other is admitted to the hall of shame.[182] Few states in today's globalized world of transnational networks can afford the potential disruption in international relations that adversarial dispute resolution can cause.[183] Arguably then, non-adversarial processes are more suitable than the law of state responsibility for handling nonconformity, at least in certain specific fields of international law. The rigidity of the idea of wrongfulness is not supported by state practice,[184] which often evinces the search for alternatives to the confrontational basis of the law of state responsibility. Findings of state responsibility are inferior to the substantive goals to be achieved within specific branches of international law.

#### 3.3.2.3 Difficulty of Determining Wrongfulness

Another implication of the term 'an internationally *wrongful* act' is that the actor in question has the option of choosing between behaviour which qualifies as legal, and unlawful conduct. However, such a construction of state behaviour is not always possible; it is not always easy to tell when one sees 'wrongs' in international law.[185] As Martin Dixon states: '[i]t sometimes seems that many of the disputes between states occur precisely because the rule of international law governing their conduct is not clear, rather than that one state is deliberately behaving illegally.'[186] The international obligations may simply be too vague to make clear how a state is to fulfil the obligation in question.

182 For critical accounts of non-compliance procedures, see e.g., Jan Klabbers, 'Compliance Procedures', in Daniel Bodansky, Jutta Brunnée and Ellen Hey (eds.), *The Oxford Handbook of International Environmental Law* (Oxford: Oxford University Press, 2007), pp. 995–1009; Martti Koskenniemi, 'The Fate of Public International Law: Between Technique and Politics' (2007) 1 *The Modern Law Review* 1–30 at 13.

183 Peters, 'International Dispute Settlement', 6. One example of the constraint interstate litigation places on the relations between states is the dispute between two Nordic countries before the ICJ, *Finland* v. *Denmark in the Great Belt* case. Martti Koskenniemi, one of the counsels for Finland in the case, noted in the aftermath of the case that the prolongation of the dispute had become a substantial encumbrance upon the political relations between Finland and Denmark [Siltakiistan pitkittymisestä oli tullut olennainen rasite Suomen ja Tanskan välisille poliittisille suhteille] (Martti Koskenniemi, 'Ison-Beltin siltariita', *Lakimies* 8/1992, 1300–1332 at 1331).

184 Jean-Marc Sorel, 'The Concept of "Soft Responsibility"?' in James Crawford, Alain Pellet and Simon Olleson (eds.), *The Law of International Responsibility* (Oxford: Oxford University Press, 2010), pp. 165–171 at 170.

185 For more on 'seeing wrongs', see Hugo Strandberg, *Escaping My Responsibility: Investigations into the Nature of Morality* (Frankfurt am Main: Peter Lang, 2009).

186 Dixon, *Textbook*, p. 15. In similar terms Jutta Brunnée notices that 'the primary rules of general international law are often too open-textured to lend themselves easily to determinations of

Although vagueness can be blamed on the design features of primary obligations, the rigidity of wrongfulness as a breach threshold only serves to accentuate the problematic character of imprecise international obligations.

Unclear or open-ended international obligations appear, for example, in the field of international economic, social and cultural rights, international environmental law and in the law of the sea. For instance, the International Covenant on Economic, Social and Cultural Rights (ICESCR) contains a number of vague expressions which make decisions regarding violations and justiciability in general difficult.[187] How does one determine, for example, when provisions containing concepts such as 'progressive realization' or 'to the maximum of its available resources' have been violated? For example, the determination of when the right to 'the highest attainable standard of physical and mental health' (ICESCR, Art. 12) has been violated cannot be stated in general terms. Rather, the determination 'will depend on the conditions prevailing in a particular State party'.[188] The threshold of wrongfulness thus varies from case to case. International environmental law has also frequently faced charges of containing vague and uncertain obligations. The United Nations Framework Convention for Climate Change (UNFCCC) is often cited as an example. It has been asserted that, in the absence of a commitment to the Kyoto Protocol as well, the UNFCCC is incapable of providing the grounds for state liability.[189] Similarly, the delimitation of maritime boundaries has been unclear in the law of the sea. The notions of 'continental shelf' and 'Exclusive Economic Zone' (EEZ) have remained imprecise. The provisions in UNCLOS III state: '[t]he delimitation of the continental shelf between States with opposite or adjacent coasts shall be affected by agreement on the basis of international law, as referred to in Article 38 of the Statute of the International Court of Justice, in order to achieve an equitable solution.'[190] Such vagueness, however, causes problems – especially with regard to the determination of

wrongfulness'. See Brunnée, 'International Legal Accountability', 27. James Crawford and Jeremy Watkins also note that in a large portion of cases that are brought before international arbitral tribunals the primary goal is the 'clarification of a confused or contested legal situation'. See Crawford and Watkins, 'International Responsibility', 292.

187 Similarly, Jutta Brunnée holds that open-ended rules do have the 'ability to influence international environmental policy', but that their vagueness rather affects 'their usefulness in litigation context'. See Brunnée, 'International Legal Accountability', 27.

188 See the Committee on Economic, Social and Cultural Rights, 22nd session, General Comment No. 14 (2000) on the right to the highest attainable standard of health, UN Doc. E/C.12/2000/4 (11 August 2000), para. 12.

189 Michael G. Faure and André Nollkaemper, 'International Liability as an Instrument to Prevent and Compensate for Climate Change' (2007) 43A *Stanford Journal of International Law* 123–179 at 143.

190 Art. 83(1) of the UNCLOS.

a possible breach. According to Churchill and Lowe, 'their wording is sufficiently imprecise for the provisions to be capable of application in more than one way'.[191] The vagueness or indeterminacy of international legal rules exists at the cost of compliance: '[i]ndeterminate normative standards not only make it harder to know what conformity is expected, but also make it easier to justify noncompliance.'[192] Thus, the issue at hand is not always about the intention to behave wrongfully, but instead it concerns the lack of certainty when it comes to the precise obligation.[193] Hence, a bifurcation of state behaviour into categories of 'right' or 'wrong' becomes useless in such circumstances, since 'there may be no objectively "right" answer'.[194] A further reason behind difficulties in assessing compliance can be evidentiary issues in connection with the covert nature of some activities.[195] Clinging to the concept of wrongfulness in such instances seems of little value.

## 3.4 DIFFICULTIES PERTAINING TO CONTENT

The content of state responsibility relates to the legal consequences ensuing upon states following the commission of an internationally wrongful act. In terms of functionality, this means that two separate but connected aspects of this concept must be explored: first, whether the consequences stipulated in the ASR reflect the explicit and implicit functions of state responsibility; and second, whether these rules operate to such an extent that the functions can be realized in practice.

### 3.4.1 *Functional Diversity*

When academics and practitioners discuss concrete cases of state responsibility, opinions may differ over the question of whether state responsibility has materialized or not. Behind such disagreement lie not inconclusive facts or evidence, but rather varying perceptions of state responsibility and its true function(s). On the one hand, the view can be sustained that state responsibility is primarily about reparation for injuries in which one state, due to its internationally wrongful act against another state or other states, is obliged to provide reparation. This represents the traditional private law origin of the state responsibility project. Indeed,

[191] Robin R. Churchill and Alan Vaughan Lowe, *The Law of the Sea* (2nd ed., Manchester: Manchester University Press, 1988), p. 159.

[192] Thomas M. Franck, 'Legitimacy in the International System' (1988) 82 *American Journal of International Law* 705–759 at 714.

[193] Dixon, *Textbook*, p. 13.

[194] Ibid.

[195] With respect to terrorism, the opposite is claimed by Trapp, *State Responsibility*, p. 266, who asserts the margin of appreciation related to primary obligations to be a bigger problem.

the rules on the content of the general law of state responsibility largely deal with reparation for injury and the various forms reparation can take.

But on the other hand, it can be argued that state responsibility has a more abstract function, according to which it ensures legality by virtue of upholding the rule of law in the international legal system. By providing legal consequences for an internationally wrongful act, state responsibility law ensures that international law is really law in the first place. At the same time, legal consequences seek to restrain the future behaviour of states. This plurality of functions means that different assessments of state responsibility may emerge, all equally entitled to assess state responsibility from their respective perspectives. However, it is important to acknowledge the possibility of construing state responsibility in different ways and exploring whether this functional diversity actually enhances the operation of state responsibility, or whether deplorable consequences follow from it. The following will argue that the mixed composition of the ASR results in tensions between bilateral and community interests, leaving both aspects of state responsibility incomplete. Although this incompleteness enables a wide range of lawyering regarding the ILC Articles, it nevertheless fails to contribute to the development of systemic and functionally complete wholes.

#### 3.4.1.1 A Mixture of Bilateral and Community Relations

The connection of state responsibility to domestic private law is hard to dispute, despite the fact that state responsibility has been described as 'simply "international"' or '*sui generis*'.[196] Although state responsibility has been compared to various responsibility models, most scholars take the view that state responsibility resembles domestic private law.[197] Similarly to private law, state responsibility has a bilateral basis which seeks to protect from infringements the relations between two or several equals. Consequently, reparation is, and has traditionally been, viewed as the basic function of the general law of state responsibility.[198]

However, the turn in the late 1960s to general and secondary rules of state responsibility in international law sought to ensure responsibility also as a

[196] Pellet, 'Can a State', 433; Nollkaemper, 'Constitutionalization', 541.

[197] For example, André Nollkaemper has held that 'responsibility in international law has been based primarily on a private rather than a public law model'. See Nollkaemper, 'Constitutionalization', 542. Martti Koskenniemi, however, notes concerning whether the proper analogy is with private or public law, that 'doctrinal controversy is ripe and both extreme positions as well [as] a large number of mediating ones have been taken'. See Koskenniemi, 'Doctrines', 47.

[198] Pellet, 'The Definition of Responsibility', 5.

component of a viable and credible legal system. A system-building function then emerged in the ILC's construction of state responsibility, alongside the traditional bilateral and reparational role state responsibility had played to that point.[199] This 'new' function with a multilateral, or even communitarian, dimension protected the international legal system as a whole from violations. Violations were now perceived not only as a threat to interstate relations but also to the rule of international law and legality.[200] Indeed, these two quite different functions of state responsibility now coexist, and one is certainly entitled to claim that '[t]he law of international responsibility fullfils essentially two functions: reparation for injury and protection of the rule of law and global order'.[201] A further complication relates to the dual nature of legality itself:[202] legality may be protected by virtue of generally upholding international commitments, but it may also relate to the sifting out of principles that possess a constitutional character. Consequently, it can be alleged that the many purposes of the law of state responsibility include: the protection of bilateral, subjective obligations; the protection of international law generally; and the safeguarding of norms of a higher rank that pertain to a process of the constitutionalization of the international legal order.

The idea of community interests, or the fact that some international obligations are more fundamental than others, was unavoidable for the ILC.[203] Special Rapporteur Roberto Ago, who led the reconceptualization of state

199 See Section 1.1.2, 'Systemic Importance'.

200 The reparational function of state responsibility has been called the 'old' concept, and the protection of the world order as the 'new' concept of international responsibility. See Manfred Mohr, 'The ILC's Distinction between "International Crimes" and "International Delicts" and Its Implications', in Marina Spinedi and Bruno Simma (eds.), *United Nations Codification of State Responsibility* (New York: Oceana Publications, 1987), pp. 115–141 at 116–117.

201 Nollkaemper, 'Constitutionalization', 535. Already in 1929, Dionisio Anzilotti had recognized the interest of other states in ensuring that reparation was made and 'the international legal order restored'. However, recognition of the legal rights of third states was not a part of the corpus of state responsibility at that time. See Dionisio Anzilotti, *Cours de droit international* (trans. Gidel, 1929, Paris: Panthéon-Assas/LGDJ, 1999), p. 517, cited in Pellet, 'The Definition', 5–6.

202 Pierre-Marie Dupuy describes the duality of legality as follows: 'Alongside an ordinary legality with a bilateral dimension, a higher legality was affirmed, which was not merely multilateral in nature, but also universal'. See Dupuy, 'A General Stocktaking', 1057. Concerning the system of aggravated responsibility, Pierre Klein states that 'the institution of a system of aggravated responsibility has the specific aim of uniting the international community in the defence of its fundamental values', see Pierre Klein, 'Responsibility for Serious Breaches of Obligations Deriving from Peremptory Norms of International Law and United Nations Law' (2002) 13 *European Journal of International Law* (2002) 1241–1255 at 1252.

203 Common attributes of community interests that have been identified are: (1) they relate to the community as a whole; (2) they are too important for unilateral implementation; and (3) some of them concern non-state actors as well. See Andreas Paulus, 'Whether Universal Values Can Prevail over Bilateralism and Reciprocity', in Antonio Cassese (ed.), *Realizing Utopia: The Future of International Law* (Oxford: Oxford University Press, 2012), pp. 89–104 at 89.

responsibility toward a unitary set of secondary and general rules, had also served as the President of the Conference on the Vienna Convention on the Law of Treaties, a project which for the first time had dealt with the question of relative normativity in international law.[204] The Vienna Convention on the Law of Treaties (VCLT) recognized the differentiation of international obligations. On the one hand, the convention divided treaty obligations into derogable and non-derogable commitments. On the other hand, it also distinguished among classic bilateral obligations, collective obligations of a bilateral character and those establishing objective regimes.[205] Special Rapporteur Ago expressly recognized that the ghost of the VCLT haunted the work on state responsibility. According to Ago, 'it would be hard to believe that the evolution of the legal consciousness of States with regard to the idea of the inadmissibility of any derogation from certain rules has not been accompanied by a parallel evolution in the domain of State responsibility.'[206] A departure from the categorization of international obligations would have been even more difficult after the ICJ judgment in the 1970 *Barcelona Traction* case, which confirmed the existence of erga omnes obligations. According to the World Court's obiter dictum,

> In particular, an essential distinction should be drawn between the obligations of a State towards the international community as a whole, and those arising vis-à-vis another State in the field of diplomatic protection. By their

[204] Dupuy, 'A General Stocktaking', 1054; Pierre-Marie Dupuy, 'The Deficiencies of the Law of State Responsibility Relating to Breaches of "Obligations Owed to the International Community as a Whole": Suggestions for Avoiding the Obsolescence of Aggravated Responsibility', in Antonio Cassesse (ed.), *Realizing Utopia: The Future of International Law* (Oxford: Oxford University Press, 2012), pp. 210–226 at 211–212.

[205] See Arts. 53 and 64 on jus cogens in the Vienna Convention on the Law of Treaties (VCLT), Vienna, 22 May 1969, in force 27 January 1980, 1155 *United Nations Treaty Series* 331. Art. 53, which defines a peremptory norm of international law, reads: 'A treaty is void if, at the time of its conclusion, it conflicts with a peremptory norm of general international law. For the purposes of the present Convention, a peremptory norm of general international law is a norm accepted and recognized by the international community of States as a whole as a norm from which no derogation is permitted and which can be modified only by a subsequent norm of general international law having the same character'.

[206] Roberto Ago, *Fifth Report on State Responsibility*, UN Doc. A/CN.4/291 and Add.1 and Add.2 (1976), p. 32, para. 99. Nevertheless, the significance of the VCLT in the 'evolution of the legal consciousness of States' is downplayed by James Crawford, who claims that the VCLT was a diplomatic success because it only marginally dealt with the community interests: 'Only peripherally does it deal with the "public order" aspects of multilateral treaties, and then usually indirectly'. He further states that the VCLT's 'approach is, so to speak, bifocal'. See Crawford, 'Responsibility to the International', 311.

very nature the former are the concern of all States. In view of the importance of the rights involved, all States can be held to have a legal interest in their protection; they are obligations *erga omnes*.[207]

There were efforts made by the ILC to explicitly embrace a distinction between international obligations. This gradation of norms had materialized in the Draft Article 19 on state crimes and delicts, which recognized the existence of certain specifically heinous acts as international crimes, whereas 'ordinary' violations of international law were labelled as international delicts.[208] Unacceptable to many states that not only rejected the terminology of penalization of state violations but also the distinction in kind, the provision and the idea it represented was nevertheless deleted from the Articles.[209] In the end, no formal differentiation of obligations was recognized in the ASR,[210] and in its later deliberations the ILC elected to deal with collective obligations from a pragmatic viewpoint rather than comprehensively as part of the general setting.[211]

The ILC shifted its focus from the formal status of the rule to defining separate consequences for breaches of a higher ranking.[212] To begin with, the

207 *Barcelona Traction, Power, and Light Company, Limited (Belgium* v. *Spain)* Second Phase, Judgment, ICJ Reports 1970, p. 3, at 32, paras. 33.

208 For analyses of Draft Article 19, see Mohr, 'The ILC's Distinction'; Joseph H. H. Weiler, Antonio Cassese and Marina Spinedi (eds.), *International Crimes of States: A Critical Analysis of the ILC's Draft Article 19 on State Responsibility* (Berlin and New York: de Gruyter, 1988); Pellet, 'Can a State Commit'.

209 James Crawford, *Third Report on State Responsibility*, UN Doc. A/CN.4/507/Add. 4 (2000), at paras. 411–412.

210 The choice to focus on more pragmatic aspects such as consequences and the right of invocation with respect to 'serious breaches of obligations under peremptory norms of general international law' instead of an outright recognition of distinct categories is explicitly recognized by the ILC: 'Accordingly, the present articles do not recognise the existence of any distinction between State "crimes" and "delicts"'. See Commentary to Chapter III of the ASR, at para. 7. It was also noted that the ICJ had taken a pragmatic approach in the 1970 *Barcelona Traction* case, when it had focused on issues of 'invocation, not with the status of the norm breach', see James Crawford, 'International Crimes of States' in James Crawford, Alain Pellet and Simon Olleson (eds.), *The Law of International Responsibility* (Oxford: Oxford University Press, 2010), pp. 405–414 at 410.

211 Disagreement prevails among scholars over the question of whether the ILC created a distinction in kind or degree. It is the view of the present author that the method adopted builds on a differentiation in degree rather than on kind. Such an interpretation is held by Alain Pellet, who notes: *'qu'il s'agisse d'une "violation grave" ou d'un autre fait internationalement illicite, le seul fait de la violation d'une obligation engage la responsabilité de son auteur; la distinction ne produit d'effet qu'au plan des conséquences de la responsabilité'*, see Alain Pellet, 'Les Articles de la C.D.I. sur la responsabilité de l'état pour fait internationalement illicite. Suite-et fin?' (2002) 48 *Annuaire francais de droit international* 1–23 at 11.

212 Crawford, 'International Crimes of States', 410.

law of the ILC failed to impose additional consequences on the state committing a serious breach of a peremptory norm of international law. No punitive or degrading consequences upon the wrongdoer were accepted; a state committing a serious breach would not face punitive damages or have its '"dignity" attacked'.[213] Instead, the Commission opted to focus on the rights of the injured state and of third states to take measures in cases of grave breaches.[214] Its work therefore needed to resolve the question of to whom the right to react to serious breaches belonged and of how such reactions of states not directly injured were to be arranged. If community interests were to be enforced through the actions of individual states only, how would one control such exercises of enforcement and how would such use be collectively legitimized? But if this right also belonged to the community of states, could enforcement take place only through institutional settings, or could community reactions be non-institutionalized? The discussion of these issues was thorny, and the debate has spurred comments depicting the issue of enforcement of community interests as a stumbling block for the ILC in its codification of state responsibility.[215]

[213] Dupuy, 'A General Stocktaking', 1062. During Special Rapporteur Arangio-Ruiz' mandate, special consequences upon the wrongdoer were discussed in the ILC. See Gaetano Arangio-Ruiz, *Second Report on State Responsibility*, UN Doc. A/CN.4/425 & Corr.1 and Add.1 & Corr.1 (1989).

[214] Community interests are often described as containing by necessity the element of collective enforcement. Thus, Bruno Simma describes community interests as 'a consensus according to which respect for certain fundamental values is not to be left to the free disposition of States individually or *inter se* but is recognized and sanctioned by the law as a matter of concern to all States', see Simma, 'Bilateralism and Community Interest in the Law of State Responsibility', in Yoram Dinstein (ed.), *International Law at a Time of Perplexity: Essays in Honour of Shabtai Rosenne* (Dordrecht: Martinus Njihoff Publishers, 1989), pp. 821–844 at 823. Similarly, Andreas Paulus notes that among the common features of community interests is the consideration that they are so important that 'it is not enough to leave their implementation to the usual interplay between states', see Paulus, 'Whether Universal Values', 89. Similarly, James Crawford notes that the international legal order lacks a '*parens patriae* who can act securely on the collective behalf'. See Crawford, 'Responsibility to the International', 315.

[215] Special Rapporteur James Crawford noted in his first report on State responsibility in 1998 that '[t]he single most controversial element in the draft articles on State responsibility [adopted in 1996] is the distinction between international crimes and international delicts', see his *First Report on State Responsibility*, UN Doc. A/CN.4/490/Add.1 (1998), at para. 43. Similarly, according to Bruno Simma the insertion of community interests into the law of state responsibility 'led to an undeniable crisis of the United Nations codification machinery', see, Simma, 'Bilateralism and Community Interest', 821. Pierre-Marie Dupuy explains that 'it was the introduction of the multilateral aspect into the codification work which constituted the main stumbling block of the successive drafts', Dupuy, 'A General Stocktaking', 1058.

Having discarded both extreme alternatives, enforcement by injured states only, and only institutionalized responses,[216] the Commission pursued a method whereby injured states could both invoke responsibility and take countermeasures, but in which third states were entitled only to invoke responsibility. The question of countermeasures taken in the collective interest was left undecided.[217] Arguably then, the ILC only partially departed from the traditional bilateral structure of state responsibility, according to which '[i]t is up to each State to protect its rights.'[218] The basic principles of the ASR fail to reflect the gradation of norms to its full extent.

#### 3.4.1.2 Failure to Fully Differentiate between International Obligations

The ILC was between a rock and a hard place when it decided to include principles on community interests in the law of state responsibility. On the one hand, the early appearance of the state crime notion into the codification work embodying community interests was strongly rejected by both states and experts on international law; on the other hand, these interests could hardly be left out altogether. Thus, the decision to include community interests in a pragmatic fashion rather than pursuing a formal categorization of international obligations was probably the only solution acceptable to all concerned parties. As such, the inclusion of both bilateral and community aspects in the codification has been praised as creative legal craftsmanship. It has been noted that '[l]ike any good compromise, the ILC text can be cited as a victory of the "bilateralist" as well as the "communitarian" school'.[219] Thus, as Martti Koskenniemi puts it, 'whether one wishes to interpret the ILC text of 2001 from a "bilateralist" or an "international community" standpoint remains largely a matter of taste'.[220] However, the partial or halfway solution adopted

[216] There were intrinsic proposals for institutional implementation of responsibility set forth, for example, by Special Rapporteur Arangio-Ruiz. His proposal involved all major UN organs in a system of compulsory dispute settlement before the ICJ. See Gaetano Arangio-Ruiz, *Seventh Report on State Responsibility*, UN Doc. A/CN.4/469 and Add. 1–2 (1995). For a discussion of this proposal, see Dupuy, 'The Deficiencies'; and Klein, 'Responsibility for Serious Breaches'.

[217] Article 54 of the ASR reads: 'This Chapter does not prejudice the right of any State, entitled under article 48, paragraph 1 to invoke the responsibility of another State, to take lawful measures against that State to ensure cessation of the breach and reparation in the interest of the injured State or of the beneficiaries of the obligation breached'. It was noted in the commentary that 'the current state of international law on countermeasures taken in the general or collective interest is uncertain'. See Commentary to Art. 54, para. 6.

[218] Simma, 'Bilateralism and Community', 821.

[219] Koskenniemi, 'Doctrines', 49; Anna Sotaniemi, 'Elements of the Nordic Practice: The Nordic Countries in Co-ordination' (2003) 72 *Nordic Journal of International Law* 521–535 at 525.

[220] Ibid., 51.

by the ILC has also been criticized. It has been described as a 'compromise',[221] and 'unsatisfactory … both in theory and in practice'.[222]

The insertion into state responsibility of principles relating to community interests can be analyzed from two different perspectives: first, one can look into what the insertion of the function relating to the protection of legality does to the system of state responsibility; and second, one can evaluate whether state responsibility is capable of adequately protecting community interests. A first point of critique can be raised against the decision to encompass different functions in the law of state responsibility without fully addressing the tensions created thereby. It appears doctrinally unclear whether the ASR contain one unified or two different orders of state responsibility. At any rate, the unity of the rules adopted by the ILC can be questioned.[223]

Second, the decision to abandon the differentiation of international obligations into crimes and delicts and to focus instead on pragmatic consequences is disappointing both from conceptual and practical perspectives. The treatment of aggravated responsibility is left incomplete and without a firm understanding that some international obligations are more important than others. The decision to include community interests in the traditional law of state responsibility should have been supported by consequent and credible means of asserting those interests. Under the present conditions, the system of aggravated responsibility has not induced resort to the law of state responsibility in cases falling under its scope. In sum, it is argued here that the alternatives of leaving out aggravated responsibility entirely or developing it fully in a separate regime in the long run would have constituted more viable solutions for the general law of state responsibility.[224]

It seems warranted to claim that the law of state responsibility as it stands today contributes little to the advancement of community interests. Yet, few states contest the relevance of community interests for state responsibility. In the course of the work of the Commission, only Japan raised the argument

[221] Crawford, 'International Crimes', 409.

[222] Dupuy, 'A General Stocktaking', 1058.

[223] Arguably, the unity of the law of state responsibility had been built upon the fact that the law pertained only 'to one essential function, namely, reparation'. Paul Reuter, 'Principes de droit international public', 103 *Recueil des Cours de l'Academie de Droit International* (1961–II) 425, as cited in Dupuy, 'A General Stocktaking', 1054.

[224] Some have argued that there was no option to omit aggravated responsibility altogether. For example, Pierre-Marie Dupuy commends Special Rapporteur Ago for having 'had the courage to find that it was already too late to confine the law of responsibility to the area of reparations alone', see Dupuy, 'A General Stocktaking', 1079. However, it is noteworthy that Special Rapporteur James Crawford held that the criminal responsibility of states was not automatically to be excluded, as long as it was to be dealt with outside the ASR. See Report of the ILC on the Work of Its Fiftieth Session, UN Doc. A/53/10 (1998), paras. 329–330.

that community interests should not be included in state responsibility, as it is 'not a "core function" of the law of State responsibility'.[225] Given that most states accept the gradation of norms to a certain extent,[226] the adopted solution seems disappointing. As acknowledged also by the ILC during its work, it is possible to affirm that 'within the field of general international law there is some hierarchy of norms, and that the importance of at least a few basic substantive norms is recognized as involving a difference not merely of degree but of kind'.[227] Yet, what is missing from the ILC law on state responsibility is a full-fledged recognition of the idea that some norms are more important than others. There is no categorization of international obligations according to their importance, and no additional consequences are imposed upon the wrongdoing state in cases of more serious breaches.

Although the terminology of 'international crimes and delicts' may have been inappropriate since it was taken as indicating a criminalization of state responsibility, the gradation of internationally wrongful acts into separate categories was nevertheless called for. The violation of a trade treaty should not be treated in the same way as, for example, the violation of aggression or genocide. As argued by the Czech Republic in 1998 in its comments upon Draft Article 19, with respect to the distinction:

> It would be a retrograde step—conceptually, at least—if the International Law Commission were now to reverse the decision it took over 20 years ago to include the concepts of 'delicts' and 'crimes' in the articles in order to distinguish between two separate categories of wrongful acts; such a step, which would not be in keeping with the unquestionably vigorous trends and developments in related fields of international law … might well paralyze and freeze the law of State responsibility as a result of an excessively conservative, static approach.[228]

[225] James Crawford, *Fourth Report on State Responsibility*, UN Doc. A/CN.4/517 and Add.1 (2001), p. 11, para. 39. The Japanese government noted: 'it is not desirable to bestow too much power on the law of State responsibility. Rather, this might blur the importance of its core function, which is to define the relationship between injured States and responsible States'. See *Comments and Observations Received from Governments*, UN Doc. A/CN.4/515 and Add.1–3 (2001), p. 8.

[226] In its commentary to Draft Article 19, for example, France that rejected the provision still admitted that 'it can hardly be denied that some wrongful acts are more serious than others'. See *Comments and Observations Received by Governments*, UN Doc. A/CN.4/488 (1998) and Add. 1–3, p. 115. In a similar vein, Ireland noted that '[a]lthough Ireland rejects the distinction drawn in draft article 19 between international crimes and international delicts, it nonetheless considers that there is some merit in regarding international obligations *erga omnes* as a distinct category and the responsibility of States for a breach of these obligations as of a different order than the breach of an obligation owed to a particular State or States'. See Ibid., at 118.

[227] Crawford, *First Report*, para. 71.

[228] *Comments and Observations Received by Governments*, UN Doc. A/CN.4/488 and Add. 1–3 (1998), p. 114.

It can be argued that the Czech Republic's warning has come true. The compromise solution reached between principles on reparation and those pertaining to legality has contributed to the marginalization of state responsibility in cases of serious breaches.[229] Instead of resorting to the mechanisms of state responsibility with respect to serious breaches, states mostly rely on other mechanisms. André Nollkaemper notes that 'states and international organizations do not treat public order questions in terms of responsibility'.[230]

The tendency to set aside the law of state responsibility in cases of community interest protection is further exacerbated by the lack of genuine collective enforcement mechanisms in the ILC Articles.[231] Admittedly, institutional development is far from being capable of efficient community interest protection.[232] As a consequence, the bilateral basis and mechanisms of state responsibility also came to form the foundation for obligations with a collective dimension. The inclusion of community interest into what essentially is a bilateral system nevertheless remains a paradox: can one truly assert the interests of the community of states as a whole with means that have been created for bilateral state relations, based on subjective obligations? A sceptical attitude towards this certainly seems well-founded:[233] '[t]he underlying rationale of a bilateralist system does not fit into the most important considerations of our time.'[234] As aptly summarized by Pierre-Marie Dupuy:

[229] This will be discussed in Section 3.4.2.2, 'Marginalization in Serious Violations of International Law'.

[230] Nollkaemper, 'Constitutionalization', 558.

[231] The opposite argument could also plausibly be made. Powerful states could prefer to act outside defined collective frameworks in order to maintain their own power. For a discussion of the instrumentalization of state responsibility, see Section 3.5, 'Problematic Implementation'.

[232] For a discussion of existing mechanisms and suggestions regarding collective enforcement mechanisms, see Klein, 'Responsibility for Serious'.

[233] Pierre-Marie Dupuy holds that the rules on the so-called aggravated responsibility 'do not provide a comprehensive and a substantial legal regime'. See Dupuy, 'The Deficiencies', 210; Bruno Simma has also drawn attention to the ill-fittingness of functions and means within the law of state responsibility: 'This scheme provides a rather impressive illustration of the difficulty of fitting the pursuit of "objective" community interests into the Procrustean bed of the bilateralist model of state responsibility'. See Simma, 'From Bilateralism to Community Interest', 318; With respect to systemic crimes, André Nollkaemper holds that '[s]tate responsibility principally remains confined within a bilateralist straitjacket and has made little progress towards communitarian responses'. See André Nollkaemper, 'State Responsibility for International Crimes: A Review of Principles of Reparation', in Aristotle Constantinides and Nikos Zaikos (eds.), *The Diversity of International Law: Essays in Honour of Professor Kalliopi K. Koufa* (Leiden: Martinus Nijhoff Publishers, Leiden, 2009), pp. 487–518 at 511–512; According to Andreas Paulus, 'the ILC did not satisfactorily solve the riddle of how to protect community interests in the framework of the bilateralist international law of state responsibility'. See Paulus, 'Whether Universal Values', 102.

[234] Paulus, 'Whether Universal Values', 96.

> the international legal order is left in the twenty-first century with a situation in which the multilateral dimension of the law of state responsibility is affirmed without at the same time providing states with a clear indication of what would be the content of this responsibility and, in particular, what would be the measures to be taken and how they should be implemented.[235]

This meagre solution clearly has consequences on state responsibility's potential to contribute to a just and safe world. Victims of serious breaches of peremptory norms of international law might experience the inadequacy of the legal consequences of the commission of genocide, for example. In addition, the capacity of state responsibility rules to affect the behaviour of actors will also be minimal.

#### 3.4.1.3 (Non) Deterrence

A crucial consequence of the failure to appropriately address many violations of the most important contemporary issues is the inability of the present system of state responsibility in preventing serious violations from taking place. Put more crudely, state responsibility is unlikely to deter any actor from engaging in activity that breaches the fundamental values of the international community. Although deterrence is normally described as a function of criminal law rather than civil law based systems, it can hardly be disputed that a general system of responsibility in any legal system ought to be capable of some degree of deterrence or prevention. Responsibility in law should be both forward- and backward-looking: 'A well-functioning and successful legal system is one in which non-compliance with prospective responsibilities, and hence occasions for the imposition of historic responsibility, are minimised.'[236]

International law is not different in this regard. It has been claimed that the 'primary function of international law is to discourage harmful acts',[237] and more specifically, that one of the purposes of any remedy is deterrence.[238] Indeed, the retrospective character of responsibility regimes in international law in general is considered inadequate.[239] Still, deterrence rarely features in discussions of

[235] Dupuy, 'The Deficiencies', 217.

[236] Cane, *Responsibility in Law*, p. 35.

[237] Eric A. Posner and Alan O. Sykes, 'An Economic Analysis of State Responsibility and Individual Responsibility under International Law' (2007) 9 *American Law and Economics Review* 72–134 at 76.

[238] Shelton, *Remedies in International*, pp. 13–14.

[239] See Jan Klabbers, 'Law, Ethics and Global Governance: Accountability in Perspective' (2013) 11 *New Zealand Journal of Public and International Law* 309–321 at 315, who states that the retrospective nature of responsibility regimes is 'somewhat unsatisfactory'. James Crawford and Jeremy Watkins admit that '[o]n the face of it, state responsibility seems to be a very poor instrument for discouraging behaviour that is deemed undesirable by the international community'. See Crawford and Watkins, 'International Responsibility', 290.

state responsibility,[240] and it is only mentioned in connection with Article 30 of the ASR dealing with cessation and non-repetition. Admittedly, there is a forward-looking component in the provision of assurances or guarantees of non-repetition. However, these measures seem unable to alleviate concerns that states feel free to behave as they want irrespective of the law of state responsibility.[241]

Deterrence is clearly not the main rationale for state responsibility and the legal consequences prescribed by it: reparations. The reason for the meagre role of deterrence in the law of state responsibility most likely resides in the general connection between deterrence and punishment: the assumption is that an actor will be discouraged from violating the law out of fear of punishment. However, punishment and punitive damages are disputed and even rejected in international law, particularly in the law of state responsibility. The sovereign equality of states mitigates the idea of punishment in international legal relations.[242] No state is thus assumed to possess the right to impose punishments on other states. In accordance with this view, states and, consequently, also the ILC 'were extremely reluctant to accept a full-scale penal regime, or indeed any punitive elements at all' into the ASR despite attempts to do so by some Special Rapporteurs.[243] Punitive or so-called aggravated damages reflecting the gravity of the violation were completely discarded from the ASR.[244]

Nevertheless, the lack of consequences commensurating with the seriousness of the violation fails to deter states from committing aggression, genocide, crimes against humanity or similar serious violations. Reparations of a symbolic nature, or mere compensation, will hardly substitute for more robust action against a wrongdoer. For example, the EU has accepted the idea of imposition of financial penalties upon its member states in situations of persistent breaches of community law. According to Article 228 of the Lisbon

240 A few accounts discuss deterrence and state responsibility. These are: Posner and Sykes, 'An Economic Analysis'; Crawford and Watkins, 'International Responsibility'; Peter Margulies, 'Sovereignty and Cyber Attacks: Technology's Challenge to the Law of State Responsibility' (2013) 14 *Melbourne Journal of International Law* 1–24; Shelton, *Remedies*, pp. 13–14.

241 As an example of the non-deterrent effect of state responsibility, Jan Klabbers mentions the violations of the 1963 Vienna Convention on Consular Relations which generated three different cases against the United States before the ICJ in six years. These cases were: *Vienna Convention on Consular Relations (Paraguay* v. *United States of America) (Provisional Measures)* ICJ Reports 1998, p. 248; *LaGrand (Germany* v. *United States of America)(Merits)* ICJ Reports 2001, p. 466; and *Avena and Other Mexican Nationals (Mexico* v. *United States of America)(Merits)* ICJ Reports 2004, p. 12. See Klabbers, 'Law, Ethics and Global Governance', 315.

242 Stephan Wittich, 'Punitive Damages', in James Crawford, Alain Pellet, and Simon Olleson (eds.), *The Law of International Responsibility* (Oxford: Oxford University Press, 2010), pp. 667–675 at 668.

243 Crawford, *'The International Law Commission's'*, p. 19. The final Special Rapporteur James Crawford suggested discussion on punitive damages in the case of gross or egregious breach. See Crawford, *Third Report*, para. 380.

244 Crawford, *The International Law Commission's*, p. 19.

Treaty, the European Court of Justice (ECJ) is able to impose penalty payments and lump sums to be paid by a member state in non-compliance of its obligations.[245] In this system, an accumulation of sanctions is even possible in order to reach the level corresponding to 'the nature, seriousness and persistence of the breach of obligations established'.[246] This arrangement within the EU suggests that principled opposition to levying sanctions above the ordinary level against wrongdoing states can be overcome. However, as the rules of state responsibility fail to provide different nuances to the consequences of a breach, their usefulness in upholding the rule of law can be questioned.[247] It is not sufficient for a functioning responsibility regime that strives to uphold legality merely to repair wrongs when such take place. It should be equally concerned with inducing good outcomes or deterring bad outcomes from happening.

#### 3.4.1.4 Disunity

The assertion of community interests (however mild its form) in the law of state responsibility alongside the traditional role of reparations clearly poses a challenge to the unity and uniformity of the system of state responsibility. This challenge is revealed first by the quite doctrinal debate on whether the insertion of community aspects into state responsibility gave rise to one or two systems of state responsibility.[248] A more important point, however, relates to

245 Treaty of Lisbon Amending the Treaty on the European Union and the Treaty Establishing the European Community, Lisbon, 13 December 2007, in force 1 December 2009, *Official Journal* C 306, 17 December 2007, Article 228.

246 European Commission, *Financial Penalties for Member States who Fail to Comply with Judgments of the European Court of Justice: European Commission Clarifies Rules*, MEMO/05/482, Brussels, 14 December 2005, p. 3.

247 Dinah Shelton is one of the few to recognize this, at least explicitly. She notes that '[t]he near absence of deterrence and punishment in considering reparations … seems inconsistent with the expressed concern for restoring and upholding the rule of law in the interest of the international community', see Shelton, 'Righting Wrongs', 845.

248 See Pierre-Marie Dupuy, who states: 'while the introduction of a twofold system for state responsibility in the end failed, the outlines of a differentiation of degrees of responsibility are perhaps discernible'. See Dupuy, 'A General Stocktaking', 1058. In the same vein, Bruno Simma held in 1989 that '[t]he ILC intends to link the crimes/delicts dichotomy with different regimes of responsibility'. See Simma, 'Bilateralism and Community', 827. Special Rapporteur James Crawford nonetheless held the view that the adoption of Draft Article 19 would not automatically have created two distinct regimes of responsibility. See James Crawford, *First Report on State Responsibility*, UN Doc. A/CN.4/490/Add.2 (1998), para. 71. Some scholars nonetheless hold that even though Draft Article 19 was abolished, a dual regime of state responsibility was installed. Georges Abi-Saab claims that '[t]he recommended alternative course of action of reverting to a unitary regime while making special allowance for the effects of violating *jus cogens* norms (and *erga omnes* obligations) would necessarily reintroduce a binary regime'. See Georges Abi-Saab, 'The Uses of Article 19' (1999) 10 *European Journal of International Law* 339–351 at 339.

the discussion of the effectiveness of a system which contains different – and potentially even opposing – legal ideas. Is such a system mainly for remedying wrongs in bilateral relations, or are the rules of state responsibility primarily aimed at creating or upholding the "climate of legality"?[249] Or, can the ASR promote both functions with one set of rules? Admittedly, it appears highly ambitious to include issues of attribution, defences, countermeasures and serious violations of peremptory norms of international law all in one single regime.[250]

The main objection against a unified system of state responsibility is the incongruity between the reparative function and the aim to uphold legality, coupled with the difficulty of constructing one set of rules capable of effectively asserting both. To begin with, it appears impossible to formulate efficient rules that apply to such different functions. The reparative function is based on a private law paradigm of responsibility which is victim-based, whereas the purpose of a public law–oriented model of responsibility is essentially to set boundaries to the use of public power. The former paradigm is 'concerned with the rights and obligations *inter se*' of individual states, the latter with 'accountability for the performance of public functions'.[251] Consequently, it cannot be assumed that the same rules of responsibility can be automatically applicable to both the private and public law paradigms.[252]

The construction of common rules for these diverse functions is necessarily built upon the least common denominator: 'value is attached to protecting the common ground'.[253] Thus a certain degree of normative ambiguity is unavoidable in such underdeveloped rules. A variety of consequences follow from this. First, some rules or concepts may be relevant to one of the functions but not to the other. One example is the concept of injury, which features prominently in the rules of state responsibility. The concept of 'injury' is naturally highly significant in a reparative system, but for a public law approach it becomes 'much less central and arguably even superfluous'.[254] There are also other concepts and parts of the ASR that are difficult to bring under one common responsibility framework. For instance, the rules providing for circumstances precluding

[249] Aust, *Complicity*, p. 86.

[250] See Christian Tams, 'Unity and Diversity in the Law of State Responsibility', in Andreas Zimmerman and Rainer Hoffmann (eds.), *Unity and Diversity in International Law: Proceedings of an International Symposium of the Kiel Walther Schücking Institute of International Law November 4–7, 2004* (Berlin: Duncker & Humblot, 2006), pp. 435–458 at 435.

[251] Cane, *Responsibility in Law*, p. 51. For his discussion of three responsibility paradigms, see p. 49 *et seqq*.

[252] Ibid.

[253] Nollkaemper, 'Constitutionalization', 560.

[254] Nollkaemper and Jacobs, 'Shared Responsibility in International Law', 404.

wrongfulness are irreconcilable within the communitarian aspects of state responsibility, since there can be no justifications or excuses for breaches of peremptory norms of international law.

Second, principles – and the ideas that they represent – may have different meanings in the private and public law contexts of responsibility.[255] The 'principle of necessity' is often used as an example to illuminate existing differences or disunity.[256] In state responsibility, the purpose of the principle is to protect a state's essential interests against 'grave and imminent peril', such as the extinction of certain animal species.[257] However, the principle of necessity has also been invoked in another instance by an international organization (in its capacity as an employer) to justify access to the confidential data of an employee.[258] Indeed, it has been argued that concepts moved from the traditional law of state responsibility into more 'public-law type relationships would have a somewhat different form and meaning'.[259] Even more disunity-related controversies appear as legal bodies attempt to apply the principle of necessity to specific cases. Necessity has been described as 'one of the most striking examples' of state disagreement when it comes to the content of the ILC codified ASR.[260] In several cases of investment dispute arbitration relating to Argentina and its pleas of necessity based on financial crisis,[261] the same facts have been interpreted incongruously. In *CMS Gas Transmission* v. *Argentina* the necessity plea was rejected, whereas in the *LG & E Award* the financial crisis was taken as fulfilling the requirements of necessity.[262] This inconsistency in arbitration and its concomitant understandings of necessity has been interpreted as reflecting the division within state responsibility,[263] in which the ILC public law model clashes with the traditional reparative role.

[255] As an example, André Nollkaemper mentions the principle of necessity. See Nollkaemper, 'Constitutionalization', 556.

[256] For an in-depth discussion, see Sloane, 'On the Use and Abuse of Necessity'.

[257] Commentary to Art. 25 of the ASR.

[258] *Responsibility of International Organizations. Comments and Observations Received from International Organizations*, UN Doc. A/CN.4/568 and Add.1 (2006), p. 137.

[259] Nollkaemper, 'Constitutionalization', 556.

[260] Alan T. Nissel, 'The Duality of State Responsibility' (2013) 44 *Columbia Human Rights Law Review* 793–858 at 852.

[261] Sarah Heathcote, 'Necessity', in James Crawford, Alain Pellet and Simon Olleson (eds.), *The Law of International Responsibility* (Oxford: Oxford University Press, 2010), pp. 491–501 at 500–501.

[262] *CMS Gas Transmission Company* v. *Argentine Republic*, ICSID Case No. ARB/01/8, Award (12 May 2005), para. 331, and *LG & E Energy Corp. and others* v. *Argentine Republic*, ICSID Case No. ARB/02/1, Decision on Liability (3 October 2006), para. 261. For a discussion of the inconsistent application of necessity and its consequences, see Nissel, 'The Duality', 852–854.

[263] Nissel, 'The Duality'.

A third consequence of the normative ambiguity is that '[b]oth the principles of responsibility applying to reparation for injury and the principles seeking a more constitutional function may remain relatively undeveloped as a result of the attempt to keep them together.'[264] In the worst case, '[m]aintaining unity may [...] hinder the refinement of the law of international responsibility that is necessary to deal with the various types of responsibility and accountability issues of modern international law, thereby marginalizing the law of responsibility'.[265] Not only do the rules on community interest remain undeveloped; the law of reparations still contains issues such as the question of interest, punitive damages, causality, shared responsibility, and so forth that require further elaboration.[266]

International institutions applying the law of state responsibility are also affected by the law's functional diversity (or incongruity, if you will). International adjudicatory bodies are increasingly concerned with issues of legality in general alongside decisions on reparations. For example, a shift in focus can be discerned in the practice of the ECtHR from a compensatory function to that of a supervisor of legality.[267] In the judgments of the ECtHR attention has come to increasingly focus on legal change and guarantees of non-repetition rather than on purely injury related aspects.[268] A similar trend is also discernible with respect to the Inter-American Court of Human Rights (IACtHR). For example, in the case of the *Detention Center of Catia* it ordered Venezuela to publicly admit international responsibility, to change its domestic legislation, to publish the judgment and give guarantees of non-repetition.[269] Clearly, such measures go beyond reparation for injury to the victims of the case. However, emphasizing the protection of legality at the cost of the reparative function may result in lessened opportunities for injured parties to obtain redress.[270]

Whereas many special procedures for the implementation of state responsibility reflect the purposive tension in the rules of state responsibility, international

[264] Nollkaemper, 'Constitutionalization', 560.

[265] Ibid., 535.

[266] Nollkaemper, 'Constitutionalization', 560. On many outstanding issues with respect to reparations, see Shelton, 'Righting Wrongs'.

[267] Nollkaemper, 'Constitutionalization', 537; Valerio Colandrea, 'On the Power of the European Court of Human Rights to Order Specific Non-monetary Measures: Some Remarks in Light of *Assanidze, Broniowski* and *Sejdovic* Cases' (2007) 7 *Human Rights Law Review* 396–411; Markus Fyrnys, 'Expanding Competences by Judicial Lawmaking: The Pilot Judgment Procedure of the European Court of Human Rights' (2011) 12 *German Law Journal* 1231–1260.

[268] See e.g., ECtHR, *Sejdovic* v. *Italy*, Application No. 56581/00, Judgment (1 March 2006), in which the Court held that the respondent's domestic legislation did not correspond to the stipulations of the ECHR.

[269] *Case of Montero-Aranguren et al. (Detention Centre of Catia)* v. *Venezuela*, IACtHR, Judgment (5 July 2006).

[270] Nollkaemper, 'Constitutionalization', 559.

practice exists that goes the opposite way and remains unaffected by the ILC law of state responsibility. It has been argued that imbuing the law of state responsibility with diversified functions has actually fragmented it into a 'spoken' and 'unspoken' version of the law. This 'duality of state responsibility' is composed of the codified ILC Articles and rules of state responsibility as applied within the framework of arbitration in investment protection in the Americas.[271] Disunity can thus be understood in broader terms; the way the ILC formulated the rules, which includes the protection of legality, departs from the traditional understanding of state responsibility in its purely reparative function.

### 3.4.2 *Remedial Insufficiencies: A Turn to Other Systems*

This subchapter explores whether or not the secondary rules of state responsibility pertaining to the content of responsibility are made use of to such a degree that the functions of the law are fulfilled. It will be contended that when it comes to the so-called aggravated breaches regime, which embodies communitarian protection of legal obligations of a higher rank, other (legal) responses have emerged that have affected the willingness of states to resort to the general law of state responsibility. The same phenomenon is visible concerning transnational large-scale environmental pollution and degradation. States seem to have shifted their attention from the general law of state responsibility to 'conventional or liability regimes',[272] as they allow for improved compensation schemes and avoid the confrontational character of state responsibility. Although state responsibility remains normatively applicable in the situations discussed below, its status as 'the default regime' has been questioned.[273]

#### 3.4.2.1 From Wrongfulness to Loss Allocation

The law of state responsibility formally applies to all international obligations, and thus it also covers the field of international environmental obligations and related breaches. But, state responsibility is often sidestepped as a response to cases of serious environmental harm. We can discern two separate reasons that have contributed to the rise of the use of alternative regimes in these instances: first, the emphasis on wrongfulness inherent in the law of state responsibility, and second, the inadequacy of the available means of reparation for large-scale environmental harm.

When actual and widespread harm (as opposed to legal damage) is done, the rules of state responsibility are of limited utility. Indeed, states have traditionally

[271] Nissel, 'The Duality'.
[272] Proulx, *Institutionalizing*, p. 52. See also Redgwell, 'The Wrong Trousers', 259.
[273] Proulx, *Transnational Terrorism*, p. 138.

avoided the state responsibility approach in cases of serious environmental harm, even in cases of clear wrongdoing by the state.[274] For example, this was the case with the Soviet Union in the *Chernobyl* incident, and Switzerland's role in the pollution of the Rhine River. Recent years have witnessed, however, a number of environmental cases before the ICJ, which in the long run can affect the willingness of states to pursue interstate adjudication.[275] Yet, few have attempted to approach the *Deepwater Horizon* oil spill or the *Fukushima* nuclear accident in terms of state responsibility, in spite of allegations of due diligence violations by the respective home states. A claim that the United States alone should be responsible for the shortcomings in security arrangements by BP seems farfetched and difficult to sustain.[276] Similarly, holding the state of Japan fully responsible for the radiation from the Fukushima reactor seems misplaced. The problem in the state responsibility regime and its insistence on wrongfulness relates to the dogmatic setting it embodies: either a state is separately and fully responsible for a wrongful act, or it is not. Two problems emerge from this basic proposition. First, in the normal course of affairs transboundary harm derives from *lawful* activity. As a rule, such activity does not constitute an internationally wrongful act of the state because it is not a breach of the state's obligations. The state's responsibility is usually founded upon an 'indirect' approach, according to which the state violates a due diligence obligation. As the ICJ noted in the *Pulps Mills* case, '[a] State is thus obliged to use all the means at its disposal in order to avoid activities which take place in its territory, or in any area under its jurisdiction, causing significant damage to the environment of another State.'[277] However, it is far from evident that a state violation of due diligence exists behind a transboundary harm.

[274] Proulx, *Institutionalizing*, p. 52; Proulx, *Transnational Terrorism*, p. 138; Alexandre Kiss, 'L'accident de Tchernobyl: ses consequences au point de vue du Droit international' (1986) 32 *Annuaire français de droit international* 139–152.

[275] For example, *Pulp Mills on the River Uruguay (Argentina* v. *Uruguay), Judgment*, ICJ Reports 2010, p. 14: *Certain activities carried out by Nicaragua in the Border Area (Costa Rica* v. *Nicaragua)* and *Construction of a Road in Costa Rica along the San Juan River (Nicaragua* v. *Costa Rica), Judgment*, ICJ Reports 2015, p. 665.

[276] On the face of it, the prime responsible entities are both private companies: Halliburton and BP. Halliburton designed the well around the oil pipeline that broke down, and BP constructed the well in a different manner than was recommended. Some scholars still maintain that, although states are not fully responsible, they still may be so in part. Alan Boyle notes that 'it is far from clear that states are fully responsible [for transboundary harm] in international law for damage to neighbouring states', see Alan E. Boyle, 'Globalising Environmental Liability: The Interplay of National and International Law' (2005) 17 *Journal of Environmental Law* 3–26 at 6.

[277] *Pulp Mills on the River Uruguay* (*Argentina* v. *Uruguay*), *Judgment*, ICJ Reports 2010, p. 14, at pp. 55–56, para. 101.

Moreover, adopting an indirect approach to serious transboundary harms is inadequate because, among other things, it distorts the true nature of the activity. Second, the state should not be held responsible for industrial (i.e., private) activity that causes harm. At least, it should not be the primary respondent. However, the rules of state responsibility contain no possibility for apportioning of responsibility to several actors, not to mention the possibility for construing shared or joint responsibility between state and non-state actors.[278]

There are further limitations to the efficacy of state responsibility in dealing with environmental harms. Restitution and compensation, the primary remedies under the general law of state responsibility, are problematic in the environmental context. Restitution may prove impossible to realize, and monetary compensation – which is the only efficient way of dealing with substantial transboundary harm deriving from lawful activities – is both disputed and inadequate under the law of state responsibility.[279] Furthermore, it is often argued that monetary compensation is not the sole or primary objective of reparation under the law of state responsibility, which often is built on more symbolic reparations such as apologies or acknowledgment of wrongdoing. The practice of the ICJ with regard to compensation has also so far been relatively scarce.[280] On the other hand, the ILC has noted that compensation is the primary form of reparation sought, and that compensation is relevant in cases of pollution, for example.[281] To illustrate, the UN Claims Commission

[278] For the question of shared responsibility, see Nollkaemper and Jacobs, 'Shared Responsibility in International Law'; André Nollkaemper and Ilias Plakokefalos (eds.), *Principles of Shared Responsibility in International Law* (Cambridge: Cambridge University Press, 2014).

[279] For example, Malgosia Fitzmaurice holds that the rules on compensation do not 'take full account of the particular demands of environmental valuation'. See Fitzmaurice, 'International Responsibility and Liability', in Daniel Bodansky, Jutta Brunnée and Ellen Hey (eds.), *The Oxford Handbook of International Environmental Law* (Oxford: Oxford University Press, 2007), pp. 1010–1035 at 1020.

[280] See e.g., *Corfu Channel* case *(United Kingdom* v. *Albania) (Judgment)*, ICJ Reports 1949, p. 4, and *Corfu Channel* case, *Judgment of December 15th*, 1949, ICJ Reports 1949, p. 244. In 2012 the ICJ decided on compensation in the case of *Ahmadou Sadio Diallo (Republic of Guinea* v. *Democratic Republic of the Congo)*, Merits, Judgment, ICJ Reports 2010, p. 639, and *Ahmadou Sadio Diallo (Republic of Guinea* v. *Democratic Republic of the Congo)*, Compensation, Judgment, ICJ Reports 2012, p. 324.

[281] See Commentaries to the ASR, Arts. 34 on Restitution and 36 on Compensation, esp. paras. 2, 13–15 to the latter article. For discussions of the various forms of reparation, see Christine Gray, 'The Different Forms of Reparation: Restitution', in James Crawford, Alain Pellet and Simon Olleson (eds.), *The Law of International Responsibility* (Oxford: Oxford University Press, 2010), pp. 589–597 at 589; Yann Kerbat, 'Interaction between the Forms of Reparation', in James Crawford, Alain Pellet and Simon Olleson (eds.), *The Law of International Responsibility* (Oxford: Oxford University Press, 2010), pp. 573–587; John Barker, 'The Different Forms of Reparation: Compensation', in James Crawford, Alain Pellet and Simon Olleson (eds.), *The Law of International Responsibility* (Oxford: Oxford University Press, 2010), pp. 599–611.

awarded compensation for environmental harms committed by Iraq during the 1990–1991 Gulf War. Nevertheless, the significance of compensation is highlighted in mixed claims involving states and other actors such as individuals or companies, whereas in pure interstate cases it has less value.[282]

In the environmental framework, the rules on compensation nevertheless display difficulties that are hard to overcome. International practice has affirmed the relevance of compensations for, among other things, 'restoration, clean-up costs, and harm to persons and private property',[283] but the value of many environmental harms is incalculable. It is unclear how to evaluate harm done to biodiversity or the ecosystem. Perhaps the development of more precise rules on compensation has been hindered by the wide array of forms of reparation within the sphere of state responsibility. Compensating for harm may be seen as representing the traditional law of state responsibility with its foundation in tort law, whereas the 'public law' side of state responsibility thrives on more 'preventive as opposed to reparative remedies'.[284] Accordingly, an approach which focuses not on preventing unlawfulness as such, but instead on how to provide relief adequately and promptly, appears better suited to handling a range of issues under international law.

Models of loss allocation offer a pragmatic approach to large-scale harm. It has been acknowledged that '[i]t may be simpler, quicker, and economically more efficient to make polluters or those who cause harm pay rather than States.'[285] In 1978, a turn to loss allocation was taken by the ILC when it separated lawful activities and concomitant issues of liability from the law of state responsibility.[286] The so-called liability framework seems more capable of channelling liability to the appropriate actor, in spite of the actor's private character. Such a model can also include the possibility of apportioning liability to several actors, which would seem to better correspond to globalization than does the either-or

282 Barker, 'The Different Forms of Reparation', 604.

283 Fitzmaurice, 'International Responsibility and Liability', 1019.

284 Cane, *Responsibility in Law*, p. 261.

285 Alan E. Boyle, 'Liability for Injurious Consequences of Acts not Prohibited by International Law', in James Crawford, Alain Pellet and Simon Olleson (eds.), *The Law of International Responsibility* (Oxford: Oxford University Press, 2010), pp. 95–104 at 98. This may certainly hold true when it comes to private companies compensating for generated harm.

286 The ILC was mandated in 1977 by GA Res. 32/151 of 19 December 1977 to commence its work on the topic of 'International liability for injurious consequences arising out of acts not prohibited by international law'. Due to difficulties in the work and difficulties regarding the concept of international liability, in 1997 the ILC decided to subdivide the liability topic into two parts, one on 'Prevention of transboundary damage from hazardous activities', and another on 'International liability in case of loss from transboundary harm arising out of hazardous activities'. See Report of the ILC on its Work on the Forty-ninth Session, UN Doc. A/52/10 (1997), Chapter VII, at para. 168, and UNGA Res. 52/156, 15 December 1997.

approach of state responsibility. The ILC Principles on Loss Allocation, which consist of eight principles, recognizes the need for the division of economic compensation. The aim of the Principles is that victims have resort to 'appropriate and effective measures' that enable them to receive 'prompt and adequate compensation'.[287] In its work in constructing efficient and victim-oriented liability principles, the Commission changed its target from states to private actors. Thus, civil liability has largely come to replace state liability.[288] This approach seems more in accord with real-life circumstances, in which private actors rather than states are behind transboundary environmental harm. It also seems reasonable to target those actors endowed with the capacity to provide substantial compensation. The plausibility of this argument finds support in the settlements in the *Deepwater Horizon* case, which involved three multinational companies that in total provided USD 6.7 billion in settlement for the oil pollution caused by the accident.[289] Redressing substantial transboundary harm outside the state responsibility framework certainly appears to achieve more than what can be achieved under the rules of state responsibility.

#### 3.4.2.2 Marginalization in Serious Violations of International Law

When it comes to atrocity crimes and other serious violations of international law, international practice shows that states employ other mechanisms besides the law of state responsibility. One such alternative legal avenue is international criminal law, another is having recourse via political organs such as the UN Security Council. While these avenues of redress remain intrinsically different, they both bring to the fore the fact that the remedies under the general law of state responsibility are considered 'toothless' with regard to the most serious violations of international law. The special consequences that follow from serious breaches of jus cogens obligations – that is, the duty to cooperate and not to recognize the unlawful situation – are formulated in terms of obligations arising for third states. No special consequences are imposed

[287] See Report of the ILC, Fifty-eighth Session, UN Doc. A/61/10 (2006), Chapter V, pp. 101–182, paras. 51–67. The General Assembly took note of the principles in: Allocation of loss in the case of transboundary harm arising out of hazardous activities, GA Resolution A/RES/61/36, 18 December 2006. The ILC Principles on Loss Allocation allocate responsibility in the first place to the operator of the hazardous activity, but also mandate that liability may be imposed on some other actor. See Principle 4. Alan E. Boyle has interpreted this as allowing for joint and several responsibility', see, Boyle, 'Liability', 102.

[288] Fitzmaurice, 'International Responsibility and Liability', 1023.

[289] Halliburton has reserved USD 1.3 billion for the settlement, BP USD 4 billion, and TransOcean USD 1,4 billion. See Tuomas Niskakangas, 'Halliburton tuhosi todisteita Meksikonlahden öljyturmasta', *Helsingin Sanomat*, 27 July 2013, p. B4.

upon the lawbreaker, leaving the ordinary sphere of reparation applicable also in the case of the serious breaches–regime. Accordingly, it has been argued that 'this regime holds less than the notion of "aggravated responsibility" suggests'.[290] The question of punitive damages, or the lack thereof, in the final ILC Articles has been especially debated.

The recent decades have witnessed a predilection for an international criminal legal approach, which has 'triggered skepticism toward other justice mechanisms',[291] including the general law of state responsibility. In fact, it has been argued that state responsibility and international criminal law are not equals in preference or in resources.[292] The principle of duality of responsibility regimes is claimed to prevail, yet the ICJ Judges Shi and Vereschetin noted in the *Bosnian Genocide* case that '[t]he determination of the international community to bring *individual perpetrators* of genocidal acts to justice, irrespective of their ethnicity or the position they occupy, points to the most appropriate course of action.'[293] The recent criticism against the ICC may, however, decrease the enthusiasm for resorting to international criminal law institutions.

But the marginalization of state responsibility cannot be explained only in terms of the development of international criminal law. When heinous crimes are committed, the first choice often is not to resort to *legal* mechanisms. Instead, it is generally acknowledged that political responses via international organizations have become the preferred route of action.[294] The nature of serious violations of international law requires efficient responses that usually must be collective and institutionalized in order to meet the level of violence in question. This can most easily be arrived at through international institutions, most notably of course the UN Security Council. The powers of the Security Council are so broad that they encompass all relevant measures – political, economic and military – for halting serious crimes. The Security Council's competence to ultimately use force, if necessary, far exceeds the options available under the state responsibility regime, thus leaving the latter mechanism an unattractive choice.[295] Thus, 'it is because the Security Council has the competence to take positive

[290] Tams and Asteriti, 'Erga Omnes, Jus Cogens', 182.

[291] Drumbl, 'Collective Responsibility', 30.

[292] For a general discussion, see Creutz, 'International Responsibility'.

[293] *Application of the Convention on the Prevention and Punishment of the Crime of Genocide (Bosnia and Herzegovina* v. *Yugoslavia) (Preliminary Objections)* ICJ Reports 1996, p. 595, at 632 (emphasis in original).

[294] See Nigel D. White, 'Responses of Political Organs to Crimes by States', in André Nollkaemper and Harmen van der Wilt (eds.), *System Criminality in International Law* (Cambridge: Cambridge University Press, 2009), pp. 314–337 at 316.

[295] Ibid., p. 319.

action that can be directed at stopping state crimes that it is an attractive mechanism, and one that is likely to be more effective than a pure state responsibility regime.'[296]

Although it is debated whether the actions and decisions of the Security Council fall within the state responsibility domain and to what degree,[297] some scholars have attempted to portray acts taken in the Security Council as measures of state responsibility. The issue of institutionalizing state responsibility has indeed received greater attention in the recent years,[298] as scholars increasingly stress the need to understand the Security Council as one way of implementing state responsibility. Indeed, it has been claimed that, when 'there is a finding of a breach of an international obligation [by the Security Council], and one of a fundamental nature; there is a process of attribution; despite the evident political origin of this qualification, this finding forms the basis for the application of legal sanctions'.[299] In fact, the acts of the Security Council can be seen as measures taken on behalf of the injured state. Accordingly, the Council is 'not acting as an impartial arbitrator or third party, but in lieu and place of the injured States in matters which affect the interest of the international community as a whole'.[300] The Security Council actions can thus be viewed as institutionalized countermeasures provided by the legal institution of state responsibility.[301]

Even though a strict and formal separation between the legal and political spheres in line with the intentions of the founding fathers of the UN might no longer be tenable,[302] one should be cautious in interpreting institutional responses as clear-cut cases of state responsibility. Admittedly, there are overlaps between the law of state responsibility and political responses. For example, in situations of flagrant violations the Security Council has shown a willingness to determine on breaches of international law. The 1990 Iraq–Kuwait crisis demonstrated quite clearly how the Security Council can come to influence and address issues of state responsibility: in its resolution 687 of 1991, the Security Council famously held Iraq to be responsible for its

296 Ibid.
297 Proulx, *Institutionalizing*, p. 224.
298 Ibid.
299 Vera Gowlland-Debbas, 'Security Council Enforcement Actions and Issues of State Responsibility' (1994) 43 *International & Comparative Law Quarterly* 55–98 at 63.
300 Ibid., 73.
301 Ibid.
302 According to Oscar Schachter, '[i]t seems probable that the principal draftsmen believed that the primary task of the Council ... would not be served and, indeed, might possibly be impeded if the Council had to decide which side had been guilty of violating its legal obligations'. See Oscar Schachter, 'The Quasi-Judicial Rôle of the Security Council and the General Assembly' (1964) 58 *American Journal of International Law* 960–965 at 960.

aggression against Kuwait.[303] The Security Council has also used its powers to create extensive reparation regimes for repairing internationally wrongful acts: for example, the UN Compensation Commission established to administer reparations for the Iraqi aggression against Kuwait, and the Ethiopia–Eritrea Claims Commission following the ending of that war. Yet, the political element of taking matters before the Security Council should not be ignored or downplayed. It is important to recognize that 'by seeking action by international organizations states are making a choice to deal with such crimes at political or institutional level'.[304] International politics dominates Security Council actions with respect to responses to serious violations, not the law of state responsibility – although such considerations surely encroach upon Security Council actions.

## 3.5 PROBLEMATIC IMPLEMENTATION

The implementation of state responsibility is highly decentralized and dependent on state consensuality as a result of the lack of centralized enforcement in international law.[305] Despite the recent proliferation of international courts and tribunals and other dispute settlement bodies, judicialization still plays an inferior role in the implementation of state responsibility. To a large extent, the process is characterized by auto-determinations of responsibility and self-help,[306] marked by some uncertainty in the rules about who is entitled to invoke responsibility, by which modalities it is to be invoked and how it can be enforced. Moreover, it is widely held that political considerations affect the law of state responsibility, especially when it comes to diplomatically important incidents. The implementation of state responsibility consequently takes place mostly 'in the context of asymmetric and disparate diplomatic relations', to the detriment of less powerful states and communitarian obligations.[307]

303 UNSC Res. 687 (1991), 8 April 1991 (Iraq), para. 16: 'Iraq … is liable under international law for any direct loss, damage, including environmental damage and the depletion of natural resources, or injury to foreign Governments, nationals and corporations as a result of Iraq's unlawful invasion and occupation of Kuwait'.

304 White, 'Responses of Political Organs', 317.

305 Roland Pierik, 'Shared Responsibility in International Law: A Normative-Philosophical Analysis', in André Nollkaemper and Dov Jacobs (eds.), *Distribution of Responsibilities in International Law* (Cambridge: Cambridge University Press, 2015), pp. 36–61 at 59.

306 Proulx, *Institutionalizing*, p. 27.

307 Vincent-Joël Proulx, 'The World Court's Jurisdictional Formalism and Its Lost Market Share: The *Marshall Islands* Decisions and the Quest for a Suitable Dispute Settlement Forum for Multilateral Disputes' (2017) 30 *Leiden Journal of International Law* 925–946 at 939.

### 3.5.1 *State Discretion*

The first problem that the implementation of state responsibility encounters is the necessity of state interest – or more precisely, the possible lack of it. State responsibility is not an automatically activated regime, despite claims to the contrary. No obligatory judicial processes follow; instead, the implementation of state responsibility relies on state interest and activity to become operative. The injured state (or states acting on behalf of the injured party or the international community at large) must have and show interest in addressing the wrongs under the law of state responsibility. Furthermore, the injured state is free to unilaterally determine the existence of an internationally wrongful act as well as the specific legal consequences following the breach in question.[308] Whereas this may be unproblematic in a true interstate situation, in certain situations other actors – such as individuals and corporations – may be forced to rely on state interest due to the state-to-state fiction that state responsibility is built upon. This configuration becomes a constraint with regard to private actors and their access to remedy. To pursue claims of state responsibility 'is not an option that is at the disposal of private injured parties'.[309] They must rely on a state's discretion to pursue their matter, and cannot compel a state to exercise diplomatic protection on their behalf.

The protection of aliens is built upon the artifice of diplomatic protection, which equates wrongs committed against individuals abroad with wrongs committed against their state of nationality.[310] The individual is thus incapacitated: private interests are merged with the interests of the state with respect to internationally wrongful acts in which aliens are ill-treated.

[308] Proulx, *Institutionalizing*, p. 27.

[309] André Nollkaemper, 'Cluster-litigation in Cases of Transboundary Environmental Harm', in Michael Faure and Song Ying (eds.), *China and International Environmental Liability: Legal Remedies for Transboundary Pollution* (Cheltenham: Edward Elgar Publishing, 2008), pp. 11–37 at 22.

[310] John Dugard, the second Special Rapporteur on the subject, defines diplomatic protection as follows: 'Diplomatic protection is the procedure employed by the injured alien's State of nationality to secure compliance with the primary rules of international law governing the treatment of aliens or to claim reparation for the injury inflicted upon the alien', see 'Diplomatic Protection', in James Crawford, Alain Pellet and Simon Olleson (eds.), *The Law of International Responsibility* (Oxford: Oxford University Press, 2010), pp. 1051–1071 at 1051. It is not the only available mechanism in the law of state responsibility for protecting injured individuals, but it is the 'obvious remedy' and 'the remedy with the longest history and a ... proven record of effectiveness'. See Report of the ILC, Fifty-eighth Session, UN Doc. A/61/10 (2006), the ILC Articles on Diplomatic Protection, p. 13, commentary to Art. 19, at para. 2. For a discussion of the relationship between the individual and the state in the context of international responsibility, see Bollecker-Stern, *Le préjudice*, esp. p. 94 *et seqq*.

Nationality provides the link between the individual and the state whereby the state is entitled to exercise diplomatic protection.[311] This legal construct emerged in times when the individual lacked legal personality and corresponding rights in international law. The purpose of this so-called Vattelian fiction,[312] is not only to protect the individual from abuse but to simultaneously assert the inviolability of the state. This transfer of injury from the individual to the state was sustained by the PCIJ in the *Mavrommatis Palestine Concessions* case, where the Court held: '[b]y taking up the case of one of its subjects and by resorting to diplomatic action or international judicial proceedings on his behalf, a State is in reality asserting its own right – its right to ensure, in the person of its subjects, respect for the rules of international law.'[313] This leaves the question of who actually is injured – the individual or the state – undecided. The traditional approach maintains that the state asserts its right of diplomatic protection because it itself has been injured, but a more recent view holds that the '[s]tate acts as agent on behalf of the injured individual and enforces the right of the individual rather than that of the State.'[314] Such a reading could also be supported in light of the ICJ's statement in the *Diallo* case, where it noted that 'the sum awarded to Guinea in the exercise of diplomatic protection of Mr. Diallo is intended to provide reparation for the latter's injury'.[315] However, the ILC Articles on Diplomatic Protection (ADP) adopt a neutral position, thereby avoiding the issue of whose rights are asserted by way of diplomatic protection. Instead, the role of the state is stressed because the state is anyhow 'the entity in which the right to bring a claim vests'.[316]

The state has no obligation under international law to help its nationals through the exercise of diplomatic protection; the state's interest in pursuing claims lies completely in its own hands.[317] Hence, individuals and corporations are placed at the mercy of their home state. Some persons are automatically in a legally inferior position, such as refugees or stateless persons;

[311] The PCIJ stated in the *Panevezys-Saldutiskis Railway* case that 'it is the bond of nationality between the State and the individual which alone confers upon the State the right of diplomatic protection'. See *Panevezys-Saldutiskis Railway* (*Estonia* v. *Lithuania*) PCIJ Series A/B, No. 76 (1939), p. 16.

[312] de Vattel, *The Law of Nations*.

[313] *Mavrommatis Palestine Concessions (Greece v. United Kingdom)*, PCIJ Series A, No 2 (1924), p. 12.

[314] Dugard, 'Diplomatic Protection', 1052.

[315] *Ahmadou Sadio Diallo (Republic of Guinea* v. *Democratic Republic of Congo), Compensation, Judgment*, ICJ Reports 2012, p. 324, at para. 57.

[316] Report of the ILC (2006), p. 13 *et seqq.*, Commentary to Art. 2, at para. 1.

[317] Ibid., Commentary to Art. 2.

in some instances, it may even be impossible to ascertain the nationality of victims.[318] Others may suffer from lack of protection as a result of political circumstances.[319] States may also 'be reluctant to exercise their right to protect their nationals for fear of deterioration of the relation with the host State'.[320] The individual that has suffered an injury is thus a bystander in his or her own affair, with no control over the procedure. It is hardly surprising that diplomatic protection has been described as 'imperialist and old-fashioned',[321] and as a mechanism that 'paternalizes individuals and prevents ownership and agency'.[322] Diplomatic protection as a discretionary right highlights once again the difficulty of fitting state responsibility not only into the structures of a globalized world, but also to an international community in which the individual arguably ought to benefit from possession of universal human rights.

Although states still view diplomatic protection as a discretionary right, some attempts have been made to bring diplomatic protection more in line with a human rights–based international community.[323] Special Rapporteur John Dugard in a progressive fashion sought to make the exercise of diplomatic protection an obligation in cases of grave breaches of peremptory norms of international law.[324] There have also been cases from national courts opening the door to the possibility of a duty of diplomatic protection, as well as national legislation establishing such a right.[325] The ILC has also sought to

318 In the case of *Armed Activities on the Territory of the Congo* before the ICJ, the claim included 17 individuals that Uganda had sought to protect but whose nationalities could not be ascertained. It is noted that the Court had 'no information whatsoever as to their nationality', *Case Concerning Armed Activities on the Territory of Congo (Democratic Republic of the Congo* v. *Uganda), Judgment*, ICJ Reports 2005, p. 168, Separate Opinion of Judge Simma, para. 25.

319 For example, with respect to the detainees at Guantánamo Bay, the Australian national David Hicks sought to acquire British citizenship in order to get better diplomatic protection than Australia had exercised on his behalf. Indeed, the phenomenon of 'nationality-shopping' had been recognized also by the ILC when drafting the ILC Articles on Diplomatic Protection. See Report of the ILC (2006), Commentary to Art. 5, at para. 1.

320 Annemarieke Vermeer-Künzli, 'A Matter of Interest: Diplomatic Protection and State Responsibility *Erga Omnes*' (2007) 56 *International and Comparative Law Quarterly* (2007) 553–581 at 581.

321 Annemarieke Vermeer-Künzli, 'As If: The Legal Fiction in Diplomatic Protection' (2007) 18 *European Journal of International Law* 37–68 at 56.

322 Peters, 'Membership', 166.

323 The ILC recognizes that '[t]he protection of human beings by means of international law is today one of the principal goals of the international legal order'. See Report of the ILC (2006), Commentary to Art. 19, at para. 2. See also the 2005 *World Summit Outcome*, A/RES/60/1 (2005), esp. para. 119.

324 John Dugard, *First Report on Diplomatic Protection*, UN Doc. A/CN.4/506 (2000), paras. 74–87.

325 Ibid., para. 80. For example, the German Constitution recognizes the right of its nationals to receive diplomatic protection, as do constitutional provisions of many other states (Ibid., para. 81). Cases that can be partly cited in support of an obligation to exercise diplomatic protection include,

mitigate the issue.[326] Article 19 of the ADP stipulates that a state which has the right to exercise diplomatic protection should '[g]ive due consideration to the possibility of exercising diplomatic protection, especially when a significant injury has occurred'.[327] The views of the individual should also be taken into account when it comes to the matters of resort to diplomatic protection, reparation sought, and the transfer of compensation. The ILC has held that 'there is growing support for the view that there is some obligation, however, imperfect, on States, either under international law or national law, to protect their nationals abroad when they are subjected to significant human rights violations.'[328]

There has been a slight shift from complete discretion to the possibility of perceiving diplomatic protection as a duty of the state of nationality in some grave situations. Despite this, the tension between the protection of community interests in the law of state responsibility and the law of diplomatic protection still exists. This has left scholars highlighting pragmatic solutions. Judge Simma of the ICJ has held that 'no gaps exist in the law that would deprive the affected persons of any legal protection'.[329] These conciliatory efforts to reconcile progressive features of international law with its more traditional rudiments are nonetheless too few to alleviate incongruities between the law of state responsibility and that of diplomatic protection.

### 3.5.2 *Lack of International Claimant(s)*

The problem with the bilateral foundation of the law of state responsibility extends beyond the discretionary practice of diplomatic protection. The state-to-state implementation of responsibility leaves it unclear as to who, if anyone, acts on behalf of the international community when its particular stakes are

among others, the *Abbasi and another* v. *Secretary of State for Foreign and Commonwealth Affairs & Secretary of State for the Home Department*, [2002] EWCA Civ 1598 (Eng.), and *Samuel Kaunda et al.* v. *President of the Republic of South Africa* before the Constitutional Court of South Africa, 44 *International Legal Materials* (2005), p. 173, esp. paras. 30, 63, 69–70. The Court held that '[t]here may thus be a duty on government… to take action to protect one of its citizens against a gross abuse of international human rights norms' (Ibid., para. 69).

326 The ILC also attempted to reflect on the non-privileged position of refugees and stateless persons by means of the insertion of Article 8 in the ADP, which stipulates that states may extend diplomatic protection to such persons as well, if they are 'lawfully and habitually resident in that State'. For the ADP, see Report of the ILC (2006), Commentary to Article 8, paras. 1–3. However, the ILC itself admitted that the threshold of protection by virtue of Article 8 is high, consequently still excluding some individuals from the sphere of diplomatic protection (Ibid., para. 4).

327 Report of the ILC (2006), the ILC Articles on Diplomatic Protection, text of the draft articles with commentaries thereto, paras. 49 and 50, Article 19.

328 Ibid., Commentary to Article 19, at para. 3.

329 *Case Concerning Armed Activities on the Territory of Congo (Democratic Republic of the Congo* v. *Uganda), Judgment*, ICJ Reports 2005, p. 168 Separate Opinion of Judge Simma, at para. 19.

at concern. When it comes to communitarian norms 'there is no collective entity with capacity to act',[330] and yet the practice of the ICJ shows the difficulties involved in 'bilateralizing' disputes that are genuinely of a multilateral nature.[331] Community interests are thus also subjected to state discretion: no one is obliged to act, even though the fundamental values of the international community may be under attack. This inconsistency becomes untenable, particularly in situations of internal atrocities in which the victims may fall completely outside the parameters of the state responsibility rules. The same applies to the protection of global commons.

Although the ILC's Articles create no enforcement mechanism of true international character for serious violations of international law that are in the interest of the whole international community, the ASR do expand the scope of possible claimants. Accordingly, those norms that are of utmost importance to the international community can be upheld by states that are not directly injured themselves or, to use the ILC language, are 'other than an injured state'.[332] Their indirect injury relates to the general legal interest of seeing international law upheld. Third states are thus categorized differently from directly injured states. This differentiation is also reflected in the modalities of invocation. Third states can invoke responsibility, but only to the extent that they demand cessation of the violation, non-repetition and fulfilment of the international obligations in question.[333]

It is noteworthy that in the ASR the right to take solidarity measures or countermeasures in defence of general interests is left undecided due to the unclear state of international law on the matter, as has been argued by the ILC.[334] The ILC thus created a regime in which the absence of a directly injured state generates a situation for which the set of responses to serious violations is smaller or more limited than with respect to 'ordinary' wrongs.[335] According to the ILC, too little practice on third-party countermeasures or 'lawful measures' exists, which reveals that third states generally hesitate to resort to countermeasures in situations in which community interests

330 James Crawford, 'Responsibility for Breaches of Communitarian Norms: An Appraisal of Article 48 of the ILC Articles on Responsibility of States for Internationally Wrongful Acts', in Ulrich Fastenrath et al. (eds.), *From Bilateralism to Community Interest: Essays in Honour of Bruno Simma* (Oxford: Oxford University Press, 2011), pp. 224–240 at 226.

331 *Obligations concerning Negotiations relating to Cessation of the Nuclear Arms Race and to Nuclear Disarmament (Marshall Islands* v. *United Kingdom), Preliminary Objections, Judgment*, ICJ Reports 2016, p. 833; Proulx, 'The World Court's Jurisdictional', 932.

332 See Arts. 48 and 54 of the ASR.

333 Art. 48 (2) of the ASR.

334 Art. 54 of the ASR.

335 Denis Alland, 'Countermeasures of General Interest' (2002) 13 *European Journal of International Law* 1221–1239 at 1239.

are violated, unless they somehow have a connection to the wrong.[336] The ILC's decision to leave the issue of third-party countermeasures open on the grounds of too little and inconsistent practice was later criticized. Arguably, the practice of such countermeasures is broader than the ILC holds it to be. In addition, *opinio juris* exists supporting the conclusion that 'third-party countermeasures are permissible under international law'.[337] Despite this finding, the great hopes placed upon the law of state responsibility with respect to enforcement of communitarian obligations have simply not materialized.[338]

However, not only with respect to the right of third states to take countermeasures in the public interest is the legal framework incomplete. Another way of realizing *actio popularis* (action to protcctive collective interests) is by initiating international proceedings against a wrongdoer when community interests are at stake.[339] Nonetheless, international practice reveals that the right of third states to bring a claim in the public interest is disputed, to say the least. Since the ICJ's rejection of *actio popularis* in the *South West Africa* cases,[340] some cases with a public interest aspect have arisen. For example, the genocide in the former Yugoslavia spurred separate complaints by Bosnia-Herzegovina and Croatia before the ICJ in order to hold the state of Serbia responsible for genocide. Both state claimants had nationals of their own among the victims: Bosniaks were massacred in Srebrenica, which gave the Bosnian state a clear interest in invoking Serbia's responsibility. Similarly, Croatia had an interest in pursuing the responsibility of Serbia for Croatians killed in the conflict. However, in the proceedings before the ICJ, Bosnia and Herzegovina recognized the non-bilateral nature of the Serbian obligation to prevent and punish genocide.[341] According to the Bosnian evidence, Serbia had also committed genocide in other parts of the former Yugoslavia,

336 See Commentary to Art. 54 of the ASR.

337 Dawidowicz, *Third-Party Countermeasures*, p. 283; Similarly, concerning state practice, see Linos-Alexander Sicilianos, 'The Classification of Obligations and the Multilateral Dimension of the Relations of International Responsibility' (2002) 13 *European Journal of International Law* 1127–1145 at 1143.

338 Dawidowicz, *Third-Party Countermeasures*, p. 1.

339 The notion of *actio popularis* is commonly used to denote questions of standing: i.e., the right of every state to initiate proceedings in the general interest, although it is used in other meanings as well. For a discussion of its usage, see Tams, *Enforcing Obligations*, p. 161.

340 In the *South West Africa Cases* the ICJ held that *actio popularis* is 'not known to international law'. See *South West Africa Cases* (*Ethiopia* v. *South Africa*, *Liberia* v. *South* Africa), Second Phase, Judgment, ICJ Reports 1966, p. 6, at para. 88. For a different assessment of the case, see Tams, *Enforcing Obligations*, p. 68.

341 *Case concerning the Application of the Convention on the Prevention and Punishment of the Crime of Genocide* (*Bosnia-Herzegovina* v. *Federal Republic of Yugoslavia*), Reply of the Government of Bosnia and Herzegovina (23 April 1998) Chapter 8, Section 12, p. 754, para. 477.

not only in the territory of the Bosnian state. Thus, the Bosnian suit also concerned nationalities other than its own citizens; expressly mentioned were Kosovo Albanians, Croats, Sandzak Muslims, and Hungarians.[342] The state of Bosnia and Herzegovina explicitly argued that it was entitled to act 'even when the claimant State or its nationals are not the direct victims of the genocidal acts', because it was a logical consequence to the erga omnes character of the Genocide Convention.[343] However, the jurisdictional basis of Bosnia-Herzegovina's claim was not *actio popularis* in international law, but Article IX of the Genocide Convention.[344]

Although the ASR admit the right of third states to invoke responsibility in the name of collective interest, the rules do not list public interest litigation within the means of enforcement.[345] Thus, litigation on behalf of non-nationals is explicitly not accepted under the general law of state responsibility because the bilateral origin of the law holds third states to be 'affected to a degree in a more theoretical or "legal" way'.[346] However, in the aftermath of the *Bosnian Genocide* case some scholars have begun to question the general rejection of third states pursuing altruistic claims. The silence of the ICJ regarding this particular issue has been interpreted as a tacit acceptance of Bosnia and Herzegovina's 'right to bring a claim in respect of atrocities committed against persons who are not its nationals'.[347] The question of public interest litigation has also been associated with the general aims of international proceedings in which arguably reparational claims would be inadmissible, but those seeking declaratory judgments

342 Ibid.

343 Ibid., Chapter 17, Section 1, p. 956, para. 4.

344 Ibid., Chapter 6, Section 4, p. 355.

345 Article 48 of the ASR reads:

1. 'Any State other than an injured State is entitled to invoke the responsibility of another State in accordance with paragraph 2 if:
   (a) The obligation breached is owed to a group of States including that State, and is established for the protection of a collective interest of the group, or;
   (b) The obligation breached is owed to the international community as a whole.
2. Any State entitled to invoke responsibility under paragraph 1 may claim from the responsible State:
   (a) Cessation of the internationally wrongful act, and assurances and guarantees of non-repetition in accordance with article 30; and
   (b) Performance of the obligation of reparation in accordance with the preceding articles in the interest of the injured State or the beneficiaries of the obligation breached;
   (c) The requirements for the invocation of responsibility by an injured State under articles 43, 44 and 45 apply to an invocation of responsibility by a State entitled to do so under paragraph 1.'

346 *Comments and Observations by Governments*, UN Doc. A/CN.4/515 and Add.1–3 (2001), Comments by the Netherlands under Article 43, p. 75.

347 Okowa, 'State and Individual Responsibility', 164.

would be acceptable. Third states would thus have a right to litigate in order to receive a 'judgment aimed at elucidating an interpretation of the peremptory obligation in issue and/or an authoritative finding that breach had occurred'.[348] Judge Simma of the ICJ has also taken a positive stance on public interest litigation. In the case of *Armed Activities on the Territory of the Congo*, he opined the right of Uganda to file a claim on behalf of maltreated private persons at the Ndjili Airport, whose nationalities could not be ascertained.[349]

Nevertheless, what has appeared as a discernible tendency toward more lenient positions on public interest litigation before the ICJ,[350] has suffered a blow with the *Marshall Islands* case.[351] In that case, the Marshall Islands sought a judgment from the World Court that a group of nuclear weapon states were in violation of their obligations to negotiate in good faith on nuclear disarmament. Among other things, the Applicant based its application to the Court on ILC Articles 42 and 48,[352] arguing that 'every State has a legal interest' in concluding negotiations leading to nuclear disarmament.[353] Nevertheless, the ICJ did not embrace the opportunity to advance the law on public interest litigation concerning communitarian norms, a decision which has been criticized for keeping the Court from bringing about 'more justice and fairness in international affairs'.[354] The recent *Myanmar Genocide* case filed by Gambia to the ICJ will, however, present the Court with another opportunity to position itself on the issue.[355]

348 Iain Scobbie, 'The Invocation of Responsibility for the Breach of "Obligations under Peremptory Norms of General International Law"' (2002) 13 *European Journal of International Law* 1201–1220 at 1219.

349 See Judge Simma, in *Case Concerning Armed Activities on the Territory of Congo (Democratic Republic of the Congo* v. *Uganda), Judgment*, ICJ Reports 2005, p. 168 Separate Opinion of Judge Simma, p. 334, esp. at paras. 19, 32–37.

350 See Christian J. Tams, 'Individual States as Guardians of Community Interests', in Ulrich Fastenrath, Rudolf Geiger, Daniel-Erasmus Khan et al. (eds.), *From Bilateralism to Community Interest: Essays in Honour of Judge Bruno Simma* (Oxford: Oxford University Press, 2011), pp. 379–405 at 386.

351 *Obligations concerning Negotiations relating to Cessation of the Nuclear Arms Race and to Nuclear Disarmament (Marshall Islands* v. *United Kingdom)*, Preliminary Objections, Judgment, ICJ Reports 2016, p. 833.

352 *Obligations concerning Negotiations relating to the Cessation of the Nuclear Arms Race and to Nuclear Disarmament (Marshall Islands* v. *Pakistan)*, Memorial of the Marshall Islands, 12 January 2015, p. 17, para. 39.

353 Ibid., p. 13, para. 31.

354 Bianchi, 'Choice and (the Awareness of)', 86. See also Ingo Venzke, 'Public Interests in the International Court of Justice – A Comparison between *Nuclear Arms Race* (2016) and *South West Africa* (1966)' (2017) 111 *AJIL Unbound* 68–74; Vincent-Joël Proulx, 'The *Marshall Islands* Judgments and Multilateral Disputes at the World Court: Whither Access to International Justice?' (2017) 111 *AJIL Unbound* 96–101; Proulx, 'The World Court's Jurisdictional'.

355 *Application of the Convention on the Prevention and Punishment of the Crime of Genocide (The Gambia* v. *Myanmar)*, Order of 23 January 2020.

The modalities for when third states can litigate for communitarian interests still remain unclear.[356] The viability of state responsibility with respect to situations of serious wrongs is dependent on third states and their right and desire to take actions: 'unless third states can bring claims, there is little possibility that these states would be held to account'.[357] The construction of state responsibility thus hinders the international community from truly acting when important concerns are at stake. At least it can be claimed that coupling the most important violations with the current unclear and insufficient means of enforcement fails to provide a much-needed incentive to act. The possible right to pursue altruistic litigation is a different matter than the making use of that right. At present, state practice indicates a general reluctance by third states to initiate public interest litigation.[358]

Thus, one ends up with serious violations for which state responsibility provides little relief. The Rwandan genocide shows that apart from general protests and condemnations, no third state either separately or jointly invoked the Rwandan state's responsibility for the genocide.[359] Pursuing an interstate responsibility claim on behalf of Tutsis remained in nobody's express interest or right. Not only were the factual circumstances different from those in the *Bosnian Genocide* case, but also those circumstances involving jurisdictional questions: Rwanda had issued a reservation on the provision on dispute settlement of the Genocide Convention of 1948 which provided the legal basis for the *Bosnian Genocide* case. Moreover, since international law remains obscure with regard to *actio popularis*, state responsibility was not going to

356 According to Pierre-Marie Dupuy, 'the conditions for an *actio popularis* in international law remain, today as previously, thoroughly imprecise'. See Dupuy, 'A General Stocktaking', 1075.

357 Okowa, 'State and Individual Responsibility', 165.

358 See Tams, 'Individual States as Guardians', 388.

359 It has been argued that '[s]tates have been very slow or reluctant to act' with respect to the Rwandan atrocities. See Luc Reydams, 'Universal Jurisdiction over Atrocities in Rwanda: Theory and Practice' (1996) 4 *European Journal of Crime, Criminal Law and Criminal Justice* 18–47 at 47. The actions of specific states with regard to the Rwandan atrocities mostly relate to international criminal law and the arrest and prosecution of Rwandan people accused of crimes falling under the principle of universal jurisdiction. Cases have been initiated in Belgium, France, Switzerland and Finland. (Ibid.) Certainly, many states protested the atrocities committed in Rwanda, but whether these can be considered as invocations of responsibility is difficult to assess. Iain Scobbie notes that 'it might be difficult to distinguish protest clearly from invocation where a state is acting under Article 48 in the collective interest'. See Scobbie, 'The Invocation of Responsibility', 1206.

help the Rwandan genocide victims.[360] The rules of state responsibility thus fail to protect with appropriate seriousness the most fundamental values of the international community.

### 3.5.3 *Factual Inequality of States*

A third problem regarding the implementation of responsibility concerns the inequality of states. Although at the normative level all states are equal in terms of enforcement,[361] at the practical level states are far from being equally capable of starting a process of state responsibility and advancing their rights through a system that foremostly relies on self-help. Influential states undeniably have more credible power in asserting their rights than less powerful states; they have a 'natural advantage' in the enforcement of their rights.[362] This is confirmed both in practice and by international legal scholars.

[360] According to the 1948 Convention on the Prevention and Punishment of the Crime of Genocide (hereinafter the Genocide Convention), New York, 9 December 1948, in force 12 January 1951, 78 *United Nations Treaty Series* 277, Art. IX: 'Disputes between the Contracting Parties relating to the interpretation, application or fulfilment of the present Convention, including those relating to the responsibility of a State for genocide or any of the other acts enumerated in article III, shall be submitted to the International Court of Justice at the request of any of the parties to the dispute'. The crux here lies with the interpretation of 'any of the parties to the dispute', which remains unclear. In situations of internal genocide, which of the contracting parties are ultimately to be considered as parties to the dispute? Three options seem available: (1) every contracting party irrespective of direct injury towards them; (2) a party directly affected by the internal genocide if, for example, its citizens are being slaughtered; (3) no state, if none is directly affected. In the *Bosnian Genocide case*, the ICJ noted that a legal dispute exists between two states when they 'hold clearly opposite views concerning the question of performance or non-performance of certain treaty obligations.' See *Application of the Convention on the Prevention and Punishment of the Crime of Genocide (Bosnia and Herzegovina* v. *Yugoslavia) (Preliminary Objections)*, ICJ Reports 1996, at para. 29. Moreover, the Court notes that the nature of the international conflict does not affect the jurisdiction of the Court due to the *erga omnes* character of the obligations to prevent and punish genocide: 'the Convention is applicable, without reference to the circumstances linked to the domestic or international nature of the conflict' (Ibid., para. 31). Arguably then, any contracting party to the Genocide Convention could have taken Rwanda to the World Court for non-performance of its obligations under the 1948 Genocide Convention, had it not issued a reservation against Article IX, stating that it does not consider itself bound by this article.

[361] According to Christian Tams, '[a]t some level, this simplistic, egalitarian approach is liberating and refreshing. It is notable for its rejection (if only implicitly) of notions of *regional "core states"* keeping order within their respective sphere of dominance, or world hegemonic powers asserting a general competence to police the world'. See Tams, 'Individual States as Guardians', 403 (emphasis in original). See also Aust, 'The Normative Environment', 24, who states that '[a]t least in theory, the rules of State responsibility are at the disposal of all States'.

[362] Margo Kaplan, 'Using Collective Interests to Ensure Human Rights: An Analysis of the Articles on State Responsibility' (2004) 79 *New York University Law Review* 1902–1933 at 1919.

The "every-man-for-himself" doctrine … 'unveils, and, even endorses, the crucial dependence of the enforceability of a State's international rights upon a favourable distribution of power'.[363] A state's interest in invoking state responsibility is therefore clearly dependent upon the leverage it possesses at the international level. As a result, situations may emerge where state responsibility remains a theoretical avenue only, leaving its use highly improbable. The 2003 illegal invasion of Iraq by the US-led Coalition Forces is often mentioned as an example of an internationally wrongful act against which states were highly unlikely to make use of the law of state responsibility.[364]

The general problem of less powerful states' reluctance to invoke responsibility and enforce their own rights by way of countermeasures is noticeable within specific branches of international law. The problem is striking in WTO law and international trade. For example, small or less powerful states are less likely to make use of the WTO dispute settlement system or to resort to countermeasures under the general rules of state responsibility, as these are of little value in the pursuit of making more powerful counterparties abide by their commitments.[365] More importantly, however, the states would themselves suffer by way of internal losses.[366] Thus, the downside to countermeasures in international trade is 'that the state imposing these measures may injure itself as much as the state against which they are directed; this is particularly so when one cuts off trade with another state'.[367] One example of the unwillingness to resort to countermeasures in trade issues is the

363 Bruno Simma, 'Bilateralism and Community', 822. In the same vein, Andreas Paulus holds that '[i]t is highly understandable why weak States object to countermeasures because they will seldom be able to induce strong States to comply with their international obligations by violating their own obligations in response'. See Andreas Paulus, 'Reciprocity Revisited', in Ulrich Fastenrath, Rudolf Geiger, Daniel-Erasmus Khan et al. (eds.), *From Bilateralism to Community Interest: Essays in Honour of Judge Bruno Simma* (Oxford: Oxford University Press, 2011), pp. 113–137 at 126.

364 Aust, 'The Normative Environment', 25.

365 Statistics show that the United States and the EU are the predominant users of the WTO legal system, and noticeably so to a much higher degree than their share of global trade would suggest. See Roderick Abbott, ECIPE Working Paper, No. 01/2007, 'Are Developing Countries Deterred from Using the WTO Dispute Settlement System? Participation of Developing Countries in the DSM in the Years 1995–2005', at 9, ecipe.org/wp-content/uploads/2014/12/are-developing-countries-deterred-from-using-the-wto-dispute-settlement-system.pdf (accessed 31 July 2019).

366 Victor Mosoti holds that '[t]he instrument of retaliation will usually involve raising trade barriers, decreasing the flow of goods on which LDCs [least developed countries] are dependent'. See Victor Mosoti, 'In Our Own Image, Not Theirs: Damages as an Antidote to the Remedial Deficiencies in the WTO Dispute Settlement Process; A View from Sub-Saharan Africa' (2001) 19 *Boston University International Law Journal* 231–256 at 254.

367 Malanczuk, *Akehurst's Modern*, p. 4.

reluctance of the East African states of Uganda, Mozambique, Kenya and Tanzania to pursue a claim against the European Union with regard to its fish import bans in 1997 and 1999.[368] The EU imposed a ban on fishery products from the region due, allegedly, to the outbreak of cholera in the East African states. This measure was criticized as overly cautious by the World Food and Agriculture Organization (FAO) and the African states in question, as arguably no scientific justification for the measure existed.[369] Thus, even though it has been asserted that the affected African states had a strong case against the EU because the imposition of the ban was considered to be a trade barrier rather than a justifiable measure aimed 'for the protection of human, animal or plant life or health', and the affected states lost several hundred million dollars in lost revenues, these less powerful states chose to outlive the ban. Instead of fighting the ban, the states proceeded to take measures in order to meet the demands set by the EU. However, the ban was in place for almost two years, during which time the states lost 'more than $300 million in foreign revenue' and many people within the fishing industry lost their jobs.[370]

When it comes to serious violations of international law, the unequal distribution of power among nations may exacerbate the inferior position of small or less powerful states, unless they have powerful friends. In cases of aggression or genocide, for example, self-help remains inadequate. Nigel D. White claims that '[c]rimes by states are almost always committed against defenceless victims (states or individuals), and the international legal system of sovereign equals is not really designed to help them.'[371] Moreover, the victim may not constitute a state, and thereby formally lack the right to self-help, or, no victim might exist to begin with.[372] The question of collective countermeasures or so-called solidarity measures undertaken by third states on behalf of the

[368] See Commission Decision 1999/253/EC, 12 April 1999 on 'Protective measures with regard to certain fishery products from or originating in Kenya and Tanzania'.

[369] According to the Food and Agriculture Organization of the United Nations (FAO), 'Epidemiological data suggests that the risk of transmission of cholera from contaminated imported fish is negligible'. Further, the FAO held that the ban was not 'the most appropriate response'. See FAO Press Release 98/21, 25 March 1998. In addition, the affected states held that their fish "were safe for human consumption", see Mosoti, 'In Our Own Image', 250.

[370] Mosoti, 'In our Own Image', 251. Similarly, it has been argued that the ban was lifted only 20 months after EU inspectors were satisfied with the operation of Kenyan authorities and no pesticides were found. See Cerina Banu Issufo Mussa, René Vossenaar and Nimrod Nakisisa Waniala, 'Eastern and Southern Africa: The Experience of Kenya, Mozambique, The United Republic of Tanzania and Uganda', in Veena Jha (ed.) *Environmental Regulation and Food Safety: Studies of Protection and Protectionism* (Cheltenham: Edward Elgar Publishing, 2005), pp. 103–144 at 117 *et seqq.*

[371] White, 'Responses of Political Organs', 315.

[372] See Crawford, *Third Report*, paras. 378–379.

victim state will not be able to alleviate concerns over the poorer position of less powerful states in asserting their rights. Instead, solidarity measures raise a new thorny issue: vigilantism and the risk for political abuse. Against this background, it comes as no surprise that powerful states generally object to stringent systems of collective or centralized enforcement that would mitigate the element of power inequality.[373]

There are clear risks involved in taking the enforcement of law into one's own hands, particularly when all states are involved as is the case with the enforcement of community interests. Under current conditions, the danger of vigilantism mainly relates to Western states and their pursuance of a world police role, as international practice has shown that non-Western states have not equally often resorted to countermeasures on behalf of the international community.[374] However, James Crawford argues that the situation would have been even worse had the notion of international crimes been adopted, since the notion of crime builds on the understanding that somebody must be punished. Under a system of criminal responsibility, powerful states, especially the permanent members of the Security Council, could more easily have made use of 'name-calling'[375] and 'illegitimate coercion'[376] in order to accentuate their power. It has also been pointed out that 'not every erroneous invocation of State responsibility can be seen as a form of abuse' since it may be difficult to separate misuse from differences of interpretation of the law.[377]

To what level the danger of political abuse is real under the current system remains open. Although it does not appear commonplace for Western states to couch their policies in the language of responsibility, this does happen, as the EU Cholera case demonstrates. State responsibility or specific implementation procedures can be used as tools of self-interest. Although Western states often have been the driving force behind countermeasures in cases of serious violations of international law,[378] and consequently, are those primarily able to

373 For a general discussion of the international legal order and power inequality, see Nico Krisch, 'International Law in Times of Hegemony: Unequal Power and the Shaping of the International Legal Order' (2005) 16 *European Journal of International Law* 369–408.

374 In his review of state practice with respect to collective countermeasures, Special Rapporteur James Crawford notes that 'it has to be frankly admitted that practice is dominated by a particular group of States (i.e. Western States). There are few instances in which, for example, States from Africa or Asia have taken collective countermeasures'. See Crawford, *Third Report*, para. 396.

375 Crawford, 'International Crimes of States', 413.

376 Koskenniemi, 'Doctrines', 49.

377 Aust, 'The Normative Environment', 24.

378 Third party countermeasures have been little protested. See Tams, *Enforcing Obligations*, p. 231.

misuse this mechanism, many other states have also resorted to countermeasures.[379] State responsibility is thus an instrument in the hands of the powerful states. The implementation of state responsibility in the contemporary world with its asymmetric distribution of power is thus characterized by a paradox: state responsibility serves as both a safeguard to any state (including the less powerful) in the world against internationally wrongful acts committed by other states, and a mechanism whereby more powerful states may preserve, and even advance, their power.

### 3.5.4 *Elusiveness*

In international law, third party dispute settlement does not play a predominant role in the enforcement of rules and principles in the way that it does in national legal systems. Instead, the implementation of state responsibility can take a variety of forms ranging from bilateral negotiations to binding adjudication. Most disputes are of a bilateral nature and occur outside the institutional structures of international legal relations. From this it follows that the prevailing means of dispute settlement are direct negotiations between the conflicting parties, as judicial settlement in international legal relations is still relatively rare.[380] In fact, in many cases of conflict, diplomacy and negotiations are 'the only means to settle disputes that the parties employ'.[381] As a result, the implementation of state responsibility is rarely a legal matter alone, especially when it comes to diplomatically important incidents. The mixing of legal and political spheres in itself may not constitute a problem, but certain consequences follow that affect the appeal of state responsibility, and may even lead states to avoid pursuing claims under the law. For example, the Soviet Union was clearly responsible for the 1986 *Chernobyl* nuclear accident, yet invocations of state responsibility were manifestly lacking. This was due at least in part to the difficulties surrounding effective implementation of

379 Dawidowicz, *Third-Party Countermeasures*, p. 283.

380 Kazuhiro Nakatani, 'Diplomacy and State Responsibility', in Maurizio Ragazzi (ed.), *International Responsibility Today: Essays in Memory of Oscar Schachter* (Leiden: Martinus Nijhoff Publishers, 2005), pp. 37–47 at 38; Michael Waibel, 'The Diplomatic Channel', in James Crawford, Alain Pellet and Simon Olleson (eds.), *The Law of International Responsibility* (Oxford: Oxford University Press, 2010), pp. 1085–1097 at 1085.

381 Waibel, 'The Diplomatic Channel', 1087. For a discussion of the benefits and disadvantages of such a method, see esp. 1090 *et seq.* Thomas Skouteris notes that secondary rules of international law, such as those of state responsibility 'operate at their best before tribunals, where the language of law is spoken with as few diversions as possible', see Skouteris, *The Notion of Progress*, p. 166.

state responsibility, which arguably had even led to a broader tendency among states during that time to avoid putting state responsibility into practice.[382]

First, because state responsibility can be situated in the middle ground between law and politics, and between informal and formal means of implementation, it can be difficult to identify the operation of state responsibility. One reason for this is that in the diplomatic context, deviations from the general law of state responsibility are common.[383] This means that the 'law in the books' may differ from the 'law in action'.[384] At times state responsibility may operate without responsibility being formally admitted. In other situations, a 'false' admission of responsibility may characterize the process. The settlement between Japan and the United States in the 1954 *Fukuryu Maru* case exemplifies how disputes can be settled through diplomatic negotiations without ever formally addressing the questions of wrongfulness and responsibility. The United States conducted nuclear tests in the Bikini Atoll causing injury, among others, to the personnel of the *Fukuryu Maru*, a Japanese fishing vessel. One crewmember died of radiation and 26 others were injured. There was no mention of legal responsibility in the settlement, yet the United States paid two million dollars in damages.[385] Arguably, the states reached 'a desirable legal result', even though 'no legal issues were formally resolved between Japan and the United States'.[386]

Another example is the Hainan airplane collision between the United States and China in 2001, which displayed similar features. In spite of the 'two very sorries' by the United States, it was argued that no international legal obligations had been violated.[387] The United States clearly apologized without accepting

382 Alexandre Kiss, 'L'accident de Tchernobyl: ses consequences au point de vue du Droit international' (1986) 32 *Annuaire français de droit international* 139–152 at 143–145.

383 Nakatani, 'Diplomacy and State Responsibility', 38. In fact, according to Nakatani, '[t]he more important a case involving State responsibility is in the diplomatic context, the more unlikely it is that the general law of State responsibility be applied without modifications' (Ibid.). In general, the significance of international law in diplomacy is disputed. See Waibel, 'The Diplomatic Channel', 1091.

384 Cane, *Responsibility in Law,* p. 225 *et seqq.*

385 Michael Waibel has indeed noticed that '[a]n undertaking to compensate assumed in diplomatic negotiations may, but need not reflect an underlying internationally wrongful act'. See Waibel, 'The Diplomatic Channel', 1095.

386 Myres S. McDougal and Norbert A. Schlei, 'The Hydrogen Bomb Tests in Perspective: Lawful Measures for Security' (1954–1955) 64 *Yale Law Journal* 648–710 at 695.

387 See Margaret K. Lewis, 'An Analysis of State Responsibility for the Chinese-American Airplane Collision Incident' (2002) 77 *New York University Law Review* 1404–1441. On the specific question of the institution of apology for an internationally wrongful act, see Sir Arthur Watts, 'The Art of Apology', in Maurizio Ragazzi (ed.), *International Responsibility Today: Essays in Memory of Oscar Schachter* (Leiden: Martinus Nijhoff Publishers, 2005), pp. 107–116.

any legal responsibility.[388] However, the intention behind the admission by the United States was to achieve the release of the American airplane crew that had been apprehended by China. There are similar cases in which state responsibility is instrumental to achieving goals outside the aim of normalizing interstate relations. For example, in the *USS Pueblo* case of 1968 the United States admitted full responsibility for having violated North Korea's territorial waters in order to get North Korea to release a ship and its crew of eighty-two men.[389]

Second, many international incidents in which the issue of state responsibility has arisen and has been implemented according to the standard rules remain unknown to the general public. This can be illustrated with the recent dispute between Turkey and Israel concerning the events on the vessel *Mavi Marmara*.[390] As a result of the killing of nine Turkish activists on the *Mavi Marmara* by Israeli forces in 2010, Turkey demanded an apology from Israel and compensation for the families of the killed activists. Israel, however, denied having done any wrong as it argued it had acted in self-defence, whereupon Turkey severed diplomatic relations with Israel. Further, Turkey suspended military cooperation with Israel. After a few years of diplomatic crisis between the two states involving several punches and counterpunches, in March 2013 Israeli Prime Minister Benjamin Netanjahu – with President Obama of the United States acting as a mediator – called his Turkish counterpart and apologized for the excessive use of violence on the *Mavi Marmara*. The two states agreed to re-establish diplomatic relations, in addition to which Turkey stated that it would not proceed with trials that had been instigated against four Israeli soldiers. In addition, Israel promised to compensate for the Turkish losses. This classic case of state responsibility and its existence, content and implementation was never portrayed as a legal process.[391] Instead, it was described in terms

388 See Lewis, 'An Analysis of State Responsibility', 1436. Contradictory views have been expressed regarding the fact of whether the United States admitted responsibility or not. For a comment interpreting the US behaviour as admitting responsibility, see Nakatani, 'Diplomacy and State Responsibility', 39. Generally it can be maintained that 'saying "sorry" may also imply an admission of legal liability.' See Watts, 'The Art of Apology', 107.

389 The sole purpose of releasing the crew members was admitted in an attachment to the document, in which General Woodward, acting on behalf of the United States, declared the following: the United States '[s]houlders full responsibility and solemnly apologizes for the grave acts of espionage'. See Statement by the Department of State Spokesman, 'Release at Panmunjom of Crew of U.S.S. Pueblo' (1969) 63 *American Journal of International Law* 682–684 at 684.

390 In 2010, the Israeli army killed nine Turkish activists on the ship *Mavi Marmara*, which attempted to break the Gaza embargo in order to deliver humanitarian goods to the Palestinians.

391 See Aishi Zidan, 'Israel pyysi Turkilta anteeksi laivaiskua', *Helsingin Sanomat*, 23 March 2013, p. B3; Jodi Rudoren and Mark Landler, 'With Obama as Broker, Israel and Turkey End Dispute', *The New York Times*, 22 March 2013, www.nytimes.com/2013/03/23/world/middleeast/president-obama-israel.html?_r=0 (accessed 31 July 2019).

of international politics, in which President Obama had mediated between the two states, and reached a political consensus on normalizing relations. Indeed, international politics was part of the dispute and its settlement. However, the international legal side operated in the shadows of international politics, however much it was intertwined with it.[392]

Third, the heightened role of negotiation and settlement as a form of implementing state responsibility generates both practical and more principled questions about the nature of state responsibility. Some scholars have questioned whether 'the practice of settling legal claims without recourse to a third-party, legally underwritten, dispute-resolution mechanism, can rightly be called a "legal responsibility practice"' to begin with.[393] Although settlement might overall be a preferable solution for an internationally community based on cooperation, it must be recognized that settlement is largely dependent on the 'relative resources and bargaining strengths of the parties'.[394] Moreover, the practice of settlement may impede the clarification of the norms involved in the dispute. This holds true especially for norms that involve public interest.

Clearly, state responsibility operates in the complex setting of both international and domestic politics. On the one hand, states strive to remedy wrongs so that they can normalize their relations with the conflicting party or parties; on the other hand, they desire to save face and appear resilient before their domestic public. As a result, it can be difficult to pinpoint clear-cut cases of state responsibility; responsibility can take different forms and it may operate behind the scenes. It may even lead an intangible life altogether.[395] Perhaps this is one reason why state responsibility seems to lack appeal, at least in comparison to more visible forms of international justice such as international criminal trials. Its elusiveness may not leave the issue of responsibility

392 Interestingly, the Communication of Comoros to the ICC regarding the same incident has received much more attention than the settlement between the involved states. See Statement 14/05/2013 of the ICC, 'ICC Prosecutor Receives Referral by the Authorities of the Union of the Comoros in relation to the Events of May 2010 on the Vessel of "Mavi Marmara"', www.icc-cpi.int/Pages/item.aspx?name=otp-statement-14-05-2013 (accessed 19 September 2019).

393 Cane, *Responsibility in Law,* p. 229.

394 Ibid., p. 232.

395 Daniel Betlehem has noted that international law in general can operate behind the scenes of the international public. According to him, '[m]ost of it [the law], however, is invisible to the world at large because it happens internally within governments and never needs to be, and sometimes would not appropriately be, made public ... It is really the invisible life of international law, that part of international law that is not readily open to the public gaze'. Daniel Betlehem, 'The Secret Life of International Law' (2012) 1 *Cambridge Journal of International and Comparative Law* 23–36 at 24.

undecided, but it certainly leaves questions of predictability and transparency open. Or, as Daniel Betlehem puts it: 'conduct must be public in order to be appreciable for reasons of the law'.[396]

## 3.6 THE WAY FORWARD – A TURN INWARDS OR OUTWARDS?

The aim of the above analysis was to discuss existing problems in the general law of state responsibility from the perspective of functionality. As noted in the first chapter of this book, functionality encompasses two dimensions: first, whether the general rules fit the functions of state responsibility; and second, whether the rules are operationalised to such an extent that those functions are achieved. The analysis showed that many problems are to be found in several aspects of the law: in the form of the rules, in the internationally wrongful act and its elements, as well as in the content and implementation of responsibility. The internal tensions of the state responsibility system leave the law oscillating between a number of poles: public and private; individual and collective; ordinary and serious wrongs; lawful and wrongful acts; the particular and the general. These dilemmas are insoluble under the rules of state responsibility, but more importantly they hinder the creation of a system or several systems that would both respond to modern demands and display higher functionality.

One specific factor behind many of these problems is the multiple functions of state responsibility. As a unique system without comparison in any domestic legal systems, it comprises elements from private, criminal and public law. International legal scholars thus expect it to perform a range of functions: a reparative function, a sanctioning function, as well as a function of protecting obligations that are in the shared interest of all states. In addition to these primary functions, state responsibility is expected to have a prospective effect upon state conduct, thus contributing to upholding legality or legal predictability and stability, and ultimately leading to an effective international legal system that guarantees peace.

Certainly, some of the problems that have been discussed above have been magnified for reasons beyond state responsibility. The customary law aspect of the rules makes it almost unavoidable that the rules are sometimes too abstract and difficult to apply to concrete situations. State responsibility is naturally also affected by the decentralized nature of international law when it comes to both lawmaking and enforcement. Consequently, state responsibility rules may have a hard time operating well if, for example, the primary obligations are imprecise or the states concerned are unwilling to make use of this particular legal avenue.

396 Ibid., 36.

It is also clear that, although the general rules of state responsibility cannot be described as being highly functional outside the basic reparative function of the law, the option of resorting to special rules compensates to a certain extent for the inherent shortcomings of the general law. Thus, state responsibility may still be highly relevant in some regimes having a strong basis in special rules. Such fields of international law are, for example, international human rights law and international investment law. But international environmental law proves that this is not always the case; in many matters, the special law sets off on a completely different track from that envisioned by the general rules.

The analysis of the problems of state responsibility shows that its core remains normal, everyday actions between states. In situations falling outside this routine, the rules of state responsibility seem ambiguous and appear to have less clear guidance to offer. On the one hand, state responsibility has proven to be inapt in responding to serious violations of international law, but on the other hand it seems incapable of repairing large scale harm that follows from lawful activities as well. A general responsibility regime cannot include everything: it is too broad a concept to be equally applicable across the broad range of existing international obligations, particularly in matters that are truly important for the international community. This breakdown has triggered a turn away from state responsibility, towards a broader search for alternative forms and notions of responsibility, and even of accountability.[397]

The purpose of the following chapter will be to examine alternative constructions of responsibility by way of looking into the systems of international liability and international criminal law. These two regimes merit scrutiny, not only because their development has in practice reduced the realm of state responsibility, but also because they allow the analysis to remain within the confines of *legal* responsibility/liability. The proliferation of accountability mechanisms will not be included here, as they generally fall outside legal parameters. Admittedly, a number of accountability mechanisms that can be described as legal exist as well: for example, the project of Global Administrative Law (GAL). However, theories and mechanisms of accountability represent a shift in focus that moves too far away from the aims of this book. It is also important to note that, due to limitations of scope, the alternative responsibility regimes will be explored through three themes embodying in a condensed way the functionality requirement set forth in this book.[398] These themes are: (1) social control; (2) collectivity; and (3) signalling effect.

[397] See Yarwood, *State Accountability*.
[398] See Section 1.4.2.2, 'Functionality in Focus'.

# 4

# Alternative Constructions of Responsibility

## A Thematic Analysis

As early as 1989 Pierre-Marie Dupuy drew attention to the theoretical fragmentation of classic state responsibility into two distinct routes: one of which sought to sanction or penalize the commission of international crimes, the other seeking to expand the compensatory dimension of responsibility.[1] Hence, this chapter will be devoted to an examination of alternative constructions of international responsibility embodying these developments, namely international liability and international criminal law. Although they constitute separate regimes, their underlying ideas about what responsibility should cover are featured in the thinking and codification of the general law of state responsibility as well.

These regimes deal, respectively, with sets of social problems that state responsibility is ill-equipped to handle. On the one hand, there are harms arising out of hazardous activities that are lawful and have been decoupled from the law of state responsibility; on the other hand, there are international obligations the violation of which is so repugnant that punishment in the name of the international community is arguably merited. In practical terms, international liability and international criminal law have shortened the continuum of acts that effectively fall under the general rules of state responsibility.

Consequently, the aim of this chapter is to analyze how these other responsibility constructions respond to some of the functionality problems that the law of state responsibility struggles with as discussed in the previous chapter. This study suggests that particularized responsibility regimes display higher practical usefulness than does the general law of state responsibility. The following analysis will start with an exploration into the practical

[1] Dupuy, 'Revolution or Evolution?'.

foundations of international liability and international criminal law. Real-world problems have been met with tailor-made rules of responsibility that do not aim to be generally applicable in international law, but rather to deal efficiently with the problems they were tasked with solving. This quality arguably makes both international liability and international criminal law fare better than the state responsibility rules in terms of the three themes chosen in this chapter to represent the requirement of functionality: (1) social control; (2) collectivity; and (3) signalling effect. Each theme will be separately explored from the perspective of both international liability and international criminal law, thus leaving room for comparative assessment. The aim is to answer questions about the way in which these regimes, in contrast to the law of state responsibility, manage to produce good outcomes, if they have flexible understandings of collectivity, and if they are capable of signalling normativity.

## 4.1 THE DEVELOPMENT OF PARTICULARIZED RESPONSIBILITY: INTERNATIONAL LIABILITY AND INTERNATIONAL CRIMINAL LAW

### 4.1.1 *Hazardous Activities as Catalysts of Change*

The difficulties surrounding the state responsibility project and its formation in the ILC in the 1950s and 1960s had brought the codification work on the topic to a standstill. Great controversy surrounded Special Rapporteur García Amador's approach to codifying state responsibility as a set of primary obligations drawing on the field of injuries to aliens. The decision introduced by Roberto Ago to embark upon the road of general and secondary state responsibility rules in 1969 salvaged the codification project.[2] Still, standard ideas of state responsibility faced almost insurmountable obstacles in dealing with contemporary challenges brought about by technological and industrial progress, the growing demand of natural resources, and increasing interdependence.[3]

In the 1960s, severe impacts on the environment and human beings started to emerge due to incidents of air and sea pollution, atmospheric and underground atomic testing, dumping of toxic waste and a number of accidents involving nuclear energy or transportation of oil. Although transnational environmental pollution had already caused problems in interstate relations

[2] See Section 2.4.1, 'ILC and the Difficulty of Finding a Suitable Approach'.

[3] According to the ILC, new rules were needed to respond to a 'revolution in technology' which 'has extended dramatically man's power to control his environment'. See Report of the ILC on the Work of Its Thirtieth Session, UN Doc. A/33/10 (1978), p. 150, para. 10.

earlier, with the *Trail Smelter* case in the 1930s being a prime example,[4] a new era of economic activities brought the question of industrial and technological harms to the forefront of responsibility concerns. These problems were distinct from the classic wrongful act: they were generated from activities that could be highly risky in nature, yet lawful. They contained an element of fatality which was unknown to the rules on state responsibility; beyond resulting from human conduct, these harms could arise from technical errors which could not be evaluated in traditional terms of responsibility.[5] Their technological or industrial origin thus contributed to the separation of these harms from traditional wrongful acts. Moreover, such harms often had a transnational and collective character because they affected people's lives beyond national frontiers and extended into many segments of life.

The idea that these harms could not sufficiently be remedied by classic state responsibility began to gain ground when a number of harmful and even devastating events took place.[6] Three types of activities that were considered of a high-risk nature and for which, after a number of accidents, conventional solutions were sought outside classic state responsibility were: (1) use of nuclear energy; (2) launching of objects into space; and (3) marine oil pollution.

The use of nuclear power – in the international arms race as well as for peaceful energy purposes – clearly represented one category of activity that was extremely dangerous but still considered lawful. In 1954, with its testing of nuclear weapons in the Pacific Ocean at the Bikini Islands, the United States caused harm to the inhabitants of the Marshall Islands and Japanese fishermen on the vessel *Fukuryu Maru*. The United States agreed to pay compensation of 2 million USD without admitting to have committed any wrong. The question of legal responsibility was not pursued any further, but the decision by the United States to pay compensation opened the door for arguments that high-risk activity entailed a duty to compensate harm.[7]

4 *Trail Smelter* case *(United States of America* v. *Canada)*, Judgment of 16 April 1938 and 11 March 1941, III Reports of International Arbitral Awards, p. 1905.

5 Pierre-Marie Dupuy, *La responsabilité internationale des États pour les dommages d'origine technologique et industrielle* (Paris: Éditions A. Pedone, 1976), p. 8.

6 René Lefeber, *Transboundary International Interference and the Origin of State Liability* (The Hague: Kluwer Law International, 1996), p. 7, who mentions in particular the *Torrey Canyon*, *Cosmos* 954, and *Chernobyl* accidents as having a decisive effect on the topic of liability.

7 For instance, during the discussions in the ILC of García Amador's report in 1957, Mr. Padilla Nervo raised the issue that the 'experimental explosion of nuclear weapons sheds doubts on the advisability of maintaining the traditional rule' [of no liability without wrongful acts or omissions]. See Summary Records of the Ninth Session, ILC Yearbook 1957, vol. I, p. 156, para. 55.

Early on the fatal consequences that a peaceful use of nuclear energy could entail generated conventions dealing with issues of liability. These were, for example, the 1960 Convention on Third Party Liability in the Field of Nuclear Energy,[8] the 1962 Convention on the Liability of Operators of Nuclear Ships,[9] and the 1963 Vienna Convention on Civil Liability for Nuclear Damage.[10] A second generation of nuclear liability conventions came about as a consequence of the 1986 *Chernobyl* accident.

Another high-risk activity recognized by the international community as deviating from the standards of state responsibility was space exploration – in particular, the launch of objects into orbit. There were a number of incidents where space activities had caused harm when satellites crashed into earth, causing loss to persons and property. In September 1960, the debris of an American satellite crashed into a South African farm, causing damage; in November of the same year a Cuban cow was killed by space debris; and in September 1962 a 10-kilo chunk of iron from the Sputnik IV satellite hit the streets of the city of Manitowoc, Wisconsin.[11] In 1963, the UNGA laid down the principle that the state launching an object into outer space was automatically liable for damage caused by the object 'on the earth, or in the air space, or in outer space'.[12] This principle of absolute liability was later incorporated into the 1972 Convention on International Liability for Damage Caused by Space Objects.[13] It was applied in practice in the case of *Cosmos* 954 when a Soviet surveillance satellite crashed to the ground in Canada and caused devastation and radiation contamination.[14]

After a number of accidents with widespread effects, specialized conventional solutions outside classic state responsibility were also sought in connection with oil pollution. A number of international conventions on marine oil pollution were concluded in the aftermath of the eye-opening disaster caused

[8] Convention on Third Party Liability in the Field of Nuclear Energy, Paris, 29 July 1960, in force 1 April 1968, 956 *United Nations Treaty Series* 251.

[9] Convention on the Liability of Operators of Nuclear Ships, Brussels, 25 May 1962, not in force, reproduced in (1963) 57 *American Journal of International Law* 268–278.

[10] Vienna Convention on the Civil Liability for Nuclear Damage, Vienna, 21 May 1963, in force 12 November 1977, 1063 *United Nations Treaty Series* 265.

[11] Dupuy, *La responsabilité internationale*, p. 45.

[12] UNGA Res. 1962 (XVIII), 13 December 1963 (Declaration of Legal Principles Governing the Activities of States in the Exploration and Use of Outer Space), para. 8.

[13] UNGA Res. 2777 (XXVI), 29 November 1971 (Convention on International Liability on Damage Caused by Space Objects), in force 1 October 1972, 961 *United Nations Treaty Series* 187.

[14] See e.g., Edward G. Lee and D. W. Sproule, 'Liability for Damage Caused by Space Debris: The Cosmos 954 Claim' (1988) 26 *Canadian Yearbook of International Law* 273–279.

by the oil tanker *Torrey Canyon* in 1967, which severely devastated French and British coastlines after it ran aground in the English Channel.[15] The accident – which resulted in a 117,000 ton crude oil spill and caused damage in the amount of 6 million GBP – highlighted two liability deficiencies: the lack of civil liability for such incidents and the inadequate focus on prevention of oil pollution.[16] States responded with the 1969 International Convention on Civil Liability for Oil Pollution Damage[17] and the 1971 International Convention on the Establishment of an International Fund for Compensation for Oil Pollution Damage.[18]

The lack of a general international legal regime on liability clearly showed how victims of various nationalities were placed in unequal positions regarding their right to obtain compensation. Hence, the common goal of all these exceptional regimes was to ensure compensation for caused harm, not to prohibit the activity in question, despite the potential for great damage. This kind of activity was necessary for economic progress and was, except for nuclear testing, never seriously questioned. Thus, the leitmotif became the provision of victims with adequate and prompt compensation when they suffered harm caused by industrial or technological activities. The rationale is thus different from the corrective aim of state responsibility, although it has been considered an 'outgrowth of the failure to exercise "due care" or "due diligence"'.[19]

### 4.1.2 *Liability in the International Sphere*

The creation of specialized international regimes on liability brought to the fore the question of the existence of a general regime of liability. The regulation of lawful but hazardous activities was known to many national legal systems. Its origins were traceable back to Roman law, in which the owner of a

[15] For an account of the Torrey Canyon Oil Spill, see Patrick Barkham, 'Oils Spills: Legacy of the Torrey Canyon', *The Guardian*, 24 June 2010, www.theguardian.com/environment/2010/jun/24/torrey-canyon-oil-spill-deepwater-bp (accessed 18 June 2019).

[16] Wang Hui, *Civil Liability for Marine Oil Pollution Damage: A Comparative and Economic Study of the International, US and Chinese Compensation Regimes* (Alphen aan den Rijn: Kluwer Law International, 2011), pp. 22, 53.

[17] International Convention on Civil Liability for Oil Pollution Damage, Brussels, 29 November 1969, in force 19 June 1975, 973 *United Nations Treaty Series* 3.

[18] International Convention on the Establishment of an International Fund for Compensation for Oil Pollution Damage, Brussels, 18 December 1971, in force 16 October 1978, 1110 *United Nations Treaty Series* 57.

[19] *Survey of Liability Regimes Relevant to the Topic of International Liability for Injurious Consequences Arising Out of Acts Not Prohibited by International Law (International Liability in Case of Loss from Transboundary Harm Arising Out of Hazardous Activities)* UN Doc. A/CN.4/543 (2004), p. 128, para. 216.

wild beast was liable for damage done by it. Later doctrines such as the Anglo-Saxon doctrine of ultra-hazardous liability developed the connection between extremely dangerous activity and the obligation to compensate. Its counterpart in the United States, the doctrine of absolute responsibility, similarly concerned activities that were hazardous and which could generate damage despite diligent behaviour.[20] However, the widespread and transnational ramifications of harm caused by new technology called for solutions of liability in the international sphere as well. Dealing with transnational harm by means of national solutions had proven insufficient from the perspective of the victim in many cases. To seek compensation in foreign courts was time-consuming because of difficulties in ascertaining the right forum. It was also problematic in terms of the execution of sentences and other problems that an alien might face, such as language differences, high costs or general hostility.[21]

As a consequence, the principle of liability for hazardous activities was transposed into the international sphere. However, different options prevailed as to who was to be held liable for such losses. Although the responsibility of the state for lawful activities was still advocated by some, either by way of a due diligence violation or on different grounds than the classic state responsibility doctrine, in specialized regimes the costs for harm were increasingly distributed among those actors directly benefitting from the activity. Whereas the state alone remains liable for harm caused by space objects, nuclear energy conventions adopted a solution which shares the burden of the cost between corporations and the state. A third variant is provided for in the area of oil pollution, which constructs another kind of collectivity for allocating loss compensation.

International liability thus developed through the creation of specialized international conventions, work by international organizations such as the International Maritime Organization (IMO) and the International Atomic Energy Agency (IAEA), and scholarly debate as to the principles regarding compensation for lawful but hazardous activities. The only international convention ever established on general liability is the Lugano Convention, which has yet to enter into force.[22] The proliferation of such principles was

20 Dupuy, *La responsabilité internationale*, p. 161.

21 Martti Koskenniemi, *Valtion kansainvälinen vastuu yksityisen toiminnan aiheuttamasta kansainvälisestä ympäristövahingosta*, Kansainvälisoikeudellinen päälaudaturkirjoitus (Turku: Turun Yliopisto, 1981), p. 14.

22 Lugano Convention on Civil Liability for Damage Resulting from Activities Dangerous to the Environment, Lugano, 21 June 1993, not in force, 32 *International Legal Materials*, 1228 (1993). It is generally held to be unlikely that the convention will ever enter into force. See Philippe Sands, *Principles of International Environmental Law* (2nd ed., Cambridge: Cambridge University Press, 2003), p. 933.

considered markedly different from the doctrine of state responsibility, which continuously occupied the ILC's agenda. The development of liability both in conventional law and international practice was also noticed within the ILC, which discussed liability under the aegis of its work on state responsibility. The topic, however, vastly divided members of the Commission; some perceived it as an integral part of state responsibility, others argued for its independent nature. In 1973, the topic of liability was separated from state responsibility into an independent subject on the ILC agenda,[23] after which it occupied the Commission for the next thirty years.

The newborn topic of liability was thorny from the very beginning, and with respect to all its aspects: its title, scope and conceptual basis were all disputed. One dilemma that the Commission was confronted with was that of the close connection between prevention and liability. Another problem was how to limit the scope of activities to be covered by liability: should it include both hazardous activities and noxious activities, or only the latter? Or should it be confined to ultra-hazardous activities?[24] And would it be limited to environmental issues only, or should liability also cover transboundary harm arising, for example, out of monetary devaluation or even harmful newspaper articles?[25] Further, it remained unclear how risk, which is essential to liability, was to be defined.[26] A main stumbling block was also the question of to whom liability would be attached. Should the state ultimately be held liable, or rather, should the private entities operating the hazardous activities be held liable as they most often functioned in states with a market economy? It was especially this last issue that divided states as well as ILC members into two groups: those who were 'dead set against the idea of the existence of State liability in general international law and, consequently, against the codification of the topic', and those who wanted to continue the topic, mainly representatives from developing states.[27]

After numerous reports of Special Rapporteurs Quentin-Baxter and Barboza, in 1997 the ILC divided the topic into two parts: one on prevention

[23] UNGA Res. 3071 (XXVIII), 30 November 1973 (Report of the ILC).

[24] Barboza, *The Environment*, p. 83, see also note 43. Daniel Barstow Magraw argues that one problem relating to the scope of liability is that the category of 'lawful acts' is much broader than that pertaining to wrongfulness. See Daniel Barstow Magraw, 'Transboundary Harm: The International Law Commission's Study of "International Liability"' (1986) 80 *American Journal of International Law* 305–330 at 322.

[25] Summary Records, UN Doc. A/C.6/37/SR.46 (1982), pp. 4, 8, 22, cited in Barstow Magraw, 'Transboundary Harm', 324.

[26] Barboza, *The Environment*, p. 93.

[27] Ibid., p. 77.

and another on liability. While the issue of prevention had progressed in the deliberations of the ILC, 'a serious attempt was made in the Commission to eliminate liability from the draft articles'.[28] Although liability was kept on the ILC agenda, its disputed status called for a change in approach: from having originally conceived of liability as belonging to the state of origin, the Commission now decided to go along with international practice, which had shifted to emphasizing the civil responsibility of the operators. Thus, after the finalization of the Articles on Prevention of Transboundary Harm in 2001,[29] the Commission resumed its work on liability. The decision to abandon state liability, together with the move away from hard obligations to softer language, bore fruit. In 2006, the ILC adopted the 'Draft Principles on the Allocation of Loss in the Case of Transboundary Harm Arising out of Hazardous Activities' (hereinafter Loss Allocation Principles).[30]

The Loss Allocation Principles are based on the assumption that, despite diligent behaviour, 'accidents or other incidents may nonetheless occur and have transboundary consequences that cause harm and serious loss to other States and their nationals'.[31] Thus, the core of the general liability regime lies in a balance of interests. On the one hand, the Loss Allocation Principles recognize the importance of hazardous activities for economic and societal development. On the other hand, however, they seek to guarantee that the risk involved in hazardous activities is balanced by 'prompt and adequate compensation' for transboundary damage. The Loss Allocation Principles are clearly modelled upon existing international conventions that place primary liability on the operator. This liability is objective, which means that the victims do not have to prove fault on the part of the operator. In the further interest of victims, the Loss Allocation Principles call for supplementary funding which seeks to ensure compensation beyond the capacity of the operator. Compensation is thus spread among multiple actors, which may or may not include the state. The actors are further obliged to create financial securities by way of, for example, industry funds in order to sufficiently cover potential compensation claims. Although the state recedes

[28] Ibid., p. 125.

[29] Draft Articles on the Prevention of Transboundary Harm from Hazardous Activities, with commentaries, Report of the International Law Commission on the Work of Its Fifty-third Session, UN Doc. A/56/10 (2001), Chapter V, text of the Draft Articles, p. 146, para. 97.

[30] International Liability for Injurious Consequences Arising Out of Acts Not Prohibited by International Law (International Liability in Case of Loss from Transboundary Harm Arising out of Hazardous Activities), Report of the International Law Commission on the Work of Its Fifty-eighth Session, UN Doc. A/61/10 (2006), Chapter V, p. 106, paras. 66–67.

[31] Ibid., Chapter V, General Commentary, para. 67 (2).

into the background when it comes to liability, its role on the preventive side is highlighted. It is expressly acknowledged that the state remains responsible under the standard rules of state responsibility for breaches of its due diligence obligations.

### 4.1.3 *Dealing with Acts That Shock the Conscience of Mankind*

Liability, the first offshoot from the doctrine of state responsibility, was accompanied by the revival of a different form of responsibility in the 1990s: international criminal law. In the course of the ILC's work on both state responsibility and international liability, it had simultaneously been staking out rules on individual criminal responsibility inspired by the international military tribunals following the Second World War. During the thirty years that the ILC worked on the topic of liability, it had even momentarily set aside liability in order to seize the opportunity to create a penal code for the international community in the favourable post–Cold War climate.[32] International criminal law is also closely related to the state responsibility doctrine, as the thorny issue of state criminality had occupied the ILC for years.

The idea, creation and rise of international criminal law are strongly connected to the conduct of warfare and the protection of human lives and dignity. The idea of dealing differently with acts that rise above acceptable standards of warfare is very old: some even trace them back to antiquity as the search for longevity has characterized the international criminal law project.[33] Still, strides in development have taken place. The driving force behind creating rules aimed at penalizing the most horrific acts that shock the conscience of mankind is to be found in atrocities committed during conflicts. When the worst imaginable acts have been committed, a parallel push for advancing the international criminal law project has also occurred. An important dimension of the efforts to punish individuals who violate the laws of war has been the endeavour to create an institution for that very purpose. Through sentencing of actors judged guilty of international crimes, such an institution would allocate reproach and blameworthiness on behalf of the international community.

It has been claimed that scholarly writings of the sixteenth century contain ideas about the criminal nature of certain international conduct. Yet, no

[32] Barboza, *The Environment*, p. 118.

[33] Cryer, *Prosecuting*, p. 21.

definitive doctrinal origin for international criminal law can be said to exist.[34] The 1474 trial of von Hagenbach is generally considered to be the landmark trial with regard to the practice of holding individuals answerable for violations of the laws of war.[35] Sir Peter von Hagenbach was tried and convicted for his brutal regime as a governor of Alsatian territories before an ad hoc tribunal in Breisach composed of twenty-eight judges from various regional city-states. Von Hagenbach was found guilty and sentenced to death for his rule of terror, which included murders and rapes. This first international criminal trial did not, however, lead to a broader practice of trying perpetrators for commission of atrocities. Suggestions for a permanent international criminal institution were first introduced centuries later by Gustave Moynier, whose concerns over belligerent misconduct in the Franco-Prussian War spurred him to set forth a proposal for a permanent international criminal court in 1872.[36]

A significant leap forward in international criminal law was taken in the aftermath of the First World War, which lacked precedents in terms of its scale and number of casualties. Nine million fatalities and twenty-one million injured as a result of trench warfare, aerial combat, an extensive use of chemical weapons and even famine contributed to the belief that no more wars would be fought. In January 1919, the Allies established the Commission on the Responsibility of the Authors of the War and on the Enforcement of Penalties, which proposed the creation of a 'High Tribunal' to try a number of high officials of the Central Powers for the outbreak of war and for violations of the laws of war.[37] Based on the Commission's suggestions, the Allies and Associated Powers declared the individual criminal responsibility of the

34 For a discussion of international legal scholars such as Vittoria, Gentili and Grotius, and international criminal law, see Cryer, *Prosecuting International Crimes*, pp. 22–24. Hersch Lauterpacht declared both Vittoria and Grotius to be the founders of international criminal law. Nevertheless, such a view has been refuted by Robert Cryer. Ibid., p. 23.

35 Several reasons have been advanced for the significance of the trial. For example, the trial was held before an *international* tribunal, it was a *war crimes* trial, and it developed an early version of the concept of the crime against humanity. See Gregory S. Gordon, 'The Trial of Peter von Hagenbach: Reconciling History, Historiography and International Criminal Law', in Kevin Jon Heller and Gerry Simpson (eds.), *The Hidden Histories of War Crimes Trials* (Oxford: Oxford University Press, 2013), pp. 13–49; Cryer, *Prosecuting International Crimes*, pp. 17–21.

36 Christopher Keith Hall, 'The First Proposal for a Permanent International Criminal Court' (1998) *International Review of the Red Cross* 57–74.

37 For the report, see 'Commission on the Responsibility of the Authors of the War and on Enforcement of Penalties, Report presented to the Preliminary Peace Conference, 29 March 1919', reproduced in (1920) 14 *American Journal of International Law* 95–154.

German emperor Kaiser Wilhelm and other persons accused of having violated the laws of war in the 1919 Treaty of Versailles.[38] Nevertheless, these efforts to impose individual criminal responsibility failed to materialize following the decision of the Netherlands to provide the emperor refuge. Despite the shortcomings in executing criminal responsibility, the foundation of modern international criminal law was established. For the first time, individual criminal responsibility for war crimes was explicitly situated in the international legal order rather than in the domestic sphere.[39] The idea of individual criminal responsibility and an international criminal court also continued to influence the inter-war era. As stipulated by the Treaty of Sèvres in 1920,[40] the Allies attempted to bring Turkish perpetrators of the Armenian genocide to justice, and the League of Nations sketched up plans for an international criminal court for trying terrorist crimes in 1937 following the assassination of King Alexander of Yugoslavia.[41]

Yet, the world had to witness the horrendous acts of the Second World War before an international criminal tribunal became a reality. Aggressive warfare and the killing of six million Jews as part of the Holocaust was considered to be so outrageous that these acts needed to be fiercely condemned. For this purpose, in 1945 the International Military Tribunal at Nuremberg (IMT), or the so-called Nuremberg Tribunal, was established by the Allied Powers. Its counterpart, the International Military Tribunal for the Far East (IMTFE), or the so-called Tokyo Tribunal, was created in 1946 to prosecute Japanese war criminals. For the first time, individual criminal responsibility

[38] Treaty of Peace between the Allied and Associated Powers and Germany, Versailles, 28 June 1919, in force 10 January 1920, reproduced in (1919) 13 *American Journal of International Law Supplements* 151–386, Arts. 227–230.

[39] Cryer, *Prosecuting International Crimes*, pp. 32–33.

[40] Treaty of Peace between the Allied Powers and Turkey (Treaty of Sèvres), 10 August 1920, reprinted in (1921) 15 *American Journal of International Law Supplements* 179–295, acknowledged in Art. 226: 'The Turkish Government recognises the right of the Allied Powers to bring before military tribunals persons accused of having committed acts in violation of the laws and customs of war'. The peace treaty was, however, never ratified and subsequent events in Turkey, accompanied by disunity between the Allied Powers, paved the way for the Treaty of Lausanne which did not deal with the individual criminal responsibility of the perpetrators. See Treaty of Peace between the Allied Powers and Turkey (Treaty of Lausanne), Lausanne, 24 July 1923, in force 6 August 1924, reprinted in (1924) 18 *American Journal of International Law Supplements* 1–53.

[41] Convention for the Creation of an International Criminal Court, Geneva, 16 November 1937, not in force, *League of Nations Official Journal*, Special Supplement 156 (1938), League of Nations Doc. C.547(I)M.384(I)1937V, reprinted in (1935–1937) 7 *International Legislation* 878 (Manley D. Hudson, ed. 1941).

was recognized at the international level with respect to the following crimes: crimes against peace, crimes against humanity and war crimes. The aim was to finally penetrate the abstraction of the state in order to hold real flesh-and-blood perpetrators accountable before the international community. The essence of international criminal law is clear in the opening statement of Chief Prosecutor Robert H. Jackson of the IMT: 'The wrongs which we seek to condemn and punish have been so calculated, so malignant, and so devastating, that civilization cannot tolerate their being ignored, because it cannot survive their being repeated.'[42] Retribution and deterrence were thus at the heart of the Nuremberg trials.[43]

The Nuremberg tribunal tried major war criminals of the highest rank ranging from former German foreign ministers to Nazi party leaders for the atrocities. On 1 October 1946, the Nuremberg judgment convicted 18 of 21 defendants to imprisonment or to a death sentence. Despite many problematic aspects of the trials,[44] they represented a paradigmatic shift in international law. Never before had senior state officials been held personally responsible for international crimes; individuals now became duty-holders under international law that could be tried in court not only nationally, but also internationally.

Within the newly created UN, the pursuit of dealing with the most egregious breaches of international law in a different way from ordinary breaches

42 Justice Robert H. Jackson, 'Opening Statement before the International Military Tribunal (1945)', reproduced in Larry May and Jeff Brown (eds.), *Philosophy of Law: Classic and Contemporary Readings* (Malden and Oxford: Wiley-Blackwell, 2010), pp. 435–440 at 435.

43 George A. Finch stated regarding the purposes of the Nuremberg trials: 'Retribution for the shocking crimes and atrocities committed by the enemy during World War II was made imperative by the overwhelming demands emanating from the public conscience throughout the civilized world'. See George A. Finch, 'The Nuremberg Trial and International Law' (1947) 41 *American Journal of International Law* 20–37 at 20.

44 Criticism has been directed against the Nuremberg trials (at least) on the basis of the following aspects of the trials: jurisdiction, retroactivity, and selectivity. For example, George A. Finch has criticized the Nuremberg trials for punishing individuals for aggressive warfare, despite express agreement by the Allies to that effect, and for disregarding the legal principle of *nullum crimen sine lege, nulla poena sine lege*. See Finch, 'The Nuremberg Trial', 33–35. With regard to selectivity, see Norman Birkett, 'International Legal Theories Evolved at Nuremberg', in Guénaël Mettraux (ed.), *Perspectives on the Nuremberg Trial* (Oxford: Oxford University Press, 2008), pp. 299–307 at 307. On a more principled level, critique has been raised against the trials as being show trials and examples of so-called victor's justice. See Edwin Borchard, 'International Law and International Organization' (1947) 41 *American Journal of International Law* 106–108 at 107. For similar criticism, see Martti Koskenniemi, 'Between Impunity and Show Trials' (2002) 6 *Max Planck Yearbook of United Nations Law* 1–35.

intensified in the aftermath of the Second World War. The ILC, which was tasked with codification of the subject, addressed the issue in a number of ways. As a first step, the Commission was asked to formulate the Nuremberg principles as a part of the overall task of creating an international criminal code for the international community.[45] It formulated seven principles on the basis of the Charters of the IMTs in Nuremberg and Tokyo, as well as on their jurisprudence. The principles recognized the existence of the following international crimes – crimes against peace, crimes against humanity and war crimes – to which head-of-state immunity did not apply. From the Nuremberg Principles, the Commission proceeded to the preparation of a Draft Code of Crimes against the Peace and Security of Mankind. This task was divided into two parts: the creation of a penal code and the planning of an implementation mechanism in the form of a draft statute for an international criminal court.[46] The purpose of the former was to establish a penal code for the international community which would list crimes under international law that were directly applicable to individuals. The problems involved in defining the crime of aggression, however, caused the work to be postponed indefinitely in 1954.[47] Another contributing factor standing in the way of the finalization of the topic was the configuration of the political constellations created by the Cold War.

Even though work on international criminal law came to a virtual standstill within the UN framework in the early 1950s, progress was made on the creation of substantive rules bearing on the topic. First, the 1948 Convention on the Prevention and Punishment of the Crime of Genocide recognized that genocide is 'a crime under international law'.[48] Moreover, the Convention establishes individual criminal responsibility for acts of genocide alongside the responsibility of states. It also laid down a provision for the possible jurisdiction of an international penal tribunal if such were to come into existence. Another major development was the adoption of the four 1949 Geneva

[45] See Jean Spiropoulos, *Report on the Formulation of the Nürnberg Principles*, UN Doc. A/CN.4/22 (1950).

[46] The mandate to draft a statute for an international criminal court or an 'international penal tribunal' derived from the Genocide Convention, Article VI. See Convention on the Prevention and Punishment of the Crime of Genocide, New York, 9 December 1948, in force 12 January 1951, 78 *United Nations Treaty Series* 277.

[47] UNGA Res. 897(IX), 4 December 1954 (Draft Code of Offences against the Peace and Security of Mankind).

[48] Art. I of the Genocide Convention.

Conventions.[49] Individual criminal responsibility was established for war crimes; that is, grave breaches of the rules of international humanitarian law embodied in the Geneva Conventions. These include, among others, wilful killing, torture, inhumane treatment, taking of hostages and extensive destruction of property. Similarly, the 1977 Additional Protocols are of importance to international criminal law.[50]

The idea of punitive responsibility prevailed after the IMTs of Nuremberg and Tokyo, both with regard to Nazi war criminals and with regard to other incidents. After the initial phase of military and civilian proceedings against Nazi war criminals in the direct aftermath of the war, many civilian proceedings were held against Nazis in various jurisdictions during the 1960s.[51] The most famous trial of the 1960s is undisputedly the *Eichmann* trial before Israeli courts in 1960–1962.[52] Outside the Nazi context, the 1968 My Lai incident in the Vietnam War resulted in death, torture and rape of numerous civilians – acts which led to the prosecution of several American soldiers.[53] A third wave of high-profile prosecutions took place in the 1980s and 1990s. French courts convicted Klaus *Barbie* in 1987, Paul *Touvier* in 1994, and Maurice *Papon* in 1998 for their respective contributions to the Nazi atrocities.[54]

49 First Geneva Convention for the Amelioration of the Condition of the Wounded and Sick in Armed Forces in the Field, Geneva, 12 August 1949, in force 21 October 1950, 75 *United Nations Treaty Series* 31; Second Geneva Convention for the Amelioration of the Condition of Wounded, Sick and Shipwrecked Members of Armed Forces at Sea, Geneva, 12 August 1949, in force 21 October 1950, 75 *United Nations Treaty Series* 85; Third Geneva Convention Relative to the Treatment of Prisoners of War, Geneva, 12 August 1949, in force 21 October 1950, 75 *United Nations Treaty Series* 135; Fourth Geneva Convention Relative to the Protection of Civilian Persons, Geneva, 12 August 1949, in force 21 October 1950, 75 *United Nations Treaty Series* 287.

50 Protocol Additional to the Geneva Conventions of 12 August 1949, and Relating to the Protection of Victims of International Armed Conflicts (Protocol I) and Protocol Additional to the Geneva Conventions of 12 August 1949, and Relating to the Protection of Victims of Non-International Armed Conflicts (Protocol II), Geneva, 8 June 1977, in force 7 December 1978, 1125 *United Nations Treaty Series* 3 and 609 respectively.

51 Mark Drumbl, *Atrocity, Punishment, and International Law* (New York: Cambridge University Press, 2007), pp. 110–122.

52 For an account of the Eichmann Trial, see David Lasok, 'The Eichmann Trial' (1962) 11 *International and Comparative Law Quarterly* 355–374; Hannah Arendt, 'Eichmann in Jerusalem', *The New Yorker*, 16 February 1963, p. 40.

53 See Jordan J. Paust, 'My Lai and Vietnam: Norms, Myths and Leader Responsibility' (1972) 57 *Military Law Review* 99–187.

54 For an overview of French prosecutions of war criminals, see Leila Nadya Sadat, 'The French Experience', in M. Cherif Bassiouni (ed.), *International Criminal Law: Volume III. International Enforcement* (3rd ed., Leiden: Martinus Nijhoff Publishers, 2008), pp. 329–358.

Despite some progress in substantive law and national prosecutions of war criminals, the project of international criminal law still remained unsettled. The aggression committed by Saddam Hussein in 1990 against Kuwait did not lead to any prosecution, in spite of the reference to individual criminal responsibility in the Security Council resolutions dealing with the Kuwaiti situation.[55] Although some scholars tried to keep the creation of an international criminal court on the agenda, even their focus shifted from atrocity crimes to transnational crimes such as drug trafficking and organized crime.[56]

Against this background, the revival of international criminal law in the wake of the atrocities committed during the Yugoslav dissolution war in the early 1990s came as a surprise to some commentators.[57] Admittedly, the ILC had resumed its work on drafting a penal code for the international community in 1981 as well as continued preparations for a draft statute for an international criminal court.[58] However, it was only with the creation of the ad hoc International Criminal Tribunal for the former Yugoslavia that international criminal law gained momentum. The end of the Cold War, along with Saddam Hussein's aggression upon Kuwait, paved the way for the creation of the ICTY.[59] In response to the ongoing atrocities in the Western Balkans, the Security Council created a Commission of Experts in 1992 to investigate the violations of international humanitarian law in the former Yugoslavia. The Commission recommended the establishment of an international criminal tribunal, an idea which was widely supported by the international community.[60] In February 1993, the Security Council established ICTY, the ad hoc tribunal for the former Yugoslavia, authorized to prosecute

55 UNSC Res. 670 (1990), 25 September 1990 (Iraq), para. 13, in which it was stated that individuals are liable under the Geneva Conventions for the commission of or ordering the commission of grave breaches.

56 See M. Cherif Bassiouni and Christopher L. Blakesley, 'The Need for an International Criminal Court in the New International World Order' (1992–1993) 25 *Vanderbilt Journal of Transnational Law* 151–182.

57 For example, Ian Brownlie noted in 1990 that 'the likelihood of setting up an international criminal court is very remote'. See Ian Brownlie, *Principles of Public International Law* (4th ed., Oxford: Clarendon Press, 1990), pp. 563–564.

58 UNGA Res. 36/106 (1981), 10 December 1981 (Draft Code of Offences against Peace and Security of Mankind).

59 William A. Schabas, *An Introduction to the International Criminal Court* (3rd ed., Cambridge: Cambridge University Press, 2007), p. 11.

60 Ibid.; See also, Philippe Kirsch, John T. Holmes, and Mora Johnson, 'International Tribunals and Courts', in David M. Malone (ed.), *The UN Security Council: From the Cold War to the 21st Century* (London: Lynne Rienner Publishers, 2004), pp. 281–294 at 283.

'persons responsible for serious violations of international humanitarian law committed in the territory of the former Yugoslavia since 1991'.[61] Shortly after the creation of the ICTY, the Security Council was forced to deal with the humanitarian tragedy in Rwanda which eventually killed over 800,000 persons. A similar route was chosen for Rwanda, and in 1994 the Security Council established the ad hoc International Criminal Tribunal for Rwanda (ICTR).[62]

### 4.1.4 A *Penal Code and Procedure for the International Community*

The statute of the ICTY revived several aspects of the ILC's work on the Draft Code of Crimes and the Draft Statute for an International Criminal Court, both originally from 1954.[63] No longer were these two projects pursued separately; the criminal code and the statute merged into a combined effort.[64] In 1994, the ILC resumed its work on the creation of an international criminal court, and the work culminated in the adoption of the Statute of an International Criminal Court on 17 July 1998 at a diplomatic conference convened in Rome.[65]

The statute was adopted by a vote of 120 states in favour of the statute, 21 abstentions, and 7 against. The most vocal objector to the newly created court was the United States, but the Court was also unsupported by other major powers such as Israel and China.[66] Yet, the creation of an international criminal court is an unprecedented historical moment which has been described as 'the culmination of a Century of hard work and false starts'.[67] The required number of sixty ratifications in order for the Rome Statute to enter into force was reached quickly, and the Court came into existence on 1 July 2002. Although major powers such as the United States, China,

61 UNSC Res. 808 (1993), 22 February 1993 (Tribunal (Former Yugoslavia)), para. 1.
62 UNSC Res. 955 (1994), 8 November 1994 (Tribunal (Rwanda)).
63 Schabas, *An Introduction to the International*, p. 12.
64 Ibid., p. 16.
65 For accounts of the Diplomatic Conference of Plenipotentiaries on the Establishment of an International Criminal Court, see Schabas, *An Introduction to the International*, pp. 18–21; Immi Tallgren, 'We Did It? The Vertigo of Law and Everyday Life at the Diplomatic Conference on the Establishment of an International Criminal Court' (1999) 12 *Leiden Journal of International Law* 683–707; Leila Nadya Sadat, *The International Criminal Court and the Transformation of International Law: Justice for the New Millennium* (Ardsley, New York: Transnational Publishers Inc., 2002).
66 Schabas, *An Introduction to the International*, p. 21.
67 Sadat, *The International Criminal Court*, p. 4.

Russia, and India remain outside the jurisdiction of the Court, 122 states have accepted the Court's jurisdiction.[68]

The jurisdiction of the ICC is complementary, which means that the prosecution of international crimes is in the first hand to be accomplished by national courts. The ICC may step in only if national courts are unable or unwilling to pursue prosecutions. Further, the jurisdiction of the Court is limited to core international crimes: crimes against humanity, genocide, war crimes and aggression. However, the crime of aggression was left undefined in the Rome Statute, which meant that the ICC became operational without having jurisdiction over that particular crime. The Kampala review conference in 2010 managed to agree upon a definition of the crime,[69] and the Court's jurisdiction in the matter was activated in July 2018.

The ICC operates on the basis of individual criminal responsibility and formally has no effect on claims of state responsibility.[70] The individual is seen as the central actor: it is always an individual or a group of individuals who acts unlawfully, and hence the proper locus of punishment rests with the individual. The veil of abstraction is removed: 'everyone, regardless of place of activity or formal position, should be accountable for their deeds'.[71] Thus, individualized international criminal law and the ICC as its institutional arm are seen as tools for dealing with actors in both the public and private spheres.

The ICC Statute recognizes jurisdiction over individual or joint acts of natural persons over eighteen years of age when the crimes are committed with intent and knowledge.[72] It is further set forth that a person who commits a crime is individually responsible and liable for punishment.[73] Penalties that can be imposed vary from imprisonment to fines. The Court is not limited by claims of head-of-state immunity or functional immunity,[74]

68 The International Criminal Court, 'The States Parties to the Rome Statute as of 6 June 2019', https://asp.icc-cpi.int/en_menus/asp/states%20parties/pages/the%20states%20parties%20to%20the%20rome%20statute.aspx (accessed 6 June 2019).

69 *Official Records of the Review Conference of the Rome Statute of the International Criminal Court*, Kampala, 31 May–11 June 2010 (RC/11), part II, RC/Res. 6, annex I.

70 See Arts. 25 (1) and 25 (4) of the Rome Statute, Rome, 17 July 1998, in force 1 July 2002, 2187 *United Nations Treaty Series* 90.

71 Koskenniemi, 'Between Impunity', 2.

72 See Arts. 25 and 26 of the Rome Statute.

73 See Art. 25 (2) of the Rome Statute.

74 Art. 27 of the Rome Statute. In practice, head-of-state immunity has been a central issue in the operation of the Court and remains a debated topic. In the case of *al-Bashir*, the Appeals Chamber of the Court held that '[t]here is neither State practice nor *opinio juris* that would support the existence of Head of State immunity under customary international law *vis-à-vis* an international court'. *Prosecutor* v. *Omar Hassan Ahmad Al-Bashir*, Judgment in the Jordan Referral re Al-Bashir Appeal, ICC-02/05-01/09 OA2, 6 May 2019.

but certain grounds such as mental disease or self-defence may exclude criminal responsibility.

According to Article 25 (3) of the Rome Statute, grounds for individual criminal responsibility are: (1) committing a crime under the statute; (2) ordering, soliciting or inducing the commission of such a crime; (3) facilitating, aiding or abetting, or otherwise assisting in the commission of a crime; (4) intentionally contributing to the commission of a crime in any other way through a group of persons acting with a common purpose; or (5) attempting to commit a crime.[75] The first mode of participation is quite clear; any individual who commits genocide, crimes against humanity or war crimes is clearly responsible. This entails that the perpetration of the crime was physically committed by the offender him- or herself.[76]

In addition, the statute extends the definition of commission to include co-perpetration, meaning situations in which the crime is committed jointly with another. Cases of mass atrocities often involve co-perpetration, since 'the crimes are often carried out by groups of individuals acting in pursuance of a common criminal design'.[77] A crime can also be committed through another person, an action termed 'perpetration by means'. This means that behind the perpetrator is a mastermind, an organizer, who exercises effective control over the perpetrator. Ultimately, the mastermind is also responsible for the act.[78] Based on the above, perpetration can be divided into three levels: (1) those perpetrators who 'belong to the leadership level', and 'who plan and organize the criminal events as a whole'; (2) mid-level hierarchy perpetrators who 'exercise some form of control over a part of the organization'; (3) 'those who execute the crimes'.[79]

Besides direct participation, the ICC Statute recognizes other modes of participation in a crime. First, there is responsibility for ordering, soliciting or inducing the commission of crimes. This covers a range of situations in which

75 See Art. 25 (3) (a)–(d)(ii) of the Rome Statute. For a comprehensive assessment of different modes or forms of responsibility in international criminal law in general, see Gideon Boas, James L. Bischoff and Natalie L. Reid, *International Criminal Law Practitioner Library, Volume I: Forms of Responsibility in International Criminal Law* (Cambridge: Cambridge University Press, 2007).

76 Kai Ambos, 'Article 25: Individual Criminal Responsibility', in Otto Triffterer (ed.), *Commentary on the Rome Statute of the International Criminal Court* (2nd ed., Munich: C. H. Beck, 2008), pp. 743–770 at 748.

77 *Prosecutor* v. *Tadić*, IT–94–1–A, ICTY Appeals Chamber (15 July 1999), para. 191.

78 This doctrine was used, for example, by the German Supreme Court in holding members of the National Defence Council and Army generals indirectly responsible for the shootings at the East German border. See Ambos, 'Article 25', 753.

79 Ambos, 'Article 25', 755.

a person prompts another person (or persons) to commit a crime. Specific to the concept of 'ordering' is the idea that there exists a superior–subordinate relationship.[80] Second, 'aiding and abetting' is an even weaker form of complicity that generates criminal responsibility before the ICC[81]; it aims to cover that which does not fall under ordering, soliciting or inducing commission. It encompasses 'any assistance, physical or psychological, that has a substantial effect on the commission of a crime'.[82] The third mode, and that with the lowest threshold for participation, is contributing in 'any other way' to the crime. The requirement for this mode is that the contribution takes place intentionally, with the knowledge of a common purpose.

Finally, there exists one additional ground for criminal responsibility in the ICC Statute: superior responsibility. Article 28 clearly lays down that a superior is responsible for crimes committed by his 'subordinates under his or her effective authority and control, as a result of his or her failure to exercise control properly'.[83] Superior responsibility is not limited only to military personnel: civilians as well can exercise such command that may generate responsibility. This means, for example, that those in control of a private military and security company and its employees cannot be held responsible only for having ordered crimes to be committed, but also for having failed to 'take all necessary and reasonable measures within his or her power to prevent or repress' the commission of crimes.[84]

During the first years of its existence, the Court struggled with how to interpret the Statute, with substantive legal issues of international criminal law, as well as with the issue of how to meet the high expectations placed upon individualized justice for acts that are the worst imaginable to mankind. Seventeen years after becoming operational, the results of the Court are meagre. It took the Court ten years to render its first judgment,[85] and as of June 2019 the ICC has handled 27 cases, of which it has convicted eight and acquitted three. The initial exhilaration over the ICC has faded:

80 Marja Lehto, *International Responsibility for Terrorist Acts: A Shift towards More Indirect Forms of Responsibility* (Rovaniemi: University of Lapland, 2008), p. 257.

81 Ambos, 'Article 25', 756.

82 Ibid., 759. One example from case law on aiding and abetting is the situation in which a person continues to interrogate a victim while the victim is being raped by another person. See Ambos, 'Article 25', 757, note 108.

83 Art. 28 (b) of the Rome Statute.

84 Art. 28 (b)(iii) of the Rome Statute.

85 *Situation in the Democratic Republic of the Congo in the Case of the Prosecutor* v. *Thomas Lubanga Dyilo* Judgment, ICC-01/04-01/06 (14 March 2012).

states parties are increasingly critical of the Court's performance,[86] and some states have even threatened to withdraw or have withdrawn from the Rome Statute.[87] Among other things, the Court has faced accusations of ineffectiveness in the form of too-lengthy and costly trials, selectivity of cases, and poor balancing of law and politics.[88] In conjunction with the lack of cooperation from states parties and increased hostility from major powers, such as the visa ban imposed by the United States upon ICC investigators in spring 2019, the Court increasingly appears to be in trouble.

## 4.2 SOCIAL CONTROL

Social control refers to the control a society exercises over its members in order to handle deviant behaviour. It can indicate bringing disobedient members under control or back in line,[89] or it can refer to encouraging others to maintain their conformity to societal norms. Thus, it is contingent upon norm-breaking conduct; '[i]t reacts to and seeks to eradicate or contain deviance, and is something positive and ameliorative that facilitates social life.'[90] Social control exists in many forms; it can be formal or informal, public or private, traditional or modern.[91] Although social control is a sociological concept, it has relevance for other disciplines as well, including legal theory. Law is a formal means of exercising social control, and therefore can be described as an 'instrument

86 For example, the statement of the United Kingdom at the 17th session of the Assembly of States Parties held that '[a]fter 20 years, and 1.5 billion Euros spent we have only three core crime convictions'. See UK Statement to the ICC Assembly of States Parties 17th Session, Statement by Andrew Murdoch, Legal Director to the International Criminal Court Assembly of States Parties, at its 17th Session in The Hague, *Foreign and Commonwealth Office*, 5 December 2018, www.gov.uk/government/speeches/uk-statement-to-icc-assembly-of-states-parties-17th-session (accessed 10 June 2019).

87 Pádraig McAuliffe and Christine Schwöbel-Patel, 'Disciplinary Matchmaking: Critics of International Criminal Law Meet Critics of Liberal Peacebuilding' (2018) 16 *Journal of International Criminal Justice* 985–1009.

88 F. Jessberger and J. Geneuss, 'Down the Drain or Down to Earth? International Criminal Justice under Pressure' (2013) 11 *Journal of International Criminal Justice* 501–503; Payam Akhavan, 'The Rise, and Fall, and Rise, of International Criminal Justice' (2013) 11 *Journal of International Criminal Justice* 527–536.

89 Peter Berger, *Invitation to Sociology: A Humanistic Perspective* (Doubleday: Anchor Books, 1963), p. 83.

90 Sharyn L. Roach Anleu, 'The Role of Civil Sanctions in Social Control: A Socio–Legal Examination' (1998) 9 *Crime Prevention Studies* 21–43 at 24.

91 Donald Black, *The Behavior of Law* (1st ed. 1976, special ed. 2010, Bingley: Emerald Group Publishing Limited, 2010), pp. 31–32.

of constraint'.[92] In contrast to other means of social control, '[l]aw is governmental social control' and relates to 'the normative life of a state and its citizens'.[93]

A role of all law is to function as a mechanism of social control, but its particular legal branches contribute to this goal to varying extents. Legal responsibility is a branch which, along with the broader aims of law, explicitly purports to induce society's members to act in accordance with society's rules in addition to providing rules that facilitate social relations.[94] Criminal law in particular has been described as one of the most powerful formal devices to exert social control.[95] At the same time, different developments in the society, such as privatization, have highlighted the role of civil remedies, including compensation.[96] As instruments of social control evolve, it has been argued that a general movement from penal to compensatory law has taken place.[97]

Social control is also central to the international legal order, despite the fact that international law surely differs from law in national societies, and contains fewer types of social control than its domestic counterparts. This is due in part to the lack of centralized enforcement and the element of coercion.[98] At the same time, it cannot be refuted that the responsibility regimes and institutions of international law do exercise social control, even though perhaps to a lesser extent than does national law. The following will explore the capacities of international liability and international criminal law to control undesired behaviour; that is, behaviour causing transboundary harm or seriously impairing human dignity. In what follows, social control will be understood as including both a deterrent and a preventive side. As long as the members of the international community comply with international norms, it is irrelevant if this compliance takes place as a result of special deterrence not to act illegally, or if they are induced on a general level to act with better care.[99]

92 Lon L. Fuller, 'Law as an Instrument of Social Control and Law as a Facilitation of Human Interaction' (1975) *Brigham Young University Law Review* 89–96 at 89.

93 Black, *The Behavior of Law*, p. 2.

94 See Fuller, 'Law as an Instrument'.

95 Justin Miller, 'Criminal Law – An Agency for Social Control' (1934) 43 *Yale Law Review* 691–715; Christopher M. V. Clarkson, *Understanding Criminal Law* (4th ed., London: Sweet & Maxwell, 2005), p. 253 *et seqq.*

96 Roach Anleu, 'The Role of Civil Sanctions', 24.

97 Emile Durkheim, 'Two Laws of Penal Evolution' (1973) 2 *Economy and Society* 285–308, cited in Roach Anleu, 'The Role of Civil Sanctions', 39.

98 See Ian Hurd, 'Legitimacy and Authority in International Politics' (1999) 53 *International Organization* 379–408.

99 'Prevention' is usually understood as a broader term than 'deterrence'. Kevin C. Kennedy defines deterrence as 'control or alteration of present and future criminal behavior which is effected by fear of adverse extrinsic consequences resulting from that behavior'.

The aim of social control is still the same, namely, to produce behaviour conforming to societal norms and expectations (i.e., good outcomes). The starting point of the analysis is the view that particularized regimes of responsibility will fare better than the law of state responsibility in the task of social control because they consist of tailor-made rules that can respond to specific features of the problems they attempt to deal with.

### 4.2.1 *The Preventive Function of Liability*

Three different but connected functions are traditionally ascribed to the concept of liability: the preventive, corrective and reparative.[100] Whereas the corrective and reparative functions both relate to ex post facto measures to deal with the consequences of an act whether unlawful or not, the preventive role of liability highlights the attempts to avoid liability arising from its other functions. In general theory, prevention has been understood in different ways; some emphasize liability as a means of prevention, whereas others see it as by-product or side-effect of the primary compensatory function of liability.[101] Although the preventive role of liability in both national and international law has been widely acknowledged, it still features mainly in theoretical discussions; its actual effect in deterring transboundary harm remains questionable.

Irrespective of the importance one affords to the preventive side of liability, there is a close connection between prevention of harm and compensation for it. This relationship becomes obvious in the case of hazardous activities which contain an inherent risk for damage, thus 'making prevention all the

See Kevin C. Kennedy, 'A Critical Appraisal of Criminal Deterrence Theory' (1983–1984) 88 *Dickinson Law Review* 1–13 at 2. Others have used the term 'deterrence' to indicate special or individual prevention, whereas the effects of criminal law and punishment upon society at large is termed 'general prevention'. To this effect, see Johannes Andenaes, 'The General Preventive Effects of Punishment' (1966) 114 *University of Pennsylvania Law Review* 949–983 at 949.

100 René Lefeber, *Transboundary Environmental*, p. 1. See also Louise Angélique de La Fayette, 'International Liability for Damage to the Environment', in Malgosia Fitzmaurice, David M. Ong and Panos Merkouris (eds.), *Research Handbook on International Environmental Law* (Cheltenham: Edward Elgar Publishing Ltd, 2010), pp. 320–360, who similarly recognize three functions of liability but have replaced the corrective function with 'the peaceful resolution of disputes'. Ibid., p. 328.

101 For example, Alan E. Boyle holds that the preventive aspect of liability cannot be the principal purpose since it is questionable if it has any such effects. See Boyle, 'Globalising Environmental Liability', 9.

more necessary'.[102] This link between prevention and liability for loss also surfaced in the ILC work on international liability, which from the beginning was covered as one topic but eventually came to be divided into two separate parts, one on prevention and the other on loss allocation.[103] According to the ILC, these two topics 'were distinct from one another, though related'.[104]

Having noted the connection between prevention and liability, a few caveats are in order. The purpose here is not to explore prevention as an international obligation. The ILC's work on prevention related directly to what obligations there are on states to ensure that potentially harmful activities are conducted with sufficient care.[105] Moreover, the draft articles target the state of origin rather than the actual actor in whose hands the activity lies. This means that the violation of these preventive obligations falls squarely within the parameters of state responsibility because they are based on wrongful behaviour. There is also one further way in which the notion of prevention is used that falls outside the present discussion. In the oil pollution regime, for example, the liable party is obliged to take 'preventive measures'.[106] In this context, prevention refers to measures undertaken *after* an accident in order to prevent further damage. In our current analysis we will focus on what effects the likelihood of responsibility for monetary compensation can have on the conduct of actors engaged in hazardous activities. The focus will thus be on prevention as a 'by-product' of liability,[107] not as an obligation of prevention. The preventive function discussed below consequently concerns the actor who would be liable to compensate for harm, which usually means that the actor will be a private entity unless the state itself is directly engaged in business activity.

#### 4.2.1.1 Incitement to Minimize Risk

The preventive side of liability builds on the assumption that the obligation to compensate for harm will, in fact, prevent harm from taking place to begin with. This so-called preventive function of liability is widely recognized,

[102] Barboza, *The Environment*, p. 14.

[103] Report of the International Law Commission on the Work of its Forty-ninth Session, UN Doc. A/52/10 (1997), Chapter VII.

[104] Pemmaraju Sreenivasa Rao, *First Report on Prevention of Transboundary Damage from Hazardous Activities*, UN Doc. A/CN.4/487 (18 March 1998), para. 7.

[105] Draft Articles on the Prevention of Transboundary Harm from Hazardous Activities, Report of the ILC (2001), Chapter V, text of the Draft Articles, p. 146, para. 97.

[106] See the International Convention on Civil Liability for Oil Pollution Damage, which in Art. I (7) defines 'preventive measures' as measures taken after an incident to minimize damage.

[107] Barboza, *The Environment*, p. 14.

despite it not being the foremost function usually assigned to liability.[108] Prevention is dependent on the primary function of liability, which is to provide compensation to victims; the underlying rationale being that the threat of economic compensation for caused harm will trigger preventive action. Liability thus becomes more than a 'reactive tool'; it 'can contribute to preventive goals by providing additional economic incentives for actors to take into account the potential social and ecological consequences of their activities'.[109] By 'reducing the number of accidents' and thereby lowering the 'costs of compensation',[110] in addition to encouraging research in improving knowledge and facilitating technological innovations,[111] liability serves both 'as a deterrent to carelessness and an incentive to safety'.[112]

The preventive effect of liability is often recognized implicitly in the negotiation and formation of international instruments,[113] but explicitly so only in a few instruments, mostly adopted within the confines of the EU. For example, the EU White Paper on Environmental Liability stresses the capacity for liability to change the behaviour of actors: environmental liability is expected to bring about a 'change of attitude [that] should result in an increased level of prevention and precaution'.[114] In similar terms, the EU

[108] See e.g., Lefeber, *Transboundary Environmental*, pp. 1–4, 313; Barboza, *The Environment*, p. 14; Koskenniemi, *Valtion kansainvälinen vastuu*, p. 181; Faure and Grimeaud, 'Financial Assurance', 19; Faure and Nollkaemper, 'International Liability as an Instrument', 141. On the other hand, de La Fayette emphasizes the importance of the preventive function of liability. See 'International Liability', 329. Similarly, European Parliament, 'Cross-border Nuclear Safety, Liability and Cooperation in the European Union', *Policy Department for Citizens' Rights and Constitutional Affairs*, Directorate General for Internal Policies of the Union PE 608.860, February 2019, p. 42; Institute of International Law, 'Responsibility and Liability under International Law for Environmental Damage' (4 September 1997), article 13, www.idi-iil.org/app/uploads/2017/06/1997_str_03_en.pdf (accessed 18 June 2019).

[109] Michael Mason, 'Transnational Compensation for Oil Pollution Damage: Examining Changing Spatialities of Environmental Liability', *LSE Research Papers in Environmental and Spatial Analysis, no 69* (2002), Department of Geography and Environment, London School of Economics and Political Science, London, UK, 1–24, p. 16.

[110] Barboza, *The Environment*, p. 29.

[111] European Commission, White Paper on Environmental Liability, COM (2000) 66 final, Brussels, 9 February 2000, Section 3.1, p. 14.

[112] De La Fayette, 'International Liability', 329.

[113] For example, during the negotiations of the Cartagena Protocol of Biosafety it was held that the liability rules should be part of the package in order to strengthen the compliance incentive of states and companies to act in accordance with the Protocol and to exercise caution. See Kate Cook, 'No Liability, No Protocol', in Christoph Bail, Robert Falkner and Helen Marquard (eds.), *The Cartagena Protocol on Biosafety: Reconciling Trade in Biotechnology with Environment & Development* (London: Earthscan Publications, 2002), pp. 371–384 at 373.

[114] Foreword, White Paper on Environmental Liability.

Environmental Liability Directive confirms the preventive side of liability by calling for financial liability 'in order to induce operators to adopt measures and develop practices to minimise the risks of environmental damage so that their exposure to financial liabilities is reduced'.[115]

Naturally, the actual preventive effect of liability is dependent on many factors, and cannot be decontextualized. Empirical market based studies, however, show that the ability of liability to change the behaviour of actors should not be overstated; liability remains one instrument among many for reducing the risk of transboundary harm.[116] Those who question the adequacy of the capacity of liability to engender prevention often emphasize that special rules on prevention are needed in order to anchor prevention in law.[117] It has been argued that 'making safety standards dependant [*sic*] on the perceptions of individuals regarding their potential liabilities may not guarantee adequate steps for prevention'.[118] Thus, sceptics call for the creation of legally binding rules on prevention in addition to reliance on the preventive side of compensation. This expressed cautiousness regarding liability as a mechanism for producing prevention finds support in recent international agreements which increasingly oblige state parties to ensure that operators take preventive measures.[119] However, the preventive effect of liability should not be dismissed altogether. It should be recognized that the role of liability as a dissuasive power has been downplayed by internal limits on international liability regimes. The optimal preventive effect of liability is rarely reached as a result of mechanisms and practices within international liability rules and regimes themselves. Thus there is room for improving the incentivizing role of liability.

115 Directive 2004/35/CE of the European Parliament and of the Council, 21 April 2004, On Environmental Liability with regard to the Prevention and Remedying of Environmental Damage, para. 2.

116 There are a number of studies on the preventive effect of liability. See, for example, the 1990 Lahnstein study on the effect of liability upon environmental damage cases. See Michael Faure, 'Concluding Remarks', in Michael Faure (ed.), *Deterrence, Insurability, and Compensation in Environmental Liability: Future Developments in the European Union* (Wien: Springer, 2003), pp. 331–343 at 333. Malgosia Fitzmaurice notes that '[s]adly, there are no clear indications that they [strict liability regimes] shape the behaviour of the polluter'. See Fitzmaurice, 'International Responsibility and Liability', 1034.

117 Barboza, *The Environment*, p. 14; Faure 'Concluding Remarks', 334.

118 Barboza, *The Environment*, p. 14.

119 de La Fayette, 'International Liability', 354. See The Liability Annex to the Treaty on the Antarctica, which lays down in Article 3 that '[e]ach Party shall require its operators to undertake reasonable preventive measures that are designed to reduce the risk of environmental emergencies and their potential adverse impact'. Annex VI to the Protocol on Environmental Protection to the Antarctic Treaty: Liability Arising from Environmental Emergencies, Stockholm, 14 June 2005, not yet in force.

#### 4.2.1.2 Internal Limits

In the aftermath of the 1999 and 2002 *Erika* and *Prestige* oil spills, the preventive or deterrent effect of the international civil liability regimes was heavily criticized.[120] The European Commission in particular questioned the capacity of the oil pollution regime to control relevant business actors, and noted that civil liability regimes were unable 'to discourage those involved in the transport of dangerous or polluting goods by sea from engaging in negligent practices and is therefore of limited value for helping to prevent accidents from happening in the first place'.[121] There are indeed a number of problems justifying the questioning of the preventive effect of liability. The actors' temperaments may contribute to the level of risk management they exercise, the applicable standard of care in liability law may influence conduct, the existence of insurance may leave actors unsympathetic to the potential damages of the activity, as may other means of spreading and socializing liability as well. Ascertaining the ultimate preventive effect of liability is considered to be difficult because various factors may affect the conduct of the actor, thus undermining the preventive dimension of having to pay for caused damages. Therefore, the close connection to liability's compensatory function also poses challenges to prevention.

The first issue that affects the preventive side of liability is the applicable standard of care that liability is grounded in. In the literature it has been convincingly argued that with respect to deterrence of accidents, '[o]nly with strict liability would the potential injurer also have an incentive to adopt an optimal activity level.'[122] If liability is made absolute in the sense of being automatic and unlimited, the point of prevention is lost: if companies or other actors know that they have to pay for damages in any case, the incentive

[120] The critique related to, inter alia, the insufficiency of the compensation and too low financial caps on liability. It resulted in increased compensation limits and a third tier of liability being created with the 2003 Supplementary Fund Protocol. See e.g., Sophia Kopela, 'Civil and Criminal Liability as Mechanisms for the Prevention of Oil Pollution: The *Erika* Case' (2011) 20 *Review of the European Community & International Environmental Law* 313–324; de La Fayette, 'International Liability', 336; Wang Hui, 'Transboundary Vessel-Source Marine Pollution – International Legal Framework and Its Application to China', in Michael Faure and Song Ying (eds.), *China and International Environmental Liability: Legal Remedies for Transboundary Pollution* (Cheltenham: Edward Elgar Publishing, 2008), pp. 64–106 at 76.

[121] Proposal for a Directive of the European Parliament and of the Council on ship-source pollution and on the introduction of sanctions, including criminal sanctions, for pollution offences (presented by the Commission), Explanatory Memorandum, COM/2003/0092 final – COD/2003/0037, 5 March 2003, para. 2.2.

[122] Faure and Grimeaud, 'Financial Assurance', 197.

to prevent such liability becomes null. In addition, if fault or negligence is set as the applicable standard it would allow the potential injurer to know in advance the difficulty the victim would have in proving the standard, which would lessen the incentive to reduce risk. Therefore, strict liability in itself prompts preventive acts.[123] As Kenneth Abraham has noted, '[a] finding of strict liability makes a statement about an activity, not an actor alone, and is therefore a statement about all who are engaged in the activity.'[124]

Another question relevant to the preventive function of liability is that of how the financial security of the potential injurer is arranged, and by what kind of compensation mechanisms. There is a delicate balance among arrangements of financial assurance, collectivity and prevention. International practice reveals that private enterprises often create cooperative arrangements in order to reduce the cost of compensation. These risk-sharing agreements may include, for example, pools or Protection and Indemnity Clubs (P&I), from which compensation is paid in case of harm. As a result, liability or the payment of compensation is 'to a large part transferred from the single plant owner to the collective guarantee fund mutually owned' by all in the same industry in the contracting states.[125] By collectivizing compensation, there is a common interest in reducing compensation claims by means of acting with a higher degree of care. The capacity of such financial security arrangements to induce change is dependent upon the mutuality between similar actors. In other words, they must share a sense of solidarity and trust in order for mutuality to work. Indeed, actors involved in the same business more easily find motivation to cooperate, because they wish to reduce claim costs. Thus, for example, it can be argued that all owners of cargo ships carrying oil who belong to a certain pool (or so-called P&I Club) have 'an interest in seeing that the claims of his fellow members are as infrequent and as small as possible'.[126] However, the preventive effect is in danger of being lost if the collectivizing effects are too broad. Kenneth Abraham argues that 'the more collective responsibility a given rule entails – on its face or because of the collectivizing effects

[123] Kenneth S. Abraham, 'Individual Action and Collective Responsibility: The Dilemma of Mass Tort Reform' (1987) 73 *Virginia Law Review* 845–907 at 857.

[124] Abraham, 'Individual Action', 859.

[125] Faure and Grimeaud, 'Financial Assurance', 230.

[126] J. Donaldson, *Safer Ships, Cleaner Seas: Report of Lord Donaldson's Inquiry into the Prevention of Pollution from Merchant Shipping* (London: HMSO, 1994), p. 273, cited in Paul Bennett, 'Mutual Risk: P & I Insurance Clubs and Maritime Safety and Environmental Performance' (2001) 25 *Marine Policy* 13–21 at 14.

of liability insurance – the less optimal is its effect on the safety incentives of those to whom it applies.'[127] Free riders can emerge, who follow the economic rationale that it will be cheaper for an individual shipowner to 'take *less* care once insured because they know that the costs of any accident will be shared amongst all'.[128]

A third feature of liability regimes which can negatively affect the capacity to persuade actors to act with care is the practice of channelling liability. Channelling constitutes a deviation from the general principle that 'only the injurer who caused the damage should be held fully liable for the loss'.[129] The fact that compensation claims are directed only to one specific actor leaves other actors outside the scope of liability. This means that different actors involved in hazardous activities know beforehand who the first addressee of claims will be. The international oil pollution regime, for example, channels liability to shipowners. Other actors, such as the charterer or cargo owner, will thus benefit from the rules of channelling liability because they will automatically be excluded from liability.[130] Indeed, channelling has been said to lead to the '"de-responsibilization" of actors involved in the incidents'.[131] Thus, the effect of channelling liability upon prevention is twofold. On the one hand, it can be argued that the deterrent effect of having to pay compensation is greater for shipowners than others involved; on the other hand, it is easy to see how the practice of channelling undermines the deterrent effect in general. All those actors against whom liability cannot be directed will have even *less* incentive to prevent harm. As a result, the practice of channelling liability has met with criticism. Especially within the international oil pollution regime, several critical voices have demanded a re-evaluation of the channelling rules in order to take account of a broader spectrum of actors involved in any specific hazardous activity.[132] Overall, it seems well-founded that '[c]hannelling can hence hardly be considered as an efficient mechanism for the prevention of accidents.'[133]

Another condition for the success of liability as a preventive mechanism is that the costs of harm all fall back onto the operator of the activity. The maximum effect on the conduct of actors is provided only if the amount of compensation is fully transferred onto them. This is due to economic theory

127 Abraham, 'Individual Action', 863.
128 Bennett, 'Mutual Risk', 15 (emphasis in original).
129 Faure and Grimeaud, 'Financial Assurance', 165.
130 Wang, *Civil Liability*, p. 349.
131 Kopela, 'Civil and Criminal Liability', 319.
132 See Proposal for a Directive, para. 2.2.
133 Faure and Grimeaud, 'Financial Assurance', 165.

and a cost/benefit analysis which explains that in order for liability to deter, the costs of care-taking must equal the costs in compensation reduction.[134] International liability rules nonetheless limit the financial liability of actors by using caps or ceilings on the amounts to be compensated. Financial caps or limits upon liability could thus result in lesser care by the potential injurer since '[t]here is a direct linear relationship between the magnitude of the accident risk and the amount spent on care.'[135] Liability caps exist both in the international oil pollution regime and in the nuclear energy regime. Therefore, it can be argued that the ability of liability to control actors in business is not fully utilized.

The inadequacy of international liability regimes to deal with expectations of prevention has generated demands for more robust measures against harm caused by hazardous activities. For example, the European Commission has held that 'only criminal sanctions will be sufficiently effective for ensuring the intended effects of the ship-source pollution rules'.[136] Accordingly, penal sanctions have been taken as constituting better deterrence than civil liability rules alone. Despite the perceived 'greater dissuasive effect' of criminal liability,[137] not everyone is prepared to disenfranchise civil liability. Some signatory states and the European Union have called for changing the rules on, for example, financial caps and the channelling of liability within the international oil pollution regime.[138] These rules are classic hallmarks of balancing between the interests of the victims and of those engaged in the relevant business. Indeed, it seems that some states feel the need to shift the emphasis from the corrective function of liability to its preventive function. The preventive side of liability is, perhaps, increasingly being accepted.[139]

#### 4.2.1.3 Optimizing Prevention

There are mechanisms to be found in international practice that strive to ensure the maximum preventive effect of liability. One such mechanism is the creation of so-called dual compensation schemes, which establish different models of liability based upon the conduct of the person or entity in question. The general model of strict liability is to be followed if the person has acted

[134] Ibid., 21.
[135] Ibid., 197.
[136] 2003 Proposal for a Directive, para. 2.2.
[137] Ibid.
[138] Ibid.
[139] Kopela, 'Civil and Criminal Liability', 323.

with due care, but if fault actually can be proven on the part of the person, broader liability is to be imposed. In short, specialized rules stipulate limited liability as the standard model, but unlimited liability if fault can be proven.[140] The Civil Liability Convention of the international oil pollution regime, for example, stipulates that a shipowner normally has the right to limit his or her liability, but that this does not apply to cases in which 'it is proved that the pollution damage resulted from his personal act or omission, committed with the intent to cause such damage, or recklessly and with knowledge that such damage would probably result'.[141]

A similar strategy of stressing the individual actor's conduct in order to optimize prevention can be said to exist within pools that collectivize liability. Undesirable behaviour is deterred by the re-individualization of collective responsibility,[142] which means that the individual actor or member in a pool receives higher premiums in the long run if he has been involved in harmful incidents.[143] The incentive to prevention would thus be maintained by the creation of internal rules on how to 'reapportion' or channel liability back, at least to a certain extent, to the individual actor who caused the harm.[144] As Gunther Teubner notes: 'Collective liability makes sure that victims will be compensated in situations where no individual causation can be established; individual reapportionment creates incentives for individual actors to reduce the ecological risk.'[145]

### 4.2.2 *International Criminal Law and Deterrence*

One of the fundamental purposes of all criminal law is to prohibit or inhibit behaviour that is harmful to individual or public wellbeing.[146] Through the fear of punishment, criminal law attempts to control persons or entities that

[140] Barboza, *The Environment*, p. 35.

[141] See Art. 6 of the 1984 Protocol to the 1969 International Convention on Civil Liability for Oil Pollution Damage, Brussels, 29 November 1969, in force 19 June 1975, 973 *United Nations Treaty Series* 3.

[142] For discussions on re-individualization of collective responsibility, see Günther Teubner, 'The Invisible Cupola: From Causal to Collective Attribution in Ecological Liability' (1994–1995) 16 *Cardozo Law Review* 429–464.

[143] Bennett, 'Mutual Risk', 15.

[144] Teubner, 'The Invisible Cupola', 458.

[145] Ibid., 455.

[146] David Ormerod, *Smith and Hogan Criminal Law* (12th ed., Oxford and New York: Oxford University Press, 2008), p. 3. Nigel Walker identifies three justifications for criminal law and punishment: (1) retributive; (2) reductive; and (3) denunciatory reasons. See Nigel Walker, *Punishment, Danger and Stigma: The Morality of Criminal Justice* (Totowa: Barnes and Noble Books, 1980), preface.

are inclined to perpetrate crime. Criminal law theories generally acknowledge that deterrence or prevention is one of the main functions that criminal law is expected to serve, alongside other objectives such as retribution or rehabilitation.

Three different justifications are frequently used in explaining the capacity of criminal law and punishment to act as a deterrent. First, the utilitarian theory as formulated by Cesare Beccaria and Jeremy Bentham emphasizes the rationality of the actor.[147] This 'rational actor theory', which is also called the 'economic model', builds on the assumption that a person who contemplates committing a crime will weigh the benefits of that crime against the costs of breaking the law. Accordingly, if the costs of the crime are higher than the potential gains, law will act as a deterrent.

A second rationale for the deterrent effect of criminal law and punishment is provided by theorists who highlight the 'moral influence of the law as a preventive factor'.[148] It is believed that the value transmitted through criminalizing certain types of behaviour will prevent the commission of such crimes. Thus, the moralizing and educational side of criminal law will also have preventive effects: '[b]y means of the criminal law, and by means of specific applications of this law, "messages" are sent to members of a society'.[149] Punishment thus has a 'moral or socio-pedagogical influence'[150] which rational choice theorists often overlook. The preventive effect of criminal law and punishment thus resides in the willingness of a society and its members to respect the law in general and in relation to the particular values that the law seeks to protect.[151] The legitimacy of the social order is hence accentuated by the general prevention of undesirable behaviour.[152]

A third motivation for the deterrence rationale of criminal law is found in its habituating effect. Punishment is thus taken to induce law-abiding conduct.[153] Although no settled understanding exists about the exact meaning and scope of the rationale of habituation, it implies that law is followed because people are predisposed to follow the law: 'observance of the law eventually becomes

[147] Cesare Beccaria, *Of Crimes and Punishments* (*Dei delitti e delle pene*) (trans. Edward D. Ingraham, Philadelphia: R. Bell, 1774); Jeremy Bentham, *An Introduction to the Principles of Morals and Legislation* (London: The Athlone Press, London, 1789).

[148] Kennedy, 'A Critical Appraisal', 3.

[149] Andenaes, 'The General Preventive', 949.

[150] Ibid., 950 (emphases omitted).

[151] Ibid., 950.

[152] See e.g., Kennedy, 'A Critical Appraisal', 4–6.

[153] Johs Andenaes, 'General Prevention – Illusion or Reality?' (1952) 43 *Journal of Criminal Law and Criminology* 176–198 at 180.

a habit which is followed automatically without reflection'.[154] This habituating effect is naturally closely connected to criminal law's other rationales, deterrence and the moralizing effect. Whether it constitutes an independent justification for criminal law or is merely a secondary effect of deterrence has been debated, but irrespective of how it is categorized it constitutes an important argument in the discussion on the general preventive effect of criminal law and punishment.[155]

Yet, it is important to note that not even the deterrence theory enjoys unquestionable support. There are both principled and practical problems with respect to deterrence. First, the deterrence theory is based on many presuppositions that need to be met in order for the theory to be effective. There is ample agreement about the importance of the certainty and severity of punishment, in addition to which some scholars emphasize the necessity of delivering swift punishments.[156] Thus, the higher the probability that conviction will follow, and that the more severe forms of punishment will be inflicted upon the perpetrator, the greater deterrent effect will follow.[157] But deterrence will result only if the threat of punishment is communicated to members of the society and the swiftness, certainty and severity of punishment is accompanied by a belief that the system is able to apprehend and punish offenders.[158]

Second, the deterrence argument is arguably unconvincing on a more principled level. Fear of punishment will never lead to a crime-free world, not only because the resources of any criminal justice system are limited, but also because there are no conclusive evidence to support the existence of deterrence even though all necessary conditions of swiftness, severity and certainty are met. The idea of the economic model is manifestly flawed because it leaves out moral elements such as the social validity of the criminal justice system; it fails to pay attention to socio-economic

[154] Gordon Hawkins 'Punishment and Deterrence: The Educative, Moralizing, and Habituating Effects' (1969) *Wisconsin Law Review* 550–565 at 564.

[155] Scholarly discussion identifies Johannes Andenaes as the one who highlighted that '[t]o the lawmaker, the achievement of inhibition and habit is of greater value than mere deterrence'. See Andenaes, 'General Prevention', 180.

[156] See Andenaes, 'The General Preventive', 964, who claims that '[a]t least since the time of Beccaria, it has been commonly accepted that the certainty of detection and punishment is of greater consequence in deterring people from committing crimes than is the severity of the penalty'.

[157] See Kennedy, 'A Critical Appraisal', 4–5.

[158] Ibid., 4–6.

factors that contribute to proclivity to crime; and because it dismisses crimes of passion.[159]

Despite the many unanswered questions that characterize the discourse around deterrence, deterrence and prevention theories through which national criminal justice is validated have been transposed directly onto the international sphere. These accounts usually pay no attention to the differences between the national and international settings, but assume by analogy that what is workable domestically will also be workable internationally.[160] However, the starting point for a discussion of the deterrent effect of international criminal law and its institutions must differ from a comparative discussion of national legal systems. It seems more accurate to discuss not how much deterrence can be achieved through international criminal law, but instead to discuss whether it possess a deterrent function to begin with. In the following, the potential of international criminal justice to act as a deterrent will be discussed from a doctrinal and institutional point of view. Alongside the question of whether international criminal law can be said at all to have a (credible) deterrent effect, the analysis will explore how this potential is used by international criminal law institutions, and to what degree deterrence is a legitimate function of international criminal law.

#### 4.2.2.1 Contested Deterrence

The deterrence argument proceeds from the assumption that a credible danger of prosecution and punishment before an international criminal tribunal will cause potential offenders to refrain from committing international crimes.[161] Consequently, in addition to punishing crime, international criminal law will also seek to prevent or deter crime. This capacity of international criminal law and its institutions is widely discussed and highly disputed. Its importance stems from the fact that deterrence has been used to justify the creation of international criminal institutions. Deterrence thus constitutes

[159] See Kennedy, 'A Critical Appraisal', 7–11.

[160] See Immi Tallgren, 'The Sense and Sensibility of International Criminal Law' (2002) 13 *European Journal of International Law* 561–595 at 565–566; Robert Sloane, 'The Expressive Capacity of International Punishment: The Limits of National Law Analogy and the Potential of International Criminal Law' (2007) 43 *Stanford Journal of International Law* 39–94 at 41; Pádraig McAuliffe, 'Suspended Disbelief? The Curious Endurance of the Deterrence Rationale in International Criminal Law' (2012) 10 *New Zealand Journal of Public and International Law* 227–262 at 231.

[161] Immi Tallgren has described the deterrence argument more vividly: 'the more gas we give to the punishing machine, the less criminality we end up with'. See Tallgren, 'We Did It?', 686.

one of the main reasons for the existence of international criminal law: it is not a by-product of any kind. Characteristic of the deterrence debate is the division of commentators from various fields into two groups: supporters of the deterrence argument and those strongly opposing it. There is relatively little empirical research on the matter, and ideology more than evidence-based research has supposedly dominated the debate.[162] The ultimate question is one of how it can be proven that international criminal law can deter potential offenders and, conversely, how it can be shown that it cannot.[163]

Relentless enthusiasm about the deterrent capacities of international criminal law seems to prevail not only among international criminal lawyers themselves, but also among many journalists and NGOs. Naturally, the deterrence argument is also upheld by international criminal law institutions themselves. The importance of punishment in preventing international crimes has been emphasized, especially surrounding the establishment of international criminal tribunals, but also in the tribunals' case law. The ICTY noted in the *Erdemović* case the importance of the tribunal as a powerful means of deterring future crimes.[164] Similarly, the ICTR held in the case of *Jean Kambanda* that the primary purposes of sentencing are retribution and deterrence.[165] Reliance on the deterrent effects of prosecution of international crimes has endured the early years of international criminal law and has constituted a part of the ICC vocabulary as well. Prosecutor Bensouda of the

[162] Mark Drumbl, 'Collective Violence and Individual Punishment: The Criminality of Mass Atrocity' (2005) 99 *North Western University Law Review* 539–610 at 548. See also, Kate Cronin-Furman, 'Managing Expectations: International Criminal Trials and the Prospects for Deterrence of Mass Atrocities' (2013) *International Journal of Transitional Justice* 434–454.

[163] It has been pointed out that it is next to impossible to prove either deterrence or non-deterrence. David J. Scheffer has stated, '[f]or people to say there will be no deterrence at all is as factually unprovable as to say there will be deterrence'. See David J. Scheffer, 'Milosevic, Killing Fields, and "Kangaroo" Courts: Symposium on an Emerging International Criminal Justice System. Should the United States Join the International Criminal Court?' (2002) 9 *University of California Davis Journal of International Law & Policy* 45–52 at 51. David Wippman has emphasized the plausibility of the deterrence argument, but maintained that it is 'largely untested'. See David Wippman, 'Atrocities, Deterrence, and the Limits of International Justice' (1999) 23 *Fordham International Law Journal* 473–488 at 474. For a discussion of and effort toward how to possibly measure the deterrent effect of international criminal tribunals, see Julian Ku and Jide Nzelibe, 'Do International Criminal Tribunals Deter or Exacerbate Humanitarian Atrocities?' (2006) 84 *Washington University Law Review* 777–833.

[164] *The Prosecutor* v. *Drazen Erdemović*, IT–96–22–T, ICTY Trial Chamber, Sentencing Judgment (29 November 1996), para. 58.

[165] *The Prosecutor* v. *Jean Kambanda*, ICTR–97–23–S, Trial Chamber, Judgment and Sentence (4 September 1998), para. 28.

ICC repeatedly stresses the 'shadow of the ICC' as one of the main functions of international criminal law. In her case against President Uhuru Kenyatta of Kenya, the Prosecutor firmly took the stance that in its decisions the ICC should also reflect upon the Court's deterrent effect. According to Bensouda: 'Deterrence, like a currency, can be debased or devalued. We can reasonably differ about the strength of the Court's deterrent effect, but there is no doubt that that effect does exist.'[166] In the Court's practice, deterrence has been recognized as one of the central aims of sentencing. For example, in the *Bemba* sentencing decision, as well as in other corresponding decisions, the Trial Chamber held that 'a sentence should be adequate to discourage a convicted person from recidivism (specific deterrence) as well as to ensure that those who would consider committing similar offences will be dissuaded from doing so (general deterrence)'.[167] At times trust in deterrence has been so great that it has even been considered as a more important justification for international criminal law than retribution.[168]

General international legal scholars usually do not share this optimism about the ability of international criminal law to function as a deterrent. Sceptical views have frequently been presented, claiming that the actual deterrent effect of international criminal law is uncertain, if not altogether non-existent.[169] Belief in the deterrence argument is said to bring about disappointment.[170] It may even cause some to overlook the many counterproductive effects of international criminal trials.[171] This is so because perpetrators of international crimes do not always act rationally. Moreover, the institutional setup of the ICC is considered troublesome from the point of deterrence.

[166] *The Prosecutor* v. *Uhuru Muigai Kenyatta*, ICC–01/09–02/11, Trial Chamber, Status Conference (5 February 2014), p. 36.

[167] *The Prosecutor* v. *Jean-Pierre Bemba Gombo, Aimé Kilolo Musamba, Jean-Jacques Mangenda Kabongo, Fidèle Babala Wandu and Narcisse Arido*, ICC-01/05-01/13, Trial Chamber VII, Decision on Sentence (22 March 2017), para. 19.

[168] The Trial Chamber of the ICTR, which held in the *Kambanda* case in 1998: 'The penalties imposed on accused persons found guilty by the Tribunal must be directed, on the one hand, at retribution of the said accused, who must see their crimes punished, and over and above that, on the other hand, at deterrence, namely dissuading for good those who will attempt in future to perpetrate such atrocities ...'. *The Prosecutor* v. *Jean Kambanda*, ICTR–97–23–S, Trial Chamber, Judgment and Sentence (4 September 1998), para. 28.

[169] Jan Klabbers, 'Just Revenge? The Deterrence Argument in International Criminal Law' (2001) XII *Finnish Yearbook of International Law* 249–267; Martti Koskenniemi, 'Between Impunity', 7–8; Wippman, 'Atrocities', 474.

[170] See Klabbers, 'Just Revenge?', 254.

[171] For a discussion on the potentially counterproductive effects of international criminal trials, see Ku and Nzelibe, 'Do International Criminal', 783; Jack Goldsmith, 'The Self-Defeating International Criminal Court' (2003) 70 *University of Chicago Law Review* 89–104 at 95.

Only a few scholars have attempted to model, test or measure the deterrent effect of international criminal tribunals.[172] Michael Gillian has found that the ICC may 'deter some atrocities at the margin', but will not be 'a cure-all' solution to international crimes.[173] According to Gillian, the contribution by the ICC mainly relates to regime change, as it will help more palatable leaders to take over.[174] Another attempt to analyze the deterrent effect of international criminal tribunals is provided by Julian Ku and Jide Nzelibe, who question the underlying assumption of the deterrence argument, which is that offenders operate in a culture of impunity. They seek to show that in fact, and contrary to the argument set forth by international criminal lawyers, potential offenders often face certain and severe sanctions at the local level. According to Ku and Nzelibe, potential perpetrators of atrocities 'are not likely to be significantly deterred by the prospect of further prosecution by ICTs [International Criminal Tribunals]'.[175] More recent studies do suggest, however, that international criminal justice may indeed deter in certain specific situations and with regard to a limited range of persons.[176] For example, Hyeran Jo and Beth Simmons have argued that 'the ICC can deter some governments and those rebel groups that seek legitimacy'.[177]

The special features of international criminal law clearly downplay its capacity of functioning as a deterrent.[178] International criminal law is a place of last resort, and even then it is applied selectively, with numerically very few prosecutions. Moreover, one should distinguish between what international

[172] Relevant studies are, for example, Jack Snyder's and Leslie Vinjamuri's comparative study of prosecution and amnesties from 2003 to 2004. See Jack Snyder and Leslie Vinjamuri, 'Trials and Errors: Principle and Pragmatism in Strategies of International Justice' (2003–2004) 28 *International Security* 5–44. For an overview of the few studies, see James F. Alexander, 'The International Criminal Court and the Prevention of Atrocities: Predicting the Court's Impact' (2009) 54 *Villanova Law Review* 1–56, esp. 45–49.

[173] In 2006 Michael J. Gilligan explored deterrence in the absence of credible enforcement through game theory. See Michael J. Gilligan, 'Is Enforcement Necessary for Effectiveness? A Model of the International Criminal Law Regime' (2006) 60 *International Organization* 935–967 at 935, 958.

[174] Ibid., 956–957.

[175] Ku and Nzelibe, 'Do International Criminal', 807.

[176] Hyeran Jo and Beth A. Simmons, 'Can the International Criminal Court Deter Atrocity?' (2016) 70 *International Organization* 443–475; Courtney Hillebrecht, 'The Deterrent Effect of the International Criminal Court: Evidence from Libya' (2016) 42 *International Interactions* 616–643.

[177] Jo and Simmons, 'Can the International', 443.

[178] For discussions on the special feature of international criminal law, see Mikaela Heikkilä, *Coping with International Atrocities through Criminal Law: A Study into the Typical Features of International Criminality and the Reflection of These Traits in International Criminal Law* (Turku: Åbo Akademi University Press, 2014), esp. pp. 94–113.

criminal law might be able to achieve at its best on a theoretical level, and what it can do in reality. Both procedural and political constraints exist that weaken the capacity of international criminal tribunals to dissuade potential offenders from committing international crimes.

For example, the low number of cases dealt with by international criminal tribunals will undoubtedly impact its potential to deter international crimes. Although it could be argued that there are simply too few prosecutions and trials to make broad generalizations on the deterrent effect of international criminal law, it seems justified to conclude that the low number of cases will affect deterrence negatively. The capability of single sentences to influence people's behaviour has been called into question, as it has been noted that '[on]ly rarely does a single sentence bring about significant preventive effects.'[179] Although international criminal law has never striven to have all perpetrators of international crimes tried for their deeds, international criminal tribunals are still underperforming. The ICTR has been estimated to have prosecuted around 0,005 per cent of the potential perpetrators in the Rwandan genocide, a figure which has been considered to be so low that its deterrent effect is marginal at best.[180]

Selective prosecution is another feature of international criminal law which affects its dissuasive force. Although the basic idea of international criminal law is that everyone irrespective of place or status should be responsible for his deeds,[181] in practice international criminal tribunals have focused on the so-called 'big fish'. Government leaders and other high-ranking officials are more likely to face prosecution than the low-level perpetrator with blood on his or her hands. The choice between prosecuting leaders or underlings has played a decisive role in the debate over deterrence. On the one hand, those seeking to punish leaders claim that this has a maximizing effect on deterrence. On the other hand, it has been questioned whether the threat of punishment has any impact on government leaders. It has been argued that the special nature of the crime and of these perpetrators as human rights violators leaves them altogether indifferent to deterrence.[182] Their essentially political motives make them unaffected by calculations of costs and benefits.

Another relevant point in assessing international criminal law's deterrent power is the question of the degree to which it is enforced. In order for international criminal law to constitute a viable deterrent, its actions must be

[179] Andenaes, 'The General Preventive', 970.

[180] Ku and Nzelibe, 'Do International Criminal', 808.

[181] Martti Koskenniemi, 'Between Impunity', 2.

[182] Klabbers, 'Just Revenge?', 253.

implemented. The absence of an international police force to execute arrest warrants, protect witnesses, seal evidence and execute sentences has a negative impact. International criminal tribunals are left at the mercy of relevant states parties, which are under legal obligation to cooperate with the tribunals. Yet, non-cooperation is a material problem. For many years, Balkan states failed to detain notorious war criminals such as Ratko Mladić and Radovan Karadžić. The former President of Sudan Omar Al-Bashir remained in office for many years despite the ICC's issuance of an arrest warrant in 2009. Most recently, Kenya has managed to impede the work of the ICC with its policy of obstructionism. Among other things, Kenya has refused to hand over evidence, and it has bribed and threatened witnesses to such an extent that the prosecutor has been forced to withdraw her charges against Uhuru Kenyatta, the President of Kenya.[183] Although the enforcement problem may be exaggerated, it has been noted that 'what is decisive is not the actual practice but how this practice is conceived by the public'.[184] To this effect, perception will not save international criminal law as a deterrent.

The interplay between international criminal law as a doctrine and the way its institutions implement it,[185] shows that general deterrence is difficult to maintain. The remote possibility of ending up before the ICC as a result of having committed international crimes is unlikely to have any significant impact on people who have the opportunity and will to perpetrate international crimes. As research has shown, 'no institution can deter all actors'.[186] What is more, the prevailing understanding that the ICC and international criminal justice more broadly are in the descendent is unhelpful to the deterrence argument, as are the acquittals by the ICC of Bemba, Gbagbo and Blé Goudé.[187] But deterrence examined from a more limited perspective may

[183] See *Prosecutor* v. *Uhuru Muigai Kenyatta*, ICC-01/09-02/11, Notice of withdrawal of the charges against Uhuru Muigai Kenyatta (5 December 2014).

[184] Andenaes, 'The General Preventive', 970.

[185] For a comprehensive recent study, see Jennifer Schense and Linda Carter (eds.), *Two Steps Forward, One Step Back: The Deterrent Effect of International Criminal Tribunals* (Brussels: Torkel Opsahl Academic EPublisher, 2017).

[186] Jo and Simmons, 'Can the International Criminal Court', 443.

[187] With respect to the practice of the ICTR, it has been held that acquittals lowered its deterrent effect. See Mackline Ingabire, 'Exploring the Boundaries of the Deterrence Effect of the International Criminal Tribunal for Rwanda', in Jennifer Schense and Linda Carter (eds.), *Two Steps Forward, One Step Back: The Deterrent Effect of International Criminal Tribunals* (Brussels: Torkel Opsahl Academic EPublishers, 2017), pp. 77–107 at 88. For a general take on acquittals, see Richard Goldstone, 'Acquittals by the International Criminal Court', *European Journal of International Law*: Talk!, 18 January 2019, www.ejiltalk.org/acquittals-by-the-international-criminal-court/ (accessed 10 June 2019).

reveal different results. There is some emerging evidence suggesting that 'the ICC does have a direct deterrence effect on particular actors in specific situations'.[188] Although the difference between deterrence on a general level and deterrence on a more specific level may be arbitrary and even artificial at times,[189] it is worth examining deterrence arising from a more case-specific perspective.

### 4.2.2.2 Targeted Deterrence

The examples adduced in support of international criminal law's deterrent effect are often local rather than general. Moreover, it seems that evidence for deterrence can be found more often in ongoing conflicts rather than in peacetime situations. After exploring the case of Libya and the deterrent effect of the ICC, Courtney Hillebrecht concludes that 'the ICC can have an effect on ongoing violence and dampen the level of violence committed against civilians'.[190] In the following, it will be argued that international criminal law and its institutions are more likely to deter specific individuals and groups within societies from committing international crimes. The concept of targeted deterrence has been formulated to examine this form of limited deterrence, in which deterrence is targeted at particular individuals or groups within societies.[191]

Examples of successful targeted deterrence are to be sought in those countries where international criminal tribunals have been active. Practitioners have indeed argued that their monitoring or investigation of a situation has helped to deter particular leaders not to engage in violence or, alternatively,

[188] Christen Romero Philips, 'The International Criminal Court & Deterrence. A Report to the Office of Global Criminal Justice, U.S. Department of State', *Stanford Law School: Law & Policy Lab*, June 2016, p. 1.

[189] Andenaes, 'The General Preventive', 951.

[190] Hillebrecht, 'The Deterrent Effect', 637.

[191] Targeted deterrence is used differently from 'specific deterrence', which relates to the capability of deterring individuals who have already been punished once for international crimes, from perpetrating crimes anew. With respect to the commission of international crimes, specific deterrence seems redundant. It is arguably difficult, for example, to find individuals who have been convicted for genocide and are engaged in similar atrocities after having served their sentence. Indeed, James Alexander notes: 'One struggles to name any historical occurrence in which an individual has been convicted of a crime like genocide by an international tribunal, served time, was released, and then found himself or herself in a second situation in which he or she might again commit genocide'. See Alexander, 'The International Criminal Court', 22. The notion has been used, inter alia, by Bosco, but is less common in international legal circles. See, David Bosco, 'The International Criminal Court and Crime Prevention: Byproduct or Conscious Goal?' (2010–2011) 19 *Michigan State Journal of International Law* 163–200 at 170.

that it has contributed to the restriction of the methods of fighting. The prosecution of Kenyan leaders for the post-election violence in 2007–2008 has been adduced as a successful example of deterrence. According to Prosecutor Fatou Bensouda of the ICC, '[i]t was perhaps the very threat of ICC prosecution which deterred election-related violence in Kenya in 2013.'[192] With regard to the ICC cases against Ugandan rebels, it has been argued that the number of crimes committed by the Lord's Resistance Army in Northern Uganda has 'drastically decreased' as a result of the ICC prosecution of Ugandan rebel leaders.[193]

There are several concrete ways in which the Court can pinpoint its effect on specific individuals or groups. These actions may be undertaken in different phases of the proceedings, and even before formal authorizations to investigate alarming situations. First, public monitoring has proven to be an important preventive tool for the ICC.[194] According to Article 15 of the Statute, the Prosecutor is free to analyze different situations that have been brought to his or her attention. The Prosecutor may seek to obtain further information in order to make a determination on the seriousness of the situation in order to decide whether to ask a Pre-Trial Chamber for permission to launch formal investigations into the matter.[195] The ICC's Rules of Procedure and Evidence, however, leave it to the discretion of the Prosecutor to decide for how long a certain situation is to be under investigation, and how such monitoring is to be conducted. This prosecutorial latitude has been used by the ICC to send particular individuals and groups the message that they are in danger of being scrutinized by the Court. Furthermore, the Court explicitly stated that one of its priority objectives for the period 2013–2017 was to '[f]urther increase the preventive impact of preliminary examinations through the actions of the Office of the Prosecutor.'[196]

The strategy of public monitoring of 'situations-under-analysis' has been extensively used in a number of different conflicts. The OTP has combined public statements with visits and talks aiming at strengthening the impact of ICC involvement. In 2006, the then Prosecutor Luis Moreno-Ocampo publicly

192 See *Uhuru Muigai Kenyatta, Status Conference*, p. 36.

193 ICC, Fifth Session of the Assembly of the State Parties, Opening Remarks by Prosecutor Luis Moreno-Ocampo, The Hague, 23 November 2006, p. 2, www.iccnow.org/documents/DARFUR_StatementToUNSC_1593_14Dec2006_eng.pdf (accessed 19 September 2019).

194 Bosco, 'The International Criminal Court', 178.

195 Art. 15 (2) and (3) of the Rome Statute.

196 ICC, Strategic Plan, 2013–2017 of 18 April 2013, p. 4, www.icc–cpi.int/iccdocs/registry/ICC–Strategic–Plan–2013–2017–190413.pdf (accessed 19 September 2019).

stated that the OTP was examining alleged international crimes in Colombia. According to Moreno-Ocampo, the effects of such scrutiny revealed the power of the ICC to influence potential offenders; as a result, the Court never formally opened investigations against Colombian actors. In 2010, the OTP also openly targeted Charles Blé Goudé – a political leader of Cote D'Ivoire – for violence during the presidential elections in November 2010.

In the case of armed hostilities between Georgia and Russia in 2008, the Court openly declared that it was looking into possible crimes committed during the operation of armed forces. It thus appears that the ICC has attempted not only to prevent crimes from taking place, but that it has also tried to influence the conduct of hostilities.[197] An attack in 2004 against the Barlonya refugee camp in Uganda also led to OTP statements on the launching of investigations into the incident.[198] These statements have been interpreted as an effort to prevent revenge attacks and spirals of violence.[199]

The role of deterrence as a decisive factor in the decision to launch formal investigations into a situation has been debated. First, it has been discussed in the context of ongoing peace negotiations. It has been argued that the decision in some situations *not* to launch an investigation may have greater deterrent effects than a decision to the contrary. Consequently, if peace negotiations are ongoing, the decision to abstain from prosecution may induce perpetrators to refrain from further violence better than a decision to begin investigations. Second, the prosecutorial strategy with respect to indictments may display targeted deterrence. The rank of the prosecuted may be relevant for targeted deterrence. In the case of *Ntaganda*, the ICC's chambers held differing views on the prosecution of low-level perpetrators. The Pre-Trial Chamber argued that the maximum deterrent effect would be achieved if prosecutions targeted leading figures instead of persons of lower rank. The Appeals Chamber, however, disagreed. According to it, '[i]t seems more logical to assume that the deterrent effect of the Court is highest if no category of perpetrators is *per se* excluded from potentially being brought before the Court.'[200]

197 Bosco, 'The International Criminal Court', 180.

198 ICC-OTP-20040223-45, Statement by the Prosecutor Related to Crimes Committed in Barlonya Camp in Uganda, 23 February 2004, www.legal-tools.org/doc/022076/pdf/ (accessed 19 September 2019).

199 Bosco, 'The International Criminal Court', 180.

200 *Situation in the Democratic Republic of Congo,* Case No. ICC–01/04, Appeals Chamber, Judgment on the Prosecutor's Appeal Against the Decision of Pre-Trial Chamber I Entitled 'Decision on the Prosecutor's Application for Warrants of Arrest, Article 58' (13 July 2006), p. 19, para. 73 (emphasis in original).

After the authorization of formal investigations, the Court can employ a variety of mechanisms to control potential perpetrators. One way of optimizing the deterrent effect in specific situations is to increase the visibility of the ICC in the place under investigation. Such heightened international presence is achieved through active investigation in the field. However, whether or not an increased presence of the Court would truly increase its deterrent function has been questioned by the Court itself.[201] One obvious, and also acknowledged, way of trying to impact ongoing hostilities is by issuing arrest warrants for the suspects. The preventive, or rather incapacitating,[202] effect of issuing arrest warrants for such persons is recognized in the Rome Statute, which stipulates that arrest warrants seek to 'prevent the person from continuing with the commission of that crime or a related crime which is within the jurisdiction of the Court and which arises out of the same circumstances'.[203] With respect to the Congolese war lord Thomas Lubanga, it has been argued that the ICC seized the opportunity to remove him from the field when it was offered the opportunity to do so.[204] It has also been suggested that the issuance of arrest warrants could 'lead the individual in question to modify his behavior, perhaps in anticipation of an eventual trial or out of desire to demonstrate to observers "clean hands"'.[205] A further consequence of the issuance of arrest warrants is that it limits the ability of the indicted person to perform his official tasks; the arrest warrant sets limits (or boundaries) on international travel. For example, since the issuance of the ICC arrest warrant in 2009, the former President of Sudan Omar Al-Bashir was unable to attend UN meetings. Although this might be considered as casting the state in question into disrepute,[206] in practice, however, the arrest warrant did not substantially incapacitate the former Sudanese leader.

The foregoing analysis has shown that the ICC can utilize a number of measures in different phases of proceedings in order to maximize its deterrent

201 *Situation in Darfur, Sudan*, Case No. ICC–02/05-21, Prosecutor's Response to Arbour's Observations of the United Nations High Commissioner for Human Rights Invited in Application of Rule 103 of the Rules of Procedure and Evidence (19 October 2006), p. 7, para. 14, in which the Pre-Trial Chamber I held that 'any principle that the presence of international investigators, or international personnel, can be expected to increase security, on balance, as applied in Darfur, would seem to be counterfactual'.

202 See Alexander, 'The International Criminal Court', 23.

203 Art. 58 (1)(b)(iii) of the Rome Statute.

204 Bosco, 'The International Criminal Court', 193.

205 Ibid., 175.

206 Otto Triffterer, 'The Preventive and Repressive Function of the International Criminal Court', in Mauro Politi and Giuseppe Nesi (eds.), *The Rome Statute of the International Criminal Court: A Challenge to Impunity* (Aldershot: Ashgate, 2001), pp. 137–175 at 168.

effect with respect to specific conflicts, and relevant persons therein. These concrete measures taken by the ICC naturally serve the larger purpose of marginalizing indicted leaders. Accordingly, when an investigation by the ICC is launched against a leader, it is assumed that isolation and marginalization of the leader will follow. This isolation has to do with both the immediate network of power, such as government or rebel groups, and the international community.[207] Radovan Karadžić and Ratko Mladić were successfully isolated and excluded from politics after their indictments before the ICTY. However, Sudan's toppled president Omar Al-Bashir never remained very marginalized. Targeted deterrence is thus no panacea for the problem of controlling notorious individuals or groups. The ICC itself has acknowledged: '[w]hether prevention is interpreted as a long-term objective, i.e., the overall result of the Court's activities generally, or as a factor in a specific situation, the preventive role of the Court may depend on many factors, much broader than the capacity of an individual to prevent crimes.'[208] Although it may have an impact on these actors, this effect may not always be as substantial as assumed.

It has been claimed that the Court could more actively seek targeted deterrence.[209] It seems, however, that the Court has an ambiguous stance towards deterrence and its importance in the everyday activities of the Court. On many occasions, the OTP has underlined deterrence as one of the main justifications for the Court, but at times it has downplayed its significance.[210] The Court and its bodies seem to be undecided on the issues of whether deterrence is ultimately a by-product of – or the main reason for – the Court's very existence and of how the deterrent function should be reflected in specific cases. As long as the Court seems ambivalent on the role to be played by deterrence, it will be difficult to increase its deterrent effect, either general or targeted.

[207] Mark Kersten, 'A Little Less Isolated and a Lot More Troubling: Ban Ki-moon meets Bashir', 5 September 2012, *Justice in Conflict*, justiceinconflict.org/2012/09/05/a-little-less-isolated-and-a-lot-more-troubling-ban-ki-moon-meets-bashir/ (accessed 10 June 2015).

[208] *Situation in the Democratic Republic of Congo*, Case No. ICC-01/04, Appeals Chamber, Judgment on the Prosecutor's Appeal Against the Decision of Pre-Trial Chamber I Entitled 'Decision on the Prosecutor's Application for Warrants of Arrest, Article 58' (13 July 2006), p. 20, para. 74.

[209] Bosco, 'The International Criminal Court', 197.

[210] See e.g., *Situation in Darfur, Sudan*, Case No. ICC-02/05-21, Prosecutor's Response to Arbour's Observations of the United Nations High Commissioner for Human Rights Invited in Application of Rule 103 of the Rules of Procedure' (19 October 2006), at para. 12, in which the OTP claimed that 'deterrence is a consequence of prosecution and accountability, not an independent objective'.

#### 4.2.2.3 Complementarity Prevention

The ICC allegedly also has the potential to foster prevention or to achieve forward-looking goals without a single case being brought to the Court. The former Prosecutor of the ICC Luis Moreno-Ocampo has stated that, even without holding trials the Court contributes to prevention of crimes through encouraging national systems to prosecute international crimes.[211] Indeed, he has gone as far as to state that 'the absence of trials before this Court, as a consequence of the regular functioning of national institutions, would be a major success' for the ICC.[212] Hence, the effect of international criminal tribunals upon the national legal system must also be explored in order to arrive at a comprehensive picture of the deterrent function of international criminal law.[213]

The principle of complementarity stipulates that the Court is to function as an instance of last resort, and the Preamble and Article 1 of the Rome Statute explicitly state that the ICC 'shall be complementary to national criminal jurisdiction'.[214] Complementarity is primarily explained as a principle that seeks to assuage concerns around possible erosion of national sovereignty.[215] The states will be protected from ICC intervention if they manage their affairs well: when national legal and justice systems function properly, the ICC is superfluous. The operation of the Court is thus limited to situations in which states appear 'unwilling or unable' to proceed with proper investigations or prosecutions.[216] This limitation can be interpreted as both a weakening and a strengthening factor of the Court and its ability to impact the conduct of actors. On the one hand, the ICC deals with fewer cases than it would under the principle of primacy, but on the other hand, national courts are expected to be more likely to address international

[211] Luis Moreno-Ocampo noted in his inaugural statement that: 'As a consequence of complementarity, the number of cases that reach the Court should not be a measure of its efficiency'. See Statement made by Mr. Luis Moreno-Ocampo, Chief Prosecutor, Ceremony for the Solemn Undertaking of the Chief Prosecutor of the International Criminal Court, 16 June 2003, The Hague, p. 2, www.iccnow.org/documents/MorenoOcampo16June03.pdf (accessed 31 July 2019).

[212] Ibid., 2.

[213] See Alexander, 'The International Criminal Court', 22.

[214] Art. 1 of the Rome Statute.

[215] For a discussion of different rationales for the complementarity principle, see Markus Benzing, 'The Complementarity Regime of the International Criminal Court: International Criminal Justice between State Sovereignty and the Fight against Impunity' (2003) 7 *Max Planck Yearbook of United Nations Law* 591–632.

[216] Art. 17 (1)(a) of the Rome Statute.

crimes themselves.[217] The general attitude, however, leans towards the latter option, which emphasizes the beneficial effects of complementarity.

The preventive effect of complementarity builds on the indirect influence of the ICC upon national legislators and courts to act according to relevant international legal standards, as well as to investigate and prosecute international crimes themselves.[218] The importance of ratifying and implementing the Rome Statute domestically for the success of the whole ICC project has been highlighted by a number of scholars.[219] States are required to adapt their national legislation – both substantive and procedural law – so that it covers the jurisdiction of the Court and is compatible overall with the ICC Statute. Although states are free to choose how they implement the Rome Statute so that it corresponds to their own legal culture, the important threshold is that national legislation does not leave them reluctant or incapable of conducting investigations and prosecutions of international crimes.[220] In addition to necessary legislation, the state must also display preparedness and willingness to investigate and prosecute. The existence and independence of the judiciary has been stressed as an indicator of such willingness. Thus, states with a collapsed judiciary are unable to fulfil the requirements of the ICC Statute.

Optimism has flourished around the capability of the ICC to trigger complementarity, and it has widely been claimed that 'the ICC's impact for domestic law and national capacity building will be significant and far-reaching'.[221] Among other things, support for such argument has been found in the increased number of national prosecutions following the creation of

[217] Alexander, 'The International Criminal Court', 20.

[218] William Burke-White, 'Proactive Complementarity: The International Criminal Court and National Courts in the Rome System of International Justice' (2008) 49 *Harvard International Law Journal* 53–108 at 57–58.

[219] See e.g., Antonio Cassesse, 'On the Current Trends towards Criminal Prosecution and Punishment of Breaches of International Humanitarian Law' (1998) 9 *European Journal of International Law* 2–17 at 13; Matthias Goldmann, 'Implementing the Rome Statute in Europe: From Sovereign Distinction to Convergence in International Criminal Law' (2005) XVI *Finnish Yearbook of International Law* 5–29 at 5; Jo and Simmons, 'Can the International', 452.

[220] Goldmann, 'Implementing the Rome Statute', 12.

[221] Mark S. Ellis, 'The International Criminal Court and Its Implication for Domestic Law and National Capacity-Building' (2002) 15 *Florida Journal of International Law* 215–242 at 241; See also Jane Stromseth, who claims: 'these processes also have a wider impact on public perceptions of justice and potentially can influence a society's ability to embrace rule of law norms'. See Jane Stromseth, 'Justice on the Ground: Can International Criminal Courts Strengthen Domestic Rule of Law in Post–Conflict Societies?' (2009) 1 *Hague Journal on the Rule of Law* 89–97 at 87.

the ICTY and ICTR.[222] Thousands of perpetrators were tried in Rwandan courts, hybrid tribunals led to prosecutions in Sierra Leone, Cambodia and East Timor, and the resurgence of universal jurisdiction gave reason to believe in the fight against impunity at the national level as well. The ICC was seen as strengthening this culture of national prosecutions of international crimes. As the result of an improved national approach toward international crimes, more perpetrators face punishment, and one can argue that the deterrent effect of national criminal law has been strengthened. In sum, even if the capability of international criminal law and its institutions, notably the ICC, to directly control potential perpetrators is modest, it has an inhibitory effect at the national level. In fact, it has been argued that the greatest deterrent effect of the ICC may lie in its complementary role.[223] As Jo and Simmons have argued, 'there is strong evidence of a reduction in intentional civilian killing by government actors when states implement ICC-consistent statutes in domestic criminal law, which we can reasonably attribute – at least indirectly – to the ICC's influence'.[224]

The general assumption, that complementarity will motivate states to handle the investigation and prosecution of perpetrators of international crimes themselves without interference from the ICC,[225] has rarely been questioned. Although little knowledge exists about tangible effects,[226] it seems that complementarity has not pushed states to aggressively 'retain control over prosecuting nationals charged with violating international humanitarian law'.[227] Besides increased national capacity-building, complementarity has also spurred two different kinds of state behaviour: states either surrender the task to the ICC altogether, or they obstruct justice at any price.

[222] Jonathan I. Charney, 'Editorial Comments: International Criminal Court and the Role of Domestic Courts' (2001) 95 *American Journal of International Law* 120–123.

[223] Alexander, 'The International Criminal Court', 22. In a similar vein, Robert Cryer has noted that the ICC can at best act 'as a repository of those ideas, and persuading states, through the incentive to them to adopt domestic legislation, and oversight of prosecutions, to prosecute international crimes'. See Robert Cryer, 'International Criminal Law vs State Sovereignty: Another Round?' (2006) 16 *European Journal of International Law* 979–1000 at 995; Burke-White, 'Proactive Complementarity'.

[224] Jo and Simmons, 'Can the International', 469.

[225] Charney, 'Editorial Comments', 122–123. For a critical account of the role of the ICC to induce change, see Katja Creutz, 'The Problem of Regulation and the Role of the International Criminal Court', in Thomas Mandrup (ed.), *Privatisation of Security: The Concept, Its History and Its Contemporary Application* (Conference Proceedings, Copenhagen: Royal Danish Defence College, 2012), pp. 63–81.

[226] See Stromseth, 'Justice on the Ground', 88.

[227] Ellis, 'The International Criminal Court', 222.

One factor devaluing complementary prevention has been the practice of self-referrals, which means that states themselves have brought their cases to the ICC. The Rome delegates never envisioned the practice of self-referrals.[228] Rather, they thought that both national authorities and the ICC would end up competing for jurisdiction because they thought states would prima facie 'be reluctant to admit to judicial inadequacies'.[229] The use of self-referrals has been explained by the existence of risk of social upheaval that would follow from national prosecution of perpetrators such as rebel leaders who might enjoy broad support at home. Therefore, the expectation that the ICC would have a positive effect on national capacity-building can partly be questioned. Self-referrals can be described as 'deliberate inactivity on the part of a state'.[230]

Another misapprehension with regard to the effectiveness of the international criminal justice system has been that states which have ratified the ICC statute unconditionally have accepted the prosecution of international crimes. The case of the Kenyan post-election violence in 2007–2008 exemplifies the reality that complementary prevention at times remains a distant ideal. The calls of the Waki Commission to establish a special tribunal to try those responsible for the violence were ignored, and not even the ICC has managed to persuade Kenya to undertake national action. Rather than investing in its own judiciary, Kenya has sought to obstruct the ICC in its investigations. The relevant question has not been which party should be the one to try and punish alleged perpetrators, but rather whether or not impunity should reign.

### 4.2.3 *Conclusions on Social Control*

The starting point for the analysis of the capacity of the regimes of international criminal law and international liability to influence the conduct of actors – either through dissuading them from committing wrong or through inducing them to greater care – was that they exert social control to a higher

[228] Mark J. Osiel notes that '[i]t's far easier to strap them firmly into a seat on a KLM jet bound for The Hague'. See Osiel, 'The Demise of International Criminal Law', *Humanity Journal*, 10 June 2014.

[229] Ellis, 'The International Criminal Court', 223.

[230] Andreas Th. Müller and Ignaz Stegmiller, 'Self–Referrals on Trial: From Panacea to Patient' (2010) 8 *Journal of International Criminal Justice* 1267–1294 at 1282. The consequences are, however, often described as far worse than just the lack of national prosecutions. For example, Mark J. Osiel holds that the legitimacy of the Court suffers as a result of the ICC having become 'a distant dumping site for political rivals'. Osiel, 'The Demise'.

degree than does the state responsibility doctrine. Indeed, prevention features in discourses about both regimes: they are forward-looking to an extent not present in the general law of state responsibility. These two regimes differ, however, in one notable aspect: the role ascribed to prevention. Whereas prevention is considered to be a by-product in the liability regimes, deterrence features more prominently in the discourse on international criminal law. They also differ with respect to the best way of achieving desired outcomes.

The potential of liability regimes to control the conduct of actors involved in hazardous activities by way of imposing an obligation to compensate is generally accepted. However, transforming this potential into real effect has failed, at least to a certain degree. Specialized rules on civil liability create obstacles to realizing the full preventive effect of liability; this especially concerns the practices of channelling liability to certain actors, the imposition of financial caps and the applicable standards of care. A focus on adequate and prompt compensation thus dominates and overshadows the preventive function of liability. However, shifting the focus to the preventive side of liability is possible. This requires the will to change rules favouring the compensatory side of liability. Of late, international practice exhibits increasing support for emphasizing the deterrence effect of liability. This backing is exemplified, for example, by the creation of dual compensation schemes which attempt to combine the level of care undertaken by the actor with the level of compensation due. Similarly, demands by signatory states to international agreements and the European Union to alter international rules so that they are more in tune with prevention display the potential of liability as a tool for controlling relevant actors. Thus, international liability rules have the capacity at their best to serve a function that cannot easily be transposed into the law of state responsibility.

Nevertheless, the current defects of the concept and practice of liability have triggered calls for criminal liability as opposed to civil liability under international law. The sentiment is that civil liability cannot exercise an adequate deterrent function. In international law in general, as well as in the regulation of hazardous activities, the idea of harsh sanctions has fully emerged. Criminal law and penalties are seen as the ultimate deterrent. Against this background, the desire to strengthen the international criminal law–project becomes understandable. However, this study has shown that the high expectations around the deterrent potential of international criminal law are unrealistic. Deterrence is questioned even in national criminal law, and taking into account the special features of international criminal law, it becomes difficult to maintain the deterrence argument. Yet, the deterrence argument prevails because it is as difficult to disprove as it is to prove. It has even gained an instrumental value beyond any attempts to control potential offenders, which makes it even more important to take a pragmatic view towards prevention in international criminal law.

The idea that a general preventive effect of international criminal law exists is difficult to uphold. Deterrence, which emphasizes the rational mind of an offender, relies on swiftness, severity and certainty in order to manifest itself. At this point, none of these criteria are sufficiently fulfilled by international criminal law and its institutions. Instead, it seems more realistic to limit expectations of deterrence to concrete situations dealt with by the ICC. The Court can publicly monitor situations and attempt to dissuade perpetrators to refrain from atrocities – or change their conduct in war. The lack of any significant proof for complementarity prevention also supports the conclusion that targeted deterrence may be the most important footprint left by international criminal tribunals.

## 4.3 COLLECTIVITY

Having established that in many instances the doctrine of state responsibility is unable to directly address groups or collectives that play an important role in international legal relations, the analysis will now move on to discussing how liability and international criminal law attend to the problem of collectivity. The recognition of collectives in different forms – whether loose in structure or highly organized – is important for several reasons. Greater harm can be inflicted by groups than can be done by individuals in the group acting separately. In addition, corporations increasingly exercise power affecting the lives of people beyond and across territorial boundaries. Hence, a well-functioning responsibility system should be flexible enough to recognize the direct role of non-state groupings. Not everything can be deconstructed into state or individual actions without losing sight of the real actor behind the wrong.

With regard to collectivity in international liability, the study will argue that the liability project is capable of handling the intersection of the public and private. In fact, the state usually plays a residual role where it adopts a position as a guarantor. Liability is able to spread the costs to a broader sphere of actors, thereby including the actor who is actually involved in the harmful activity, instead of relying merely on legal constructs. On the other hand, international criminal law seems to struggle with the collective character of international crimes. For a system of individual criminal responsibility, collective thinking and adaptation do not come naturally; instead, international tribunals have been forced to respond by means of analogies of domestic law to the systematic nature of aggression, genocide, war crimes and crimes against humanity.

### 4.3.1 *Loss Allocation: From States to Networks of Liability*

International liability, and in particular loss allocation, is strongly attached to the concept of collectivity. A number of different entities ranging from states to corporations and insurance pools are involved in loss allocation under the international conventions establishing civil liability. In fact, liability serves the purpose of distributing costs of hazardous activities and is thus intrinsically linked to collectivity. From the perspective of the question concerning to which entity – or to which collective – liability attaches, two different but fundamental approaches to collectivity emerge. On the one hand, many scholars ask if states of origin are accountable in international law for transboundary damage caused by hazardous but lawful activities, and if so, 'are they subject to liability or to responsibility?'.[231] On the other hand, there are those who accept liability and ask whether liability should fall upon the state or the private entity. There are indeed various positions with regard to liability and to which entity it attaches. At the one end of the spectrum there are those who deny liability and maintain the relevance of state responsibility based on wrongfulness; at the other end there is the view that in all instances harmful activities should be guaranteed by the state. A mediating position has nonetheless won ground, according to which liability lies on those engaged in the activity. Spreading the costs of uncertainty to many involved parties appears to be the preferred pattern of liability.

#### 4.3.1.1 State Centrism

The state's position with regard to compensation for transboundary harm has been disputed in jurisprudence as well as in international practice; sometimes states are placed at the forefront of liability, and at other times they remain on the margins. This section will deal with models of liability that place the state in the centre rather than in a supplementary or subsidiary role. Three different models of liability that centre around the state can be identified: (1) emphasis on the due diligence obligations of the state which remain within the classic state responsibility doctrine; (2) objective responsibility of the state, or so-called state liability, for hazardous activities that cause transboundary

[231] Barboza, *The Environment*, p. 64.

harm; and (3) so-called alternative liability, for situations in which identifiable entities that could compensate the harm are lacking. The question of due diligence obligations of states will not be dealt with here since such obligations fall under the category of responsibility, not liability.[232] But since the line between state responsibility for due diligence violations and state liability for lawful but hazardous acts appears thin at times, a few words about due diligence are in order. Those who emphasize the role of the state appear to remain within the confines of classic state responsibility by emphasizing the state's duty to act diligently. Alan Boyle, who has criticized the liability project, has argued that '[o]n the most widely held view, the responsibility of states for transboundary damage depends principally on objective fault, i.e., a failure to act with due care or diligence, or a breach of treaty, or the commission of a prohibited act.'[233]

Contrary to what one might expect, the separation of liability from the doctrine of state responsibility did not doom the state to irrelevance as the liable entity. For a number of reasons, the ILC's Special Rapporteurs on the liability subject attempted to keep the state in their focus. Liability had originally been carved out of the state responsibility doctrine, but principles such as *sic utere tuo* (one must use his own property so as not to injure the lawful rights of another) already grounded liability in the state. From the perspective of the victims it was preferable to hold the state answerable rather than private parties, and unless liability were attached to the state, it would not be encouraged to take preventive measures with regard to hazardous activities.[234]

Despite the alleged benefits of state liability, the issue remained thorny and was by far one of the most discussed issues within the liability doctrine more broadly. When the topic of liability surfaced in the course of specialized responses to different hazardous branches, the onus of liability

[232] The due diligence doctrine has been described as an intermediate doctrine between objective state responsibility proper and liability for harmful acts. See Martti Koskenniemi, 'Doctrines of State Responsibility', in James Crawford, Alain Pellet and Simon Olleson (eds.), *International Responsibility* (Oxford: Oxford University Press, 2010), pp. 45–51 at 50. Yet, the breach of a due diligence obligation amounts to wrongfulness and therefore falls under the rules of state responsibility.

[233] Boyle, 'Globalising Environmental', 3.

[234] Sreenivasa Rao, *First Report*, para. 16. However, it is to be noted that the misplaced highlighting of state liability was unacceptable to all members of the ILC. See Barboza, *Seventh Report on International Liability for Injurious Consequences Arising Out of Acts Not Prohibited by International Law*, UN Doc. A/CN.4/437 and Corr 1. (1991), p. 85, para. 48, where he admits that not all ILC members were prepared to accept state liability.

was placed exclusively on the state within one sector only: space law. The 1972 Convention on International Liability for Damage Caused by Space Objects established strict liability of the state for harm caused by space objects launched into orbit.[235] The unique character of outer space and, consequently, activities therein made ordinary rules of state responsibility impossible to apply. Space law thus contains a unique feature compared to other types of activities that entail a risk of harm: liability is simplified and centralized on the state.

The motivations for such an approach were both ideological and pragmatic. To start with, the Soviet bloc insisted on keeping space activities the prerogative of the state; no private entities should be allowed to explore space.[236] Recognizing the strict liability of the state for harm stemming from space activities, highlighted the statal privilege of space activities. Second, states played almost an exclusive role in space activities, a fact which justifies the direction of liability to the concerned state or states from where the damage derives.[237] Liability can thus be described as functional, because states are held liable not because of the general requirements of territorial control but because they actually are the entities conducting the activities in question. This may indeed explain why space law is the only special regime in which states have accepted primary, exclusive and strict liability. Third, it can also be argued that the limitation of space activities to peaceful use had a public order–character which motivated the statal role.

Some have claimed that the liability model derived from space law should be adopted for all hazardous activities causing harm. Accordingly, state liability should be the general rule in all cases of hazardous activities. Such claims

235 Dupuy, *La responsabilité internationale*, p. 44; Convention on International Liability on Damage Caused by Space Objects. The Outer Space Treaty of 1967 mentions both responsibility and liability of states; see UNGA Res. 2222 (XXI) 19 December 1966 (Treaty on Principles Governing the Activities of States in the Exploration and Use of Outer Space, including the Moon and Other Celestial Bodies), in force 10 October 1967, 610 *United Nations Treaty Series* 205, Arts. VI and VII.

236 Dupuy, *La responsabilité internationale*, p. 59. See also, Jaqueline Dutheil De La Rochere, 'La Convention sur l'internationalisation de l'espace' (1967) 13 *Annuaire francais de droit international* 607–647, esp. at 635.

237 This perception is not completely accurate any longer, with the increasing rise of private ventures in outer space. Such ventures include, for example, space tourism by Virgin Galactic and commercially developed space aircraft. See Zach Meyer, 'Private Commercialization of Space in an International Regime: A Proposal for a Space District' (2010) 30 *Northwestern Journal of International Law and Business* 241–261.

cannot, however, be based on the functional grounds that justify state liability in the space regime. Indeed, the protagonists of state liability for hazardous activities have generally based their views on the existence of a number of doctrines from national legal systems. Their motivation for disconnecting wrongfulness and the obligation to repair so that a state would be obliged to compensate harm irrespective of fault (sensu lato) is usually grounded in three different but related doctrines: (1) theory of risk; (2) abuse of rights; and (3) *bon voisinage* or the non-harmful use of territory.[238] Yet, none of these theories have offered a persuasive foundation for state liability beyond specialized regimes.[239]

The theories considered as providing some justification for use of state liability in the case of transboundary harm resulting from hazardous activities are those of non-harmful use of territory as expressed by the maxim *sic utere tuo*, and the risks of ultra-hazardous activities. Much confusion, many contradictions and different interpretations exist between the potentially relevant doctrines and case law and their implications for customary international law in the field. This is exacerbated by the fact that both those who argue for a norm of state liability and those who reject it base their reasoning on the same cases. For example, the seminal *Trail Smelter* case is seen by some as upholding the theory of non-harmful use of territory or the principle of *sic utere tuo*. This is based on the arbitral tribunal's statement, which holds that:

> under the principles of international law, as well as of the law of the United States, no State has the right to use or permit the use of its territory in such a manner as to cause injury by fumes in or to the territory of another or the properties or persons therein, when the case is of serious consequence and the injury is established by clear and convincing evidence.[240]

Yet, this passage has been disputed. Whereas some scholars hold it to be clear that it sets the ground for state liability because it appears irreconcilable with classic state responsibility rules,[241] many oppose such an interpretation. L. F. E. Goldie belongs to the former category: he interprets the arbitral award in support of liability when he states that the 'arbitration depends upon

[238] For discussions of the merits of these theories, see Dupuy, *La responsabilité internationale*, pp. 12–37; Koskenniemi, *Valtion kansainvälinen vastuu*; Barboza, *The Environment*.

[239] See Dupuy, *La responsabilité internationale*, p. 32; Barboza, *The Environment*, p. 47.

[240] *Trail Smelter* case *(United States of America v. Canada)*, Judgment of 16 April 1938 and 11 March 1941, III Reports of International Arbitral Awards, p. 1905, at p. 1965.

[241] Dupuy, *La responsabilité internationale*, p. 32.

different standards from those usually associated with fault'.[242] The rejectionists view the award as laying down an obligation to control private actors within one's territory, thus giving rise to a due diligence obligation, which in this case was violated.[243] Under this interpretation, it belongs to the field of wrongfulness and classic state responsibility. An intermediate position is occupied by those scholars who see in the arbitration the embodiment of the principle of good-neighbourliness, which in turn can be used to justify either liability or due diligence responsibility. For the present purposes, however, it suffices to state that the *Trail Smelter* case cannot uncritically be cited in support of state liability in general international law, although it seems to indicate liability in stating that: 'if any damage as defined under Question No. 2 shall have occurred since October 1, 1940, or shall occur in the future, whether through failure on the part of the Smelter to comply with the regulations herein prescribed or *notwithstanding the maintenance of the régime*, an indemnity shall be paid for such damage.'[244] The *Corfu Channel* case is another classic and equally debated case which has been cited in support of state liability in general international law.[245] In this case, Albania was accused of having failed to notify the United Kingdom of mines allegedly laid in its territorial waters by Yugoslavia. The ICJ found that the laying of mines was impossible without the knowledge of Albania and, consequently, its failure to prevent the injury gave rise to 'a duty of Albania to pay compensation to the United Kingdom'.[246] The judgment and its grounds for compensation have divided scholars; some claim that liability was based on the breach of a due diligence obligation of failing to warn other international actors; others maintain that the dictum was based on strict liability.[247] However, the judgment in its entirety, including the separate and dissenting opinions, seems to support the latter position that the standard of strict liability was applied. Judges Winiarski and Badawi Pasha both dissented from the court's finding; in their opinion, Albania's responsibility was,

[242] L. F. E. Goldie, 'Liability for Damage and the Progressive Development of International Law' (1965) 14 *International and Comparative Law Quarterly* 1189–1264 at 1227.

[243] Dupuy, *La responsabilité internationale*, p. 32; Barboza, *The Environment*, p. 47.

[244] *Trail Smelter* case *(United States of America* v. *Canada)*, Judgment of 16 April 1938 and 11 March 1941, III Reports of International Arbitral Awards, p. 1905, at p. 1980 (emphasis added).

[245] *Corfu Channel* case *(Merits)*, Judgment of April 9th, ICJ Reports 1949, p. 4.

[246] Ibid., p. 23.

[247] *Survey of Liability Regimes Relevant to the Topic of International Liability for Injurious Consequences Arising Out of Acts Not Prohibited by International Law (International Liability in Case of Loss from Transboundary Harm Arising out of Hazardous Activities)*, UN Doc.A/CN.4/543 (2004), p. 79, para. 225.

inter alia, based on too strict standards of responsibility. Judge Badawi Pasha even explained:

> it must be stressed that international law does not recognize objective responsibility based upon the notion of risk, adopted by certain national legislations. Indeed, the evolution of international law and the degree of development attained by the notion of international co-operation do not allow us to consider that this stage has been reached, or is about to be reached.[248]

Based on international case law, it seems fair to conclude that state liability for hazardous activities is not generally accepted outside conventional regimes. States also firmly reject a general liability to compensate for transboundary harm caused by hazardous activities.[249] There are, however, some elements supporting such a principle. These include, for example, the willingness of states to pay ex gratia for harm caused by hazardous activities, and some general statements made by the ICJ on the conduct of states which might cause transboundary harm.[250] Thus, despite difficulties, the idea of state liability has not been completely buried; some scholars attempt to keep the principle of state liability alive. For example, former Special Rapporteur on the topic Julio Barboza claims that '[t]he norm imposing compensation for damage caused by hazardous activities [...] is more than an emerging principle; it is an existing principle of law not being applied.'[251] René Lefeber again maintains that state liability is necessary for filling the gaps in the specialized regimes on liability.[252]

A form of qualified state liability has also been suggested. According to this view, states would not generally have primary liability, but in some cases would function as guarantors when private entities could not be held responsible.

[248] *Corfu Channel* case *(Merits)*, Judgment of April 9th, ICJ Reports 1949, p. 4, dissenting opinion of Judge Badawi Pasha, at p. 65.

[249] Barboza, *The Environment*, p. 38.

[250] Julio Barboza maintains that the fact that states do react in some ways upon transboundary harms, and often by paying *ex gratia*, proves the existence of a state liability principle. See Barboza, *The Environment*, p. 63, and, *Survey of Liability Regimes*, p. 140, para. 421. In the *Corfu Channel* case, the ICJ held that it was 'every State's obligation not to allow knowingly its territory to be used for acts contrary to the rights of other States'. See *Corfu Channel* case *(Merits)*, Judgment of April 9th, ICJ Reports 1949, p. 4, at p. 22. In similar terms in the *Legality of the Threat or Use of Nuclear Weapons*, Advisory Opinion, ICJ Reports 1996, p. 226: '[t]he existence of the general obligation of States to ensure that activities within their jurisdiction and control respect the environment of other States or of areas beyond national control is now the corpus of international law relating to the environment'. Ibid., pp. 241–242.

[251] Barboza, *The Environment*, p. 154.

[252] Lefeber, *Transboundary Environmental*, p. 230.

This so-called alternative liability would come into effect when it would be unclear as to who else could be held liable. The state would thus substitute for the private party which originally would be considered the liable entity.[253] Situations that potentially would fall under the scope of such liability could include incidents in which it is impossible to identify the responsible entity or entities that have caused damage, either due to harm caused by cumulative pollution or due to long-range pollution.[254] Nevertheless, the prospect of the realization of so-called alternative state liability seems unclear; it has been characterized as *de lege ferenda*.[255] It also seems difficult to separate ideas of alternative liability from general state liability.

#### 4.3.1.2 Piercing the Corporate Veil

The liability regime has traditionally been more flexible and receptive than the state responsibility doctrine in recognizing and accommodating the role of private entities in issues of compensation. Several developments in international societal and legal relations helped to 'pierce the corporate veil' with respect to issues of liability for transboundary harm. To start with, the recognition that such harm mainly stems from private entities rather than the state as such helped to shift the focus away from state liability. More importantly, states were unwilling to accept liability for activities that occurred under their jurisdiction.[256] Second, international conventions in specific fields of hazardous activities discarded state centrism for civil liability models. Instead, such conventions place liability primarily on the operator of the hazardous activity, which through its business both benefits from and assumes costs for the risks involved. Third, the creation of operator liability also corresponded to the development of the Polluter-Pays principle, which in its basic form 'holds the polluter who creates an environmental harm liable to pay the costs to remedy that harm'.[257]

Operator liability was established for the first time in the 1952 Rome Convention on Damage Caused by Foreign Aircraft to Third Parties.[258]

[253] Barboza, *The Environment*, p. 38.

[254] Barboza, *Seventh Report*, ILC Yearbook 1991, vol II(1), p. 78, at para. 21; Barboza, *The Environment*, p. 38.

[255] Barboza, *The Environment*, p. 38.

[256] Boyle, 'Globalising Environmental', 6.

[257] Alexandre Kiss and Dinah Shelton, *International Environmental Law* (2nd ed., Ardsley, New York: Transnational Publishers Inc., 2000), p. 266.

[258] See Art. 2 of the 1952 Rome Convention on Damage Caused by Foreign Aircraft to Third Parties on the Surface, Rome, 7 October 1952, in force 4 February 1958, 310 *United Nations Treaty Series* 182.

With the 1960 Paris Convention on Third Party Liability in the Field of Nuclear Energy, strict liability of the operator was recognized with respect to ultra-hazardous activities as well.[259] Later international agreements on nuclear energy similarly pinpoint liability on the operator,[260] as do conventions with respect to oil pollution, such as the Civil Liability Convention.[261] Hence, it has become increasingly accepted to attach liability to private entities rather than to perceive states as primary guarantors of private and economic activities. This pattern was also acknowledged by the ILC in 2004 when it held that '[s]tate liability is an exception' among different liability patterns, and that 'there is also general agreement that liability [...] should be attached primarily to the operator'.[262] However, the abandonment of state liability in accordance with the space law model was due more to pragmatic than principled reasoning: it was simply politically unrealizable.[263]

The shift towards the civil liability of the operators was supported by the development of a general principle of environmental law (originally of an economic character): the Polluter-Pays principle (PPP).[264] Seemingly easy to grasp, it presupposes that the person or entity that causes pollution should

259 Art. 3 states: 'The operator of a nuclear installation shall be liable ... for: (i) damage to or loss of life of any person; and (ii) damage to or loss of any property ... upon proof that such damage or loss ... was caused by a nuclear incident in such installation', Convention on Third Party Liability in the Field of Nuclear Energy, Paris, 29 July 1960, in force 1 April 1986, 956 *United Nations Treaty Series* 264, as amended by the Additional Protocol of 28 January 1964, and by the Protocol of 16 November 1982.

260 These are, for example: the IAEA 1963 Vienna Convention on Civil Liability for Nuclear Damage; the 1988 Joint Protocol on the Application of the Vienna Convention and the Paris Convention, 21 September 1988, in force 27 April 1992, 1672 *United Nations Treaty Series* 293; and the 1997 Protocol to Amend the Vienna Convention on Liability for Nuclear Damage, 12 September 1997, in force 4 October 2003, 2241 *United Nations Treaty Series* 302.

261 International Convention on Civil Liability for Oil Pollution Damage.

262 Report of the International Law Commission on the Work of Its Fifty-sixth Session, UN Doc. A/59/10 (2004), Chapter VII, General Commentary to Draft Principles, p. 159.

263 Boyle, 'Globalising Environmental', pp. 6, 8.

264 On the Polluter-Pays principle in general, see e.g., Priscilla Schwartz, 'The Polluter-Pays Principle', in Malgosia Fitzmaurice, David M. Ong and Panos Merkouris (eds.), *Research Handbook on International Environmental Law* (Cheltenham: Edward Elgar Publishing Ltd, 2010), pp. 243–261; Kiss and Shelton, *International Environmental Law*, pp. 266–268; Sanford E. Gaines, 'The Polluter-Pays Principle: From Economic Equity to Environmental Ethos' (1991) 26 *Texas International Law Journal* 463–496; Dupuy, *La responsabilité internationale*, pp. 281–285; Nicolas de Sadeleer, 'The Polluter-pays Principle in EU Law – Bold Case Law and Poor Harmonisation', in Christina Voigt, Inge Lorange Backer, and Ole Kristian Fauchald (eds.), *Pro Natura: Festskrift til Hans Christian Bugge* (Oslo: Universitetsforlaget, 2012), pp. 405–419; Arne Bleeker, 'Does the Polluter Pay? The Polluter-Pays Principle in the Case Law of the European Court of Justice' (2009) *European Energy and Environmental Law Review* 289–306.

internalize its costs.[265] It is noteworthy that the PPP did not evolve as a liability principle, 'but rather is a principle for the allocation of the costs of pollution control'.[266] Thus, in its original form it merely addressed the costs for preventive measures ex ante through the creation of 'a system of charges by which polluters help finance public policy to protect the environment'.[267] It was not before the turn of the 1990s that the ex post side of the principle, namely that focusing on liability, began to develop. Since 1989, when the OECD adopted the 'Recommendation on the Application of the Polluter-Pays Principle to Accidental Pollution',[268] the principle has encompassed the internalization of both preventive and response costs. Consequently, liability for transboundary harm is one way of implementing the broader Polluter-Pays principle.[269] This other, redistributive, dimension of the principle has received increasing emphasis and attention, especially in civil liability contexts.[270] Despite the strengthening of its status as a general principle of international environmental law, the PPP is no panacea for solving liability. Its lack of clarity extends to such questions as who the polluter is, what constitutes pollution and how

265 The principle was first articulated by the Organization for Economic Cooperation and Development (OECD) in 1972 in the OECD Guiding Principles Concerning International Economic Aspects of Environmental Policies, Recommendation C(72)128, 26 May 1972, 11 *International Legal Materials* 1172. It has been subsequently endorsed by a number of international instruments such as the 1992 Rio Declaration, Principle 16: 'National authorities should endeavour to promote the internalization of environmental costs and the use of economic instruments, taking into account the approach that the polluter should, in principle, bear the cost of pollution, with due regard to the public interest and without distorting international trade and investment.' See Rio Declaration on Environment and Development, 31 *International Legal Materials*, 874 (1992). The EU has also widely endorsed the PPP in its internal regulations. See for example, the 1986 Single European Act, and the 1992 Maastricht Treaty (Art 130R(2)). Today the principle enjoys a significant position in international environmental law and policy, having been described as a 'general principle of international environmental law'. See the preamble of the 1990 London Oil Convention on Oil Pollution Preparedness, Response and Co–operation, London, 30 November 1990, in force 13 May 1995, 1891 *United Nations Treaty Series* 51.

266 Gaines, 'The Polluter-Pays Principle', 468.

267 De Sadeleer, 'The Polluter-pays Principle', 408. This preventive side of the PPP entails, for example, financial charges or taxes that are tied to the pollution level. See Gaines, 'The Polluter-Pays Principle', 473.

268 OECD, Council Recommendation on the Application of the Polluter Pays Principle to Accidental Pollution, Recommendation C(89)88, 7 July 1989, 28 *International Legal Materials*, 132 (1989).

269 De Sadeleer, 'The Polluter-pays Principle', 412.

270 Within the European Union, the liability side of the PPP has been enunciated in the Waste Framework Directive on Civil Liability, and the 2004/35/EC Directive on Environmental Liability.

much the polluter should be charged.[271] As a consequence, it has been maintained that the PPP principle is important mainly in sectors where the polluters are easy to identify and where polluters 'have sufficient economic resources to pay their way'.[272]

The connection between a number of international civil liability conventions and the Polluter-Pays principle is obvious, since under both conventional international law and the Principles of Loss Allocation adopted by the ILC, the primary liable party is the operator or comparable private entities.[273] This form of 'exclusive' liability is realized through the practice of channelling, which directs all liability to the operator. Moreover, since liability is not only exclusive but also strict, this means that the operator bears the costs for the accident irrespective of its conduct. Accordingly, if an accident takes place all liability claims are brought against the operator. The practice of channelling thus excludes from liability a number of other actors such as subcontractors – providing service or fuel – or the builders of the nuclear power plant, and steers compensation claims solely to the operator. There are several reasons for channelling liability. From the perspective of the victim, channelling simplifies the procedure: the victims do not have to determine who is liable, since the law already provides the answer. Having only one defendant to whom compensation claims are directed is easier than multi-party litigation, which inevatibly would be more complex, costly and time-consuming. The complexity and costliness of insurance for hazardous activities also justify directing claims to the operator.[274]

#### 4.3.1.3 Distributing Liability

Although the civil liability of operators constitutes the primary liability model in many conventions as well as in the 2006 ILC Principles on Loss Allocation, this model is often constrained by limitations both in time and amount. Therefore, additional safeguards have been created to ensure that these limitations do not threaten the position of the victims. Therefore, many

[271] For discussion of such problems in the interpretation and application of the PPP, see de Sadeleer, 'The Polluter-pays Principle'; Gaines, 'The Polluter-Pays Principle'; and Kiss and Shelton, *International Environmental Law*, pp. 266–268.

[272] Gaines, 'The Polluter-Pays Principle', 487.

[273] Although the logic behind the PPP and these conventions is basically the same, namely, to allocate liability irrespective of fault upon the private party engaged in the business, they also differ from each other. Whereas the primary constellation in civil liability conventions is that between the operator and victims, the PPP implies also a broader macroeconomic aspect to the question of loss allocation. See Dupuy, *La responsabilité internationale*, p. 284.

[274] Dupuy, *La responsabilité internationale*, pp. 112–113.

specialized rules prescribing strict or absolute liability create layers of liability supplementing operator liability with other mechanisms and actors. The importance of creating additional schemes of compensation was also recognized by the ILC when it noted in 2004: 'there is a consensus in favour of providing for supplementary funding in any scheme of allocation of loss and that such funding would be particularly important if the concept of limited liability is adopted. The basic understanding is to adopt a scheme of allocation of loss, spreading the loss among multiple actors, including the State.'[275] Spreading liability is necessitated by concerns both for the operator's ability to pursue his or her business and by the interests of the victims. On the one hand, limited operator liability seeks to ensure that the activity can be insured,[276] and that an accident will not wipe out the business in its entirety. On the other hand, hazardous activities are capable of causing such widespread disasters that compensation will exceed the capacities of private entities.[277] Therefore, the means and mechanisms of financial compensation usually must be established and guaranteed beforehand, either by way of taking out insurance or other financial security.[278] It is notable, however, that insurers are reluctant to 'assume full liability for the potentially colossal damage of industrial catastrophes'.[279] Spreading liability thus ensures that 'meaningful levels of compensation are available with a minimal level of litigation and difficulty'.[280] The potential enormous costs of a nuclear power plant meltdown help to illustrate the necessity of distributing costs in case of damage. The clean-up costs for the 2011 *Fukushima* Daiichi incident, for example, have risen to almost 200 billion USD,[281] potentially even far more.

275 Report of the ILC (2004), Chapter VII, General Commentary to Draft Principles, p. 159.

276 For a discussion of the reluctance of insurance companies to provide insurance for catastrophic events, See Marcus Radetzki and Marian Radetzki, 'Private Arrangements to Cover Large-Scale Liabilities Caused by Nuclear and Other Industrial Catastrophes' (2000) 25 *The Geneva Papers on Risk and Insurance* 180–195; see also Alexandre Kiss and Dinah Shelton, 'Strict Liability in International Environmental Law', in Tafsir Malick Ndiaye and Rüdiger Wolfrum (eds.), *Law of the Sea, Environmental Law and Settlement of Disputes: Liber Amicorum Judge Thomas A. Mensah* (Leiden: Brill, Leiden, 2007), pp. 1131–1151 at 1151.

277 Dupuy, *La responsabilité internationale*, p. 115.

278 See *Survey of Liability Regimes*, p. 219, para. 684.

279 Radetzki and Radetzki, 'Private Arrangements', 180.

280 World Nuclear Association, 'Liability for Nuclear Damage', www.world-nuclear.org/information-library/safety-and-security/safety-of-plants/liability-for-nuclear-damage.aspx (accessed 19 September 2019).

281 Yuka Obayashi and Kentaro Hamada, 'Japan Nearly Doubles Fukushima Disaster-related Costs to $188 Billion', *Reuters*, 6 December 2016, www.reuters.com/article/us-tepco-fukushima-costs/japan-nearly-doubles-fukushima-disaster-related-cost-to-188-billion-idUSKBN13Y047 (accessed 19 September 2019).

To begin with, the international framework for nuclear damage prescribes the operator's liability irrespective of fault, thus making strict liability the governing principle. For example, under the Vienna Convention regime, liability is – depending on the injury or damage – limited to thirty or ten years after the relevant nuclear incident, and to a maximum compensation sum of 300 million Special Drawing Rights (SDRs).[282] In order to guarantee compensation, the Vienna Convention regime obligates the operator to maintain insurance.[283] The installation state also assumes the role of a guarantor: should the operator be incapable of compensating for an amount up to 300 million SDRs, the state is obliged to pay compensation claims up to that amount.[284] Although insurance is provided for, usually it is limited and consequently may fail to cover the necessary costs, especially concerning third-party liability.[285] The costs may simply exceed the financial capacity of the operator and its insurers to compensate, thus making the costs unpayable. Thus, it has been considered necessary to create additional liability layers. The next protective layer of liability is provided for in the Convention on Supplementary Compensation adopted together with the 1997 Vienna Protocol on Civil Liability,[286] which fixes additional compensation reservoirs through contributions by contracting parties based on installed nuclear capacity and UN assessment rate.[287]

Second or additional layers of liability can consist of public or private arrangements, or even both. First, the state where the accident takes place might have supplementary liability for nuclear accidents if compensation to be paid exceeds the amount that falls upon the operator. By passing the compensation duty forward onto public actors, the risks are in effect socialized. Because the activity itself has been profitable to society at large, in the final analysis the state as a collective appears as a guarantor for the activity.[288]

282 The Convention does not use any national currency but uses the International Monetary Fund's international currency, which can be defined as a weighted average of different convertible currencies. See Arts. 7 and 8 of the 1997 Protocol to Amend the Vienna Convention on Liability for Nuclear Damage, Vienna, 12 September 1997, in force 4 October 2003, 2241 *United Nations Treaty Series* 302.

283 Art. VII of the Vienna Convention on Liability for Nuclear Damage.

284 Ibid.

285 It has been argued that insurance companies seldom cover amounts exceeding 500 million USD. See Radetzki and Radetzki, 'Private Arrangements', 181.

286 Convention on the Supplementary Compensation for Nuclear Damage, Vienna, 12 September 1997, in force 15 April 2015, reproduced in (1997) 23 *International Legal Materials* 1473.

287 Ibid., Art. IV.1; See also Ben McRae, 'Entry into Force of the Convention on Supplementary Compensation for Nuclear Damage: Opening the Umbrella' (2015) *Nuclear Law Bulletin* 7–25.

288 Dupuy, *La responsabilité internationale*, p. 125.

Holding the state as the guarantor also finds motivation in the fact that states license and control hazardous activities, which provides a link between the activity and the state. Examples of this second tier of liability can be found in the conventional regimes for nuclear damages.

But supplementary liability need not always fall upon the state. Specialized liability rules may also channel liability from the operator to private arrangements such as industry funds, thereby leaving the state outside compensation claims. For example, international conventions established to address compensation for oil pollution place the shipowner instead of the operator in the first tier of liability. In line with this, the 1969 Civil Liability Convention with concomitant amendments places the shipowner under the obligation to maintain insurance or some other kind of financial security as liability extends to 4.51 million SDR or more, depending on the gross tonnage.[289] Such financial securities are usually arranged through a Protection & Indemnity Club along with the possibility to derive supplementary funding in cases of inadequate or unobtainable compensation from the 1971 Fund Convention.[290] The maritime oil pollution regime thus relegates the state to the background, and the industry itself receives a heightened role.

#### 4.3.1.4 Liability Networks

Spreading liability among different tiers and actors serves to collectivize the transboundary harms that are caused by hazardous activities. The search for a causal connection to the harm according to the principles of individual liability has been replaced by liability networks which bring various actors under one umbrella, or cupola as Gunther Teubner calls it,[291] in order to counterweigh inherent difficulties in causally ascertaining harm caused by hazardous activities.[292] International liability schemes have accordingly developed more in the direction of collective responsibility than toward causation-based individual liability, despite appearances to the opposite.[293] The reason for this shift is not ideological, but rather is based on the nature of ecological harms,

[289] The limitation amounts of the International Convention on Civil Liability for Oil Pollution Damage have been increased with the 1992 Additional Protocol, 27 November 1992, in force 30 May 1996, as well as with Adoption of Amendments of the Limitations Amounts in the Protocol of 1992 to Amend the International Convention on Civil Liability for Oil Pollution Damage, 18 October 2000, in force 1 November 2003, Resolution LEG.1(82).

[290] International Convention on the Establishment of an International Fund for Compensation for Oil Pollution Damage.

[291] See Teubner, 'The Invisible Cupola'.

[292] Barboza, *The Environment*, p. 12.

[293] Teubner, 'The Invisible Cupola', 430.

whose complexities 'have frustrated lawyers in their attempts to construct causal links between individual actions and ecological damage'.[294] The basis for individual responsibility is simply not met; there are not easily distinguishable actions that can be attributed to particular entities,[295] as is the case with transboundary harm. Gunther Teubner has argued that, as a result, 'courts and legislatures are shifting liability away from the individual responsibility of single actors towards a new collective responsibility of risk networks'.[296] Such a shift in approach may be visible both in national and international law, as they highly interact with each other.[297]

Liability thus arises not from individual action but on the basis of a common risk and a link to other actors involved in this activity. In itself, this is not revolutionary: all models of international liability more or less adhere to this liability scheme. It is noteworthy, however, that liability in such situations has moved beyond individual liability based on loose causation requirements; whenever compensation comes from a fund, this indicates that liability has been collectivized. Not only the member of the fund that has caused the harm pays for the harm; all members do. For example, broadening the scope of liable actors has been considered necessary within the maritime oil pollution liability regime since a high number of claims have demonstrated the hindrance of existing liability limitations to effective compensation.[298] Another example illustrating how liability has been socialized and collectivized is that of the handling of liability claims regarding the 2011 *Fukushima* nuclear accident. Due to the large number of claims, in September 2012 the Japanese government established a Nuclear Damage Liability Facilitation Fund tasked with assisting in paying the astronomical sums in compensation that overwhelmed TEPCO's financial capabilities.[299] Contributions to the Fund were made by the government, TEPCO and other Japanese nuclear power companies.[300] In addition to providing adequate and prompt compensation, its aim also was to 'prevent adverse effects on business operators dealing with the accident'.[301]

[294] Ibid.
[295] Abraham, 'Individual Action', 848.
[296] Teubner, 'The Invisible Cupola', 431.
[297] See Faure and Nollkaemper, 'International Liability', 127.
[298] Michael Mason, 'Civil Liability for Oil Pollution Damage: Examining the Evolving Scope for Environmental Compensation in the International Regime' (2003) 27 *Marine Policy* 1–12.
[299] Eri Osaka, 'Corporate Liability, Government Liability, and the Fukushima Nuclear Disaster' (2012) 21 *Pacific Rim Law & Policy Journal* 433–459 at 443.
[300] Ibid., 442–443.
[301] Ibid., 443.

However, there is another, broader, understanding of network liability. Instead of viewing a network as a number of companies that cooperate for purposes of monetary compensation for transboundary harm, liability has expanded beyond organized units; that is, beyond corporate actors as such. Accordingly, a unique network is created by the involved actors for the purposes of liability. As described by Gunther Teubner, 'the law does not refer to preexisting social units but creates anew networks of ecological risks'.[302] This can entail industry wide funds, but it can also mean that liability is conceptualized in terms of geographical units, or even in terms of abstract units such as the 'bubbles' featuring in the emission trade.[303] The point of departure is not the actor(s), but the situation in which the risk has materialized into actual harm.

The oil pollution regime exemplifies how networks are created in practice, and why. Under the international liability conventions, shipowners transporting oil must have insurance or financial security in order to compensate for possible losses. Basically, they have two options to choose from: either to purchase insurance from profit-making companies, or to pool their third-party liability.[304] The vast part of the world's merchant fleet, including most oil tankers, belong to Protection and Indemnity (P&I) Clubs. These are mutual, non–profit making pools providing financial protection against third-party liability. As a result, every shipowner in the pool becomes both the 'insurer and insured'.[305] Thus 'each shipowner is liable to meet a share of the losses caused by themselves and all other members'.[306] The rationale for such pooling lies in social control; it is in each P & I Club member's interest to keep the number of claims to be compensated by the pool low. This will again ensure the lowest possible premiums to be paid, an incentive that shipowners as economic actors are likely to appreciate. The distribution of risks in the ship industry does not end here, however. The P & I Clubs 'are themselves members of a mutual structure known as the International Group of P & I Clubs'.[307] The purpose of this structure is to spread the risks even further

[302] Teubner, 'The Invisible Cupola', 437 (emphasis omitted).

[303] For example, the concept of bubbles in the emission trade means that multiple emission points are treated as one imaginary 'bubble'. This means that 'bubbles can be extended to include not only emission points within the same plant, but emission points in plants owned by other firms as well'. See Thomas H. Tietenberg, *Emissions Trading: An Exercise in Reforming Pollution Policy* (Washington, DC: Resources for the Future Inc., 1985), p. 8.

[304] Bennett, 'Mutual Risk', 13.

[305] Ibid.

[306] Ibid., 14.

[307] Ibid., 17, note 6.

in order to meet large compensation claims. Paul Bennett also notes that 'commercial reinsurers require a very large risk spread before insuring high magnitude events'.[308]

There are several benefits involved in networking liability to actors involved in a given activity or geographical unit, besides the rationale of ensuring compensation to victims. First, a collective focus may increase the likelihood of preventive measures. Second, it involves a broad array of actors without emphasizing the character of the actor; both private and public actors can become liable to compensate. In fact, the collective dimension plays a crucial role in liability; effective compensation while maintaining conditions conducive to business cannot materialize with fault-based liability since 'the complexities of causation make individual liability virtually impossible'.[309] Unless liability is collective in cases of transboundary harm, there is no liability at all.[310]

### 4.3.2 *Collectivity in International Criminal Law*

Although much of international criminal law and its history is about 'the particular and specific',[311] international criminal law is not exclusively focused on individualism in spite of the principle of individual criminal responsibility. By their very nature, international crimes are collective crimes that are conditioned 'on the activity of many individuals'.[312] The definition of the core international crimes requires collective criminality: they are committed as a result of state or organizational policies, not by lone *génocidaires* or bloodthirsty individuals. For example, the ICC holds jurisdiction only over war crimes that have been perpetrated as 'part of a plan or policy or as part of a large-scale commission of such crimes'.[313] In a similar vein, crimes against

[308] Ibid.

[309] Teubner, 'The Invisible Cupola', 438.

[310] Ibid.

[311] Immi Tallgren and Thomas Skouteris, 'Editors' Introduction', in Immi Tallgren and Thomas Skouteris (eds.), *The New Histories of International Criminal Law: Retrials* (Oxford: Oxford University Press, 2019), pp. 1–11 at 3.

[312] Bert Swart, 'Modes of International Criminal Liability', in Antonio Cassese (ed.), *The Oxford Companion to International Criminal Justice* (Oxford: Oxford University Press, 2009), pp. 82–93 at 82. In a similar vein, Shane Darcy notes: 'International crimes, such as genocide, crimes against humanity, and war crimes are rarely, if ever, the product of individual action'. See Shane Darcy, *Collective Responsibility and Accountability under International Law* (Leiden: Transnational Publishers Inc., 2007), p. 197.

[313] Art. 8 of the Rome Statute.

humanity are limited to incidents that are part of a widespread or systematic attack 'pursuant to or in furtherance of a State or organizational policy to commit such attack'.[314]

Consequently, collectivity holds a place in the discipline of international criminal law. This paradox has not escaped the attention of international legal scholars. Scholars have observed that international criminal law 'finds itself perpetually drawn back to group responsibility and communal guilt',[315] and that 'the individual's behaviour is motivated by, and can only be understood in reference to, larger communities of nation, state or tribe'.[316] Unless one recognizes the collective character of international crimes, there will be no difference between international crimes and the crimes of murder, killings or rape as defined in domestic law.[317] As a result, one should view international criminal law as a fusion between individual and collective notions of responsibility.[318]

George P. Fletcher has described this blending as follows: 'The mind of the law may speak in the language of liberal individualism, but its heart lies in the disfavored ideas of collective action and collective guilt.'[319] Hence, this coexistence of individual and collective dimensions of responsibility in international criminal law is not unproblematic. It creates a tension between the collective nature of international crimes and the desire to express moral outrage through the imposition of punishment. Indeed, international criminal tribunals have been forced to deal with this tension through a number of creative solutions that address the collective dimension of international crimes, even though it might be hard to ascertain the precise scope of the collective in each circumstance.

The group element is important not only from the perspective of perpetrators, but also in the definition of victimhood. International crimes are defined in a way which necessitates a large sphere of victims; widespread attacks, genocides and a broad policy necessitate the concept of mass victimization.[320]

[314] Art. 7 (2)(a) of the Rome Statute.

[315] Gerry Simpson, *Law, War & Crime: War Crimes Trials and the Reinvention of International Law* (Cambridge: Polity Press, 2007), p. 58.

[316] Ibid., discussing George P. Fletcher, 'The Storrs Lectures: Liberals and Romantics at War: The Problem of Collective Guilt' (2001–2002) 111 *Yale Law Journal* 1499–1573.

[317] George P. Fletcher, *Romantics at War: Glory and Guilt in the Age of Terrorism* (Princeton: Princeton University Press, 2002), p. 62.

[318] Ibid.; Simpson, *Law, War & Crime*, p. 71.

[319] Fletcher, *Romantics at War*, p. 70.

[320] See Heikkilä, *Coping with International Atrocities*, pp. 33–36.

For example, approximately 800,000 Tutsis were killed in the Rwandan genocide, thousands of girls and women were raped in the Democratic Republic of Congo and thousands were mutilated in Sierra Leone. Yet, it is important to note that no numerical figures can be presented that would define these crimes. Rather, the decisive factor is group belongingness: victims 'are targeted *en masse* based on discriminatory grounds'.[321]

#### 4.3.2.1 Legal Entities

One of the cornerstones of both national and international criminal law is that criminal responsibility is personal. Yet, there are several organized collectives that might be implicated in the commission of international crimes. Corporations are frequently implicated in serious human rights violations that at times could even amount to international crimes; the East India Company was accused of widespread torture in the nineteenth century, companies in Nazi Germany were implicated in the Nazi atrocities, and more recently PMSCs have been involved in shootings of civilians. It is not farfetched either to argue that states have a capacity to commit international crimes: Bosnia-Herzegovina accused Serbia of genocide before the ICJ, and the United States' policy of torture comes close to the most condemned crimes of the international community. Thus, the two foremost entities that are relevant for a discussion of criminal responsibility of organized collectives are the state and the corporation. Notably, the law recognizes that the state and the corporation are legal persons different from the natural persons they are composed of; still, the question of allocating criminal responsibility to such entities has been considered difficult but not unheard of. International criminal law has dealt with such entities through the theories of criminal organizations and corporate criminal responsibility.

To begin with, it must immediately be noted that international criminal law as a normative order, as well as the institutions implementing it, has fairly little to say about state criminal responsibility.[322] The focus of international criminal law upon the individual and a guilty mind means that the state fades into the background and becomes the context in which individual criminal responsibility is considered. For instance, the Versailles Treaty of 1919

[321] Drumbl, *Atrocity*, p. 41 (emphasis in original).

[322] Immi Tallgren has noted that international criminal law 'does not address the use of violence by states in general'. See Immi Tallgren, '*La Grande Illusion*' (2002) 15 *Canadian Journal of Law and Jurisprudence* 297–316 at 310. For a comprehensive account of state criminal responsibility, see Nina H. B. Jørgensen, *The Responsibility of States for International Crimes* (Oxford: Oxford University Press, 2000).

established the personal responsibility of Kaiser Wilhelm for 'supreme offence against international morality and the sanctity of treaties', whereas his underlings were to be tried for 'violation of the laws and customs of war'.[323] Although it has been pointed out that both Nazi Germany and Saddam Hussein's Iraq were held and treated as 'criminal states',[324] this was not as a result of international criminal law or its tribunals. Although nothing stands in the way of developing a regime on state criminal responsibility in the future, the contemporary legal order fails to incorporate such a concept.[325]

But to some extent, international criminal law theory and practice have dealt with and touched upon another legal entity: the corporation. However, opinions are still divided on the criminal responsibility of corporations both at the national and international level, a situation which resulted in the exclusion of corporations or legal entities in general from the ICC Statute. As long as there is no international court or tribunal competent to elaborate on the details of corporate criminal responsibility, the prerequisites for corporate criminal responsibility will remain undecided.[326] In particular, two thorny questions pose problems for the recognition of corporate criminal responsibility: first, can a corporation be a moral agent; and second, if it can, how it can be punished. The obvious difficulty of ascribing criminal responsibility to legal entities is 'the lack of a soul to be damned and a body to be kicked'.[327]

The moral agency of groups and organizations is extensively debated. Since a corporation is a legal construct composed of human beings, it is possible to delineate two opposite understandings. On the one hand, there are those who always argue for reduction of the group into individuals, and thus completely reject corporate criminal responsibility; on the other hand, others hold a reductive approach to be insufficient, and thus call for the moral agency of the group itself. For individualists who represent the former position, 'collectivities can be considered neither agents nor

[323] Arts. 227 and 228 of the Versailles Treaty.

[324] Pellet, 'Can a State Commit', 433.

[325] James Crawford, for instance, notices that 'the notion of state crimes remains a dormant legal concept'. See James Crawford, *State Responsibility: The General Part* (Cambridge: Cambridge University Press, 2013), p. 394.

[326] Andrew Clapham, 'Extending International Criminal Law beyond the Individual to Corporations and Armed Opposition Groups' (2008) 6 *Journal of International Criminal Justice* 899–926 at 918–919.

[327] Quotation of Edward First Baron Thurlow, cited in John C. Coffee, Jr, '"No Soul to Damn: No Body to Kick": An Unscandalized Inquiry into the Problem of Corporal Punishment' (1980–1981) 79 *Michigan Law Review* 386–459 at 386.

moral agents'.[328] This is expressed by the maxim *societas non delinquere potest*. But disagreement prevails even among those accepting the criminal responsibility of corporations, because the reasoning involved in determining culpability varies. Two different rationales are commonly found: the agency or identification doctrine and the constructivist approach, which believes in genuine corporate criminal responsibility. The former still sees the individual as the starting point, since it ascribes the 'minds and bodies of the officers and servants of the corporation' to the legal entity in question.[329] The acts and minds of leading senior officers are thereby attributed to the corporation. The latter view, often called the constructivist theory, places the corporation as the primary perpetrator, thus recognizing the distinct personality and guilty mind of the company. Such a model sees corporations as 'systems [...] not just aggregations of individuals'.[330] Therefore, it takes into account 'corporate culture and ethos'.[331] The corporation is thus judged based on policies, attitudes, conduct and practice.

Not all corporations, however, can qualify as moral agents capable of being held criminally responsible. Many commentators stress that such a corporation must be more than the sum of its constituent parts: it must be able to make decisions and translate them into reality; it must have a corporate identity which extends over time; and finally it must perceive itself as a unit.[332] It has further been argued that when the corporation is weak or constrained due to internal or external causes, it fails to be a moral agent in full. Moral agency thus viewed is not a binary, on/off characteristic, but rather is a matter of degree.[333] However, it has increasingly been accepted – both in national and international law – that when corporations can be considered moral agents whose freedom of action has not been curtailed in any way, 'blaming that institution for the consequences of its failure is a coherent response'.[334]

328 Toni Erskine, 'Kicking Bodies and Damning Souls: The Danger of Harming "Innocent" Individuals While Punishing "Delinquent" States', in Tracy Isaacs and Richard Vernon (eds.), *Accountability for Collective Wrongdoing* (New York: Cambridge University Press, 2011), pp. 261–286 at 265.

329 Ormerod, *Criminal Law*, p. 248.

330 Brent Fisse and John Braithwaite, 'The Allocation of Responsibility for Corporate Crime: Individualism, Collectivism and Accountability' (1986–1988) 11 *Sydney Law Review* 468–513 at 479.

331 Ormerod, *Criminal Law*, p. 257.

332 For a discussion of the criteria by which a corporation can be seen as a moral agent, see Erskine, 'Kicking Bodies'.

333 Ibid., 270–271.

334 Ibid., 272.

The field of international criminal law has been exposed to the debate over the criminality of corporations, first with regard to the Nuremberg legacy, and of late with the rise of national criminal laws which are open to the possibility of corporate criminal responsibility.[335] To start with the Nuremberg trials and the approach adopted towards legal entities, the classic maxim expressed in the Nuremberg judgment shows where the primary, if not exclusive, focus of the trial lay: 'Crimes against international law are committed by men, not by abstract entities, and only by punishing individuals who commit such crimes can the provisions of international law be enforced.'[336] Still, corporations and organizations were indirectly included in the trials. Two different means were used to address the centrality of organizations and the multitude of culprits: a first approach was to declare a certain number of organizations as 'criminal'; and in a second, a number of industrialists faced charges for their participation in the atrocities. The difference between criminal organizations and corporations lies in their corporate aims. Whereas criminal organizations are 'formed expressly to achieve criminal aims', corporations may engage in criminal acts within their ordinary sphere of activity.[337] The identity of criminal organizations, therefore, is dependent on the actual commission of crimes.

Declaring certain organizations to be criminal was unique for the Nuremberg Trials and has not extended to modern international criminal institutions. Article 9 of the Nuremberg Charter laid down that the Tribunal may declare any group or organization a criminal organization.[338] According to this provision, the Tribunal did indeed find three organizations to be criminal: the Leadership Corps of the Nazi Party; the Gestapo and the SD; and the *Achutzstaffeln der nationalsozialistischen deutschen*

335 For an account of corporate criminal responsibility, see Harmen van der Wilt, 'Corporate Criminal Responsibility for International Crimes: Exploring the Possibilities' (2013) 12 *Chinese Journal of International Law* 43–77; Norman Farell, 'Attributing Criminal Liability to Corporate Actors: Some Lessons from the International Tribunals' (2010) 8 *Journal of International Criminal Justice* 873–894; Volker Nerlich, 'Core Crimes and Transnational Business Corporations' (2010) 8 *Journal of International Criminal Justice* 895–908; Kyle Rex Jacobson, 'Doing Business with the Devil: The Challenges of Prosecuting Corporate Officials whose Business Transactions Facilitate War Crimes and Crimes against Humanity' (2005) 56 *Air Force Law Review* 167–232.

336 Schabas, *An Introduction to*, p. 211, note 64.

337 Jørgensen, 'Criminality of Organizations', 202.

338 Agreement for the Prosecution and Punishment of the Major War Criminals of the European Axis, and Charter of the International Military Tribunal, London, 8 August 1945, 82 *United Nations Treaty Series* 279.

*arbeiterparti*, SS.[339] However, because a sentence could not be imposed upon the organization, such a judgment remained declaratory. Yet, the novelty of the idea had far-reaching consequences for the members of such criminal organizations. The Tribunal saw the concept as endangering the basic principle of individual guilt. In order to mitigate the broad implications of the concept of the criminal organization, the Tribunal held that only members of the criminal organization who had knowledge of the criminal acts were to be held as criminal along with the organization.[340] In a sense, the Tribunal thus adopted a more careful approach to membership in criminal organizations than what the Charter had envisaged. However, in the so-called Subsequent Nuremberg Proceedings – which followed the Nuremberg trials and focused on major war criminals of second rank – membership was recognized as a crime.[341] In the course of those proceedings, a small number of defendants were convicted for membership in the SS.

The Subsequent Nuremberg Proceedings are important not only because of the concept of criminal organization. Article II(2) of the legal basis of these proceedings – Control Council Law No. 10 – laid down that those who 'held high position in the financial, industrial or economic life' could be guilty of crime.[342] In line with this provision, three cases in the Subsequent Proceedings concerned known industrialists and their corporations. These were the cases of *Krupp*,[343] *I. G. Farben*[344]

339 Nuremberg Judgment, *France and ors* v. *Göring (Hermann) and ors*, Judgment and Sentence, [1946] 22 *IMT* 203, 1 October 1946, reproduced in (1947) 41 *American Journal of International Law* 172. See also *The Charter and Judgment of the Nürnberg Tribunal*, UN Doc. A/CN.4/5 (1949), see p. 74 *et seqq.*, esp. 77.

340 IMT Judgment, 30 September and 1 October 1946, 'The Accused Organizations', see *France and ors* v. *Göring (Hermann) and ors.*

341 Control Council Law No. 10 of 20 December 1945, Art. II(1)(d). Control Council Law No. 10 of 20 December 1945: Punishment of Persons Guilty of War Crimes, Crimes against Peace and against Humanity, *Amtsblatt*, of the Control Council in Germany, No. 3, 31 January 1946, p. 50, Art. II(1)(d).

342 Control Council Law No. 10.

343 Alfred Krupp and eleven other defendants from the Krupp industrial concern were charged with enslavement and other war crimes, including the plunder of public and private property. *Trial of Alfred Felix Alwyn Krupp von Bohlen und Halbach and Eleven Others*, United States Military Tribunal, Nuremberg, 17 November 1947–30 June 1948, Law Reports of Trials of War Criminals (UNWCC), Vol. X, p. 69. For a discussion of the choice of defendants by the Allies, see Allison Marston Danner, 'The Nuremberg Industrialist Prosecutions and Aggressive War' (2005–2006) 46 *Virginia Journal of International Law* 651–676.

344 Twenty-four defendants from the IG Farben concern were charged with plunder and spoliation. See *Trial of Carl Krauch and Twenty-Two Others* (I. G. Farben Trial), United States Military Tribunal, Nuremberg, 14 August 1947–29 July 1948, Law Reports of Trials of War Criminals (UNWCC), Volume X, p. 1.

and *Flick*.[345] The industrialists were central to the Nazi regime due to their provision of, among other things, weapons, raw materials and Zyklon B gas. Although these cases are rarely portrayed as a central feature of the trials, some commentators claim that they contribute to a de facto recognition of corporate criminal responsibility on the part of the Nuremberg trials.[346]

Although it is true that the corporations of these industrialists featured in the trials, it cannot be maintained that in these cases the Tribunal fully accepted the criminal responsibility of the corporations themselves. One reason for this is the limited competence of the Tribunal. It was simply not endowed with the powers for making a finding of corporate criminal responsibility, since its competence was limited to natural persons. As a result, it chose a bottom-up approach in which it stressed how the industrialists had used the corporation to achieve their goals. The respective corporations were therefore seen as instruments through which criminal acts had been committed, rather than as primary actors. Such an approach nevertheless ignores the company completely or perceives it as an entity in the hands of the Nazis, not as a company functioning on the basis of the capitalistic logic in which it operates as an instrument of itself and hence is a subject of responsibility.[347] Whether the outcome would have been different had the Tribunal been able to make verdicts directly on legal persons is difficult to tell. The Tribunal noted in the *Farben* case that 'the corporate defendant, Farben, is not before the bar of the Tribunal and cannot be subjected to criminal penalties in these proceedings'.[348] At any rate, corporations were a salient part of the deliberations around international crimes in the aftermath of the Second World

345 Six members of the Flick concern were charged with using slave labour and plundering private property. *Trial of Friedrich Flick and Five Others*, United States Military Tribunal, Nuremberg, 20 April–22 December 1947, Law Reports of Trials of War Criminals (UNWCC), Vol. IX, p. 1.

346 To this effect, Andrew Clapham holds with regard to corporations: 'There are clearly violations of international criminal law that exist in the absence of any international jurisdiction to try them'. See Clapham, *Human Rights Obligations*, p. 267; and 'The Question of Jurisdiction under International Criminal Law over Legal Persons: Lessons from the Rome Conference on an International Criminal Court', in Menno Kamminga and S. Zia-Zarifi (eds.), *Liability of Multinational Corporations Under International Law* (The Hague: Kluwer Law International, 2000), pp. 139–195 at 167–168.

347 Doreen Lustig, 'The Nature of the Nazi State and the Question of International Criminal Responsibility of Corporate Officials at Nuremberg: Franz Neuhmann's Behemoth at the Industrialist Trials', *Institute for International Law and Justice Working Paper 2011/2* (History and Theory of International Law Series), Finalized 20 June 2011, p. 59.

348 *Trial of Carl Krauch and Twenty-Two Others* (I. G. Farben Trial), p. 52. Interestingly, one of the judges held that if it indeed had been before the bar, the finding would have been different.

War despite the absence of a full-fledged recognition of corporate criminal responsibility. The legacy of Nuremberg can thus be described as its having opened the door to the criminal responsibility of corporations.

The resurgence of international criminal law in the post–Cold War period did not bring about radical changes in attitudes towards corporate criminal responsibility. The statutes of the ICTY and ICTR include only natural persons under the tribunals' jurisdictions,[349] thus leaving legal entities outside their scope. At the time of the adoption of the Rome Statute of the ICC, many states whose national legal systems accepted corporate criminal responsibility advanced the idea of including legal entities within the Court's jurisdiction. But the issue of corporate criminal responsibility turned out to be one of the most contentious topics during the Rome conference. The delegations were deeply divided over the very premise of holding corporations criminally responsible.[350] France submitted a proposal to that effect, which was nevertheless rejected by the international conference.[351] Although some progress was made, consensus on the issue was impossible to achieve, as many states whose national legislative systems do not recognize the criminal liability of corporations firmly resisted the inclusion of such a principle of criminal law into the Rome Statute.[352] Although the shortage of negotiation

[349] Art. 6 of the ICTY Statute, adopted by UNSC Res. 827 (1993), 25 May 1993, and, Art. 5 of the ICTR Statute.

[350] Per Saland, 'International Criminal Law Principles', in Roy S. Lee (ed.), *The International Criminal Court: The Making of the Rome Statute* (The Hague: Kluwer Law International, 1999), pp. 189–216 at 199.

[351] The proposal reads: 'Without prejudice to any individual criminal responsibility of natural persons under this Statute, the Court may also have jurisdiction over a juridical person for a crime under this Statute. Charges may be filed by the Prosecutor against a juridical person, and the Court may render a judgement over a juridical person for the crime charged, if:

(a) The charges filed by the Prosecutor against the natural person and the juridical person allege the matters referred to in subparagraphs (b) and (c); and
(b) The natural person charged was in a position of control within the juridical person under the national law of the State where the juridical person was registered at the time the crime was committed; and
(c) The crime was committed by the natural person acting on behalf of and with the explicit consent of that juridical person and in the course of its activities; and
(d) The natural person has been convicted of the crime charged.

For the purpose of this Statute, 'juridical person' means a corporation whose concrete, real or dominant objective is seeking private profit or benefit, and not a State or other public body in the exercise of State authority, a public international body or an organization registered, and acting under the national law of a State as a non–profit organisation'.

See Working Paper on Article 23, paras. 5–6, A/Conf.183/C.1/WGGP/L.5/Rev.2, 3 July 1998.

[352] Saland, 'International Criminal', 199.

time arguably affected the outcome,[353] the importance of sealing the acceptance of the package as a whole was more important than the single issue of competence over legal entities.[354] Thus, Article 25 (1) of the Rome Statute stipulates that 'the Court shall have jurisdiction over natural persons pursuant to this Statute'.[355] Thus, the criminal responsibility of corporations is not an accepted feature of international criminal law.

#### 4.3.2.2 Other Collective Criminality

International criminal law is able to take account of a plurality of perpetrators and individuals who have contributed to differing degrees to the commission of an international crime outside the ambit of formal organizational structures. Thus, it also addresses collectives other than legal entities. These collectives may be unorganized and highly contextual, such that they exist only in relation to certain crimes in a specific environment. They are intermediate groups that are formed at a sub-state level but which still bind together a number of people directly and indirectly through the commission of an international crime. It is noteworthy, however, that there might be an infinite variety in these collectives; they may be small and unorganized, or loose collectives which are highly organized. Both the size and the organization of the group become essential elements in the discussion of how international criminal tribunals have approached collective criminality.[356] However, the issue of how to deal with loosely organized groups is far from settled because of the differences in approach and interpretation among the various international criminal tribunals.[357]

In practice, international criminal tribunals have utilized national criminal law doctrines in recognizing collective criminality. Innovative theories of collective criminality have also been developed that are specific to international criminal law. At the same time, a few caveats are in order. First, the general principle of individual criminal responsibility which forms the basis for international criminal trials makes it more difficult for international criminal tribunals to deal with larger collectives. The further away one moves from a tangible connection to the crime, the more inappropriate individual

353 William Schabas states that 'time was simply too short for the delegates to reach a consensus'. See Schabas, *An Introduction to the International*, p. 211.

354 Personal interview with former ICC Judge Erkki Kourula, 28 January 2014.

355 Art. 25(1) of the Rome Statute.

356 See the discussion in Mikaela Heikkilä, *International Criminal Tribunals and Victims of Crime: A Study of the Status of Victims before International Criminal Tribunals and of Factors Affecting This Status* (Turku: Åbo Akademi University, 2004), esp. p. 240 *et seqq.*

357 For a general discussion of the question of how to construct the criminal responsibility of loose collectives, see Boas, Bischoff and Reid, *International Criminal Law.*

criminal responsibility becomes. At some point, collectives may thus cross the threshold from a common undertaking in which the participants have knowledge of acts committed by other members of the group to what might be labelled a legal fiction in which the individual's role is remote. Clearly, efforts to determine the collective dimension of international crimes have stretched international criminal law to its margins.

In spite of international criminal law being rooted in a focus on determining the criminality of individuals, it was recognized from the start that the collective dimension of criminality must be addressed. When the Allied powers were confronted with the question of mass criminality in the aftermath of the Second World War, they strove to lay down principles of liability that were sufficiently broad to include the vast number of perpetrators in Nazi Germany. The Allied powers did not share any common principle of criminal law which accounted for liability for planning the atrocities. The idea of conspiracy or common plan was borrowed from American criminal law and reflected in the Charter of the International Military Tribunal at Nuremberg. Accordingly, '[l]eaders, organisers, instigators and accomplices participating in the formulation or execution of a common plan or conspiracy to commit any of the foregoing crimes are responsible for all acts performed by any persons in execution of such plan.'[358] This made it possible to find guilt and convict those against whom it would be very difficult to prove specific criminal acts besides planning the atrocities, but who were considered 'deserving of trial and punishment'.[359]

But conspiracy and responsibility based on criminal organization membership cast the net too wide. As a consequence, current international criminal tribunals still struggle with the collective dimension of international crimes, and particularly with the question of what international criminal legal tools to use with regard to individuals who have been non-physically involved in a crime. The doctrine developed for these purposes by the ad hoc international criminal tribunals, most notably the ICTY, is that of Joint Criminal Enterprise (JCE) responsibility.[360]

The JCE doctrine originates in the landmark case before the ICTY of *Prosecutor* v. *Duško Tadić*, in which the Tribunal had to decide whether the

358 Art. 6 of the Agreement for the Prosecution and Punishment of the Major War Criminals of the European Axis, and Charter of the International Military Tribunal, London, 8 August 1945, 82 *United Nations Treaty Series* 280.

359 See the statement by the American delegate, Minutes of Conference Session of July 23, 1945 (Document XLIV), Report of Robert H. Jackson on the International Conference on Military Trials, p. 328 at 332, cited in Darcy, *Collective Responsibility*, p. 211.

360 For accounts of the JCE, see Giulia Bigi, 'Joint Criminal Enterprise in the Jurisprudence of the International Criminal Tribunal for the Former Yugoslavia and the Prosecution of Senior Political and Military Leaders: The Krajisnik Case' (2010) 14 *Max Planck Yearbook of United Nations Law* 51–83.

accused was to be held guilty under international criminal law 'for the killing of five men from Jaskici even though there is no evidence that he personally killed any of them'.[361] In other words, the question that arose was whether the common criminal purpose of the armed group that *Tadić* belonged to was enough to find him criminally responsible for the crimes committed. In spite of the lack of any provisions establishing collective criminality in the ICTY Statute, the Appeals Chamber proceeded on the basis of the objective and purpose of the Statute when it held that '[w]hoever contributes to the commission of crimes by the group of persons or some members of the group, in execution of a common criminal purpose, may be held to be criminally liable.'[362] Because the Tribunal held that non-physical involvement in common-purpose crimes is not inferior to direct participation in the commission of the crimes,[363] the mode of 'aiding and abetting' was seen as ill-fitting. According to the Tribunal, *Tadić* was not an accomplice, but rather a co-perpetrator, of the crimes committed.

The Appeals Chamber in the *Tadić* case also developed a general theory of the JCE doctrine. It identified three different categories of joint criminal enterprise: (1) basic; (2) systemic; and (3) extended forms. The basic form was explained as cases in which the co-perpetrators act on the basis of a common purpose and all share the same criminal intent. The systemic form is represented, for example, by concentration camps where the perpetrators have knowledge of and intention to engage in maltreatment. The third category, however, is the most controversial from the perspective of criminal law's basic tenet of personal culpability. The requirements for criminal responsibility for the extended form of JCE are fulfilled if the accused had 'the *intention* to participate in and further the criminal activity or the common criminal purpose of a group and to contribute to the joint criminal enterprise or in any event to the commission of a crime by the group', and 'if, under the circumstances of the case, (i) it was *foreseeable* that such a crime might be perpetrated by one or other members of the group and (ii) the accused *willingly took that risk*'.[364]

The JCE doctrine has been substantially critiqued for a deficient normative basis,[365] but primarily because it imposes a criminal responsibility so broad that it almost represents a form of vicarious responsibility or guilt by

[361] *Prosecutor* v. *Duško Tadić*, IT-94-1-A, ICTY Appeals Chamber, Judgment (15 July 1999), para. 185.

[362] Ibid., para. 190.

[363] Ibid., para. 191.

[364] Ibid., pp. 104–105, para. 228 (emphases in original).

[365] It has widely been held that the Appeals Chamber in the *Tadić* case went too far in the interpretation of the ICTY Statute as well as of its object and purpose. According to Jens Ohlin, 'the framers of the ICTY Statute made no reference to criminal liability for a joint

association.[366] Whereas some scholars would be prepared to accept JCE in situations of mob violence and even for somewhat larger enterprises such as detention camps, including loose networks within the concept seems unacceptable to many.[367] The applicability of JCE to nationwide genocides, for example, could lead to situations in which individuals are criminally held responsible for the acts of people who they are unacquainted with. Nonetheless, the most critical point of the JCE doctrine is its extended form. In this form of JCE, an individual is held responsible based on foresight and voluntary assumption of risk for the acts of others that even could be outside of the common criminal purpose. Responsibility under the extended form of JCE is thus disconnected from intent, which is a key criminal law principle.[368] As a result, JCE has been described as a 'magic bullet' of the Prosecutor that helps to secure conviction in complex situations where it would be difficult to prove the intent or knowledge of the accused.[369] Indeed, one of the major problems with JCE is the uncertainty with which it manages to capture the reality of systematic crimes.[370]

The ICC has chosen another route than the JCE to deal with the problem of perpetrator plurality. The Rome Statute acknowledges two different modes of liability in handling cases in which several persons work collectively

criminal enterprise, a common design or plan, or any notion of conspiracy at all'. See Jens David Ohlin, 'Three Conceptual Problems with the Doctrine of Joint Criminal Enterprise' (2007) 5 *Journal of International Criminal Justice* 69–90 at 71. A similar critique has also been made by the Trial Chamber of the ICTY, which in the *Stakić* case adopted the notion of 'co–perpetratorship' instead of JCE. The Trial Chamber wanted to avoid 'the misleading impression that a new crime [membership in a criminal organization] not foreseen in the Statute of this Tribunal has been introduced through the backdoor'. See *Prosecutor* v. *Milomir Stakić*, IT–97–24–T, Trial Chamber II, Judgment (31 July 2003), para. 441. Other commentators have also described the JCE as judicial entrepreneurship, see inter alia, Steven Powles, 'Joint Criminal Enterprise: Criminal Liability by Prosecutorial Ingenuity and Judicial Creativity?' (2004) 2 *Journal of International Criminal Justice* 606–619.

366 Indeed, this critique has found expression in interpretations of the acronym for the doctrine, which has been twisted into 'Just Convict Everyone'. See Mohamed Elewa Bahar, '"Just Convict Everyone!"– Joint Perpetration: From *Tadic* to *Stakic* and Back' (2006) 6 *International Criminal Law Review* 293–302; For critical comments, see e.g., Ohlin, 'Three Conceptual Problems'.

367 Heikkilä, *Coping with International Atrocities*, p. 203.

368 This becomes particularly problematic if the crime requires special intent, such as with genocide. For relevant discussions, see Elies van Sliedregt, 'Joint Criminal Enterprise as a Pathway to Convicting Individuals for Genocide' (2007) 5 *Journal of International Criminal Justice* 184–207.

369 William A. Schabas, *War Crimes and Human Rights: Essays on the Death Penalty, Justice and Accountability* (London: Cameron May: London, 2008), p. 484.

370 Harmen van der Wilt, 'Sreberenica: On Joint Criminal Enterprise, Aiding and Abetting and Command Responsibility' (2015) 62 *Netherlands International Law Review* 229–241 at 239.

towards a joint criminal endeavour. First, according to Article 25(3)(a), there is joint perpetration or co-perpetation, in which a person commits the crime jointly with another person. Second, another hierarchically lower ground for recognizing liability of multiple persons exists in the Rome Statute as well: the common purpose doctrine modelled upon anti-terrorist conventions in the 1990s.[371] This latter theory of liability is unparalleled in international criminal law and balances the collective dimension of international crimes with the need for individual culpability.[372] It is noteworthy, however, that the Rome Statute does not criminalize mere membership in criminal organizations in a way akin to the Nuremberg IMT, and generally its stipulations on perpetrator plurality remain loyal to the criminal law principles of legality and culpability.

In its case law the ICC has addressed the plurality of perpetrators and the different modes of liability without, however, being able so far to clarify all related aspects. First, joint perpetration or co-perpetration is viewed as the 'principal liability theory that captures the responsibility of senior political and military figures who mastermind international crimes'.[373] Further, the ICC has distinguished between direct and indirect co-perpetration. As an example of the former taken from the *Lubanga* judgment, the Court identified as necessary elements: the existence of a common plan between at least two persons to engage in a crime, and that the accused 'provided an essential contribution' to that crime.[374] Indirect co-perpetration was held to exist

371 Article 25 (3)(d) of the Rome Statute stipulates: 'In any other way contributes to the commission or attempted commission of such a crime by a group of persons acting with a common purpose. Such contribution shall be intentional and shall either:

i. Be made with the aim of furthering the criminal activity or criminal purpose of the group, where such activity or purpose involves the commission of a crime within the jurisdiction of the Court; or
ii. Be made in the knowledge of the intention of the group to commit the crime'.

Cf. Article 2(3)(c) of the 1997 International Convention for the Suppression of Terrorist Bombings, adopted in the General Assembly Res. A/RES/52/164 of 15 December 1997, in force, 23 May 2001, 2149 *United Nations Treaty Series* 256.

372 Kai Ambos, 'The ICC and Common Purpose – What Contribution is Required under Article 25(3)(d)?', in Carsten Stahn (ed.), *The Law and Practice of the International Criminal Court* (Oxford: Oxford University Press, 2015), pp. 592–593 at 592–593.

373 Marjolein Cupido, 'Common Purpose Liability Versus Joint Perpetration: A Practical View on the ICC's Hierarchy of Liability Theories' (2016) 29 *Leiden Journal of International Law* 897–915 at 898.

374 *Situation in the Democratic Republic of the Congo in the case of the Prosecutor* v. *Thomas Lubanga Dyilo*, ICC–01/04–01/06, ICC Trial Chamber I, Judgment Pursuant to Article 74 of the Statute (14 March 2012), para. 1006.

when the aforementioned conditions were fulfilled, in addition to which the accused had control over a hierarchical power apparatus.[375]

In the *Lubanga* judgment, the majority of the Trial Chamber opined that there is a hierarchical relationship between the different modes of liability. Thus, it was held that 'the contribution of the co-perpetrator who "commits" a crime is necessarily of greater significance than that of an individual who "contributes in any other way to the commission" of a crime'.[376] The same position regarding the hierarchical nature of Article 25 (3) had already been taken by the Pre-Trial Chamber in the *Mbarushimana* case.[377] As a consequence, the majority of ICC judges have held common purpose responsibility as laid down in Art. 25 (3)(d) to be a residual form of responsibility.[378]

While taking due note of the resemblance of JCE doctrine developed by the ad hoc tribunals to common purpose liability, the ICC has noted the existing differences between these two theories addressing group responsibility.[379] For example, in its judgment of Congolese rebel leader Germain Katanga the Court applied strict criteria in holding Katanga criminally responsible for his accessoryship in the crimes of the Ngiti militia of the Walendu-Bindi *collectivité*. Katanga's accessoryship was based on his significant contribution to the criminal acts of a group with a common plan and on the determination that he acted with intention and with knowledge of the group's criminal intentions.[380] Katanga was not held responsible for the deeds of the militia, but only for those acts that he performed himself.[381]

Case law shows that the practice of the ICC is more flexible than what is suggested by the standards set down by the Rome Statute with regard to

[375] Heikkilä, *Coping with International Atrocities*, p. 210.

[376] *Situation in the Democratic Republic of Congo in the Case of the Prosecutor* v. *Thomas Lubanga Dyilo*, ICC-01/04-01/06, ICC Trial Chamber I, Judgment Pursuant to Article 74 of the Statute (14 March 2012), para. 996.

[377] *Situation in the Democratic Republic of Congo, Prosecutor* v. *Callixte Mbarushimana*, ICC-01/04-01/10 (16 December 2011), Pre-Trial Chamber I, Decision on the Confirmation of Charges, p. 121, para. 278.

[378] Cupido, 'Common Purpose', 914.

[379] *Situation in the Democratic Republic of Congo, Prosecutor* v. *Callixte Mbarushimana*, ICC-01/04-01/10 (16 December 2011), Pre-Trial Chamber I, Decision on the Confirmation of Charges, p. 123, para. 282.

[380] ICC, Summary of Trial Chamber II's Judgment of 7 March 2014, in the case of *The Prosecutor* v. *Germain Katanga*, para. 73.

[381] *Le Procureur* c. *Germain Katanga*, ICC–01/04–01/07, CPI, Jugement rendu en application de l'article 74 du statut (7 March 2014), para. 1619.

the different forms of perpetration and participation. Yet, the 'varied and context-dependent practice' regarding joint perpetration and common purpose liability,[382] entails a categorically stricter approach to the plurality of perpetrators than that embraced by the ad hoc tribunals. Indeed, it has been held to be problematic that there are 'two diverging bodies of international criminal law' as the methodologies utilized by the ad hoc tribunals and the ICC vary when it comes to the plurality of perpetrators.[383] The ICC definitely appears to want to take international criminal law closer to its origins instead of accepting the ICTY's relaxed standards of responsibility. Put differently, the ad hoc tribunals employed a too-broad notion of collective responsibility.

#### 4.3.2.3 Collective Victimhood

There is another dimension to collectivity in international criminal law besides collective perpetration: collective victimhood. Collectivity is essential in the identification of victims of international crimes.[384] International crimes usually target ethnic, racial, religious or other groups; thus, membership in a particular collective becomes the decisive factor separating perpetrators from victims. The crimes can thus be said to violate both the specific rights of the individual, but also the collective interests of the group in question. Another

382 Cupido, 'Common Purpose', 914.

383 Elies van Sliedregt, *The Criminal Responsibility of Individuals for Violations of International Humanitarian Law* (The Hague: T.M.C. Asser Press, 2003), p. 115.

384 For a study of the role of victims in international criminal law, See Heikkilä, *International Criminal Tribunals*. No uniform definition of a 'victim' exists in international law. The notion of a victim is usually not defined on a general plane in international human rights conventions, which means that any collective dimension of victimhood is also left undefined. Art. 1 of the 1985 *UN Declaration on Basic Principles of Justice for Victims of Crime and Abuse of Power* (1985 UN Victims' Declaration) defines a victim as follows: '"Victims" means persons who, individually or *collectively*, have suffered harm [...]'(emphasis added). For the Victim Declaration, see Annex to UNGA Res. 40/34, 29 November 1985. In a similar vein, the 2005 *Basic Principles and Guidelines on the Right to a Remedy and Reparation for Victims of Gross Violations of International Human Rights Law and Serious Violations of International Humanitarian Law* (2005 Basic Principles) emphasize the collective aspect of victimhood. See Annex to UNGA Res. 60/147, 16 December 2005. The Rome Statute's Rules of Procedure and Evidence mirrors the two UN declarations, but adds legal persons to the category of victims. Rule 85 defines a victim as follows: '(a) "Victims" means natural persons who have suffered harm as a result of the commission of any crime within the jurisdiction of the Court; (b) Victims may include organizations or institutions that have sustained direct harm to any of their property which is dedicated to religion, education, art or science or charitable purposes, and to their historic monuments, hospitals and other places and objects for humanitarian purposes'.

factor which contributes to the importance of collectivity when it comes to victims of international crimes is the sheer number of victims, which may rise to thousands and even tens of thousands. However, the irrelevance of nationality for international criminal proceedings and victim participation must be stated.[385] Contrary to the axiomatic character of nationality in the rules of state responsibility and those of diplomatic protection, international criminal law is constructed upon different communal bonds than nationality. A number of various collectives may be victims of international crimes: for example, women and children, indigenous communities, village communities, or tribal communities. Thus, victimized collectives are highly diverse. They are often subnational, but they can even be transboundary. From a legal point of view, it is also important to note that some groups may enjoy international legal personality, whereas others do not.[386] However, most collectives that fall victim to international crimes belong to the latter category, without the right to act as a group claimant.[387]

In spite of the problems connected to collective victimhood, it seems logical to acknowledge a group dimension to international crimes: if victims suffer as a group, the legal consequences of the wrong committed should benefit the group as a whole as well. To this effect, collective reparations have become a trend spreading from human rights law to international criminal law.[388] The aim of such reparations is to 'undo collective harm' through the conferral of benefits upon the affected collective.[389] The collective harm is thus seen to be greater than the sum of its parts. This associative basis of collective harm is also transferred to the form collective reparation takes: victims who are awarded collective reparation cannot enjoy it alone, but only together with other members of the collective.[390] Collective forms of reparation

385 See Marc Henzelin, Veijo Heiskanen and Guénaël Mettraux, 'Reparations to Victims before the International Criminal Court: Lessons from International Mass Claims Processes' (2006) 17 *Criminal Law Forum* 317–344 at 323.

386 Friedrich Rosenfeld, 'Collective Reparations for Victims of Armed Conflicts' (2010) 92 *International Review of the Red Cross* 731–746 at 736.

387 Ibid., at 743. In its decision establishing the principles and procedures to be applied in reparations, the ICC noted that '[t]here is a growing recognition in international human rights law that victims and groups of victims may apply for and receive reparations'. See *Situation in the Democratic Republic of Congo in the Case of the Prosecutor* v. *Thomas Lubanga Dyilo*, ICC–01/04–01/06, Decision Establishing the Principles and Procedures to be Applied to Reparations (7 August 2012), para. 217.

388 Diana Contreras-Garduño, 'Defining Beneficiaries of Collective Reparations: The Experience of the IACtHR' (2012) 4 *Amsterdam Law Forum* 40–57 at 41.

389 Rosenfeld, 'Collective Reparations', 732.

390 Ibid., 733.

usually include symbolic benefits such as apologies, creation of memorials or renaming of streets, or reparation in the form of development programmes. International human rights law, and especially the IACtHR, has been at the forefront when it comes to collective awards. In cases in which the number of victims is high, or in which an explicit group right has been violated, the Court has afforded reparations such as renovation of road systems, provision of interculturally skilled teachers, health centres and sewage systems.[391]

Due to the nature of criminal law, punishment of the offender, not reparation, traditionally stands at the core of international criminal tribunals. Yet, the Rome Statute lays the groundwork for a 'civil liability' side of international criminal trials by acknowledging the right of victims to restitution, compensation or rehabilitation.[392] This reflects 'a growing recognition in international criminal law that there is need to go beyond the notion of punitive justice, towards a solution which is more inclusive, encourages participation and recognises the need to provide effective remedies for victims'.[393] Indeed, the *Lubanga* judgment forced the ICC to ponder and decide upon which general principles of reparation were to be applicable in the Court's work. Along these lines, collective reparations were ordered in the *Katanga* case, with victims receiving inter alia housing and education help as well as psychological support.[394] Collective reparations are not, however, a unique feature of the ICC.[395] The Extraordinary Chamber in the Courts of Cambodia (ECCC) awarded collective reparations in their first judgment delivered when it ordered the convicted to apologize publically.[396]

The unique combination of individual and collective approaches to victims of international crimes before the ICC has received praise, but only time will tell whether or not the Court will be able to make a victim-inclusive

391 Contreras-Garduño, 'Defining Beneficiaries', 50. It has been questioned whether such programmatic approaches to collective reparations truly constitute reparation or simply amount to ordinary enjoyment of economic, social and cultural rights in human rights law (Ibid., 48).

392 Art. 75 of the Rome Statute. For a discussion of 'civil liability' aspects of the ICC, see Henzelin, Heiskanen and Mettraux, 'Reparations to Victims'.

393 *Situation in the Democratic Republic of Congo in the Case of the Prosecutor* v. *Thomas Lubanga Dyilo*, ICC–01/04–01/06, Decision Establishing the Principles and Procedures to be Applied to Reparations (7 August 2012), para. 177.

394 *Situation in the Democratic Republic of Congo in the Case of the Prosecutor* v. *Germain Katanga*, ICC–01/04–01/07, Order for Reparations pursuant to Article 75 of the Statute (24 March 2017), paras. 301–306.

395 Contreras-Garduño, 'Defining Beneficiaries', 40.

396 See Case 001, in which Kaing Guek Eav, *alias* Duch, was convicted to, inter alia, offering apologies to civil parties as reparations. See Case No. 001/18–07–2007/ECCC/TC, Trial Chamber, Judgment (26 July 2010), para. 668.

approach – with tangible collective reparation – a reality. There are many open questions that plague the implementation of collective reparation under the ICC.[397] First, the exact identification of the victims and beneficiaries of reparation remains problematic. Many collectives lack clear delimitations, and it might prove impossible to determine who belongs to the group and who does not.[398] Second, scholars have pointed out that what the ICC has in mind with reparation focuses on symbolic, not monetary, reparation.[399] Whereas some victims may prioritize financial compensation, the ICC is thinking in terms of, for example, rebuilding a church for the victim community or raising a memorial statue in the affected community. Third, the necessity of establishing clear and strict procedural standards has been highlighted so that the Court will be able to ascertain victims 'appropriate, adequate and prompt reparations'.[400] Thus, among other things scholars have argued for strict threshold criteria for which types of damages are eligible for reparation, relatively relaxed standards of causation, and yet sufficiently restrictive evidentiary standards.[401] Despite all the complexities involved in the collective dimension of reparation, the ICC has definitively taken a step away from methodological individualism to a world which partially recognizes the communitarian nature of society.

### 4.3.3 *Conclusions on Collectivity*

The role played by collectivity in different constructions of responsibility varies. Whereas collectivity in state responsibility is often portrayed as overinclusive and as a hindrance to the advancement of constructions of responsibility, its role in liability is central. In fact, in the liability regime collectivized efforts are crucial to the entire project of assigning responsibility. Without the

397 Henzelin, Heiskanen and Mettraux, 'Reparations to Victims'.

398 Rosenfeld, 'Collective Reparations', 742.

399 Henzelin, Heiskanen and Mettraux, 'Reparations to Victims', 340.

400 This goal was explicitly recognized by the ICC itself. See *Situation in the Democratic Republic of Congo in the Case of the Prosecutor* v. *Thomas Lubanga Dyilo*, ICC-01/04-01/06, Decision Establishing the Principles and Procedures to be Applied to Reparations (7 August 2012), para. 242.

401 Henzelin, Heiskanen and Mettraux, 'Reparations to Victims', esp. 324–30. The ICC decided in the case of Lubanga's victims that 'a less exacting standard should apply' and thus it opted for 'a balance of probabilities'. *Situation in the Democratic Republic of Congo in the Case of the Prosecutor* v. *Thomas Lubanga Dyilo*, ICC-01/04-01/06, Decision Establishing the Principles and Procedures to be Applied to Reparations (7 August 2012), paras. 251–254.

ability to distribute liability among several actors its whole objective is lost; only through including different actors via the layering of liability can one achieve the goal of adequate and prompt compensation. Collectivity is central to the liability project, which becomes clear in the application of strict liability as the standard of care.[402] A further feature of collectivity in international liability is its versatility. Different collective entities are found in liability rules, and involved actors may create new context-appropriate collectives whenever the need arises for additional targets of liability. Corporations and states are legal persons upon whom liability is distributed, but international practice shows that persons engaged in certain hazardous activities can be forced to create and join industry-wide funds. The flexibility with which liability is ascribed to different actors also disregards the traditional distinction between public and private actors.

Paradoxically, collectivity has become a relevant element for both the doctrine and the practice of international criminal law. It is vital for dealing with both the multitude of perpetrators often involved in international crimes, as well as with the vast number of victims. Despite the accentuated role of various collectives in international law, a tension exists between the personal foundation of criminal law and collectivity that cannot be eliminated. This becomes problematic, especially the larger the groups involved become. Yet, international criminal law manages to deal with intermediate groups situated between the individual and state. In fact, international criminal law situates itself in the domain between collective and individual notions of responsibility. Thus, there is potential for international criminal law to answer the criticism against methodological individualism raised by protagonists of communitarianism.

## 4.4 SIGNALLING EFFECT

One fundamental task of the law is to transmit the values embedded in society. Law can serve societal values either indirectly, or by expressing them directly.[403] On the other hand, the claim that law is based on values is thought to be a 'romantic belief'[404] which fails to acknowledge that law merely represents the legislator's interest, nothing more. For international

[402] Abraham, 'Individual Action', 854.

[403] Yehezkel Dror, 'Values and the Law' (1957) 17 *The Antioch Review* 440–454 at 440.

[404] Leslie Green, 'Introduction', in H. L. A. Hart (ed.), *The Concept of Law* (1st published 1961, 3rd ed., Oxford: Oxford University Press, 2012) at xxx.

law, the discussion around values is even more problematic. Two strands of reasoning can be identified that strive to explain the foundations of international law: first, there are international lawyers who believe in the existence of global values; and second, there are those who argue that international lawmaking is interest-based. The recognition of common values is increasingly gaining ground among international lawyers.[405] They endorse the existence of a common, although thin, set of beliefs that forms the foundations of the international legal order.[406] Although there are not many norms that express global values, the most often named candidates are norms related to respect for human dignity, peace, security and justice.[407] Nevertheless, efforts to ground international law in global or common values are always susceptible to the charge that international society is too heterogeneous to be able to have common values. Universality has been construed as an insurmountable obstacle to shared values; values are taken to be embedded in a particular individual or in a particular community.[408] The international community neither shares the same history nor the same 'common essential values' as national communities do.[409] Thus, the values that are advanced by international law are arguably Western or European, not global.

Those who question or deny the existence of common values see national interests as the driving force behind international law. International law cannot extend beyond the interests of states; the decision to conclude international agreements, accept customary international law and abide by

405 See Otto Spijkers, 'What's Running the World: Global Values, International Law and the United Nations' (2009–2010) 4 *Interdisciplinary Journal of Human Rights Law* 67–87.

406 See e.g., Stefan Kirchner, 'Relative Normativity and the Constitutional Dimension of International Law: A Place for Values in the International Legal System' (2004) 5 *German Law Journal* 47–64 at 56. See also Martha Nussbaum, 'In Defense of Universal Values', The Fifth Annual Hesburgh Lectures in Ethics and Public Policy, February 1999, philosophy.uchicago.edu/faculty/files/nussbaum/In%20Defense%20of%20Universal%20Values.pdf (accessed 20 June 2019).

407 Spijkers, 'What's Running the World', 70–71.

408 Hans Kelsen, for example, states that '[e]very system of values, especially a system of morals and its central idea of justice, is a social phenomenon, the product of a society, and hence different according to the nature of the society within which it arises'. See Hans Kelsen, *General Theory of Law and State* (1st published 1945, translated by Anders Wedberg, Clark: Lawbook Exchange, 2007), p. 8. See also Martti Koskenniemi, 'International Law in Europe: between Tradition and Renewal' (2005) 16 *European Journal of International Law* 113–124.

409 Emmanuel Voyiakis, 'International Law and the Objectivity of Value' (2009) 22 *Leiden Journal of International Law* 51–78 at 53.

international obligations is arguably steered by rational choice concerning the question of how to maximize one's own interests.[410] Recently, a mediating position has been adopted by scholars who advance the idea of 'common interests' as a basis for the international legal order.[411] The difference between common interests and common values remains unclear, however.

Without delving too deeply into the discussion about values versus interests, in my opinion there is a clear difference between norms. Some are simply more important than others, and this fact should be reflected in the way law deals with the violations thereof. Otherwise, the heightened status of some international legal norms remains inconclusive. Moreover, it seems that the contours of specific shared values are discernable. Most often, these shared values relate to the condemnation of genocide or apartheid. Indeed, 'human beings universally share certain notions of what is abhorrent and what is not, what is scandalous and what is not'.[412]

The debate about how international law ought to reflect the gradation of norms has been expressed in the doctrines of jus cogens and erga omnes, but also to some extent in the discussion of the constitutionalization of international law.[413] The hierarchization of legal norms is also reflected in the law of international responsibility. The general rules of state responsibility attempted to construct a hierarchy of norms by means of the notion of international crimes;[414] nevertheless, this attempt was rejected. The remnants of this approach fall back, however, on the techniques of jus cogens and erga omnes. Nevertheless, the purpose of the following analyses is to move beyond the ambit of state responsibility in order to describe and discuss to what degree the alternative constructions of responsibility explored here attempt to signal values, and to what extent they succeed in doing so.

410 See Jack L. Goldsmith and Eric A. Posner, *The Limits of International Law* (New York: Oxford University Press, 2006).

411 See Jean D'Aspremont, 'The Foundations of the International Legal Order' (2007) XVIII *Finnish Yearbook of International Law* 219–255.

412 Jan Klabbers, 'Constitutionalism and the Making of International Law: Fuller's Procedural Natural Law' (2008) 5 *NoFo* 84–112 at 89.

413 According to Anne Peters, one aspect of constitutionalization is that 'certain basic values, such as human rights protection, climate protection, and maybe even free trade, seem to have acquired universal acceptance'. Anne Peters, 'The Merits of Global Constitutionalism' (2009) 16 *Indiana Journal of Global Legal Studies* 397–411 at 399.

414 See Prosper Weil, who argues that '[t]his unity of the normative regime is shattered by the … distinction between international crimes and international delicts', 'Towards Relative Normativity in International Law?' (1983) 77 *American Journal of International Law* 413–442 at 423.

### 4.4.1 Liability and Thresholds of Acceptability

Every international activity or transboundary conduct that poses a risk of significant, transboundary harm must be assessed from the viewpoint of regulation and legality. The legal consequences of such harm need to be determined: the level of risk and the magnitude of harm will guide the decision as to whether the activity in question should fall under the rules on liability or the rules on responsibility. International liability thus plays a twofold role in the gradation of norms and in conveying values. First, it sets the boundary between conduct that is merely inconvenient, and conduct that is so hazardous that it entails a duty to compensate for harm caused by it. Second, it establishes the point at which a specific activity becomes unacceptable. Liability exists in a continuum between activities that entail no legal consequences and those that are categorized as wrongful. It concerns activities that fall between the minimum and maximum threshold of risk,[415] whereas activities exceeding the level of tolerable activity fall under the scope of state responsibility.

It seems paradoxical that international liability should contribute to the discussion of gradation of norms and international values, since its foundation lies in lawful activities. Values are usually discussed in the context of the question of how to separate more important norms from ordinary norms, not in the relation between ordinary norms as such. Yet, at the heart of lawful activities lies a concern for the environment and human health, but equally the desire to tolerate certain activities that are economically beneficial irrespective of their harmful potential. Either way, liability entails a political decision to accept or reject a particular risk.[416] Since it is impossible to eliminate all risks in a society, it means that the decision to tolerate or not to tolerate a certain activity ought to be based upon a discussion estimating both the prospect and range of possible harm. However, scholars have pointed out that such discussion rarely takes place.[417] Instead of discussions about desirability, it appears instead that scientists and technical experts are often given a prominent role. The lack of public disagreement about a certain technology or chemical is often understood as implied acceptance of the involved risks, although it has been shown that often distrust towards a hazardous activity has simply not been articulated.[418] An unwillingness to accept risks may actualize only with the occurrence of accidents involving widespread or devastating effects on

[415] Julio Barboza describes this as the span 'from high probability of causing significant harm to a low probability of causing disastrous harm.' Barboza, *The Environment*, p. 5.

[416] Ibid., p. 9.

[417] Beck, *Risk Society*, p. 6.

[418] Ibid.

people and their society. As noted by Plato, '[a]ccidents and calamities [...] are the universal legislators of the world.'[419]

The categorization of activities along a continuum from lawful to wrongful is, however, neither predetermined nor fixed. Setting the threshold between activities that are acceptable and those that are not can be problematic due to a number of reasons. On the one hand, the available knowledge and information may be insufficient for formulating a stance on the desirability of the activity. On the other hand, the standards according to which activities are deemed either as lawful or wrongful, may vary from time to time and between different actors. In addition, the inherent nature of law defies permanent classifications of activities as either lawful or wrongful.[420] There are always exceptions or excuses to the general rules that make it possible to perceive that which was lawful one day, as unlawful the next. Despite the fluctuant nature of law, there is still a societal need to categorize activities, and liability provides one tool for structuring the debate over what to accept and what not.

#### 4.4.1.1 Inconvenience *vs* Liability

Liability is grounded in activities that pose a risk for harm and thereby become relevant for claims under international law. However, defining 'risk' and 'harm', which are key notions in international liability, is difficult,[421] as is identifying how much risk and harm makes a particular activity 'hazardous'. In general, it has been suggested that hazardous activities entail a low risk for substantial harm. There is wide-ranging agreement that liability does not follow from endurable harm or so-called minor inconveniences.[422]

419 Plato, *The Laws* (trans. Trevor J. Saunders, London: Penguin Books, 2004), cited in Raphael J. Heffron, Stephen F. Ashley and William J. Nuttall, 'The Global Nuclear Liability Regime post Fukushima Daiichi' (2016) 90 *Progress in Nuclear Energy* 1–10 at 1.

420 Martti Koskenniemi, 'Hierarchy in International Law: A Sketch' (1997) 8 *European Journal of International Law* 566–582 at 573.

421 Oscar Schachter, 'The Emergence of International Environmental Law' (1991) 44 *Journal of International Affairs* 457–493 at 463. In 1991, Oscar Schachter noted that 'no single general definition [of harm] has emerged as authoritative' (Ibid). Among other things, risk has been described in the following terms: '"Risk" means the risk occasioned by the use of things whose physical properties, considered either intrinsically or in relation to the place, environment or way in which they are used, make them highly likely to cause transboundary injury throughout the process'. See Special Rapporteur Julio Barboza, *Fourth Report on International Liability for Injurious Consequences Arising Out of Acts Not Prohibited by International Law*, UN Doc. A/CN.4/413 (1988), p. 254, Draft Article 2 (a)(i).

422 Barboza, *The Environment*, p. 11; Xue Hanqin, *Transboundary Damage in International Law* (Cambridge: Cambridge University Press, 2003), p. 7; Schachter, 'The Emergence', 463, who notes: 'To say that a state has no right to injure the environment of another seems quixotic in the face of the great variety of transborder environmental harms that occur every day'.

The acceptance of minor inconveniences falling below the threshold of harm has been explained in terms of the need 'to acknowledge that modern technology has made every State both a victim and a source of inconveniences'.[423] The commonality of environmental interference also makes it difficult to address all levels of harms.[424] An additional reason for not addressing minor inconveniences is the desire to maintain good neighbourliness and avoid ruptures in international relations, which litigation could bring about.[425] However, the acceptance of minor harm has not, however, escaped criticism. It is problematic from at least two perspectives: first, it restricts the obligation not to cause harm; and second, it leaves it to the subjective judgment of the state causing the harm to decide when harm becomes 'appreciable'.[426]

But where does one fix the limit between tolerable harm and harm that must be compensated for if it takes place? Setting this threshold is essential, as for the purposes of liability it determines when the duty to compensate comes into effect. Yet, defining this threshold in general, yet precise, terms appears impossible.[427] The 1965 arbitration award in the *Trail Smelter* case, suggests that the limit should be fixed at 'serious consequence' and when 'the injury is established by clear and convincing evidence'.[428] The ILC has similarly resorted to vague descriptions of when acceptable inconvenience turns into harm. Special Rapporteur Barboza attempted to define legally relevant harm as 'greater than the mere nuisance or insignificant harm, which is normally tolerated'.[429] In its Principles on the Loss Allocation, the ILC set the threshold at 'significant' harm, and similarly in its Draft Articles on the Non-Navigational Use of International Waterways it is stated that harm can be caused as long as it is not 'significant'.[430] Abstract characterizations

423 Barboza, *The Environment*, p. 11.

424 Schacter, 'The Emergence', 463.

425 Barboza, *The Environment*, p. 11.

426 Alberto Székely, '"General Principles" and "Planned Measures" Provisions in the International Law Commission's Draft Articles on the Non-Navigational Uses of International Watercourses: A Mexican Point of View' (1992) 3 *Colorado Journal of International Environmental Law & Policy* 93–101 at 97–99; Schachter, 'The Emergence', 464.

427 Schachter, 'The Emergence', 464.

428 *Trail Smelter* case *(United States of America* v. *Canada)*, Judgment of 16 April 1938 and 11 March 1941, III Reports of International Arbitral Awards, p. 1905, at p. 1965.

429 Julio Barboza, *Sixth Report of International Liability for Injurious Consequences Arising Out of Acts Not Prohibited by Law*, UN Doc A/CN.4/428 & Corr.1–4 and Add.1 (1990), p. 105.

430 See Report of the International Law Commission on the Work of Its Forty-sixth Session, UN Doc. A/49/10 (1994), p. 89, para. 222, Article 7.

have constituted the primary method of defining when inconvenience or unpleasantness turns into harm to which liability rules apply,[431] and special rules on liability in international conventions mostly state that harm must be 'serious', 'significant' or 'appreciable'.[432] However, the threshold at which harm becomes subject to special liability rules varies from one context to another.[433]

International practice sheds light on the difference between minor and significant harm, and the difficulty of establishing it. States and the international community are continuously confronted with new technologies and activities that can be described as hazardous. It is thus up to the international community to decide whether such innovations are so risky that separate liability arrangements should be instigated or not, in order to deal with the risks involved. For instance, progress within biotechnology has resulted in living modified organisms (LMO),[434] which means that modified genes are inserted into an organism, thereby giving it the ability to resist cold, drought or diseases. At the same time, disagreement prevails over the risks involved with LMOs; United States agencies maintain that LMOs are safe, whereas scepticism prevails in Europe over LMOs and their implications for health, the environment and the economy. There are still many open questions about the effects of LMOs, but the possibility of LMOs causing damage due to transboundary movement is recognized. Adverse effects on the environment and biodiversity may include the following: the LMOs may outcompete other species (especially native species), LMOs may produce toxins, and LMOs may contaminate organic crops (resulting in economic damage). It has already been shown that these organisms may be dangerous to both flora and fauna, and potentially even to humans.[435] There have also been allegations that LMOs may cause cancer, allergies, infertility and other diseases.

[431] Kamen Sachariew, 'The Definition of Thresholds of Tolerance of Transboundary Environmental Injury Under International Law: Development and Present Status' (1990) 37 *Netherlands International Law Review* 193–206.

[432] See the discussion in Barboza, *The Environment*, as well as special conventions. For a discussion within the ILC on different abstract terms and their distinctions, see Barboza, *Fourth Report*, p. 258, note 12, which reproduces the relevant discussions of Special Rapporteur Schwebel on the non-navigational uses of international watercourses.

[433] Xue, *Transboundary Damage*, p. 8.

[434] The popular term for LMOs is genetically modified organisms (GMOs), but the usage here will follow that of legal texts, which has favoured the use of the term LMOs.

[435] Walden Bello and Foreign Policy in Focus, 'Twenty-Six Countries Ban GMOs – Why Won't the US?', *The Nation*, 29 October 2013.

It is debated whether LMOs can be classified as a 'hazardous activity' or not.[436] The magnitude of harm may potentially be disastrous, but on a long-term basis rather than through the occurrence of accidents. It seems that the open questions about the consequences of LMOs are the primary reasons for placing the topic on the international agenda. During the discussions on an international agreement on biosafety in general, no incidents of LMO movement with transboundary damages were identified.[437] Consequently, even the possibility of disastrous consequences, although generally considered to be low, has sufficed to name LMOs as a hazardous activity with potential transboundary effects.[438] Indeed, this technology has been compared to other hazardous activities such as maritime oil pollution, nuclear energy, hazardous waste and outer space activities.[439] Nonetheless, the option of prohibiting the genetic engineering of organisms is excluded. Its risks are balanced by economic and social needs; although developing states have worried that they will become biotechnological testing laboratories, at the same time they place hope in LMOs to counter famine. As a result, in 2010 the UN Conference on Biosafety adopted international liability rules for ecological damage resulting from genetically modified organisms.[440]

The liability rules concerning LMOs do not generally follow the models of other international instruments on liability for transboundary harm for hazardous activities. Although they do attach liability to private actors who are in control of LMOs, they neither impose strict liability nor the need for

[436] For instance, the issue was first discussed during the negotiations over an international convention on biodiversity. Due to substantial disagreement, the issue was left to be dealt with under a separate international treaty, which led to negotiation of the Cartagena Protocol on Biosafety. Even during these negotiations, states had differing opinions on the necessity of including liability rules in the convention, which led to the adoption of an enabling clause (Article 27). Based on this clause, liability rules were finally adopted in separate negotiations on what became the Supplementary Protocol. For a presentation of the different negotiations, see David Langlet, *Prior Informed Consent and Hazardous Trade: Regulating Trade in Hazardous Goods at the Intersection of Sovereignty, Free Trade and Environmental Protection* (Alphen aan den Rejin: Kluwer Law International, 2009), esp. Chapter 7.

[437] Cook, 'No Liability, No Protocol', 371.

[438] See M. V. Shiju, 'Standard of Liability under the Cartagena Protocol on Biosafety: Need for an Equitable Regime, in K. D. Raju (ed.), *Genetically Modified Organisms: Emerging Law and Policy in India* (New Delhi: Teri Press, 2007), pp. 79–91 at 88.

[439] Shiju, 'Standard of Liability'.

[440] The Nagoya-Kuala Lumpur Supplementary Protocol on Liability and Redress to the 2003 Cartagena Protocol on Biosafety, Nagoya, 15 October 2010, in force 5 March 2018, UN Doc. UNEP/CBD/BS/COP-MOP/5/17.

financial guarantees. Instead, states are urged to construct their own liability models in their own national law. The lack of a broad consensus on how to construct liability for transboundary damage caused by LMOs shows that the activity is viewed by some as not rising above the threshold of substantial harm. It constitutes a mere inconvenience, rather than falling squarely under compensable hazardous activity. However, the recently adopted Nagoya–Kuala Lumpur Supplementary Protocol has the potential to add value to the concept of international liability in general because it is the first international convention ever to define the level of damage that renders liability rules applicable beyond mere abstract words. First, the Nagoya–Kuala Lumpur Supplementary Protocol explains damage as something that is 'measurable or otherwise observable'.[441] Second, it stipulates that liability follows from 'significant harm', and that significant harm entails the following elements:

> A 'significant' adverse effect is to be determined on the basis of factors, such as:
>
> a. The long-term or permanent change, to be understood as change that will not be redressed through natural recovery within a reasonable period of time;
> b. The extent of the qualitative or quantitative changes that adversely affect the components of biological diversity;
> c. The reduction of the ability of components of biological diversity to provide goods and services;
> d. The extent of any adverse effects on human health in the context of the Protocol.[442]

At least in connection to LMOs, setting the threshold of harm will be clearer. At the same time, the definition will probably have a spillover effect on the general discussion of harm that gives rise to the duty to pay damages.

#### 4.4.1.2 Liability *vs* Prohibited Activities

There is a point at which the harm generated by lawful activities may become so substantial or so costly that the activity itself becomes undesirable. A regime of prohibition may consequently be instituted. This would mean that the boundary between lawful and prohibited acts had been crossed. Liability would no longer be the applicable regime through which such harm would be dealt with, but instead the rules of state responsibility would take over.

[441] Art. 2 of the Nagoya-Kuala Lumpur Supplementary Protocol.
[442] Arts. 2 and 3 of the Nagoya-Kuala Lumpur Supplementary Protocol.

The prohibition of an activity thus transforms liability into responsibility. Some hazardous activities have indeed been prohibited by international agreements; the testing and use of nuclear weapons in outer space is prohibited, as are nuclear tests in the atmosphere and underground,[443] or, for that matter, anywhere.[444]

The general principle that space use and exploration are allowed but qualified by the duty to compensate for potential harm that may arise, is limited by the prohibition of the use of outer space for non-peaceful purposes. This means that states cannot use space to conduct war or test weapons. This prohibition was triggered by the will to exclude such activity even before it had occurred. The rationale of the prohibition thus lies elsewhere than in a cost–benefit analysis. In addition to its potentially damaging effects, the activity was considered completely unacceptable, beyond the values of the international community. Indeed, this prohibition has been described as having a public order–character;[445] it represents the values of all states engaged in space activities.

However, it is not always clear whether a specific activity falls under the liability for lawful acts, or under the responsibility for wrongful acts; some international actors may find the activity in question acceptable, others completely reprehensible. The exact scope of the prohibition of nuclear tests in international law, for example, remains disputed, and its legal consequences are unclear.[446] Is nuclear testing in itself a violation of the international legal order which merits reparation, or is it contingent upon the causing of explicit damage to specific states? There is some indication that nuclear testing has moved towards becoming something altogether unacceptable, from having earlier been a hazardous activity which entailed a duty to compensate. Although there are no special rules on liability for damages arising out of nuclear testing, state practice already proceeded on a tacit understanding

[443] See the Treaty Banning Nuclear Weapons Tests in the Atmosphere, in Outer Space and Under Water, Moscow, 5 August 1963, in force 10 October 1963, 480 *United Nations Treaty Series* 43.

[444] The Comprehensive Test Ban Treaty (CTBT) adopted 24 September 1996 (1996) 35 *International Legal Materials* 1439, has received widespread support but has not yet entered into force because of the non-ratification of nuclear powers such as the United States and Russia. Still, with 184 signatory states and 168 ratifications as of June 2019, it indicates strong support for the prohibition of nuclear tests. A de facto moratorium has been imposed, with only North Korea currently pursuing nuclear testing.

[445] See Myres S. McDougal, Harold D. Lasswell and Ivan A. Vlasic, *Law and Public Order in Space* (New Haven: Yale University Press, 1963).

[446] See Klabbers, *International Law*, p. 36; S. Azadon Tiewul, 'International Law and Nuclear Test Explosions on the High Seas' (1974–1975) 8 *Cornell International Law Journal* 45–70 at 69.

that nuclear testing gave rise to a duty to compensate if damages occurred, irrespective of precautionary measures taken. However, with increased knowledge of the widespread harm caused by nuclear radiation, liability was considered to be an insufficient response to the testing. This was reflected in the international regulation of the subject, first by the Partial Test Ban Treaty (PTBT) in 1963,[447] and later by the Comprehensive Test Ban Treaty (CTBT) in 1996.[448] It is still disputed whether or not these conventional prohibitions have developed into a customary prohibition of nuclear testing. Nonetheless, support for such an interpretation is increasingly common, which indicates that nuclear testing no longer can be categorized as an activity not prohibited by international law; that is, an activity to which the rules of international liability apply.[449]

The use of nuclear weapons has also featured in the debate over what kinds of activities international law should prohibit. It would certainly seem logical not only to prohibit testing, but also the usage of nuclear weapons; resort to such armaments would undoubtedly entail a high probability of transnational disastrous harm. The destructive effect upon humans, the environment and even the climate are broadly accepted facts which justify a complete ban. Indeed, steps to outlaw the use of nuclear weapons have been taken. In July 2017, the Treaty on the Prohibition of Nuclear Weapons was adopted in the UNGA, with 122 signatory states.[450] As it has yet to enter into force, the position taken by the ICJ in its advisory opinion on the *Legality of Nuclear Weapons* still holds true: the usage of these weapons cannot be considered banned in all situations.[451] In circumstances in which nuclear weapons would be used, the rules of liability may instead become applicable.

Grey zones between acceptable and prohibited activities have also emerged outside the armament framework. The cloning of humans is a recent development in biotechnology which exists in the borderland of unacceptable activity, and has caught the international community's attention. The reactions to cloning are steep; it has been noted that 'it is time to ask not

447 Treaty Banning Nuclear Tests in the Atmosphere, in Outer Space and under Water, Moscow, 5 August 1963, in force 10 October 1963, 480 *United Nations Treaty Series* 43.

448 Comprehensive Nuclear Test Ban Treaty, New York, 10 September 1996, not yet in force (1996) 35 *International Legal Materials* 1439.

449 See Weil, 'Towards Relative Normativity', 435.

450 Treaty on the Prohibition of Nuclear Weapons, New York, 7 July 2017, not in force, UN Doc. C.N.475.2017.TREATIES-XXVI.9 (Depositary Notification).

451 *Legality of the Threat or Use of Nuclear Weapons*, Advisory Opinion, ICJ Reports 1996, p. 226.

*if* cloning and inheritable alterations should be regulated, but *how*?'.[452] In fact, cloning meets such fierce resistance that there have been suggestions to make it a new international crime upon which the International Criminal Court would be competent to decide.[453] Yet, the risks are far from established and the worst fears, that human nature itself will be altered, remain open to debate.[454]

### 4.4.2 *The Signalling Effect of International Criminal Law*

When discussing legal responses to serious problems in international relations – be it environmental pollution, corruption or genocide – international criminal law always seems to represent the harshest solution at the international level. This avenue of responsibility overshadows other alternatives because it is a 'highly visible' use of power undertaken on behalf of the entire international community,[455] or as some would argue, even humanity as a whole. This high-ranking position of international criminal law also highlights the importance of the violations that fall within its scope. Only violations that shock the conscience of mankind are labelled as international crimes and fall under the scope of international criminal law.

International criminal law conveys both explicit and implicit messages regarding the international obligations that are covered by it. The basic message that is spelled out by the proliferation of international criminal tribunals – and especially with the creation of the International Criminal Court – is that atrocities should not go unpunished.[456] Individuals and groups are signalled that the commission of international crimes is reproachable, and that perpetrators should fear prosecution. States are signalled that they should legislate for the investigation and prosecution of these crimes, as well as be prepared to prosecute if need be. These substantive messages are easy to identify, but what does international criminal law say on a systemic level about the international obligations that it covers?

452 George J. Annas, Lori B. Andrews, and Rosari M. Isasi, 'Protecting the Endangered Human: Toward an International Treaty Prohibiting Cloning and Inheritable Alterations' (2002) 28 *American Journal of Law & Medicine* 151–178 at 157 (emphases in original).

453 Ibid., note 11.

454 Stephen P. Marks, 'Tying Prometheus Down: The International Law of Human Genetic Manipulation' (2002) 3 *Chicago Journal of International Law* 115–136 at 115.

455 Helen Stacy, 'Criminalizing Culture', in Larry May and Zachary Hoskins (eds.), *International Criminal Law and Philosophy* (New York: Cambridge University Press, 2010), pp. 75–90 at 84.

456 Steven R. Ratner, 'The International Criminal Court and the Limits of Global Judicialization' (2003) 38 *Texas International Law Journal* 445–454 at 447; Klabbers, *International Law*, p. 233; Payam Akhavan, 'Can International Criminal Justice Prevent Future Atrocities?' (2001) 95 *American Journal of International Law* 7–31 at 8.

There is overwhelming support for a general signalling effect of international criminal law.[457] The fact that the acts that constitute international crimes are not only illegal but also criminal, conveys the message that '[a]n international crime is something more than merely a violation of international law.'[458] Yet, it is difficult to grasp the true content of such a signalling function. There are different interpretations of the real meaning behind these messages, and to what they contribute. For example, punishment has been described as communicating meaning 'about power, authority, legitimacy, normality, morality, personhood, social relations, and a host of other tangential matters'.[459] Another factor complicating the discussion on the signalling effect of international criminal law are the intrinsic connections among the different objectives of the discipline.[460] The signalling effect of international criminal law has been discussed both under the expressive function of international criminal law, as well as under general deterrence discourse.[461] In the following, we will therefore focus on the capacity of international criminal law to signal international values and the consequence of delivering messages about these values; that is, the possible long-run, transformative effect these values and their signalling has upon the international community.

#### 4.4.2.1 Value Reservoir

International criminal law represents one effort in international law to present a normative hierarchy indicating certain international obligations as being of more importance than others.[462] It aims to protect those values that the

457 See Wippman, 'Atrocities', 475, who notes: 'prosecutions might also serve an important signaling and educational function'; Claudia Hofmann, *Learning in Modern International Society: On the Cognitive Problem Solving Abilities of Political Actors* (Wiesbaden: VS Verlag für Sozialwissenschaften, 2008), p. 78; Stacy, 'Criminalizing Culture', 89.

458 The Charter and Judgment of the Nürnberg Tribunal – History and Analysis: Memorandum Submitted by the Secretary-General, UN Doc. A/CN.4/5 (1949), p. 45.

459 David Garland, *Punishment and Modern Society: A Study in Social Theory* (Oxford: Clarendon Press, 1990), p. 252.

460 The objectives of international criminal law have generally been described as retribution, deterrence and expressivism. See, the discussion in the 'Introduction'; Drumbl, *Atrocity*.

461 Expressivism can briefly be described as communication of values or attitudes. See Elisabeth S. Anderson and Richard H. Pildes, 'Expressive Theories of Law: A General Restatement' (1999–2000) 148 *University of Pennsylvania Law Review* 1503–1575 at 1505. For arguments connecting the signalling effect of ICL to deterrence, see Cassese, *International Criminal Law*, p. 442, who notes: 'In delivering punishment, the international community's purpose is not so much retribution as stigmatization of the deviant behaviour, in the hope that this will have a deterrent effect'.

462 See e.g., Dinah Shelton, 'Normative Hierarchy in International Law' (2006) 100 *American Journal of International Law* 291–323 at 317. For a discussion on relative normativity, see Weil, 'Towards Relative Normativity'.

whole international community considers the most significant, and therefore collectively wishes to suppress violations impacting those values.[463] As a consequence, international criminal law can be said to constitute 'a common reservoir of universal principles',[464] 'international values',[465] 'elementary international norms',[466] 'common values of humanity',[467] 'constitutive norms'[468] or 'international law's most fundamental norms'.[469] It 'signals the absolute immutability of core values',[470] which explains why the perpetrators of international crimes are even described as *hostes humanis generis* or 'barbarians'.[471]

The prosecution of perpetrators before international criminal tribunals should therefore not be understood only as a means of achieving the goals of retribution and deterrence; instead, the social practice of punishment is to be seen as an end in itself.[472] According to the Durkheimian understanding of punishment, the main social function of punishment is to embody the main 'moral values that society holds sacred, so that crimes that violate this "conscience collective" will tend to provoke collective moral outrage and a passionate desire for vengeance'.[473] This function of signalling what the core values of the international community are is partly embraced in the discourse on expressivism as one purpose of international criminal law.[474] Supporters of the expressivist theory indeed recognize that the practice of prosecuting perpetrators of international crime

463 The Preamble to the Rome Statute speaks of 'the most serious crimes of concern to the international community as a whole'. Robert Cryer explicitly makes international criminal law a question of values by holding that international criminal law 'provides an insight into what values the law is trying to promote'. See Cryer, 'International Criminal Law', 988.

464 Shelton, 'Normative Hierarchy', 295.

465 Stacy, 'Criminalizing Culture', 76.

466 Akhavan, 'Can International Criminal', 13.

467 Sang-Hyun Song, 'The Role of the International Criminal Court in Ending Impunity and Establishing Rule of Law', *UN Chronicle*, vol. XLIX, December 2012, unchronicle.un.org/article/role-international-criminal-court-ending-impunity-and-establishing-rule-law (accessed 20 June 2019).

468 Frédéric Mégret, 'Epilogue to an Endless Debate: The International Criminal Court's Third Party Jurisdiction and the Looming Revolution of International Law' (2001) 12 *European Journal of International Law* 247–268 at 264.

469 Simpson, *Law, War & Crime*, p. 55.

470 Drumbl, *Atrocity*, p. 175.

471 See Alette Smeulers, 'Punishing the Enemies of All Mankind' (2008) 21 *Leiden Journal of International Law* 971–993 at 973; Tom J. Farer, 'Restraining the Barbarians: Can International Criminal Law Help?' (2000) 22 *Human Rights Quarterly* 90–117.

472 David Garland, 'Sociological Perspectives on Punishment' (1991) 14 *Crime and Justice* 115–165 at 119.

473 Ibid., 122.

474 See Drumbl, *Atrocity*.

communicates social values. Accordingly, '[t]he message we get from a law' becomes central,[475] because law reflects 'society's values, what it esteems, what it abhors'.[476] Yet, expressive theories often stress instrumentality; they explain truth-telling and historical narratives that result from the conduct of trials and punishment as a necessity for national reconciliation or for a strengthened rule of law,[477] not as independent goals. International criminal law is nevertheless significant in its own right as a reservoir of values shared by the international community. The law tells us when the threshold of repugnance has been crossed; in legal terms, this means that point where the threshold between wrongful and criminal acts has been crossed. This was confirmed by the Appeals Chamber of the ICTY in the *Aleksovski* case, in which the Court noted that international criminal trials express 'the outrage of the international community at these crimes'.[478]

This signalling effect of international criminal law is highlighted by the conduct of public trials. International criminal law has a symbolic importance that appeals to the wider public. International criminal trials have become popularized, and their global reach ensures that the message of the importance of the law is conveyed to each and every one of us.[479] As Mark Drumbl explains, '[t]here is good reason to believe that the punishment inflicted by an international tribunal operating prominently on the global agenda at the cusp of history has enhanced expressive value in asserting the importance of law, the stigmatization of the offender who transgresses that law, and the authenticity of the historical narrative that ensues.'[480]

The understanding of international criminal law as a reservoir of values draws heavily upon the role played by national criminal law as an embodiment of 'the most fundamental, particularistic norms and values of a local community'.[481] Yet, international criminal law combines elements from two different legal disciplines; as a mixture of international law and national criminal

475 Diane Marie Amann, 'Message as Medium in Sierra Leone' (2001) 7 *ILSA Journal of International and Comparative Law* 237–245 at 238.

476 Diane Marie Amann, 'Group Mentality, Expressivism, and Genocide' (2002) 2 *International Criminal Law Review* 93–143 at 118.

477 Drumbl, *Atrocity*, p. 175.

478 See ICTY, *Prosecutor* v. *Zlatko Aleksovski*, IT–95–14/1–A, ICTY (24 March 2000), para. 185. Other cases which acknowledge the importance of expressing condemnation and intolerance of international crimes are, among others, *The Prosecutor* v. *Drazen Erdemović*, IT-96-22-T, ICTY Trial Chamber, Sentencing Judgment (29 November 1996) paras. 64–65; *Prosecutor* v. *Kambanda*, ICTR-97-23-S, Trial Chamber, Judgment and Sentence (4 September 1998), para. 28.

479 Drumbl, *Atrocity*, p. 175.

480 Ibid.

481 Robert D. Sloane, 'The Expressive Capacity of International Punishment', (2007) 43 *Stanford Journal of International Law* 39–94 at 40.

law, it is dependent on consensuality and 'broadly shareable norms among nation-states'.[482] Therefore, the capacity of international criminal law to express the shared values of the international community is often questioned, because the existence of 'a collective conscience of moral principles shared by all' is repudiated.[483] It is also unclear whose interests and values international criminal law purports to express. Does it send messages in the name of the contracting parties to the Rome Statute, or on behalf of the figurative international community?[484] Or, do the international criminal legal norms represent mankind as a whole, a *civitas maxima*, in which all human beings, by virtue of being human beings, share core values?[485]

These unanswered questions demonstrate the intrinsic difficulties in asserting the existence of commonly shared values in the international community. Even though it seems that the values incorporated into international criminal law may truly be shared, one should be wary of the fact that 'these rules, conducts, emotions, beliefs, and authorities may be the property of particular social groups rather than "society as a whole"'.[486] The rules that embody the core values have emerged in a particular international community, in whose vision some states have participated more than others. Thus, according to David Garland: 'it seems more appropriate to think of this as the political achievement of the dominant cultural groups, whose particular vision of social order has achieved a measure of hegemony, rather than a given set of values that are somehow consensually shared.'[487]

But the criticism levied against the existence of shared values should not be accepted unreservedly. It has increasingly been accepted that certain obligations are more important than others and that positive law reflects the

[482] Ibid.

[483] Mark J. Osiel, 'In Defense of Liberal Show Trials – Nuremberg and Beyond', in Guénaël Mettraux (ed.), *Perspectives on the Nuremberg Trial* (Oxford: Oxford University Press, 2008), pp. 704–725 at 704.

[484] The figurative international community is of course far from monolithic, and denotes 'a broad array of global actors (including but not limited to states), processes, values, and interests'. See Sloane, 'The Expressive Capacity', 53.

[485] Ibid., 48.

[486] Garland, 'Sociological Perspectives', 126.

[487] Ibid. For a similar position, see Martti Koskenniemi, 'Humanity's Law by Ruti G. Teitel' (2012) 26 *Ethics & International Law* 395–398, in which he claims: 'The language of the universal also tends to lift the speaker's values to an altogether exalted position – as the position of "humanity"'.

importance and universality of these norms.[488] The nucleus of international criminal law, which is the protection of human lives from grave and direct assaults upon the physical and spiritual human person,[489] enjoys widespread support as witnessed by the adoption of the Rome Statute. Although the Rome Statute has not been universally ratified, the participation in the conference creating the Rome Statute was nearly universal, and most states that dropped out from the Statute do not categorically reject the existence of international criminal law on a principled level.[490] One should thus separate between rules and process;[491] for example, the critique of the ICC from African states for being biased does not mean that African states are distancing themselves from international criminal law as such. This is evident from efforts by the African Union to construct an African Criminal Court Chamber in the so-called Malabo Protocol, which still awaits ratification.[492] Nevertheless, the Africans do question some substantive issues of international criminal law, one example being the immunity of heads of state. As a result, the AU has attempted to seek an advisory opinion from the ICJ concerning the issue.

What should be recognized, however, is that this 'common bond' and 'shared heritage' between all peoples is very limited.[493] Consensus does not extend beyond the repudiation of extreme evil which results from genocide, crimes against humanity or war crimes. Any further additions to the category of international crimes are difficult to envisage.[494] Moreover, even the protection of core values suffers from open-ended and disputed concepts, which leaves the

488 Pierre-Marie Dupuy, 'Some Reflections on Contemporary International Law and the Appeal to Universal Values: A Response to Martti Koskenniemi' (2005) 16 *European Journal of International Law* 131–137 at 135. For a general discussion of the potential for making universal international law, see Jonathan I. Charney, 'Universal International Law' (1993) 87 *American Journal of International Law* 529–551.

489 See Steven R. Ratner, 'The Schizophrenias of International Criminal Law' (1998) 33 *Texas International Law Journal* 237–256 at 250.

490 It is notable that over 160 governments participated in the international conference of plenipotentiaries in Rome in 1998. Only 7 states voted against the creation of the ICC, with 21 abstentions. See UN Press Release L/2889, 20 July 1998.

491 Mark Drumbl argues: 'All national legal systems know a distinction, albeit often blurred, between process and substance. Supranational legal orders also know such a distinction'. See Drumbl, *Atrocity*, p. 183.

492 For a general discussion, see Gerhard Werle and Moritz Vormbaum (eds.), *The African Criminal Court: A Commentary on the Malabo Protocol* (The Hague: T.M.C. Asser Press, 2017).

493 These notions appear in the Preamble to the Rome Statute.

494 Personal interview with former ICC Judge Erkki Kourula, 28 January 2014.

exact limits of international criminal law undecided.[495] Hence, the expansionist agenda of international criminal institutions may serve to undermine the fragile agreement on what constitutes the most important international norms. One should therefore be aware of the narrow space within which consensus prevails on the fundamentality of certain international norms. At the same time, the existence of a common platform should not be dismissed, whatever one chooses to call it. Bosnian citizens have used the concept of 'humanness' to argue that human beings are different from animals, and therefore should limit their conduct in warfare because excesses are inherently wrong.[496] One should therefore accept the role played by international criminal law in signalling the gradation of international norms.

#### 4.4.2.2 Educative Effect

The role played by international criminal law as a manifestation of core dominant values cannot be viewed in isolation from its function as a pedagogical project. Accordingly, it is frequently argued that the prosecution and punishment of perpetrators of international crimes has an educative effect upon the public. The lessons that are taught through the conduct of international criminal trials are both backward- and forward-looking: international criminal trials construct a historic memory while at the same time they take a stance on where the actors involved should be headed and on what social norms ought to govern their future. For purposes of signalling effect, the latter function of directing future conduct is crucial.

The educational effect of international criminal trials is usually widely accepted and praised.[497] The conduct of trials in general is described as a learning process in which punishment expresses social disapproval.[498] Johannes Andenaes describes the socio-pedagogical influence of punishment in the following way: '[t]he "messages" sent by law and the legal processes

495 J. Benton Heath, 'Human Dignity at Trial: Hard Cases and Broad Concepts in International Criminal Law' (2012) 44 *George Washington International Law Review* 317–366 at 322.

496 See ICRC, People on War, 'Country Report Bosnia–Herzegovina: ICRC Worldwide Consultation on the Laws of War', Report by Greenberg Research Inc., Geneva, November 1999, www.icrc.org/eng/assets/files/other/bosnia.pdf (accessed 20 June 2019).

497 For critical accounts of the educative effect of international criminal law, see e.g., Wippman, 'Atrocities'; Snyder and Vinjamuri, 'Trials and Errors'. However, as Gordon Hawkins notes: 'That punishment can be and is used as an educational technique is, of course, recognized even by those dubious about its value as an instrument of moral education'. See Hawkins, 'Punishment and Deterrence', 557.

498 Andenaes, 'The General Preventive', 950.

contain factual information about what would be risked by disobedience, but they also contain proclamations specifying that it is *wrong* to disobey.[499] Social disapproval may thus help individuals to live up to particular legal rules such as the laws of war, while it simultaneously strengthens the overall rule of law through spreading the message of rule legitimacy.[500] International criminal trials operate as a 'moral educator': they consolidate the shared understanding of the 'moral unacceptability' of repressive politics.[501] The task of international criminal trials, then, is to reveal the inverted morality of those implicated in international crimes, and to make the abidance to law 'a habit which is followed automatically without reflection'.[502]

The educative effect of international criminal trials is intrinsically linked to traditional goals of criminal law. For the most part, this educative effect is subordinated to the objectives of retribution and deterrence. The Jerusalem District Court, for example, acknowledged in its *Eichmann* judgment that the very holding of the trial had 'great educational value'.[503] Yet, it considered this a by-product of the trial, not its main goal.[504] Some scholarly writings, however, emphasize the primacy of the educative effect over retribution and deterrence.[505] Yet, internalization of legal norms should not be taken for granted, nor should the assumption that knowledge and acceptance of the rules will make actors behave according to the rules. In order for individuals and other actors to accept the rules of international criminal law, a few conditions must be met. A first requirement is that the international criminal trials themselves are perceived as legitimate.[506] This has proven to be problematic with respect to both the ad hoc tribunals of the ICTY and ICTR and the permanent ICC.[507] For example, African states have seriously criticized the

499 Ibid.
500 Wippman, 'Atrocities', 488.
501 Drumbl, *Atrocity*, p. 174.
502 Hawkins, 'Punishment and Deterrence', 564.
503 District Court of Jerusalem, Criminal Case No. 40/61, *Attorney–General* v. *Karl Adolf Eichmann*, Judgment, para. 2.
504 Ibid.
505 Osiel, 'In Defense of Liberal Show Trials', 704; Mirjan Damaska, 'What is the Point of International Criminal Justice?' (2008) 83 *Chicago-Kent Law Review* 329–365 at 346, who claims that 'the central mission of international criminal courts should be the socio-pedagogical one'. Sloane, 'The Expressive Capacity', 44.
506 Damaska, 'What is the Point', 345; Alexander, 'The International Criminal Court', 26 *et seqq.*
507 For critiques of the ad hoc tribunals, see Kingsley Chideu Moghalu, 'Image and Reality of War Crimes Justice: External Perceptions of the International Criminal Court for Rwanda' (2002) 26 *Fletcher Forum of World Affairs* 21–46, esp. 38–42.

ICC for having an anti-African bias.[508] The criticism of the African focus of the Court needs to be taken seriously. As of June 2019, there are 122 parties to the Rome Statute. Yet, all cases under investigation save one have concerned African situations and Africans.[509] Thus, the message conveyed by the practice of international criminal trials seems to differ from the idea of the universality of international criminal law. This may have consequences for efforts to build a culture of compliance, since the importance of the understood message is often highlighted in contrast to the message intended.[510]

A second factor which affects the internalization of rules is temporal. Few would deny that establishing a culture of cognizable and respectable rules takes time. Thus, it has been pointed out that educative effects might be discernable only after a longer period of time.[511] This is also linked to the question of norm differentiation; although the core of international criminal law such as discriminate killings is widely if not universally accepted, some of its rules are not as clearly perceived as valid. For example the recruitment of child soldiers is a war crime under international criminal law and can be prosecuted by the ICC, yet it is 'a practice that is accepted as normal in some environments'.[512] Consequently, by way of prosecutorial strategy the ICC can 'seek to prioritize those crimes within its jurisdiction that are lesser known and where the educational impact can be maximized'.[513]

[508] The discontent culminated in an extra AU summit in October 2013, during which the African states threatened the ICC with mass withdrawal. According to President Kenyatta, the Court 'stopped being the home of justice the day it became the toy of declining imperial powers'. See BBC, 'African Union Urges ICC to Defer Uhuru Kenyatta Case', 12 October 2013, www.bbc.com/news/world-africa-24506006 (accessed 20 June 2019).

[509] African countries currently or formerly under investigation are: Uganda, the Democratic Republic of Congo, the Central African Republic, Sudan, Kenya, Libya, Côte d'Ivoire, Mali, Burundi and the Union of the Comoros. The only non-African case under investigation is that of Georgia. However, the geographical scope of the Court's preliminary investigations is much broader, including states such as Colombia, Afghanistan, Ukraine and the Philippines.

[510] Amann, 'Message', 238.

[511] Damaska, 'What is the Point', 346, note 27; Alexander, 'The International Criminal Court', 29; ICC Judge Hans-Peter Kaul has opined that the ICC should not be judged 'in terms of the short attention spans and impatience frequently found in media-dominated societies'. See Hans-Peter Kaul, 'Developments at the International Criminal Court. Construction Site for More Justice: The International Criminal Court After Two Years' (2005) 99 *American Journal of International Law* 370–384 at 384; Catherine Lu, 'The International Criminal Court as an Institution of Moral Regeneration: Problems and Prospects', in Joanna Harrington, Michael Milde, and Richard Vernon (eds.), *Bringing Power to Justice? The Prospects of the International Criminal Court* (Montreal & Kingston: McGill's-Queen University Press, 2006), pp. 191–209 at 201.

[512] Bosco, 'The International Criminal Court', 191.

[513] Ibid., 192.

But even if the rules have been internalized to the degree that they are known and considered to be valid, it does not automatically follow that they will be respected in all situations.[514] The 1992–1995 Bosnian war showed that although rules were widely known and recognized as valid, that did not stop the commission of atrocities. The International Committee of the Red Cross (ICRC) found that while 4 out of 5 Bosnian citizens were familiar with the laws of war, yet there was a 'vast gap between the norms that limit wartime behaviour and practices on the ground'.[515] The breakdown of rules was explained, among other things, with reference to the situation on the ground where nationalist passions and hatred reigned, the fact that people lost their sense during the war, and the belief that the other side was violating the laws of war.[516] This shows the difficulty of abiding by the rules in exceptional situations. International crimes are often committed in a political environment which is manifestly distorted: the society has become criminal in the sense that crimes represent normality and there is little true freedom of action for the individual.[517] In such circumstances, 'it is implausible to believe that criminal law is able to teach people to become heroes' by resisting the machinery of evil.[518]

By way of conclusion, it can be noted that the educative effect of international criminal law is both praised and contested. At best, spreading the message of international criminal law can strengthen respect for fundamental norms concerning the protection of human lives by habituating various actors to the embedded values. Yet, many pitfalls stand in the way of the creation of such a culture of compliance. One major controversy is rarely discussed. It seems paradoxical that, if the rules of international criminal law represent humanity or mankind as many commentators claim, there should be no need to teach deviants these rules. They should already be a feature of each and every one of us by virtue of our being a human being. H. L. A. Hart has aptly stated that 'there is very little evidence to support the idea that morality is *best* taught by fear of legal punishment'.[519] Human beings do not necessarily need (international) criminal law to tell them that the commission of atrocities is wrong.

514 Amnesty International reported in 2014 that half of the state parties to the Convention against Torture still sporadically or systematically torture, despite having ratified the convention. See 'Mycket tortyr trots förbud', *Hufvudstadsbladet*, 14 May 2014, p. 14. This would indicate that other factors than mere knowledge of rules actually informs the conduct of actors.

515 See ICRC, 'Country Report Bosnia-Herzegovina', p. vi.

516 'Country Report Bosnia-Herzegovina'.

517 Koskenniemi, 'Between Impunity', 8.

518 Ibid.

519 H. L. A. Hart, *Law, Liberty and Morality* (Stanford: Stanford University Press, 1963), p. 58 (emphasis added).

### 4.4.2.3 Emerging Cosmopolitanism

International criminal law signals a commitment to internationalism or, to be precise, the belief in cooperation between states which seeks to promote the common good. It represents the idea that through international means one can influence national problems. In particular, one of the explicit objectives of international criminal law is to make states internalize the culture of responsibility. Internationalism thus becomes a means of influence rather than an end in itself. But many scholars see international criminal law, and in particular the ICC, as indicative of something beyond ordinary international cooperation. They assert that international criminal law is an important ingredient and even a step towards real transformation of international society.[520]

From the beginning of the Nuremberg trials, it was declared that international criminal law shows the '"supremacy" of international law over national law'.[521] It was noted in 1949 that the principle of individual criminal responsibility deviates from the basic tenets of international law, and that it would eventually undermine or even put an end to the notion of the state.[522] The manifestation of international criminal law and the creation of the ICC in the 1990s therefore fulfil a historic purpose; the Court allegedly represents true supranationalism, and manages to impose factual restraints upon the political

[520] These scholars include, among others, Leila Nadya Sadat, who sees the ICC as an 'extraordinary achievement' that 'opens a window to the future for humanity at the dawn of the third millennium'. See Sadat, *The International Criminal Court*, p. 281; Robert Cryer, who argues: '[a] perfectly reasonable case can be made that the ICC does represent a new era in international law'. See Cryer, 'International Criminal Law', 983; Mégret, 'Epilogue', 266 notes: 'The Rome Statute … comes as close as the international community has ever been to the realization of a cosmopolitical social contract, in that it proposes to put the sanctioning of certain international crimes that endanger the very survival of humanity above any contingent sovereign interests'; Jason Ralph, 'International Society, the International Criminal Court and US Foreign Policy' (2005) 31 *Review of International Studies* 27–44 at 35, who states that 'the Rome Statute not only forged a new consensus on universal human values, it also created a legal mechanism – the ICC – to independently protect such values'.

[521] See Principles of International Law Recognized in the Charter of the Nürnberg Tribunal and in the Judgment of the Tribunal, Report of the ILC on the Work of Its Second Session, UN Doc. A/1316 (1950), p. 375, para. 102.

[522] 'The Charter and Judgment of the Nürnberg Tribunal – History and Analysis: Memorandum Submitted by the Secretary-General', UN Doc. A/CN.4/5 (1949), p. 40. See also Luban, 'State Criminality', 64, who notes: 'International criminal law represents a major, if incomplete, effort toward deflating the state-worship that defines public international law as a subject'.

world order.[523] Therefore, international criminal law arguably has brought about an important shift from an interstate system to an international institution speaking in the name of the international community or all individuals, rather than states.[524] This shift conflicts with the traditional interstate logic of international law, and thus has the potential to 'turn the international legal order literally upside down'.[525] Indeed, international criminal law 'promises the renewal, perhaps completion of international law'.[526]

Scholarly writings occasionally stress the revolutionary character of the ICC in particular.[527] The radical feature of the ICC lies in its constituting a means of real enforcement with the ambition of protecting individuals, without giving full consideration to aspects of state sovereignty.[528] The ICC can therefore be seen as one step towards the creation of a true cosmopolitan international law,[529] in which the rule of law replaces anarchy and self-interest. Cosmopolitan theories see all human beings as belonging to one single community with shared values; the individual is a 'citizen of the world', not of a specific state.[530] According to Frédéric Mégret, the Court 'seems deeply embedded in a cosmopolitical outlook rather than geared to minimizing the undesirable side effects of sovereign co-existence'.[531] Leila Sadat concurs on the uniqueness of the ICC in the international legal order by claiming that the Rome Statute has the 'status of a constitution', and that the Court is 'the last great international institution of the Twentieth Century'.[532]

523 Leila Nadya Sadat and S. Richard Carden, 'The New International Criminal Court: An Uneasy Revolution' (1999–2000) 88 *Georgetown Law Journal* 381–474 at 385; Kirsten Fischer claims that 'the International Criminal Court… is an innovative form of cosmopolitanism'. See Kirsten J. Fischer, 'The Distinct Character of International Crime: Theorizing the Domain' (2009) 8 *Contemporary Political Theory* 44–67 at 45. Mégret, 'Epilogue', 260; Bassiouni and Blakesley, 'The Need for an International Criminal Court'.

524 Mégret, 'Epilogue', 266.

525 Ibid., 264. In a somewhat similar vein, see Ralph, 'International Society', 28.

526 Simpson, *Law, War & Crime*, p. 55.

527 The term 'revolution' is used by Sadat, *The International Criminal Court*, and Mégret, 'Epilogue'. Samuel Moyn describes the creation of the ICC as an 'unprecedented development'. See Samuel Moyn, 'Towards Instrumentalism at the International Criminal Court' (2014) 39 *Yale Journal of International Law* 55–65 at 60.

528 Mégret, 'Epilogue', 266.

529 Mégret, 'Epilogue'.

530 Drumbl, *Atrocity*, p. 185; Padraig McAuliffe, 'From Watchdog to Workhorse: Explaining the Emergence of the ICC's Burden-sharing Policy as an Example of Creeping Cosmopolitanism' (2014) 13 *Chinese Journal of International Law* 259–296 at 266.

531 Mégret, 'Epilogue', 259.

532 Leila Nadya Sadat, 'The Legacy of the ICTY: The International Criminal Court' (2003) 37 *New England Law Review* 1073–1080 at 1077; and Sadat, *The International Criminal Court*, p. 281.

The descriptions of an innovative, supranational international institution are not entirely misplaced, despite the fact that the Court was established as a result of political compromise and also that it takes state sovereignty into account. The foremost elements in the Rome Statute that serve as the foundation for arguments of an emerging cosmopolitanism are the dismissal of state consent in jurisdictional matters, and that of an independent prosecutor with proprio motu rights to initiate investigations.[533] With regard to the former feature, it appears truly groundbreaking that the ICC envisages jurisdiction over third parties without the consent of the concerned state.[534] Third-party jurisdiction may derive either from a UN Security Council referral, or, it may arise in situations in which non-party nationals have committed international crimes in the territory of a state party to the ICC. The United States in particular has fiercely objected to this as a practice contradicting the consensual basis of international law.[535]

The supranational element of the ICC is further strengthened by the institution of an independent prosecutor, who – by Article 15 of the Rome Statute – is accorded the autonomy to open investigations on his or her own initiative and to decide on indictments. This right, which was never foreseen by the draft statute adopted by the ILC in 1994, was one of the most debated aspects in the negotiations of the Rome Statute.[536] At the same time, it has been argued that '[b]y legally empowering victims of core crimes in a manner that can bypass the society of states the Rome Statute helps to constitute world society.'[537] Indeed, the prosecutor has made use of this right when launching investigations in 2010 into the Kenyan post-election violence that took place in 2007–2008. Yet, safeguards have been installed to limit the prosecutor's proprio motu right. To begin with, the prosecutor's proprio motu powers extend

533 Other features that have been characterized as revolutionary are: the lack of head of state immunity, the permanency of the Court and its unique institutional composition, the decision-making of the Assembly of State Parties which will work on the basis of supermajority, the lessened role of nationality, and the fact that the Court was created outside the UN system. See Sadat, *The International Criminal Court*, pp. 275–281.

534 For an analysis of the ICC's third party jurisdiction, see Dapo Akande, 'The Jurisdiction of the International Criminal Court over Nationals of Non-State Parties: Legal Basis and Limits' (2003) 1 *Journal of International Criminal Justice* 618–650.

535 For accounts of the US position, see Madeleine Morris, 'High Crimes and Misconceptions: The ICC and Non-State Parties' (2001) 64 *Law & Contemporary Problems* 13–66.

536 Luc Côté, 'Independence and Impartiality', in Luc Reydams, Jan Wouters and Cedric Ryngaert (eds.), *International Prosecutors* (Oxford: Oxford University Press, 2012), pp. 319–415 at 402.

537 Ralph, 'International Society', 39.

only to state parties of the Court, and they are further limited by the principle of complementarity. Accordingly, this narrows prosecutorial freedom to situations where a state party is either unwilling or unable itself to act. The prosecution is also subjected to the scrutiny of the Pre-Trial Chamber, which must approve the launch of investigations and confirm the indictments. In fact, it has even been argued that the Pre-Trial Chamber should exercise a general supervisory power over the prosecutorial discretion to exercise his or her right to launch investigations.[538] The right of the Security Council to decide on deferral of cases for a 12-month period places a more particular restraint upon the freedom of the prosecutor. So far, the Security Council has been reluctant to interfere with the Court and has never decided on deferral. The combined effect of the explicit statutory independence of the prosecutor, the Security Council's non-interference, and the fact that all international prosecutors tend 'to escape from their creators'[539] has left the Court enjoying true components of supranationalism.

The practice of the ICC has also demonstrated a willingness on the part of the Prosecutor and other ICC personnel to actively stress the cosmopolitan elements of the Statute. Instead of being perceived as a court of last resort in accordance with the complementarity principle expressed in Article 1 of the Rome Statute, the Court has arguably expanded its role in the direction of greater burden-sharing. By actively seeking self-referrals, the Prosecutors have through a number of expansive interpretative methods minimized the elements protecting state sovereignty.[540]

Notwithstanding the radical features of the Court, along with the desire to prioritize cosmopolitan elements over those protecting state sovereignty, the Court and its role in shaping the international legal order must also be assessed on the basis of its performance. Although it may be too early to tell in which direction the ICC will eventually take international law, proponents of the ICC can hardly deny assessments that the Court's operation has been disappointing, and that a transformed international legal order still awaits. The promise of international criminal law to rise above the sovereign interests of states, or power politics in the UN Security Council, has not materialized. To be sure, the interests of powerful states have prevailed over the protection of victims in the Syrian conflict, for example. Because of

[538] Frédéric Mégret, 'Accountability and Ethics', in Luc Reydams, Jan Wouters and Cedric Ryngaert (eds.), *International Prosecutors* (Oxford: Oxford University Press, 2012), pp. 416–487 at 429.
[539] Côté, 'Independence and Impartiality', 414.
[540] McAuliffe, 'From Watchdog'.

Chinese and Russian vetoes, the Security Council has been unable to refer the Syrian situation to the ICC, despite the widespread prevalence there of international crimes.[541]

Difficulties in rising above the interests of states also plague the ICC after the launching of investigations into a situation. The dependence of international criminal tribunals upon state cooperation, both when it comes to evidence and with regard to the arrest of suspects, has also left the ICC impoverished. The Court has been unable to secure the arrest of the former President of Sudan Omar Al-Bashir, despite its numerous pleas to state parties to act in accordance with the Court's warrant. Further, the Court has been unable to proceed with its cases against Kenyan leaders due to the reluctance of Kenya to cooperate with the Court to such a degree that Prosecutor Bensouda has called Kenya's inaction obstructionism.[542] The Court itself has noted that it has suffered from obstructions of justice – witness tampering in particular – in 'almost all cases in the confirmation of charges and trial phases'.[543] All in all, it must be concluded that although the jury will be out on the ICC for years to come, the promised revolution has so far not materialized.[544] The expectations placed upon the ICC as an institution of global justice have simply been too high.

### 4.4.3 *Conclusions on Signalling Values*

International criminal law is a regime highly suitable for the signalling of values. There is also a broad understanding that this signalling is one of the specific objectives of international criminal law. Its very purpose is to

[541] On 22 May 2014, the Security Council voted on the adoption of a resolution which would have referred the Syrian atrocities to the investigation of the Court. China and Russia voted against, whereas all other members of the SC voted in favour. See UN News Centre, 'Russia, China Block Security Council Referral of Syria to the International Criminal Court', 22 May 2014, www.un.org/apps/news/story.asp?NewsID=47860#.U38xgPmSxVI (accessed 20 June 2019). For a discussion of the ICC and Syria, see Annika Jones, 'Seeking International Criminal Justice in Syria' (2013) 89 *International Law Studies* 802–816.

[542] *Prosecutor* v. *Uhuru Muigai Kenyatta*, ICC–01/09–02/11, Trial Chamber V (B), Decision on Non-compliance (31 March 2014), para. 57.

[543] ICC, Office of the Prosecutor, Strategic Plan 2016–2018, 16 November 2015, p. 13, para. 27.

[544] For a different assessment of the Court's performance, see Fatou Bensouda, 'Reflections from the International Criminal Court Prosecutor' (2012) 45 *Case Western Reserve Journal of International Law* 505–511 at 506 who states: 'The International Criminal Court, by virtue of its mandate and operations in the last ten years, has introduced a new paradigm in international relations: utilizing law as a global tool to promote peace and international security'.

communicate explicit and implicit messages from the international community to the public. The discipline of international criminal law as such stands for the transformation of international society in the direction of lessened state interest for the benefit of humanity. It embodies the idea of a higher order whose ultimate goal is a cosmopolitan world order freed from state interests.

On the contrary, international liability is rarely discussed in the context of values. It relates to ordinary norms, not the most fundamental standards of mankind. There is, however, more to liability than meets the eye. It is a tool for evaluating when harm can be accompanied by legal claims, and ultimately it forms the basis for prohibiting activities that constitute indirect threats to humanity. It has also been set forth here that the boundaries fluctuate between what is acceptable and what is not. This fact must not altogether devalue the role of liability in signalling values. Its function as a tool for exchanging views on desirability remains somewhat helpful.

It is also remarkable that both regimes use similar language referring to the common good or common interest of all mankind. In this respect, they both depart from the law of state responsibility. The language of state responsibility struggles to express the language of humanity or common interests. Furthermore, new social phenomena are often discussed from the perspective of both liability and international criminal law. For example, proponents of cloning advocate for liability because they want to accept the activity in question; the reductionists again resort to criminal law argumentation to show that they are repelled by it.

## 4.5 CHAPTER CONCLUSIONS

This chapter has focused on alternative constructions of responsibility. To begin with, the development of international liability and international criminal law was traced to real-world problems which arguably made these regimes cope better with functionality demands. Having explored their respective origins, the study moved on to a thematic exploration of three themes crucial to a well-functioning and practical responsibility regime. These cross-cutting topics were: social control, collectivity, and signalling effect. Despite the contrasts in the two regimes under exploration, the starting point for the analysis was that – due to their specialization – both international criminal law and international liability can potentially offer more appropriate solutions to the themes explored here than what state responsibility can offer.

*International liability* has developed in response to extreme events that greatly affect the lives of many peoples across borders. Irrespective of the nature of the act, its purpose is to deliver compensation to those affected by serious industrial harm. Indeed, liability is imposed for activities that are lawful and beneficial to societies as a whole, but which still may produce harmful effects. At the same time, controlling the behaviour of actors involved in such activities is one, albeit not the foremost, function of liability. Prevention features commonly in the various liability schemes that have been adopted in different industrial sectors, and its relevance is commonly acknowledged. Still, the principle of strict liability, along with various practices, diminishes the preventive value of liability.

When it comes to dealing with different collectives, international liability displays flexibility. Liability arrangements recognize a variety of actors with differentiated roles in compensation schemes. They manage to hold actors below and above the state level liable by focusing on industry-wide collectives, which involve a combination of different actors such as operators and owners, without forgetting the important role that states can play in disastrous events. Overall, international liability cuts across the division between public and private by means of bringing together enterprises, pools and states into layers of liability.

However, the signalling effect of liability is insignificant. Undeniably, it sets the threshold between lawful and prohibited activities and even between harms that must be compensated and those that must not. In that sense, international liability certainly contributes to a gradation of activities in society. It also brings the importance of environmental concerns to the forefront. Yet, it is clear that international liability does not deal with the nucleus of values of the international community. On the contrary, the signalling function is the core domain of *international criminal law.* International criminal law strongly condemns transgressions upon human lives and dignity by labelling such acts as criminal, and inflicting punishment upon perpetrators of international crimes. Its very aim is indeed to send the message of reproach associated with these offences. It is often hoped that sending these messages to the international community, or to a rebel leader targeted by the Court, will have an educative effect leading to improved compliance. In fact, reliance on the educative effect has been an element of the discussion around deterrence, which has traditionally dominated the international legal discourse on the rationale for international criminal law. Agreement on its inability to provide broad general deterrence prevails in debates on deterrence in international criminal law, although there is also recognition that the deterrent effect can be evidence-based in some limited cases.

The relevance of international criminal law to systematic crimes is questioned at times. Indeed, the present author, in similar fashion to many others, has adopted a critical stance towards the international community's seemingly preferred response to collective crimes such as genocide. Yet, it cannot be denied that international criminal law seeks to recognize the collective character of international crimes. Different concepts and practices have developed that aim to recognize the plurality of actors. Indeed, international criminal law succeeds to a certain extent in taking account of collectivity. Problems start to emerge when individuals are charged and convicted for the acts of large groups, leading to guilt by association rather than individual fault.

In many respects, it seems that the promise of alternative responsibility regimes is held to be high, but that what they actually can deliver is another story. Similar to the law of state responsibility, both international criminal law and international liability have problems internal to their regimes. Still, these regimes appear to be more dynamic than the law of state responsibility. They attempt to take a prospective approach, to deal with the variety of actors, and to contribute to the discussion of what should be allowed and what should be the foremost in a hierarchy of international obligations. They are relevant to all themes analyzed here, but to a varying extent. The core of the matter is not the overall effect they have in all the matters I have chosen to explore; instead, both regimes have their own rationale from which they do not even purport to stray. As particularized regimes, it suffices that they address the problems that lie at the core of their very existence.

# 5

# Conclusions

This study has critically explored the general law of state responsibility in international law. It has discussed the role and standing of state responsibility in its own right, as well as against the backdrop of other forms of responsibility: international liability and international criminal law. The aim has been to situate state responsibility within the myriad of existing responsibility ideas, forms, rules, and practices, and to trace how recent societal transformations have come to affect its standing. The main argument set forth in this book is that the general law of state responsibility is not as uniformly relevant across the spectrum of international obligations as it once was, and that the importance of this law has diminished over time. This lessened significance is a consequence of problems internal to the law itself, but is also due to the strengthening of other responsibility regimes.

The study began with a discussion of the challenges faced by the law of state responsibility. Globalization was highlighted as an initial factor affecting state responsibility. The changed international landscape has called into question the exclusive position enjoyed by states in the international legal system, due to their reduced possibilities of acting as sole centres of power along with the increased leverage of non-state actors. Furthermore, states no longer are strong political units not only because of the rise of other actors, but also because many states suffer from internal rivalry and lack of capacity to perform traditional state functions. A blurring of public and private actors has taken place, which also has had an impact on state responsibility law. Simultaneously, the world has developed in the direction of increased regulation. More topics are being regulated, many of which affect the international community as a whole rather than the interests of single states. A common agenda extends today in areas from fighting climate change to preventing genocide.

But the challenges the law of state responsibility faces are not solely external. State responsibility has developed within and exists in a setting where it has been constantly subjected to a diversity of responsibility ideas and definitions. Its unique international nature has not prevented it from being susceptible to domestic analogy, against which, to varying degrees, it has always been evaluated. Although state responsibility is usually taken to be analogous to private law, traces of criminal law and public law thinking have also featured in the discourse surrounding state responsibility. But these different schools of thought seeking to exert influence on state responsibility are not merely doctrinal: they have also found their way into the actual practice of states. International responsibility has become highly fragmented; it no longer entails the law of state responsibility alone, but also a range of different responsibility regimes. From the perspective of this study, international liability and international criminal law are the most important systems that have emerged parallel to, but also linked with, the codification process of state responsibility. These regimes do not only interact or overlap with state responsibility but, more importantly, they represent different approaches to responsibility in international law.

This diversification of international responsibility has led to opposing developments, in which responsibility is both criminalized and made softer. Generalization is countered with specialization, and the traditional focus on states is met with efforts to expand responsibility to other subjects of international law. This development suggests that an exploration into the role of state responsibility is necessary because of the several tensions that exist in international responsibility as a whole. As a consequence, the aim of this book has been to open for discussion the degree to which the general law of state responsibility is still relevant – or practically useful – in dealing with the complexities of the world as well as with the various expectations that a general system of responsibility should be able to handle.

This book has utilized functionality as the framework for evaluating the law of state responsibility. In this regard, it must be able to deal with the multi-actor and multi-issue world. Second, it must be capable of having an impact on the conduct of a myriad of actors affecting international law and what it seeks to protect. The processes, functions, and aims of the law – rather than the rules themselves – have thus been central to this study.

Having established that the law of state responsibility has many challenges that arguably affect its functionality, this study moved on to explore the different ages and stages of state responsibility. For centuries, responsibility in international law remained only an implicit doctrine that developed over the course of the nineteenth century – through a vast amount of arbitration – into the law of injuries to aliens. Responsibility in its traditional form thus concerned violations of a contested minimum standard of justice, which sought to protect aliens from interference with their rights and properties through the practice of diplomatic protection. The development of substantive and procedural law through arbitration prompted numerous codification efforts and scholarly interest in responsibility. By the turn of the twentieth century, this increased interest and multiple codification efforts caused state responsibility to become firmly established as a separate topic of international law. Still, the road from the traditional law of injuries to aliens to a general and secondary system of responsibility was cumbersome. A gap developed between international practice and doctrine: some scholars had come to envision state responsibility as a unified system pretending to the completeness of international law rather than to the settling of concrete claims between two states. This dichotomized understanding of state responsibility also came to mark the work of the ILC on the topic, since the Commission struggled with finding a suitable approach to state responsibility. The decisive turn came in the 1960s, when the effort to codify primary obligations was replaced with the idea of creating a regime of general and secondary rules of state responsibility. As a result of this shift, the ILC managed to bring the state responsibility project to a conclusion. In 2001, it finalized the Articles on the State Responsibility, the foremost manifestation of customary international law on state responsibility.

The law of state responsibility as articulated in the ILC Articles has been widely accepted and is broadly referenced. In fact, few are willing to question the perceived relevance of the law of state responsibility in the international legal order. Yet, this study has sought to comprehensively examine, from the perspective of functionality, numerous fundamental dilemmas underlying the doctrine. A prime contention of the criticism presented in this book is that the general law of state responsibility suffers from problems in meeting the challenges of the twenty-first century. The multiplication and diversification of actors pose a challenge to the rules on state responsibility, which are constructed based on the division of public and private: an element of diminishing significance in times of globalization. In addition to being required to respond to a more complex operative landscape, state responsibility is increasingly seen as instrumental to a number of goals ranging from reparation to maintenance of international peace. Thus, international legal scholars place diversified aims and expectations upon the law of state responsibility. The transformation from a pure reparative system into a system marked by the multiplicity of functions has been problematic. State responsibility is now expected to fulfil its traditional function of reparation, and at the same time be at the vanguard of international legality and rule of law.

The different functions that state responsibility is expected to achieve are grounded in diverse perceptions of the international legal order. For some, the doctrine of state responsibility represents rules regarding how to deal with breaches so that interstate relations can proceed as smoothly as possible; for others, state responsibility in itself has normative value. This dichotomized understanding of state responsibility affects all aspects of the law, including the grounds, content, and implementation of responsibility. The bilateral, reparative dimension of state responsibility pulls it in a different direction than its multilateral aspect. This division of functions should be clearly considered not only in discourse on the state responsibility, but also when international lawyers discuss concrete cases of wrongful acts. Moreover, international legal scholars often contrast responsibility under international law to its domestic counterparts. In fact, the domestic analogy haunts every aspect of state responsibility. In particular, the function of state responsibility pertaining to the upholding of legality per se receives its strength from national legal systems and the essence of interpretation, application, and enforcement of legal rules in court. Although international courts, tribunals, and other adjudicative bodies have noticeably proliferated in recent years, the bilateral elements of negotiation and diplomacy remain the core mechanisms through which state responsibility is implemented. State responsibility remains trapped in the impasse between the bilateral and multilateral dimensions of international law.

While responsibility regimes often have multiple aims to fulfil, this study has questioned whether or not a system can embrace and effectively protect such different purposes. In my view, especially considering the way in which the codification was finalized, this duality – or even multiplicity – of purpose is problematic. The rules of state responsibility had to be formulated in both abstract and general terms in order to be able to accommodate both reparation and legality protection in a single system. The result was the streamlining of responsibility. The rules were constructed in a way that allowed for variety, but by the same token their content suffered. By streamlining responsibility, the violation of all kinds of international obligations could be brought under one system, but at the same time the system became unresponsive to the needs and features of particular problems. This is the main contradiction of the state responsibility regime: issues of responsibility have been simplified in order to create efficiency through one system. Yet, there is nothing simple or efficient about it. Because the law of state responsibility treats all violations of international law more or less the same, it appears at the same time too mild and too harsh.

Nevertheless, this generality allows state responsibility to be described as one of the building blocks of international law. A general responsibility regime is alleged to be preferable, because it is capable of providing formal rules for dealing with claims between states. State responsibility has been hailed for being a 'meta-language' that alleviates concerns over deformalization and fragmentation so characteristic of the international legal order today.[1] Such accounts, however, rarely pay attention to the variability of state responsibility; the law frequently takes forms outside the ILC Articles, or may feature as a political rather than a legal process.

My contention is that generalization and the concomitant streamlining of state responsibility, affected the very essence of this law. Although state responsibility is formally applicable to all kinds of international legal violations, international practice has shown that its solutions are in reality applicable to the broad range of international issues only to varying degrees. While findings of state responsibility are common in some areas – for example, in the area of human rights and investment arbitration – it has less to offer in cases of transnational pollution, cyberattacks or atrocity crimes. It has also proven less efficient not only within certain branches of international law, but also with respect to important functions of the law. This especially concerns three aspects of functionality which I have chosen to focus on: the ability to influence prospectively the conduct of actors (social control); the ability to respond to various groups or collectives that are on the rise in international relations (collectivity); and the ability to indicate gradation of norms (signalling effect). None of these important features are integral to the law of state responsibility. This void with respect to content has been filled by alternative constructions of responsibility.

This book's exploration of alternative constructions of responsibility has included international liability and international criminal law. They are different in kind, not degree, from state responsibility: they signify an altogether distinct approach to issues of responsibility. In many ways, they respond differently than the rules of state responsibility. Both regimes were explored in this book from a limited functionality perspective – using the three themes of social control, collectivity, and signalling effect. The starting point for the analysis was the claim that, due to their particularized nature, international liability and international criminal law presumably fare better under these three themes than the law of state responsibility. Despite their differing natures, international criminal law and international liability are both able to

[1] Aust, 'The Normative Environment', 27.

respond to situations involving all three themes; although it might be difficult to prove (or disprove) the degree to which they produce real positive outcomes. More importantly, both regimes contain a language of solidarity or common interests – language which the law of state responsibility is unable to fully integrate. These regimes also rely on institutional enforcement, to a degree completely different from the limited institutionalized means available under the law of state responsibility.

Based on the analyses here, it cannot be concluded that international liability or international criminal law can answer all concerns. But this is not as problematic as it is with state responsibility, because these two regimes do not purport to be general solutions to issues of responsibility; state responsibility does, when considered in conjunction with special rules. Hence, the point here is not that one can replace state responsibility with either international liability or international criminal law as a general regime. Instead, I am arguing that one should be open to particularized solutions, to the heterogeneity of international responsibility. Particularized solutions benefit from not striving to be all-encompassing; central features of the system are left intact and are not extended to deal with all possible issues. Moreover, this book's analysis shows that particularized regimes are flexible in finding innovative solutions to new problems. For example, international liability crosses the boundaries of public and private international law. From the perspective of the victim, it seeks to construct a way of responding to problems in the most efficient way, while at the same time seeking to reach the real actors behind a harm. The particularized regimes are far from perfect; yet they seem to respond better – not necessarily more efficiently, but more correctly – than a general regime of state responsibility to certain acts that appear beyond the efficient reach of state responsibility alone. Without such alternative responsibility thinking, the international community would have a far more difficult time in maintaining certain hazardous economically desirable activities, or to express reproach over genocide or crimes against humanity. One should not hesitate to recognize that these particularized responsibility systems with their different approaches have already encroached upon and gradually reduced the sphere in which state responsibility is highly functional.

The examination of different kinds of responsibility regimes has highlighted the significance of the domestic analogy for the field of international responsibility. The domestic analogy has greatly affected the formation of responsibility in international law and the way in which international legal scholars think about responsibility. But the application of the domestic analogy to international responsibility is built on a paradox. On the one hand, it tells international lawyers engaged in responsibility matters that one cannot respond with a homogenous regime to the heterogeneity of actors, problems, topics, and norms that characterize the international community. Hence, despite the entirely different international setting, state responsibility is expected to work similarly to tort law, international criminal law is compared to national criminal law, and liability draws from different theories of absolute responsibility applied on a national level. But on the other hand, efforts to construct one general system of responsibility capable of dealing with all types of violations are also grounded in the domestic analogy. There is a desire to build a complete system of international law reminiscent of the national legal order – one cornerstone of which is a general system of responsibility. Arguably, then, one general system of responsibility – such as that of state responsibility – is necessary in order to make international law a bit more like 'real law'.

Given that ample development outside of state responsibility has taken place in recent decades, it seems justified to critically evaluate the status of state responsibility. Indeed, in recent years an inclination to question state responsibility has become discernable. Many of these efforts primarily seek to improve the existing rules of state responsibility, whereas only a few scholars have been willing to discuss the (in)adequacy of state responsibility law. Yet, these developments – that have in part called into question the classic structure of international law as interstate law – must be taken into account also in the field of responsibility. In my opinion, an inclusive approach which takes into account the plurality of actors is vital, as many non-state actors still fly below the radar of international law. One cannot deal with private actors in all situations sufficiently through the lens of the state. In my view, it is also important to highlight the need for collectivity. Not everything can be understood in terms of individualism; many intermediate actors in between the individual and the state should be considered. Thus, the different and, at times, fluctuating collectives in both international criminal law and international liability seem to handle the contemporary scene of global actors in a more realistic and flexible way than the law of state responsibility does.

Another factor diminishing the power of state responsibility is the abstract language in which it is articulated. Without primary obligations, it seems futile to discuss responsibility. Still, much of the state responsibility discourse relates to academic discussion on the principles of reparations or the rules of attribution. This means that the importance of objectives is relegated to the background. The primary focus should be on what one wants to achieve with state responsibility. Is it upholding legality, compensation to victims, or preventing future violations? A discussion of the purposes of state responsibility reveals the shortcomings of the regime; state responsibility seems to be an academic endeavour rather than a workable solution to important world problems.

As a consequence of the uneven importance of state responsibility across the broad spectrum of subject matters that interface with international law, other regimes are left to deal with the ineffectively addressed issues. This study has sought to show that state responsibility is not functional when it comes to transboundary pollution, climate change, genocide, or crimes against humanity, for example. International liability has become the preferred option in situations where compensation or prevention are the main concerns; international criminal law imposes reproach and punishment for those acts that are considered to be egregious in character. In effect, these two regimes have come to reduce the domain in which state responsibility is viewed as functional. Admittedly, these regimes have not extinguished state responsibility. As long as international responsibility remains underdeveloped with respect to non-state actors, state responsibility will be utilized. It will remain important, but increasingly more reliant on special rules rather than on the general law alone. The core of state responsibility is increasingly being questioned, in particular regarding new challenges such as human cloning or living modified organisms, issues that are not discussed in terms of responsibility for wrongfulness. Instead, options at the extreme dominate discussions; new practices should either be accepted with a concomitant duty to compensate harms, or they should be strongly condemned for transgressing the most important values of mankind.

This study has sought to show that international responsibility is fragmented and that state responsibility no longer occupies the exclusive responsibility position it once held. The actual practice of states, in terms of international rule-making and judicial settlement of disputes, shows that the fragmentation of responsibility is both a normative and practical fact. This fragmentation grants each system of responsibility more importance in some issues, and less importance in others. As a consequence, the ideological significance of state responsibility should not be overstated. A multitude of reactive mechanisms exist today which guarantee that lawbreaking will not go unnoticed or unremedied in the international legal order, thereby guaranteeing that international law is real law – even though state responsibility no longer constitutes the sole response.

Although this study has mainly focused on state responsibility and its role in international responsibility at large, there is much to be said about the proliferation of and increased interest in issues of responsibility in international law. While responsibility as a legal category of international law has witnessed immense development, it remains unclear whether international responsibility will continue to evolve towards a mosaic of different forms and practices of responsibility, and what role international responsibility will play in the overall structure of international law. Many challenges remain to be addressed, one of which is the difficulty in grasping the forward-looking or preventive dimension of the law. A second challenge is how responsibility deals with the divided aspirations of the international community. Yet another dilemma is how international responsibility will address the multiplication of actors in the future. Nevertheless, one thing is certain: building a culture of ex post facto responsibility cannot substitute for the need to address vital concerns beforehand. Responsibility cannot compensate for disagreement on protecting territory-straddling fish stocks, or stop practices that contribute to climate change. It is not alone the answer to stopping wars or systematic killings. International responsibility should not be seen as an ultimate guarantee to solving outstanding issues: at best, it can only be part of the solution.

# Select Bibliography


Abi-Saab, Georges, 'The Uses of Article 19' (1999) 10 *European Journal of International Law* 339–351.

Abraham, Kenneth S., 'Individual Action and Collective Responsibility: The Dilemma of Mass Tort Reform' (1987) 73 *Virginia Law Review* 845–907.

Ago, Roberto, 'Le délit international' (1939–II) 68 *Collected Courses of the Hague Academy Lecture of International Law* 415–554.

Akande, Dapo, 'The Jurisdiction of the International Criminal Court over Nationals of Non-State Parties: Legal Basis and Limits' (2003) 1 *Journal of International Criminal Justice* 618–650.

Akande, Dapo, and Tzanakopoulos, Antonios, 'The Crime of Aggression in the ICC and State Responsibility' (2017) 58 *Harvard International Law Online Journal* 33–36.

Akhavan, Payam, 'Can International Criminal Justice Prevent Future Atrocities?' (2001) 95 *American Journal of International Law* 7–31.

Akhavan, Payam, 'The Rise, and Fall, and Rise, of International Criminal Justice' (2013) 11 *Journal of International Criminal Justice* 527–536.

Alexander, James F., 'The International Criminal Court and the Prevention of Atrocities: Predicting the Court's Impact' (2009) 54 *Villanova Law Review* 1–56.

Alland, Denis, 'Countermeasures of General Interest' (2002) 13 *European Journal of International Law* 1221–1239.

Allott, Philip, 'State Responsibility and the Unmaking of International Law' (1988) 29 *Harvard International Law Journal* 1–26.

Alston, Philip, 'The Myopia of the Handmaidens: International Lawyers and Globalization' (1997) 3 *European Journal of International Law* 435–448.

Amann, Diane Marie, 'Group Mentality, Expressivism, and Genocide' (2002) 2 *International Criminal Law Review* 93–143.

Amann, Diane Marie, 'Message as Medium in Sierra Leone' (2001) 7 *ILSA Journal of International and Comparative Law* 237–245.

Ambos, Kai, 'Article 25: Individual Criminal Responsibility', in Otto Triffterer (ed.), *Commentary on the Rome Statute of the International Criminal Court* (2nd ed., Munich: C. H. Beck, 2008), pp. 743–770.

Ambos, Kai, 'The ICC and Common Purpose – What Contribution Is Required under Article 25(3)(d)?', in Carsten Stahn (ed.), *The Law and Practice of the International Criminal Court* (Oxford: Oxford University Press, 2015), pp. 592–607.

Andenaes, Johannes, 'The General Preventive Effects of Punishment' (1966) 114 *University of Pennsylvania Law Review* 949–983.

Andenaes, Johs, 'General Prevention – Illusion or Reality?' (1952) 43 *Journal of Criminal Law and Criminology* 176–198.

Anderson, Elisabeth S., and Pildes, Richard H., 'Expressive Theories of Law: A General Restatement' (1999–2000) 148 *University of Pennsylvania Law Review* 1503–1575.

Anderson, Kenneth, 'The Ottawa Convention Banning Landmines, the Role of International Non-governmental Organizations and the Idea of International Civil Society' (2000) 11 *European Journal of International Law* 91–120.

Annas, Georg J., Andrews, Lori B., and Isasi, Rosari M., 'Protecting the Endangered Human: Toward an International Treaty Prohibiting Cloning and Inheritable Alterations' (2002) 28 *American Journal of Law & Medicine* 151–178.

Anscombe, Gertrude Elisabeth Margareta, 'Modern Moral Philosophy' (1958) 33 *Philosophy* 1–16.

Anzilotti, Dionisio, *Corso di diritto internazionale* (Rome: Atheneum, 1912).

Anzilotti, Dionisio, *Cours de droit international* (trans. Gidel, 1929, Paris: Panthéon-Assas/LGDJ, 1999).

Anzilotti, Dionisio, 'La responsabilité internationale des États a raison des dommages soufferts par des étrangers' (1906) 13 *Revue generale de droit international public* 5–29.

Anzilotti, Dionisio, *Teoria generale della responsabilità dello stato nel diritto internazionale* (Florence: F. Lumachi Libraio-editore, 1902).

Arendt, Hannah, 'Eichmann in Jerusalem', *The New Yorker*, 16 February 1963, p. 40.

Aust, Helmut Philipp, *Complicity and the Law of State Responsibility* (Cambridge: Cambridge University Press, 2011).

Aust, Helmut Philipp, 'The Normative Environment for Peace – On the Contribution of the ILC's Articles on State Responsibility', in Georg Nolte (ed.), *Peace through International Law: The Role of the International Law Commission. A Colloquium at the Occasion of Its Sixtieth Anniversary* (Dordrecht: Springer, 2009), pp. 13–46.

Austin, John, *The Province of Jurisprudence Determined and the Uses of the Study of Jurisprudence* (1st published 1832, London: Weidenfeld and Nicolson, 1954).

Avant, Deborah D., Finnemore, Martha, and Sell, Susan K., 'Who Governs the Globe?', in Deborah D. Avant, Martha Finnemore and Susan K. Sell (eds.), *Who Governs the Globe?* (Cambridge: Cambridge University Press, 2010), pp. 1–31.

Bahar, Mohamed Elewa, '"Just Convict Everyone!" – Joint Perpetration: From Tadic to Stakic and Back' (2006) 6 *International Criminal Law Review* 293–302.

Barboza, Julio, *The Environment, Risk and Liability in International Law* (Leiden, Boston: Martinus Nijhoff Publishers, 2011).

Barker, John, 'The Different Forms of Reparation: Compensation', in James Crawford, Alain Pellet and Simon Olleson (eds.), *The Law of International Responsibility* (Oxford: Oxford University Press, 2010), pp. 599–611.

Barkun, Michael, 'International Law from a Functional Perspective' (1970) 1 *Georgia Journal of International and Comparative Law* 19–28.

Barstow Magraw, Daniel, 'Transboundary Harm: The International Law Commission's Study of "International Liability"' (1986) 80 *American Journal of International Law* 305–330.

Bartholomeusz, Lance, 'The Amicus Curiae before International Courts and Tribunals' (2005) 5 *Non-State Actors and International Law* 209–286.

Bassiouni, M. Cherif, and Blakesley, Christopher L., 'The Need for an International Criminal Court in the New International World Order' (1992–1993) 25 *Vanderbilt Journal of Transnational Law* 151–182.

Baxter, Richard R., 'Reflections on Codification in Light of the International Law of State Responsibility for Injuries to Aliens' (1964–1965) 16 *Syracuse Law Review* 745–761.

Beaucillon, Charlotte, Fernandez, Julian, and Raspail, Hélèn, 'State Responsibility for Conduct of Private Military and Security Companies', in Francesco Francioni and Natalino Ronzitti (eds.), *War by Contract: Human Rights, Humanitarian Law, and Private Contractors* (New York: Oxford University Press, 2011), pp. 396–420.

Beccaria, Cesare, *Of Crimes and Punishments* (Dei delitti e delle pene) (trans. Edward D. Ingraham, Philadelphia: R. Bell, 1774).

Beck, Ulrich, *Risk Society: Towards a New Modernity* (trans. Mark Ritter, London: Sage Publishing, 1992).

Becker, Tal, *Terrorism and the State: Rethinking the Rules of State Responsibility* (Oxford and Portland, OR: Hart Publishing, 2005).

Bederman, David, 'Counterintuiting Countermeasures' (2002) 96 *American Journal of International Law* 817–832.

Bedjaoui, Mohammed, 'Responsibility of States: Fault and Strict Liability', in Rudolf Bernhardt (ed.), *Encyclopedia of International Law*, vol. IV (Amsterdam: North Holland, 1984), pp. 212–216.

Bennett, Paul, 'Mutual Risk: P & I Insurance Clubs and Maritime Safety and Environmental Performance' (2001) 25 *Marine Policy* 13–21.

Bensouda, Fatou, 'Reflections from the International Criminal Court Prosecutor' (2012) 45 *Case Western Reserve Journal of International Law* 505–511.

Bentham, Jeremy, *An Introduction to the Principles of Morals and Legislation* (London: The Athlone Press, 1789).

Benton Heath, J., 'Human Dignity at Trial: Hard Cases and Broad Concepts in International Criminal Law' (2012) 44 *George Washington International Law Review* 317–366.

Benzing, Markus, 'The Complementarity Regime of the International Criminal Court: International Criminal Justice between State Sovereignty and the Fight against Impunity' (2003) 7 *Max Planck Yearbook of United Nations Law* 591–632.

Berger, Peter, *Invitation to Sociology: A Humanistic Perspective* (Doubleday: Anchor Books, 1963).

Besson, Samantha, 'State and Individual Secondary Liability in Case of International Organizations' Responsibility: The Challenge of Unfairness Unveiled' (2017) 1 *Rivista di filosofia del diritto* 51–78.

Betlehem, Daniel, 'The Secret Life of International Law' (2012) 1 *Cambridge Journal of International and Comparative Law* 23–36.

Bianchi, Andrea, 'Choice and (the Awareness of) Its Consequences: The ICJ's "Structural Bias" Strikes Again in the Marshall Islands Case' (2017) 111 *American Journal of International Law Unbound* 81–87.

Bianchi, Andrea, 'State Responsibility and Criminal Liability of Individuals', in Antonio Cassese (ed.), *The Oxford Companion to International Criminal Justice* (New York: Oxford University Press, 2009), pp. 16–24.

Bigi, Giulia, 'Joint Criminal Enterprise in the Jurisprudence of the International Criminal Tribunal for the Former Yugoslavia and the Prosecution of Senior Political and Military Leaders: The Krajisnik Case' (2010) 14 *Max Planck Yearbook of United Nations Law* 51–83.

Bird, Annie, 'Third State Responsibility for Human Rights Violations' (2011) 21 *European Journal of International Law* 883–900.

Birkett, Norman, 'International Legal Theories Evolved at Nuremberg', in Guénaël Mettraux (ed.), *Perspectives on the Nuremberg Trial* (New York: Oxford University Press, 2008), pp. 299–307.

Birnie, Patricia W., and Boyle, Alan E., *International Law & the Environment* (2nd ed., Oxford: Oxford University Press, 2002).

Black, Donald, *The Behavior of Law* (1st ed. 1976, special ed. 2010, Bingley: Emerald Group Publishing Limited, 2010).

Bleeker, Arne, 'Does the Polluter Pay? The Polluter-Pays Principle in the Case Law of the European Court of Justice' (2009) 18 *European Energy and Environmental Law Review* 289–306.

Blum, Gabriella, and Lockwood, Natalie J., 'Earthquakes and Wars', in Larry May and Elisabeth Edenberg (eds.), *Jus Post Bellum and Transitional Justice* (New York: Cambridge University Press, 2013), pp. 178–216.

Boas, Gideon, Bischoff, James L., and Reid, Natalie L., *International Criminal Law Practitioner Library, Volume I: Forms of Responsibility in International Criminal Law* (Cambridge: Cambridge University Press, 2007).

Bodansky, Daniel, and Crook, John R., 'Symposium: The ILC's State Responsibility Articles. Introduction and Overview' (2002) 96 *American Journal of International Law* 773–791.

Bollecker-Stern, Brigitte, *Le préjudice dans la théorie de la responsabilité internationale* (Editions A. Paris: Pedone, 1973).

Bonafè, Beatrice I., *The Relationship between State and Individual Responsibility for International Crimes* (Leiden and Boston: Martinus Nijhoff Publishers, 2009).

Bonafè, Beatrice I., 'Reassessing Dual Responsibility for International Crimes' (2016) 73 *Seqüênica (Florianópolis)* 19–36.

Boon, Kirsten E., 'The Law of Responsibility: A Response to Fragmentation?' (2012) 25 *Global Business and Development Law Journal* 395–407.

Boon, Kristen E., 'Are Control Tests Fit for the Future: The Slippage Problem in Attribution Doctrines' (2014) 15 *Melbourne Journal of International Law* 330–377.

Borchard, Edwin, 'The "Minimum" Standard of the Treatment of Aliens' (1939) 33 *Proceedings of the American Society of International Law at Its Annual Meeting* 51–63.

Borchard, Edwin, 'International Law and International Organization' (1947) 41 *American Journal of International Law* 106–108.

Borchard, Edwin M., 'Theoretical Aspects of the International Responsibility of States' (1929) *Max-Planck-Institut für ausländisches öffentliches Recht und Völkerrecht* 223–250.

Bosco, David, 'The International Criminal Court and Crime Prevention: Byproduct or Conscious Goal?' (2010–2011) 19 *Michigan State Journal of International Law* 163–200.

Boyle, Alan, 'Liability for Injurious Consequences of Acts Not Prohibited by International Law', in James Crawford, Alain Pellet and Simon Olleson (eds.), *Oxford Commentaries on International Law: The Law of International Responsibility* (Oxford: Oxford University Press, 2010), pp. 95–104.

Boyle, Alan, and Chinkin, Christine, *The Making of International Law* (Oxford: Oxford University Press, 2007).

Boyle, Alan E., 'State Responsibility and International Liability for Injurious Consequences of Acts Not Prohibited by International Law: A Necessary Distinction?' (1990) 39 *International and Comparative Law Quarterly* 1–26.

Boyle, Alan E., 'Globalising Environmental Liability: The Interplay of National and International Law' (2005) 17 *Journal of Environmental law* 3–26.

Brownlie, Ian, *State Responsibility: Part I* (Oxford: Clarendon Press, 1983).

Brownlie, Ian, *Principles of Public International Law* (4th ed., Oxford: Clarendon Press, 1990).

Brownlie, Ian, *Principles of International Law* (6th ed., Oxford: Oxford University Press, 2003).

Brownlie, Ian, 'State Responsibility and the International Court of Justice', in Malgosia Fitzmaurice and Dan Sarooshi (eds.), *Issues of State Responsibility before International Judicial Institutions* (Oxford and Portland, OR: Bloomsbury, 2004), pp. 11–18.

Brunnée, Jutta, 'International Legal Accountability through the Lens of the Law of State Responsibility' (2005) XXXVI *Netherlands Yearbook of International Law* 21–55.

Burke-White, William, 'Proactive Complementarity: The International Criminal Court and National Courts in the Rome System of International Justice' (2008) 49 *Harvard International Law Journal* 53–108.

Cançado Trindade, Antônio Augusto, 'Complementarity between State Responsibility and Individual Responsibility for Grave Violations of Human Rights: The Crime of State Revisited', in Maurizio Ragazzi (ed.), *International Responsibility Today: Essays in Memory of Oscar Schachter* (Leiden: Martinus Nijhoff Publishers, 2005), pp. 253–269.

Cane, Peter, *Responsibility in Law and Morality* (Oxford and Portland, OR: Hart Publishing, 2002).

Caron, David D., 'The Basis of Responsibility: Attribution and Other Trans-Substantive Rules', in Richard B. Lillich and Daniel Barstow Magraw (eds.), *The Iran-United States Claims Tribunal: Its Contribution to the Law of State Responsibility* (New York: Transnational Publishers, 1998), pp. 109–184.

Caron, David D., 'The ILC Articles on State Responsibility: The Paradoxical Relationship between Form and Authority' (2002) 96 *American Journal of International Law* 857–873.

Cassesse, Antonio, 'On the Current Trends towards Criminal Prosecution and Punishment of Breaches of International Humanitarian Law' (1998) 9 *European Journal of International Law* 2–17.

Cassese, Antonio, *International Criminal Law* (2nd ed., Oxford: Oxford University Press, 2008).

Cassese, Antonio, *International Law* (Oxford and New York: Oxford University Press, 2001).

Cesar, Sylvia, 'Privatization of Water: Evaluating Its Performance in the Developing World' (2019) 90 *Annals of Public and Cooperative Economics* 5–23.

Charney, Jonathan I., 'Universal International Law' (1993) 87 *American Journal of International Law* 529–551.

Charney, Jonathan I., 'Editorial Comments: International Criminal Court and the Role of Domestic Courts' (2001) 95 *American Journal of International Law* 120–123.

Charnovitz, Steve, 'The WTO's Problematic "Last Resort" Against Noncompliance' (2002) 57 *The Swiss Review of International Economic Relations* 409–440.

Chayes, Abram, and Handler Chayes, Antonia, *The New Sovereignty: Compliance with International Regulatory Agreements* (Cambridge: Harvard University Press, 1995).

Chideu Moghalu, Kingsley, 'Image and Reality of War Crimes Justice: External Perceptions of the International Criminal Court for Rwanda' (2002) 26 *Fletcher Forum of World Affairs* 21.

Chinen, Mark, 'Complexity Theory and the Horizontal and Vertical Dimensions of State Responsibility' (2014) 25 *European Journal of International Law* 703–732.

Chinkin, Christine, 'A Critique of the Public/Private Dimension' (1999) 10 *European Journal of International Law* 387–395.

Chinkin, Christine, 'The Continuing Occupation: Issues of Joint and Several Liability and Effective Control', in Phil Shiner and Andrew Williams (eds.), *The Iraq War and International Law* (Oxford and Portland, OR: Hart Publishing, 2008), pp. 161–183.

Christenson, Gordon A., 'The Doctrine of Attribution in State Responsibility', in R. B. Lillich (ed.), *International Law of State Responsibility for Injuries to Aliens* (Charlottesville: University of Virginia Press, 1983), pp. 321–360.

Christenson, Gordon A., 'Attributing Conduct to the State: Is Anything New?' (1990) 84 *ASIL Proceedings* 51–59.

Churchill, Robin R., and Lowe, Alan Vaughan, *The Law of the Sea* (2nd ed., Manchester: Manchester University Press, 1988).

Clapham, Andrew, 'The Question of Jurisdiction under International Criminal Law over Legal Persons: Lessons from the Rome Conference on an International Criminal Court', in Menno Kamminga and S. Zia-Zarifi (eds.), *Liability of Multinational Corporations Under International Law* (The Hague: Kluwer Law International, 2000), pp. 139–195.

Clapham, Andrew, *Human Rights Obligations of Non-State Actors* (Oxford: Oxford University Press, 2006).

Clapham, Andrew, 'Extending International Criminal Law beyond the Individual to Corporations and Armed Opposition Groups' (2008) 6 *Journal of International Criminal Justice* 899–926.

Clarke, Lisa, 'Global Health Public-Private Partnerships: Better Protecting Against Disease but Creating a Gap in Responsibility under International Law' (2009) XX *Finnish Yearbook of International Law* 349–372.

Clarkson, Christopher M. V., *Understanding Criminal Law* (4th ed., London: Sweet & Maxwell, 2005).

Coffee, Jr., John C., '"No Soul to Damn: No Body to Kick": An Unscandalized Inquiry into the Problem of Corporal Punishment' (1980–1981) 79 *Michigan Law Review* 386–459.

Colandrea, Valerio, 'On the Power of the European Court of Human Rights to Order Specific Non-monetary Measures: Some Remarks in Light of Assanidze, Broniowski and Sejdovic Cases' (2007) 7 *Human Rights Law Review* 396–411.

Condorelli, Luigi, 'Les attentats du 11 septembre et leurs suites: où va le droit?' (2001) 105 *Revue Générale de Droit International Public* 829–848.

Conetti, Giorgio, 'State's Crime and Individuals' Crimes: What Relationship?' in Mauro Politi and Giuseppe Nesi (eds.), *The Rome Statute of the ICC: A Challenge to Impunity* (Dartmouth, Aldershot: Ashgate, 2001), pp. 131–133.

Contreras-Garduño, Diana, 'Defining Beneficiaries of Collective Reparations: The Experience of the IACtHR' (2012) 4 *Amsterdam Law Forum* 40–57.

Cook, Kate, 'No Liability, No Protocol', in Christoph Bail, Robert Falkner and Helen Marquard (eds.), *The Cartagena Protocol on Biosafety: Reconciling Trade in Biotechnology with Environment & Development* (London: Earthscan Publications, 2002), pp. 371–384.

Côté, Luc, 'Independence and Impartiality', in Luc Reydams, Jan Wouters and Cedric Ryngaert (eds.), *International Prosecutors* (Oxford: Oxford University Press, 2012), pp. 319–415.

Cottereau, Gilles, 'Système juridique et notion de responsabilité', in Société française pour le droit international (ed.), *La responsabilité dans le système international: Colloque du mans* (Paris: Pedone, 1991), pp. 3–90.

Crawford, James, 'Responsibility to the International Community as a Whole' (2001) 8 *Indiana Journal of Global Legal Studies* 303–322.

Crawford, James, 'The ILC's Articles on Responsibility of States for Internationally Wrongful Acts: A Retrospect' (2002) 96 *American Journal of International Law* 874–890.

Crawford, James, 'International Law as an Open System', in James Crawford (ed.), *International Law as an Open System: Selected Essays* (London: Cameron May, 2002), pp. 17–38.

Crawford, James, *The International Law Commission's Articles on State Responsibility: Introduction, Text and Commentaries* (Cambridge: Cambridge University Press, 2002).

Crawford, James, 'Responsibility of States and Non-State Actors', Speech at the Biennial Conference of the Japanese Association of International Law, Tokyo, 14 May 2005.

Crawford, James, 'International Crimes of States', in James Crawford, Alain Pellet and Simon Olleson (eds.), *The Law of International Responsibility* (Oxford: Oxford University Press, 2010), pp. 405–414.

Crawford, James, 'Investment Arbitration and the ILC Articles on State Responsibility' (2010) 25 *ICSID Review-Foreign Investment Law Journal* 127–199.

Crawford, James, 'The System of International Responsibility', in James Crawford, Alain Pellet and Simon Olleson (eds.), *The Law of International Responsibility* (Oxford: Oxford University Press, 2010), pp. 17–25.

Crawford, James, 'Responsibility for Breaches of Commmunitarian Norms: An Appraisal of Article 48 of the ILC Articles on Responsibility of States for Internationally Wrongful Acts', in Ulrich Fastenrath et al. (eds.), *From Bilateralism to Community Interest: Essays in Honour of Bruno Simma* (Oxford: Oxford University Press, 2011), pp. 224–240.

Crawford, James, 'The International Court of Justice and the Law of State Responsibility', in Christian J. Tams and James Sloan (eds.), *The Development of International Law by the International Court of Justice* (Oxford: Oxford University Press, 2013), pp. 71–86.

Crawford, James, *State Responsibility: The General Part* (Cambridge: Cambridge University Press, 2013).

Crawford, James, Grant, Thomas, and Messineo, Francesco, 'Towards an International Law of Responsibility: Early Doctrine', in Laurence Boisson de Chazournes and Marcelo Kohen (eds.), *International Law and the Quest for Its Implementation: Liber Amicorum Vera Gowlland-Debbas* (Leiden: Martinus Nijhoff Publishers, 2010), pp. 377–402.

Crawford, James, and Olleson, Simon, 'The Nature and Forms of International Responsibility', in Malcolm D. Evans (ed.), *International Law* (Oxford: Oxford University Press, 2006), pp. 451–477.

Crawford, James, Pellet, Alain, and Olleson, Simon (eds.), *The Law of International Responsibility* (Oxford: Oxford University Press, 2010).

Crawford, James, Pellet, Alain, and Olleson, Simon, 'Preface', in James Crawford, Alain Pellet and Simon Olleson (eds.), *The Law of International Responsibility* (Oxford: Oxford University Press, 2010), pp. v–vii.

Crawford, James, and Watkins, Jeremy, 'International Responsibility', in Samantha Besson and John Tasioulas (eds.), *The Philosophy of International Law* (New York: Oxford University Press, 2010), pp. 283–298.

Creutz, Katja, Transnational Privatised Security: The Erik Castrén Institute Research Reports 19/2006 (Helsinki: The Erik Castrén Institute, 2006).

Creutz, Katja, 'The Problem of Regulation and the Role of the International Criminal Court', in Thomas Mandrup (ed.), *Privatisation of Security: The Concept, Its History and Its Contemporary Application* (Copenhagen: Conference Proceedings, Royal Danish Defence College, 2012), pp. 63–81.

Creutz, Katja, 'International Responsibility and Problematic Law-making', in Rain Liivoja and Jarna Petman (eds.), *International Law-making: Essays in Honour of Jan Klabbers* (Oxon: Routledge, 2014), pp. 171–189.

Cronin-Furman, Kate, 'Managing Expectations: International Criminal Trials and the Prospects for Deterrence of Mass Atrocities' (2013) *International Journal of Transitional Justice* 434–454.

Cryer, Robert, *Prosecuting International Crimes: Selectivity and the International Criminal Law Regime* (Cambridge: Cambridge University Press, 2005).

Cryer, Robert, 'International Criminal Law vs State Sovereignty: Another Round?' (2006) *European Journal of International Law* 979–1000.

Cupido, Marjolein, 'Common Purpose Liability versus Joint Perpetration: A Practical View on the ICC's Hierarchy of Liability Theories' (2016) 29 *Leiden Journal of International Law* 897–915.

Cutler, Claire, *Private Power and Global Authority: Transnational Merchant Law in the Global Political Economy* (Cambridge: Cambridge University Press, 2003).

Dahan, Yossi, Lerner, Hanna, and Milman-Sivan, Fain, 'Shared Responsibility and the International Labour Organization' (2012–2013) 34 *Michigan Journal of International Law* 675–743.

Damaska, Mirjan, 'What Is the Point of International Criminal Justice?' (2008) 83 *Chicago-Kent Law Review* 329–365.

Darcy, Shane, *Collective Responsibility and Accountability under International Law* (Leiden: Brill, 2007).

D'Aspremont, Jean, 'The Foundations of the International Legal Order' (2007) XVIII *Finnish Yearbook of International Law* 219–255.

D'Aspremont, Jean, Nollkaemper, André, Plakokefalos, Ilias, and Ryngaert, Cedric, 'Sharing Responsibility between Non-State Actors and States in International Law: Introduction' (2015) 62 *Netherlands International Law Review* 49–67.

Dawidowicz, Martin, *Third-Party Countermeasures in International Law* (Cambridge: Cambridge University Press, 2017).

de Aréchaga, Jiménez, 'International Law in the Past Third of a Century' (1978) 159 *Collected Courses of the Hague Academy of International Law* 1–343.

DeFrancia, Cristian, 'Due Process in International Criminal Courts: Why Procedure Matters' (2001) 87 *Virginia Law Review* 1381–1489.

de La Fayette, Louise Angélique, 'International Liability for Damage to the Environment', in Malgosia Fitzmaurice, David M. Ong and Panos Merkouris (eds.), *Research Handbook on International Environmental Law* (Cheltenham: Edward Elgar Publishing Ltd, 2010), pp. 320–360.

de Sadeleer, Nicolas, 'The Polluter-pays Principle in EU Law–Bold Case Law and Poor Harmonisation', in Christina Voigt, Inge Lorange Backer, and Ole Kristian Fauchald (eds.), *Pro Natura: Festskrift til Hans Christian Bugge* (Oslo: Universitetsforlaget, 2012), pp. 405–419.

Desierto, Diane A., 'Rawlsian Fairness and International Arbitration' (2015) 36 *University of Pennsylvania Journal of International Law* 939–993.

de Than, Claire, and Shorts, Edwin, *International Criminal Law and Human Rights* (London: Sweet and Maxwell, 2003).

de Vattel, Emmerich, *The Law of Nations: Or, Principles of the Law of Nature, Applied to the Conduct and Affairs of Nations and Sovereigns* (1st published in 1758, trans. Joseph Chitty, Philadelphia: T. and J. W. Johnson, 1839).

DeWitt Dickinson, Edwin, 'The Analogy between Natural Persons and International Persons in the Law of Nations' (1917) 26 *The Yale Law Journal* 564–591.

Dixon, Martin, *Textbook on International Law* (7th ed., Oxford: Oxford University Press, 2013).

Dominicé, Christian, 'La question de la double responsabilité de l'Etat et de son agent', in Emile Yakpo and Tahar Boumedra (eds.), *Liber Amicorum Mohammed Bedjaoui* (The Hague, London, Boston: Kluwer Law International, 1999), pp. 143–157.

Dominicé, Christian, 'Attribution of Conduct to Multiple States and the Implication of A State in the Act of Another State', in James Crawford, Alain Pellet and Simon Olleson (eds.), *The Law of International Responsibility* (Oxford: Oxford University Press, 2010), pp. 281–289.

Dror, Yehezkel, 'Values and the Law' (1957) 17 *The Antioch Review* 440–454.

Drumbl, Mark, 'Collective Violence and Individual Punishment: The Criminality of Mass Atrocity' (2005) 99 *Northwestern University Law Review* 539–610.

Drumbl, Mark, *Atrocity, Punishment, and International Law* (Cambridge: Cambridge University Press, 2007).

Drumbl, Mark, 'Collective Responsibility and Postconflict Justice', in Tracy Isaacs and Richard Vernon (eds.), *Accountability for Collective Wrongdoing* (New York: Cambridge University Press, 2011), pp. 23–60.

Dugard, John, 'Diplomatic Protection', in James Crawford, Alain Pellet and Simon Olleson (eds.), *The Law of International Responsibility* (Oxford: Oxford University Press, 2010), pp. 1051–1071.

Dunn, Frederick S., 'International Law and Private Property Rights' (1928) 28 *Columbia Law Review* 166–180.

Dunn, Frederick S., *The Protection of Nationals: A Study in the Application of International Law* (New York: The Johns Hopkins Press, 1932).

Dupuy, Pierre-Marie, *La responsabilité internationale des États pour les dommages d'origine technologique et industrielle* (Paris: Éditions A. Pedone, 1976).

Dupuy, Pierre-Marie, 'International Law of State Responsibility: Revolution or Evolution?' (1989) 11 *Michigan Journal of International Law* 105–128.

Dupuy, Pierre-Marie, 'Dionisio Anzilotti and the Law of International Responsibility of States' (1992) 3 *European Journal of International Law* 139–148.

Dupuy, Pierre-Marie, *Droit International Public* (5th ed., Paris: Dalloz, 2000).

Dupuy, Pierre-Marie, 'A General Stocktaking of the Connections between the Multilateral Dimension of Obligations and Codification of the Law of Responsibility' (2002) 13 *European Journal of International Law* 1053–1081.

Dupuy, Pierre-Marie, 'International Criminal Responsibility of the Individual and International Responsibility of the State', in Antonio Cassese, Paolo Gaeta and John R. W. D. Jones (eds.), *The Rome Statute of the International Criminal Court: A Commentary (Volume II)* (Oxford: Oxford University Press, 2002), pp. 1085–1099.

Dupuy, Pierre-Marie, 'Some Reflections on Contemporary International Law and the Appeal to Universal Values: A Response to Martti Koskenniemi' (2005) 16 *European Journal of International Law* 131–137.

Dupuy, Pierre-Marie, 'The Deficiencies of the Law of State Responsibility Relating to Breaches of "Obligations Owed to the International Community as a Whole": Suggestions for Avoiding the Obsolescence of Aggravated Responsibility', in Antonio Cassesse (ed.), *Realizing Utopia: The Future of International Law* (Oxford: Oxford University Press, 2012), pp. 210–226.

Dutheil De La Rochere, Jaqueline, 'La Convention sur l'internationalisation de l'espace' (1967) 13 *Annuaire francais de droit international* 607–647.

Eagleton, Clyde, 'The Responsibility of the State for the Protection of Foreign Officials' (1925) 19 *American Journal of International Law* 293–314.

Eagleton, Clyde, *Responsibility of States in International Law* (New York: The New York University Press, 1928).

Eagleton, Clyde, 'Measure of Damages in International Law' (1929–1930) 39 *Yale Law Journal* 52–75.

Ellis, Mark E., 'The International Criminal Court and Its Implication for Domestic Law and National Capacity-Building' (2002) 15 *Florida Journal of International Law* 215–242.

Erskine, Toni, 'Kicking Bodies and Damning Souls: The Danger of Harming "Innocent" Individuals While Punishing "Delinquent" States', in Tracy Isaacs and Richard Vernon (eds.), *Accountability for Collective Wrongdoing* (New York: Cambridge University Press, 2011), pp. 261–286.

Evans, Malcolm, 'State Responsibility and the European Convention on Human Rights: Role and Realm', in Malgosia Fitzmaurice and Dan Sarooshi (eds.), *Issues of State Responsibility before International Judicial Institutions* (Oxford and Portland, OR: Bloomsbury, 2004), pp. 139–160.

Farell, Norman, 'Attributing Criminal Liability to Corporate Actors: Some Lessons from the International Tribunals' (2010) 8 *Journal of International Criminal Justice* 873–894.

Farer, Tom J., 'Restraining the Barbarians: Can International Criminal Law Help?' (2000) 22 *Human Rights Quarterly* 90–117.

Farrall, Jeremy, *United Nations Sanctions and the Rule of Law* (Cambridge: Cambridge University Press, 2009).

Faure, Michael, 'Concluding Remarks', in Michael Faure (ed.), *Deterrence, Insurability, and Compensation in Environmental Liability. Future Developments in the European Union* (Wien: Springer, 2003), pp. 331–343.

Faure, Michael, and Grimeaud, David, 'Financial Assurance Issues of Environmental Liability', in Michael Faure (ed.), *Deterrence, Insurability, and Compensation in Environmental Liability: Future Developments in the European Union* (Wien: Springer, 2003), pp. 7–302.

Faure, Michael, and Nollkaemper, André, 'International Liability as an Instrument to Prevent and Compensate for Climate Change' (2007) 43 A *Stanford Journal of International Law* 123–179.

Favre, Antoine, 'Fault as an Element of the Illicit Act' (1963–1964) 52 *Georgetown Law Journal* 555–570.

Feller, Abraham H., 'The Mexican Claims Commissions' (1933–1934) 19 *Iowa Law Review* 225–230.

Finch, George A., 'The Nuremberg Trial and International Law' (1947) 41 *American Journal of International Law* 20–37.

Finnemore, Martha, and Hollis, Duncan B., 'Constructing Norms for Global Cybersecurity' (2016) 110 *American Journal of International Law* 425–479.

Fischer, Kirsten J., 'The Distinct Character of International Crime: Theorizing the Domain' (2009) 8 *Contemporary Political Theory* 44–67.

Fisse, Brent, and Braithwaite, John, 'The Allocation of Responsibility for Corporate Crime: Individualism, Collectivism and Accountability' (1986–1988) 11 *Sydney Law Review* 468–513.

Fitzmaurice, Malgosia, 'International Responsibility and Liability', in Daniel Bodansky, Jutta Brunnée and Ellen Hey (eds.), *The Oxford Handbook of International Environmental Law* (Oxford: Oxford University Press, 2007), pp. 1010–1035.

Fitzmaurice, Malgosia A., 'International Environmental Law as a Special Field', in L. A. N. M. Barnhoorn and Karel C. Wellens (eds.), *Diversity in Secondary Rules and the Unity of International Law* (The Hague: Martinus Nijhoff Publishers, 1995), pp. 181–226.

Fletcher, George P., 'The Storrs Lectures: Liberals and Romantics at War: The Problem of Collective Guilt' (2001–2002) 111 *Yale Journal of International Law* 1499–1573.

Fletcher, George P., *Romantics at War: Glory and Guilt in the Age of Terrorism* (Princeton: Princeton University Press, 2002).

Focarelli, Carlo, 'International Law and Third-party Countermeasures in the Age of Global Instant Communication' (2016) 29 *Questions of International Law* 17–24.

Franck, Thomas, *Fairness in International Law and Institutions* (Oxford: Clarendon Press, 1995).

Franck, Thomas, 'Individual Criminal Liability and Collective Civil Responsibility: Do They Reinforce or Contradict One Another?' (2007) 6 *Washington University Global Studies Law Review* 567–573.

Franck, Thomas M., 'Legitimacy in the International System' (1988) 82 *American Journal of International Law* 705–759.

Fuller, Lon, *The Morality of Law* (New Haven and London: Yale University Press, 1964).

Fuller, Lon L. 'Law as an Instrument of Social Control and Law as a Facilitation of Human Interaction' (1975) *Brigham Young University Law Review* 89–96.

Fyrnys, Markus, 'Expanding Competences by Judicial Lawmaking: The Pilot Judgment Procedure of the European Court of Human Rights' (2011) 12 *German Law Journal* 1231–1260.

Gaines, Sanford E., 'The Polluter-Pays Principle: From Economic Equity to Environmental Ethos' (1991) 26 *Texas International Law Journal* 463–496.

Gaja, Giorgio, 'Positivism and Dualism in Dionisio Anzilotti' (1992) 3 *European Journal of International Law* 123–138.

Garcia, Frank J., 'Globalization and the Theory of International Law' (2005) 11 *International Legal Theory* 9–26.

García Amador, F. V., 'State Responsibility in the Light of New Trends of International Law' (1955) 49 *American Journal of International Law* 339–346.

García Amador, Francisco V., Sohn, Louis B., and Baxter, Richard R., *Recent Codification of the Law of State Responsibility for Injuries to Aliens* (Dobbs Ferry, NY: Oceana Publications, 1974).

Garland, David, 'Sociological Perspectives on Punishment' (1991) 14 *Crime and Justice* 115–165.

Gattini, Andrea, 'A Return Ticket to Communitarisme, Please' (2002) 13 *European Journal of International Law* 1181–1199.

Gilligan, Michael J., 'Is Enforcement Necessary for Effectiveness? A Model of the International Criminal Law Regime' (2006) 60 *International Organization* 935–967.

Goebel, Jr., Julius, 'The International Responsibility of States for Injuries Sustained by Aliens on Account of Mob Violence, Insurrections and Civil Wars' (1914) 8 *American Journal of International Law* 802–852.

Goldie, L. F. E., 'Liability for Damage and the Progressive Development of International Law' (1965) 14 *International and Comparative Law Quarterly* 1189–1264.

Goldmann, Matthias, 'Implementing the Rome Statute in Europe: From Sovereign Distinction to Convergence in International Criminal Law' (2005) XVI *Finnish Yearbook of International Law* 5–29.

Goldsmith, Jack, 'The Self-Defeating International Criminal Court' (2003) 70 *University of Chicago Law Review* 89–104.

Goldsmith, Jack L., and Posner, Eric A., *The Limits of International Law* (Oxford: Oxford University Press, 2006).

Goodwin-Gill, Guy S., 'State Responsibility and the "Good Faith" Obligation in International Law', in Malgosia Fitzmaurice and Dan Sarooshi (eds.), *Issues of State Responsibility before International Judicial Institutions* (Oxford and Portland, OR: Bloomsbury, 2004), pp. 75–104.

Gordon, Gregory S., 'The Trial of Peter von Hagenbach: Reconciling History, Historiography and International Criminal Law', in Kevin Jon Heller and Gerry Simpson (eds.), *The Hidden Histories of War Crimes Trials* (New York: Oxford University Press, 2013), pp. 13–49.

Gowlland-Debbas, Vera, 'Security Council Enforcement Actions and Issues of State Responsibility' (1994) 43 *International & Comparative Law Quarterly* 55–98.

Gray, Christine, 'The Different Forms of Reparation: Restitution', in James Crawford, Alain Pellet and Simon Olleson (eds.), *The Law of International Responsibility* (Oxford: Oxford University Press, 2010), pp. 589–597.

Green, Leslie, 'Introduction', in H. L. A. Hart (ed.), *The Concept of Law* (1st published 1961, 3rd ed., Oxford: Oxford University Press, 2012).

Griebel, Jörn, and Plücken, Milan, 'New Developments Regarding the Rules of Attribution? The International Court of Justice's Decision in *Bosnia* v. *Serbia*' (2008) 21 *Leiden Journal of International Law* 601–622.

Gros Espiell, Héctor, 'International Responsibility of the State and Individual Criminal Responsibility in the International Protection of Human Rights', in Maurizio Ragazzi (ed.), *International Responsibility Today: Essays in Memory of Oscar Schachter* (Leiden: Martinus Nijhoff Publishers, 2005), pp. 151–160.

Grossman, Claudio, and Bradlow, Daniel D., 'Are We Being Propelled Towards A People-Centered Transnational Legal Order' (1993–1994) 9 *American University Journal of International Law and Policy* 1–26.

Grotius, Hugo, *De jure belli ac pacis libri tres (1625)* (trans. Francis W. Kelsey, Oxford: Clarendon Press, 1925).

Guha Roy, S. N., 'Is the Law of Responsibility of States for Injuries to Aliens A Part of Universal International Law?' (1961) 55 *American Journal of International Law* 863–891.

Guzman, Andrew T., 'Saving Customary International Law' (2005) 27 *Michigan Journal of International Law* 115–176.

Hafner, Gerhard, 'Accountability of International Organizations' (2003) 97 *American Society of International Law Proceedings* 236–237.

Hall, Christopher Keith, 'The First Proposal for a Permanent International Criminal Court' (1998) *International Review of the Red Cross* 57–74.
Hall, William Edward, *A Treatise on International Law* (8th ed., Oxford: Clarendon Press, 1924).
Hart, Jr., Henry M., 'The Aims of the Criminal Law' (1958) 23 *Law and Contemporary Problems* 401–441.
Hart, H. L. A., *Law, Liberty and Morality* (Stanford: Stanford University Press, 1963).
Hawkins, Gordon, 'Punishment and Deterrence: The Educative, Moralizing, and Habituating Effects' (1969) *Wisconsin Law Review* 550–565.
Heathcote, Sarah, 'Necessity', in James Crawford, Alain Pellet and Simon Olleson (eds.), *The Law of International Responsibility* (Oxford: Oxford University Press, 2010), pp. 491–501.
Heffter, August Wilhelm, *Le droit international public de L'Europe* (trans. Jules Bergson, Paris: Cotillon, 1857).
Heikkilä, Mikaela, *International Criminal Tribunals and Victims of Crime: A Study of the Status of Victims before International Criminal Tribunals and of Factors Affecting This Status* (Turku: Åbo Akademi University, 2004).
Heikkilä, Mikaela, *Coping with International Atrocities through Criminal Law. A Study into the Typical Features of International Criminality and the Reflection of These Traits in International Criminal Law* (Turku: Åbo Akademi University Press, 2014).
Helfer, Laurence R., and Wuerth, Ingrid, *Custom in the Age of Soft Law* (Working Paper).
Helfer, Laurence R., and Wuerth, Ingrid B., 'Customary International Law: An Instrument Choice Perspective' (2016) 37 *Michigan Journal of International Law* 563–609.
Henzelin, Marc, Heiskanen, Veijo, and Mettraux, Guénaël, 'Reparations to Victims before the International Criminal Court: Lessons from International Mass Claims Processes' (2006) 17 *Criminal Law Forum* 317–344.
Hessbruegge, Jan Arno, 'The Historical Development of the Doctrines of Attribution and Due Diligence in International Law' (2004) 36 *New York University Journal of International Law & Politics* 265–306.
Higgins, Rosalyn, *Problems & Progress: International Law and How We Use It* (Oxford: Clarendon Press, 1994).
Higgins, Rosalyn, 'Issues of State Responsibility before the International Court of Justice', in Malgosia Fitzmaurice and Dan Sarooshi (eds.), *Issues of State Responsibility before International Judicial Institutions* (Oxford and Portland, OR: Bloomsbury, 2004), pp. 1–9.
Hillebrecht, Courtney, 'The Deterrent Effect of the International Criminal Court: Evidence from Libya' (2016) 42 *International Interactions* 616–643.
Hobe, Stephan, 'The Era of Globalisation as a Challenge to International Law' (2001–2002) 40 *Duquesne University Law Review* 655–665.
Hofmann, Claudia, *Learning in Modern International Society: On the Cognitive Problem Solving Abilities of Political Actors* (Wiesbaden: VS Verlag für Sozialwissenschaften, 2008).
Holland, Thomas Erskine, *Studies in International Law* (Oxford: Clarendon Press, 1898).

Huang, Zhxiong, 'The Attribution Rules in the ILC Articles on State Responsibility: A Preliminary Assessment on Their Application in Cyber Operation' (2014) 14 *Baltic Yearbook of International Law* 41–54.

Hudson, Manley O., *International Tribunals: Past and Future* (Washington, DC: Carnegie Endowment for International Peace & Brookings Institute, 1944).

Hurd, Ian, 'Legitimacy and Authority in International Politics' (1999) 53 *International Organization* 379–408.

Isaacs, Tracy, 'Introduction', in Tracy Isaacs and Richard Vernon (eds.), *Accountability for Collective Wrongdoing* (Cambridge: Cambridge University Press, 2011), pp. 1–19.

Jackson, Robert H., 'Opening Statement before the International Military Tribunal (1945)', reproduced in Larry May and Jeff Brown (eds.), *Philosophy of Law: Classic and Contemporary Readings* (Malden and Oxford: Wiley-Blackwell, 2010), pp. 435–440.

Jacobson, Kyle Rex, 'Doing Business with the Devil: The Challenges of Prosecuting Corporate Officials Whose Business Transactions Facilitate War Crimes and Crimes against Humanity' (2005) 56 *Air Force Law Review* 167–232.

Jamieson, Ruth, and McEvoy, Kieran, 'State Crime by Proxy and Juridical Othering' (2005) 45 *British Journal of Criminology* 504–527.

Jessberger, F., and Geneuss, J., 'Down the Drain or Down to Earth? International Criminal Justice under Pressure' (2013) 11 *Journal of International Criminal Justice* 501–503.

Jessup, Philip C., 'Responsibility of States for Injuries to Individuals' (1946) 46 *Columbia Law Review* 903–928.

Jinks, Derek, 'State Responsibility for the Acts of Private Armed Groups' (2003) 4 *Chicago Journal of International Law* 83–95.

Jo, Hyeran, and Simmons, Beth A., 'Can the International Criminal Court Deter Atrocity?' (2016) 70 *International Organization* 443–475.

Johnston, Douglas M., 'Functionalism in the Theory of International Law' (1988) 26 *Canadian Yearbook of International Law* 3–60.

Johnstone, Rachael Lorna, 'State Responsibility: A Concerto for Court, Council and Committee' (2008) 37 *Denver Journal of International Law and Policy* 63–118.

Jones, Annika, 'Seeking International Criminal Justice in Syria' (2013) 89 *International Law Studies* 802–816.

Jørgensen, Nina H. B., *The Responsibility of States for International Crimes* (Oxford: Oxford University Press, 2000).

Jørgensen, Nina H. B., 'Criminality of Organizations under International Law', in André Nollkaemper and Harmen van der Wilt (eds.), *System Criminality in International Law* (Cambridge: Cambridge University Press, 2009), pp. 201–221.

Kaplan, Margo, 'Using Collective Interests to Ensure Human Rights: An Analysis of the Articles on State Responsibility' (2004) 79 *New York University Law Review* 1902–1933.

Kaul, Hans-Peter, 'Developments at the International Criminal Court. Construction Site for More Justice: The International Criminal Court after Two Years' (2005) 99 *American Journal of International Law* 370–384.

Kelsen, Hans, 'Théorie du droit international public' (1953–III) 84 *Recueil des cours* 1–204.

Kelsen, Hans, *Principles of International Law* (3rd printing, Clark: The Lawbook Exchange Ltd, 1959).

Kelsen, Hans, *General Theory of Law and State* (1st published 1945, trans. Anders Wedberg, Clark: Lawbook Exchange, 2007).

Kennedy, Duncan, 'The Stages of the Decline of the Public/Private Division' (1981–1982) 130 *University of Pennsylvania Law Review* 1349–1357.

Kennedy, Kevin C., 'A Critical Appraisal of Criminal Deterrence Theory' (1983–1984) 88 *Dickinson Law Review* 1–13.

Kerbat, Yann, 'Interaction between the Forms of Reparation', in James Crawford, Alain Pellet and Simon Olleson (eds.), *The Law of International Responsibility* (Oxford: Oxford University Press, 2010), pp. 573–587.

Kersten, Mark, 'A Little Less Isolated and a Lot More Troubling: Ban Ki-moon meets Bashir', 5 September 2012, Justice in Conflict, justiceinconflict.org/2012/09/05/a-little-less-isolated-and-a-lot-more-troubling-ban-ki-moon-meets-bashir/ (accessed 10 June 2015).

Kingsbury, Benedict, and Donaldson, Megan, 'From Bilateralism to Publicness in International Law', in Ulrich Fastenrath, Rudolf Geiger and Daniel-Erasmus Khan et al. (eds.), *From Bilateralism to Community Interests: Essays in Honour of Judge Bruno Simma* (Oxford: Oxford University Press, 2011), pp. 79–89.

Kirchner, Stefan, 'Relative Normativity and the Constitutional Dimension of International Law: A Place for Values in the International Legal System' (2004) 5 *German Law Journal* 47–64.

Kirsch, Philippe, Holmes, John T., and Johnson, Mora, 'International Tribunals and Courts', in David M. Malone (ed.), *The UN Security Council: From the Cold War to the 21st Century* (London: Lynne Rienner Publishers, 2004), pp. 281–294.

Kiss, Alexandre, 'L'accident de Tchernobyl: ses consequences au point de vue du Droit international' (1986) 32 *Annuaire français de droit international* 139–152.

Kiss, Alexandre, 'State Responsibility and Liability for Nuclear Damage' (2006) 35 *Denver Journal of International Law and Policy* 67–83.

Kiss, Alexandre, and Shelton, Dinah, *International Environmental Law* (2nd ed., Ardsley, New York: Transnational Publishers, 2000).

Kiss, Alexandre, and Shelton, Dinah, 'Strict Liability in International Environmental Law', in Tafsir Malick Ndiaye and Rüdiger Wolfrum (eds.), *Law of the Sea, Environmental Law and Settlement of Disputes: Liber Amicorum Judge Thomas A. Mensah* (Leiden: Brill, 2007), pp. 1131–1151.

Klabbers, Jan, 'Just Revenge? The Deterrence Argument in International Criminal Law' (2001) XII *Finnish Yearbook of International Law* 249–267.

Klabbers, Jan, 'Reflections on Soft International Law in a Privatized World' (2005) XVI *Finnish Yearbook of International Law* 313–328.

Klabbers, Jan, 'Compliance Procedures', in Daniel Bodansky, Jutta Brunnée and Ellen Hey (eds.), *The Oxford Handbook of International Environmental Law* (Oxford: Oxford University Press, 2007), pp. 995–1009.

Klabbers, Jan, 'Constitutionalism and the Making of International Law: Fuller's Procedural Natural Law' (2008) 5 *NoFo* 84–112.

Klabbers, Jan, 'Setting the Scene', in Jan Klabbers, Anne Peters and Geir Ulfstein (eds.), *The Constitutionalization of International Law* (Oxford: Oxford University Press, 2009), pp. 1–44.

Klabbers, Jan, *International Law* (Cambridge: Cambridge University Press, 2013).

Klabbers, Jan, 'Law, Ethics and Global Governance: Accountability in Perspective' (2013) 11 *New Zealand Journal of Public and International Law* 309–321.

Klabbers, Jan, 'Responsibility of States and International Organisations in the Context of Cyber Activities with Special Reference to NATO', in Katharina Ziolkowski (ed.), *Peacetime Regime for State Activities in Cyberspace: International Law, International Relations and Diplomacy* (Tallinn: NATO Cooperative Cyber Defence Centre of Excellence, 2013), pp. 485–506.

Klabbers, Jan, 'Book Review on André Nollkaemper and Dov Jacobs (eds.), Distribution of Responsibilities in International Law' (2016) 27 *European Journal of International Law* 541–551.

Kleffner, Jann K., 'The Collective Accountability of Organized Armed Groups for System Crimes', in André Nollkaemper and Harmen van der Wilt (eds.), *System Criminality in International Law* (Cambridge: Cambridge University Press, 2009), pp. 238–269.

Klein, Pierre, 'Responsibility for Serious Breaches of Obligations Deriving from Peremptory Norms of International Law and United Nations Law' (2002) 13 *European Journal of International Law* 1241–1255.

Kleinlein, Thomas, 'The Language of Public International Law', in Société Française pour le droit international (ed.), *Droit international et diversité des cultures juridiques* (Paris: Pedone, 2008), pp. 199–208.

Kolb, Robert, *The International Law of State Responsibility: An Introduction* (Cheltenham: Edward Elgar, 2017).

Kopela, Sophia, 'Civil and Criminal Liability as Mechanisms for the Prevention of Oil Pollution: The Erika Case' (2011) 20 *Review of the European Community & International Environmental Law* 313–324.

Korhonen, Outi, and Selkälä, Toni, 'Theorizing Responsibility', in Anne Orford and Florian Hoffmann (eds.), *The Oxford Handbook on the Theory of International Law* (Oxford: Oxford University Press, 2016), pp. 844–861.

Koskenniemi, Martti, *Valtion kansainvälinen vastuu yksityisen toiminnan aiheuttamasta kansainvälisestä ympäristövahingosta*, Kansainvälisoikeudellinen päälaudaturkirjoitus (Turku: Turun Yliopisto, 1981).

Koskenniemi, Martti, 'International Liability for Transfrontier Pollution Damage' (1990) 2 *International Environmental Affairs. A Journal for Research and Policy* 309–316.

Koskenniemi, Martti, 'The Politics of International Law' (1990) 1 *European Journal of International Law* 4–32.

Koskenniemi, Martti, 'Ison-Beltin siltariita' (1992) 8 *Lakimies* 1300–1332.

Koskenniemi, Martti, 'Hierarchy in International Law: A Sketch' (1997) 8 *European Journal of International Law* 566–582.

Koskenniemi, Martti, 'Solidarity Measures: State Responsibility as a New International Order?' (2001) 72 *British Yearbook of International Law* 337–356.

Koskenniemi, Martti, 'Between Impunity and Show Trials' (2002) 6 *Max Planck Yearbook of United Nations Law* 1–35.

Koskenniemi, Martti, *The Gentle Civilizer of Nations: The Rise and Fall of International Law 1870–1960* (Cambridge: Cambridge University Press, 2002).

Koskenniemi, Martti, 'Hersch Lauterpacht and the Development of International Criminal Law' (2004) 2 *Journal of International Criminal Justice* 810–825.

Koskenniemi, Martti, *From Apology to Utopia: The Structure of International Legal Argument* (reissue with new epilogue, Cambridge: Cambridge University Press, 2005).

Koskenniemi, Martti, 'International Law in Europe: Between Tradition and Renewal' (2005) 16 *European Journal of International Law* 113–124.

Koskenniemi, Martti, *Fragmentation of International Law: Difficulties Arising from the Diversification and Expansion of International Law. Report of the Study Group of the International law Commission*, UN Doc. A/CN.4/L.682 (13 April 2006).

Koskenniemi, Martti, 'The Fate of Public International Law: Between Technique and Politics' (2007) 1 *The Modern Law Review* 1–30.

Koskenniemi, Martti, 'Doctrines of State Responsibility', in James Crawford, Alain Pellet and Simon Olleson (eds.), *The Law of International Responsibility* (Oxford: Oxford University Press, 2010), pp. 45–51.

Koskenniemi, Martti, *The Politics of International Law* (Oxford and Portland, OR: Hart Publishing, 2011).

Koskenniemi, Martti, 'Humanity's Law by Ruti G. Teitel' (2012) 26 *Ethics & International Law* 395–398.

Kozma, Julia, Nowak, Manfred, and Scheinin, Martin, *A World Court of Human Rights: Consolidated Statute and Commentary* (Vienna, Graz: Neuer Wissenschaftlicher Verlag, 2010).

Kramer, Matthew H., 'On the Moral Status of the Rule of Law' (2004) 63 *Cambridge Law Journal* 65–97.

Kress, Claus, 'L'organe de facto en droit international public, réflexions sur l'imputation à l'Etat de l'acte d'un particulier à la lumière des développements récents' (2001) 105 *Revue Générale de Droit International Public* 93–144.

Krieg, Andreas, and Rickli, Jean-Marc, *Surrogate Warfare: The Transformation of War in the Twenty-first Century* (Washington, DC: Georgetown University Press, 2019).

Krisch, Nico, 'International Law in Times of Hegemony: Unequal Power and the Shaping of the International Legal Order' (2005) 16 *European Journal of International Law* 369–408.

Ku, Julian, and Nzelibe, Jide, 'Do International Criminal Tribunals Deter or Exacerbate Humanitarian Atrocities?' (2006) 84 *Washington University Law Review* 777–833.

Kyriakakis, Joanna, 'Australian Prosecution of Corporations for International Crimes. The Potential of the Commonwealth Criminal Code' (2007) 5 *Journal of International Criminal Justice* 809–826.

Laithier, Lucie, 'Private Codification Efforts', in James Crawford, Alain Pellet and Simon Olleson (eds.), *The Law of International Responsibility* (Oxford: Oxford University Press, 2010), pp. 53–59.

Langlet, David, *Prior Informed Consent and Hazardous Trade. Regulating Trade in Hazardous Goods at the Intersection of Sovereignty, Free Trade and Environmental Protection* (Alphen aan den Rejin: Kluwer Law International, 2009).

Lanovoy, Vladyslav, *Complicity and its Limits in the Law of International Responsibility* (Oxford and Portland, OR: Bloomsbury, 2016).

Lanovoy, Vladyslav, 'The Use of Force by Non-state Actors and the Limits of Attribution of Conduct' (2017) 28 *European Journal of International Law* 563–585.

Lasok, David, 'The Eichmann Trial' (1962) 11 *International and Comparative Law Quarterly* 355–374.

Lauterpacht, Hersch, *The Function of Law in the International Community* (Oxford: Clarendon Press, 1933).

Lauterpacht, Hersch, *International Law: Collected Papers, Vol. 1, General Works* (ed. Elihu Lauterpacht) (Cambridge: Cambridge University Press, 1970).

Lauterpacht, Hersch, *Private Law Sources and Analogies of International Law* (first published by Longmans, Green and Co. Ltd: London, 1927, North Haven: Archon Books, 1970).

Lee, Edward G., and Sproule, D. W., 'Liability for Damage Caused by Space Debris: The Cosmos 954 Claim' (1988) 26 *Canadian Yearbook of International Law* 273–279.

Lefeber, René, *Transboundary Environmental Interference and the Origins of State Liability* (The Hague: Kluwer Law International, 1996).

Lehnardt, Chia, 'Private Military Companies and State Responsibility', in Simon Chesterman and Chia Lehnardt (eds.), *From Mercenaries to Market* (Oxford: Oxford University Press, 2007), pp. 139–157.

Lehnardt, Chia, 'Individual Liability of Private Military Personnel under International Criminal Law' (2008) 19 *European Journal of International Law* 1015–1034.

Lehto, Marja, *International Responsibility for Terrorist Acts: A Shift towards More Indirect Forms of Responsibility* (Rovaniemi: Lapland University Press, 2008).

Lehto, Marja, *Indirect Responsibility for Terrorist Acts. Redefinition of the Concept of Terrorism Beyond Violent Acts* (Leiden and Boston: Martinus Nijhoff Publishers, 2010).

Lesaffer, Randall, 'Argument from Roman Law in Current International Law' (2005) 16 *European Journal of International Law* 25–58.

Lewis, Margaret K., 'An Analysis of State Responsibility for the Chinese-American Airplane Collision Incident' (2002) 77 *New York University Law Review* 1404–1441.

Lillich, Richard B., 'The Current Status of the Law of State Responsibility for Injuries to Aliens', in Richard B. Lillich (ed.), *International Law of State Responsibility for Injuries to Aliens* (Charlottesville: University Press of Virginia, 1983), pp. 1–61.

Linderfalk, Ulf, 'The Functionality of Conceptual Terms in International Law and International Legal Discourse' (2013/2014) 6 *European Journal of Legal Studies* 27–50.

Louka, Elli, *International Environmental Law: Fairness, Effectiveness, and World Order* (New York: Cambridge University Press, 2006).

Lowe, Vaughan, 'The Iraq Crisis: What Now?' (2003) 52 *International and Comparative Law Quarterly* 859–871.

Lu, Catherine, 'The International Criminal Court as an Institution of Moral Regeneration: Problems and Prospects', in Joanna Harrington, Michael Milde and Richard Vernon (eds.), *Bringing Power to Justice? The Prospects of the International Criminal Court* (Montreal & Kingston: McGill's-Queen University Press, 2006).

Luban, David, 'State Criminality and the Ambition of International Criminal Law', in Tracy Isaacs and Richard Vernon (eds.), *Accountability for Collective Wrongdoing* (Cambridge: Cambridge University Press, 2011), pp. 61–91.

Maison, Rafaëlle, *La responsabilité individuelle pour crime d'État en droit international public* (Bruxelles: Bruylant, 2004).

Malanczuk, Peter, *Akehurst's Modern Introduction to International Law* (7th revised ed., London and New York: Routledge, 1997).

Mälksoo, Lauri, 'State Responsibility and the Challenge of the Realist Paradigm: The Demand of Baltic Victims of Soviet Mass Repressions for Compensation from Russia' (2003) 3 *Baltic Yearbook of International Law* 57–76.

Margulies, Peter, 'Sovereignty and Cyber Attacks: Technology's Challenge to the Law of State Responsibility' (2013) 14 *Melbourne Journal of International Law* 1–24.

Marks, Stephen P., 'Tying Prometheus Down: The International Law of Human Genetic Manipulation' (2002) 3 *Chicago Journal of International Law* 115–136.

Marks, Susan, 'State-Centrism, International Law and the Anxieties of Influence' (2006) 19 *Leiden Journal of International Law* 339–347.

Marston Danner, Allison, 'The Nuremberg Industrialist Prosecutions and Aggressive War' (2005–2006) 46 *Virginia Journal of International Law* 651–676.

Mason, Michael, 'Transnational Compensation for Oil Pollution Damage: Examining Changing Spatialities of Environmental Liability', LSE Research Papers in Environmental and Spatial Analysis, no 69 (2002), Department of Geography and Environment, London School of Economics and Political Science, London, UK, 1–24.

Mason, Michael, 'Civil Liability for Oil Pollution Damage: Examining the Evolving Scope for Environmental Compensation in the International Regime' (2003) 27 *Marine Policy* 1–12.

Matsui, Yoshiro, 'The Transformation of the Law of State Responsibility', in René Provost (ed.), *State Responsibility in International Law* (Dartmouth: Ashgate, 2002), pp. 3–63.

Mayer, Benoit, 'Climate Change Reparations and the Law and Practice of State Responsibility' (2017) 7 *Asian Journal of International Law* 185–216.

McAuliffe, Pádraig, 'Suspended Disbelief? The Curious Endurance of the Deterrence Rationale in International Criminal Law' (2012) 10 *New Zealand Journal of Public and International Law* 227–262.

McAuliffe, Padraig, 'From Watchdog to Workhorse: Explaining the Emergence of the ICC's Burden-sharing Policy as an Example of Creeping Cosmopolitanism' (2014) 13 *Chinese Journal of International Law* 259–296.

McAuliffe, Pádraig, and Schwöbel-Patel, Christine, 'Disciplinary Matchmaking. Critics of International Criminal Law Meet Critics of Liberal Peacebuilding' (2018) 16 *Journal of International Criminal Justice* 985–1009.

McDougal, Myres S., Lasswell, Harold D., and Chen, Lung-Chu, *Human Rights and World Public Order* (New Haven: Yale University Press, 1980).

McDougal, Myres S., Lasswell, Harold D., and Vlasic, Ivan A., *Law and Public Order in Space* (New Haven: Yale University Press, 1963).

McDougal, Myres S., and Schlei, Norbert A., 'The Hydrogen Bomb Tests in Perspective: Lawful Measures for Security' (1954–1955) 64 *Yale Law Journal* 648–710.

McRae, Ben, 'Entry into Force of the Convention on Supplementary Compensation for Nuclear Damage: Opening the Umbrella' (2015) *Nuclear Law Bulletin* 7–25.

Mégret, Frédéric, 'Epilogue to an Endless Debate: The International Criminal Court's Third Party Jurisdiction and the Looming Revolution of International Law' (2001) 12 *European Journal of International Law* 247–268.

Mégret, Frédéric, 'Accountability and Ethics', in Luc Reydams, Jan Wouters and Cedric Ryngaert (eds.), *International Prosecutors* (Oxford: Oxford University Press, 2012), pp. 416–487.

Mégret, Frédéric, 'Globalization', in Rüdiger Wolfrum (ed.), *Max Planck Encyclopedia of International Law* (Oxford: Oxford University Press, 2009).

Mégret, Frédéric, 'State Responsibility for Aggression: A Human Rights Approach' (2017) 58 *Harvard International Law Online Journal* 62–65.

Meron, Theodor, 'State Responsibility for Violations of Human Rights' (1989) 83 *American Society of International Law Proceedings* 372–385.

Meyer, Zach, 'Private Commercialization of Space in an International Regime: A Proposal for a Space District' (2010) 30 *Northwestern Journal of International Law and Business* 241–261.

Milanović, Marko, and Papić, Tatjana, 'As Bad as It Gets: The European Court of Human Rights's Behrami and Saramati Decision and General International Law' (2009) 58 *International and Comparative Law Quarterly* 267–297.

Miller, Justin, 'Criminal Law – An Agency for Social Control' (1934) 43 *Yale Law Review* 691–715.

Mohr, Manfred, 'The ILC's Distinction between "International Crimes" and "International Delicts" and Its Implications', in Marina Spinedi and Bruno Simma (eds.), *United Nations Codification of State Responsibility* (New York: Oceana Publications, 1987), pp. 115–141.

Morgenthau, Hans, 'Positivism, Functionalism, and International Law' (1940) 34 *American Journal of International Law* 260–284.

Morris, Madeleine, 'High Crimes and Misconceptions: The ICC and Non-State Parties' (2001) 64 *Law & Contemporary Problems* 13–66.

Morss, John R., *International Law as the Law of Collectives: Toward a Law of People* (Farnham: Ashgate Publishing Limited, 2013).

Mosoti, Victor, 'In Our Own Image, Not Theirs: Damages as an Antidote to the Remedial Deficiencies in the WTO Dispute Settlement Process; A View from Sub-Saharan Africa' (2001) 19 *Boston University International Law Journal* 231–256.

Moyn, Samuel, 'Towards Instrumentalism at the International Criminal Court' (2014) 39 *Yale Journal of International Law* 55–65.

Mujezinović Larsen, Kjetil, 'Attribution of Conduct in Peace Operations: The "Ultimate Authority and Control" Test' (2008) 19 *European Journal of International Law* 509–531.

Müller, Andreas Th., and Stegmiller, Ignaz, 'Self-Referrals on Trial. From Panacea to Patient' (2010) 8 *Journal of International Criminal Justice* 1267–1294.

Müller, Daniel, 'The Work of García Amador on State Responsibility for Injury Caused to Aliens', in James Crawford, Alain Pellet and Simon Olleson (eds.), *The Law of International Responsibility* (Oxford: Oxford University Press, 2010), pp. 69–74.

Murphy, Liam, 'International Responsibility', in Samantha Besson and John Tasioulas (eds.), *The Philosophy of International Law* (Oxford: Oxford University Press, 2010), pp. 299–315.

Mussa, Cerina Banu Issufo, Vossenaar, René, and Nakisisa Waniala, Nimrod, 'Eastern and Southern Africa: The Experience of Kenya, Mozambique, The United Republic of Tanzania and Uganda', in Veena Jha (ed.), *Environmental Regulation and Food Safety: Studies of Protection and Protectionism* (Cheltenham: Edward Elgar Publishing, 2005), pp. 103–144.

Nakatani, Kazuhiro, 'Diplomacy and State Responsibility', in Maurizio Ragazzi (ed.), *International Responsibility Today: Essays in Memory of Oscar Schachter* (Leiden: Martinus Nijhoff Publishers, 2005), pp. 37–47.

Nerlich, Volker, 'Core Crimes and Transnational Business Corporations' (2010) 8 *Journal of International Criminal Justice* 895–908.

Nieminen, Katja, 'The Rules of Attribution and the Private Military Contractors at Abu Ghraib: Private Acts or Public Wrongs?' (2006) XV *Finnish Yearbook of International Law* 289–319.

Nissel, Alan T., 'The Duality of State Responsibility' (2013) 44 *Columbia Human Rights Law Review* 793–858.

Nissel, Tzvika Alan, *A History of State Responsibility: The Struggle for International Standards (1870–1960)* (Helsinki: University of Helsinki, 2016).

Nollkaemper, André, 'Concurrence between Individual Responsibility and State Responsibility in International Law' (2003) 52 *International and Comparative Law Quarterly* 615–640.

Nollkaemper, André, 'Cluster-litigation in Cases of Transboundary Environmental Harm', in Michael Faure and Song Ying (eds.), *China and International Environmental Liability: Legal Remedies for Transboundary Pollution* (Cheltenham: Edward Elgar Publishing Ltd., 2008), pp. 11–37.

Nollkaemper, André, 'Towards Public Responsibility in International Law', conference presentation at Global Constitutionalism: Process and Substance, Kandersteg, 17–19 January 2008.

Nollkaemper, André, 'Constitutionalization and the Unity of the Law of International Responsibility' (2009) 16 *Indiana Journal of Global Legal Studies* 535–563.

Nollkaemper, André, 'State Responsibility for International Crimes: A Review of Principles of Reparation', in Aristotle Constantinides and Nikos Zaikos (eds.), *The Diversity of International Law: Essays in Honour of Professor Kalliopi K. Koufa* (Leiden: Martinus Nijhoff Publishers, 2009), pp. 487–518.

Nollkaemper, André, 'Procedural Aspects of Shared Responsibility in International Adjudication. Introduction' (2013) 4 *Journal of International Dispute Settlement* 277–294.

Nollkaemper, André, and Jacobs, Dov, 'Shared Responsibility in International Law: A Conceptual Framework' (2012–2013) 34 *Michigan Journal of International Law* 359–438.

Nollkaemper, André, and Jacobs, Dov (eds.), *Distribution of Responsibilities in International Law* (Cambridge: Cambridge University Press, 2015).

Nollkaemper, André, and Jacobs, Dov, 'Introduction: Mapping the Normative Framework', in André Nollkaemper and Dov Jacobs (eds.), *Distribution of Responsibilities in International Law* (Cambridge: Cambridge University Press, 2015), pp. 1–35.

Nollkaemper, André, and Plakokefalos, Ilias (eds.), *Principles of Shared Responsibility in International Law* (Cambridge: Cambridge University Press, 2014).

Nollkaemper, André, and Plakokefalos, Ilias (eds.), *The Practice of Shared Responsibility in International Law* (Cambridge: Cambridge University Press, 2017).

Nollkaemper, André, and van der Wilt, Harmen, 'Conclusions and Outlook', in André Nollkaemper and Harmen van der Wilt (eds.), *System Criminality in International Law* (Cambridge: Cambridge University Press, 2009), pp. 338–353.

Nollkaemper, André, and van der Wilt, Harmen, 'Preface', in André Nollkaemper and Harmen van der Wilt (eds.), *System Criminality in International Law* (Cambridge: Cambridge University Press, 2009), pp. vii–viii.

Nollkaemper, André, and van der Wilt, Harmen (eds.), *System Criminality in International Law* (Cambridge: Cambridge University Press, 2009).

Nolte, Georg, 'From Dionisio Anzilotti to Roberto Ago: The Classical International Law of State Responsibility and the Traditional Primacy of a Bilateral Conception of Inter-state Relations' (2002) 13 *European Journal of International Law* 1033–1098.

Nolte, Georg, and Aust, Helmut Philipp, 'Equivocal Helpers – Complicit States, Mixed Messages and International Law' (2009) 58 *International and Comparative Law Quarterly* 1–30.

Norrie, A., '"Simulacra of morality"? Beyond the Ideal/Actual Antinomies of Criminal Justice', in Antony Duff (ed.), *Philosophy and Criminal Law: Principle and Critique* (Cambridge: Cambridge University Press, 1998), pp. 101–155.

Noyes, John E., and Smith, Brian D., 'State Responsibility and the Principle of Joint and Several Liability' (1988) 13 *Yale Journal of International Law* 225–267.

Ohlin, Jens David, 'Three Conceptual Problems with the Doctrine of Joint Criminal Enterprise' (2007) 5 *Journal of International Criminal Justice* 69–90.

Okowa, Phoebe, *State Responsibility for Transboundary Air Pollution in International Law* (Oxford and New York: Oxford University Press, 2000).

Okowa, Phoebe, 'State and Individual Responsibility in Internal Conflicts: Contours of an Evolving Relationship' (2009) 20 *Finnish Yearbook of International Law* 143–188.

Olleson, Simon, 'Attribution in Investment Treaty Arbitration' (2016) 31 *ICSID Review* 457–483.

Ormerod, David, *Smith and Hogan Criminal Law* (12th ed., Oxford: Oxford University Press, 2008).

Osaka, Eri, 'Corporate Liability, Government Liability, and the Fukushima Nuclear Disaster' (2012) 21 *Pacific Rim Law & Policy Journal* 433–459.

Osiel, Mark J., 'In Defense of Liberal Show Trials–Nuremberg and Beyond', in Guénaël Mettraux (ed.), *Perspectives on the Nuremberg Trial* (Oxford: Oxford University Press, 2008), pp. 704–725.

Paddeu, Federica, 'To Convene or Not to Convene? The Future Status of the Articles on State Responsibility: Recent Developments' (2018) 21 *Max Planck Yearbook of United Nations Law* 83–123.

Palojärvi, Pia, *A Battle in the Bits and Bytes: Computer Network Attacks and the Law of Armed Conflict. The Erik Castrén Institute Research Reports 27/2009* (Helsinki: The Erik Castrén Institute, 2009).

Paparinskis, Martins, 'Circumstances Precluding Wrongfulness in International Investment Law' (2016) 31 *ICSID Review* 484–503.

Parlett, Kate, 'The Application of the Rules on Countermeasures in Investment Claims. Visions and Realities of International Law as an Open System', in Christine Chinkin and Freya Baetens (eds.), *Sovereignty, Statehood and State Responsibility: Essays in Honour of James Crawford* (Cambridge: Cambridge University Press, 2015), pp. 389–405.

Paulus, Andreas, 'From Territoriality to Functionality: Towards a Legal Methodology', in Ige F. Dekker and Wouter G. Werner (eds.), *Governance and International Legal Theory* (Leiden: Martinus Nijhoff, 2004), pp. 59–96.

Paulus, Andreas, 'Reciprocity Revisited', in Ulrich Fastenrath, Rudolf Geiger, Daniel-Erasmus Khan et al. (eds.), *From Bilateralism to Community Interest: Essays in Honour of Judge Bruno Simma* (Oxford: Oxford University Press, 2011), pp. 113–137.

Paulus, Andreas, 'Whether Universal Values can Prevail over Bilateralism and Reciprocity', in Antonio Cassese (ed.), *Realizing Utopia: The Future of International Law* (Oxford: Oxford University Press, 2012), pp. 89–104.

Paust, Jordan J., 'My Lai and Vietnam: Norms, Myths and Leader Responsibility' (1972) 57 *Military Law Review* 99–187.

Payne, Christian, 'International Law Cannot Keep Up with Cyber-Criminals', *World Economic Forum*, 25 February 2019, www.weforum.org/agenda/2019/02/why-international-law-is-failing-to-keep-pace-with-technology-in-preventing-cyber-attacks/ (accessed 20 May 2019).

Pellet, Alain, 'Can a State Commit a Crime? Definitely, Yes!' (1999) 10 *European Journal of International Law* 425–434.

Pellet, Alain, 'Les Articles de la C.D.I. sur la responsabilité de l'État pour fait internationalement illicite. Suite-et fin?' (2002) 48 *Annuaire francais de droit international* 1–23.

Pellet, Alain, 'The ILC's Articles on State Responsibility for Internationally Wrongful Acts and Related Texts', in James Crawford, Alain Pellet and Simon Olleson (eds.), *The Law of International Responsibility* (Oxford: Oxford University Press, 2010), pp. 75–94.

Pellet, Alain, 'The Definition of Responsibility in International Law', in James Crawford, Alain Pellet and Simon Olleson (eds.), *Oxford Commentaries on International Law* (Oxford: Oxford University Press, 2010), pp. 3–16.

Pellet, Alain, 'Responsibility of States in Cases of Human-Rights or Humanitarian-law Violations', in James Crawford, Abdul B. Koroma, Said Mahmoudi and Alain Pellet (eds.), *The International Legal Order: Current Needs and Possible Responses. Essays in Honour of Djamchid Momtaz* (Leiden and Boston: Brill Nijhoff, 2017), pp. 230–251.

Peters, Anne, 'International Dispute Settlement: A Network of Cooperational Duties' (2003) 14 *European Journal of International Law* 1–34.

Peters, Anne, 'Membership in Global Constitutional Community', in Jan Klabbers, Anne Peters and Geir Ulfstein (eds.), *The Constitutionalization of International Law* (Oxford: Oxford University Press, 2009), pp. 153–262.

Peters, Anne, 'The Merits of Global Constitutionalism' (2009) 16 *Indiana Journal of Global Legal Studies* 397–411.

Phillimore, Robert, *Commentaries upon International Law* (3rd ed., London: Butterworths, 1879).

Pierik, Roland, 'Shared Responsibility in International Law. A Normative-Philosophical Analysis', in André Nollkaemper and Dov Jacobs (eds.), *Distribution of Responsibilities in International Law* (Cambridge: Cambridge University Press, 2015), pp. 36–61.

Pitea, Cesare, 'The Legal Status of NGOs in Environmental Non-Compliance Procedures: An Assessment of Law and Practice', in Pierre-Marie Dupuy and Luisa Vierucci (eds.), *NGOs in International Law: Efficiency in Flexibility?* (Cheltenham: Edward Elgar Publishing, 2008), pp. 181–203.

Plakokefalos, Ilias, 'The Use of Force by Non-state Actors and the Limits of Attribution of Conduct: A Reply to Vladyslav Lanovoy' (2017) 28 *European Journal of International Law* 587–593.

Posner, Eric, and Sykes, Alan O., 'An Economic Analysis of State and Individual Responsibility under International Law' (2007) 9 *American Law and Economics Review* 72–134.

Postema, Gerald J., 'Custom in International Law: A Normative Practice Account', in Amanda Perreau-Saussine and James Bernard Murphy (eds.), *The Nature of Customary Law: Legal Historical and Philosophical Perspectives* (Cambridge: Cambridge University Press, 2007), pp. 279–306.

Powles, Steven, 'Joint Criminal Enterprise: Criminal Liability by Prosecutorial Ingenuity and Judicial Creativity?' (2004) 2 *Journal of International Criminal Justice* 606–619.

Prost, Mario, 'Hierarchy and the Sources of International Law: A Critique' (2017) 39 *Houston Journal of International Law* 285–330.

Proulx, Vincent-Joël, *Transnational Terrorism and State Accountability: A New Theory of Prevention* (Oxford and Portland, OR: Hart Publishing, 2012).

Proulx, Vincent-Joël, 'An Uneasy Transition? Linkages between the Law of State Responsibility and the Law Governing the Responsibility of International Organizations', in Maurizio Ragazzi (ed.), *Responsibility of International Organizations: Essays in Memory of Sir Ian Brownlie* (Leiden: Martinus Nijhoff Publishers, 2013), pp. 109–120.

Proulx, Vincent-Joël, *Institutionalizing State Responsibility: Global Security and UN Organs* (Oxford: Oxford University Press, 2016).

Proulx, Vincent-Joël, 'The Marshall Islands Judgments and Multilateral Disputes at the World Court: Whither Access to International Justice?' (2017) 111 *AJIL Unbound* 96–101.

Proulx, Vincent-Joël, 'The World Court's Jurisdictional Formalism and Its Lost Market Share: The Marshall Islands Decisions and the Quest for a Suitable Dispute Settlement Forum for Multilateral Disputes' (2017) 30 *Leiden Journal of International Law* 925–946.

Proulx, Vincent-Joël, 'International Civil Individual Responsibility and the Security Council: Building the Foundations of a General Regime' (2019) 40 *Michigan Journal of International Law* 215–287.

Provost, René (ed.), *State Responsibility in International Law* (Dartmouth: Ashgate, 2002).

Quéneudec, Jean-Pierre, *La responsabilité internationale de l'État pour les fautes personelles de ses agents* (Paris: Pichon et Durand-Auzias, 1966).

Radetzki, Marcus, and Radetzki, Marian, 'Private Arrangements to Cover Large-Scale Liabilities Caused by Nuclear and Other Industrial Catastrophes' (2000) 25 *The Geneva Papers on Risk and Insurance* 180–195.

Ragazzi, Maurizio (ed.), *International Responsibility Today: Essays in Memory of Oscar Schachter* (Leiden and Boston: Martinus Nijhoff Publishers, 2005).

Ralph, Jason, 'International Society, the International Criminal Court and US Foreign Policy' (2005) 31 *Review of International Studies* 27–44.

Ratner, Steven R., 'The Schizophrenias of International Criminal Law' (1998) 33 *Texas International Law Journal* 237–256.

Ratner, Steven R., 'The International Criminal Court and the Limits of Global Judicialization' (2003) 38 *Texas International Law Journal* 445–454.

Raz, Joseph, 'The Rule of Law and Its Virtue', in Joseph Raz (ed.), *The Authority of Law: Essays on Law and Morality* (Oxford: Clarendon Press, 1970), pp. 210–229.

Recalde Vela, Maria Jose, 'Statelessness at the United Nations Compensation Commission', *Institute on Statelessness and Inclusion*, Statelessness Working Paper Series No. 2015/03, December 2015.

Redgwell, Catherine, 'The Wrong Trousers: State Responsibility and International Environmental Law', in Malcolm Evans and Panos Koutrakos (eds.), *The International Responsibility of the European Union: European and International Perspectives* (Oxford and Portland, OR: Hart Publishing, 2013), pp. 257–274.

Reid, Natalie L., 'Bridging the Conceptual Chasm: Superior Responsibility as the Missing Link between State and Individual Responsibility in International Law' (2005) 18 *Leiden Journal of International Law* 795–828.

Reis, Tarcísio Hardman, *Compensation for Environmental Damages under International Law: The Role of the International Judge* (Alphen aan den Rijn: Wolters Kluwer, 2011).

Reisman, Michael W., 'Legal Responses to Genocide and Other Massive Violations of Human Rights' (1996) 59 *Law & Contemporary Problems* 75–80.

Reuter, Paul, 'Principes de droit international public' (1961–II) 103 *Receuil des Cours Annuaire de Droit International* 425.

Reuter, Paul, *Droit International Public* (Paris: Dalloz, 1973).

Reuter, Paul, 'Trois observations sur le codification de la responsabilité international des Etats pour fait illicite' (1991) *Le droit international au service de la paix, de la justice et du développement. Etudes dédiées à la mémoire de Michel Virally* 389–398.

Reydams, Luc, 'Universal Jurisdiction over Atrocities in Rwanda: Theory and Practice' (1996) 4 *European Journal of Crime, Criminal Law and Criminal Justice* 18–47.

Roach Anleu, Sharyn L., 'The Role of Civil Sanctions in Social Control: A Socio-Legal Examination' (1998) 9 *Crime Prevention Studies* 21–43.

Roberts, Anthea, 'Traditional and Modern Approaches to Customary International Law: Reconciliation' (2001) 95 *American Journal of International Law* 757–791.

Romero Philips, Christen, 'The International Criminal Court & Deterrence. A Report to the Office of Global Criminal Justice, U.S. Department of State', *Stanford Law School: Law & Policy Lab*, June 2016.
Root, Elihu, 'The Basis of Protection to Citizens Residing Abroad' (1910) 4 *American Journal of International Law* 517–528.
Rosenfeld, Friedrich, 'Collective Reparations for Victims of Armed Conflicts' (2010) 92 *International Review of the Red Cross* 731–746.
Rosenstock, Robert, 'The ILC and State Responsibility' (2002) 96 *American Journal of International Law* 792–797.
Roth, Kenneth, 'Africa Attacks the International Criminal Court', *New York Review of Books*, 6 February 2014.
Roucounas, Emmanuel, 'Non-State Actors: Areas of International Responsibility in Need of Further Exploration', in Ragazzi, Maurizio (ed.), *International Responsibility Today: Essays in Memory of Oscar Schachter* (Leiden: Martinus Nijhoff Publishers, 2005), pp. 391–404.
Sabahi, Borzu, *Compensation and Restitution in Investor-State Arbitration: Principles and Practice* (New York: Oxford University Press, 2011).
Sachariew, Kamen, 'The Definition of Thresholds of Tolerance of Transboundary Environmental Injury Under International Law: Development and Present Status' (1990) 37 *Netherlands International Law Review* 193–206.
Sadat, Leila Nadya, *The International Criminal Court and the Transformation of International Law: Justice for the New Millennium* (Ardsley, New York: Transnational Publishers, 2002).
Sadat, Leila Nadya, 'The Legacy of the ICTY: The International Criminal Court' (2003) 37 *New England Law Review* 1073–1080.
Sadat, Leila Nadya, 'The French Experience', in M. Cherif Bassiouni (ed.), *International Criminal Law: Volume III. International Enforcement* (3rd ed., Leiden: Martinus Nijhoff Publishers, 2008), pp. 329–358.
Sadat, Leila Nadya, (ed.), *Seeking Accountability for the Unlawful Use of Force* (Cambridge: Cambridge University Press, 2018).
Sadat, Leila Nadya, and Carden, Richard S., 'The New International Criminal Court: An Uneasy Revolution' (1999–2000) 88 *Georgetown Law Journal* 381–474.
Saland, Per, 'International Criminal Law Principles', in Roy S. Lee (ed.), *The International Criminal Court: The Making of the Rome Statute* (The Hague: Kluwer Law International, 1999), pp. 189–216.
Sands, Philippe, *Principles of International Environmental Law* (2nd ed., Cambridge: Cambridge University Press, 2003).
Schabas, William A., *An Introduction to the International Criminal Court* (3rd ed., Cambridge: Cambridge University Press, 2007).
Schabas, William A., *War Crimes and Human Rights: Essays on the Death Penalty, Justice and Accountability* (London: Cameron May, 2008).
Schachter, Oscar, 'The Quasi-Judicial Rôle of the Security Council and the General Assembly' (1964) 58 *American Journal of International Law* 960–965.
Schachter, Oscar, 'The Emergence of International Environmental Law' (1991) 44 *Journal of International Affairs* 457–493.
Schachter, Oscar, *International Law in Theory and Practice* (Dordrecht: Martinus Nijhoff Publishers, 1991).

Scheffer, David J., 'Milosevic, Killing Fields, and "Kangaroo" Courts: Symposium on an Emerging International Criminal Justice System. Should the United States Join the International Criminal Court?' (2002) 9 *University of California Davis Journal of International Law & Policy* 45–52.

Schense, Jennifer, and Carter, Linda (eds.), *Two Steps Forward, One Step Back: The Deterrent Effect of International Criminal Tribunals* (Brussels: Torkel Opsahl Academic EPublisher, 2017).

Schmalenbach, Kirsten, 'Dispute Settlement', in Jan Klabbers and Åsa Wallendahl (eds.), *Research Handbook on the Law of International Organizations* (Cheltenham: Edward Elgar Publishing, 2011), pp. 251–284.

Schmitt, Michael N. (ed.), *Tallinn Manual 2.0 on the International Law Applicable to Cyber Operations* (Cambridge and New York: Cambridge University Press, 2017).

Schmitt, Michael N., and Vihul, Liis, 'Proxy Wars in Cyberspace: The Evolving International Law of Attribution' (2014) 1 *Fletcher Security Review* 53–72.

Schoen, Paul, *Die völkerrechtliche Haftung der Staaten aus unerlaubten Handlungen*, Ergänzungsheft 2, zur Zeitschrift für Völkerrecht Band X (Breslau: J. U. Kern's Verlag, 1917).

Schwartz, Priscilla, 'The Polluter-Pays Principle', in Malgosia Fitzmaurice, David M. Ong and Panos Merkouris (eds.), *Research Handbook on International Environmental Law* (Cheltenham: Edward Elgar Publishing Ltd, 2010), pp. 243–261.

Scobbie, Iain, 'The Invocation of Responsibility for the Breach of "Obligations under Peremptory Norms of General International Law"' (2002) 13 *European Journal of International Law* 1201–1220.

Scott, Sterling, 'Codification of State Responsibility in International Law: A Review and Assessment' (1985) 9 *ASILS International Law Journal* 1–36.

Scovazzi, Tullio, 'Some Remarks on International Responsibility in the Field of Environmental Protection', in Maurizio Ragazzi (ed.), *International Responsibility Today: Essays in Memory of Oscar Schachter* (Leiden: Martinus Nijhoff Publishers, 2005), pp. 209–222.

Shelton, Dinah, 'Protecting Human Rights in a Globalized World' (2002) 25 *Boston College International and Comparative Law Review* 273–322.

Shelton, Dinah, 'Righting Wrongs: Reparations in the Articles on State Responsibility' (2002) 96 *American Journal of International Law* 833–856.

Shelton, Dinah, 'Normative Hierarchy in International Law' (2006) 100 *American Journal of International Law* 291–323.

Shelton, Dinah, *Remedies in International Human Rights Law* (2nd ed., Oxford: Oxford University Press, 2006).

Shiju, M. V., 'Standard of Liability under the Cartagena Protocol', in K. D. Raju (ed.), *Genetically Modified Organisms: Emerging Law and Policy in India* (New Delhi: Teri Press, 2007), pp. 79–91.

Short, Nicola, 'The Role of NGOs in the Ottawa Process to Ban Landmines' (1999) 4 *International Negotiation* 481–500.

Sicilianos, Linos-Alexander, 'The Classification of Obligations and the Multilateral Dimension of the Relations of International Responsibility' (2002) 13 *European Journal of International Law* 1127–1145.

Simma, Bruno, 'Bilateralism and Community Interest in the Law of State Responsibility', in Yoram Dinstein (ed.), *International Law at a Time of Perplexity: Essays in Honour of Shabtai Rosenne* (Dordrecht: Martinus Njihoff Publishers, 1989), pp. 821–844.

Simma, Bruno, 'From Bilateralism to Community Interest in International Law' (1994–VI) 250 *Receuil des Cours* 217–384.

Simma, Bruno, 'Universality of International Law from the Perspective of a Practitioner' (2009) 20 *European Journal of International Law* 265–297.

Simma, Bruno, and Pulkowski, Dirk, 'Of Planets and the Universe: Self-Contained Regimes in International Law' (2006) 17 *European Journal of International Law* 483–529.

Simma, Bruno, and Pulkowski, Dirk, 'Leges Speciales and Self-Contained Regimes', in James Crawford, Alain Pellet and Simon Olleson (eds.), *The Law of International Responsibility* (Oxford: Oxford University Press, 2010), pp. 139–163.

Simpson, Gerry, *Law, War & Crime: War Crimes Trials and the Reinvention of International Law* (Cambridge, Malden: Polity Press, 2007).

Skouteris, Thomas, 'The Vocabulary of Progress in Interwar International Law: An Intellectual Portrait of Stelios Seferiades' (2005) 16 *European Journal of International Law* 823–856.

Skouteris, Thomas, *The Notion of Progress in International Law Discourse* (The Hague: T. M. C. Asser Press, 2010).

Sloane, Robert, 'The Expressive Capacity of International Punishment: The Limits of National Law Analogy and the Potential of International Criminal Law' (2007) 43 *Stanford Journal of International Law* 39–94.

Sloane, Robert D., 'On the Use and Abuse of Necessity in the Law of State Responsibility' (2012) 106 *American Journal of International Law* 447–508.

Smeulers, Alette, 'Punishing the Enemies of All Mankind' (2008) 21 *Leiden Journal of International Law* 971–993.

Smeulers, Alette, and van Niekerk, Sander, 'Abu Ghraib and the War on Terror – A Case Against Donald Rumsfeld?' (2009) 51 *Crime, Law and Social Change* 327–349.

Snyder, Jack, and Vinjamuri, Leslie, 'Trials and Errors: Principle and Pragmatism in Strategies of International Justice' (2003/2004) 28 *International Security* 5–44.

Sohn, Louis B., and Baxter, Richard, 'Responsibility of States for Injuries to the Economic Interests of Aliens' (1961) 55 *American Journal of International Law* 545–584.

Soltau, Friedrich, *Fairness in International Climate Change Law and Policy* (New York: Cambridge University Press, 2009).

Sorel, Jean-Marc, 'The Concept of "Soft Responsibility"?' in James Crawford, Alain Pellet and Simon Olleson (eds.), *The Law of International Responsibility* (Oxford: Oxford University Press, 2010), pp. 165–171.

Sotaniemi, Anna, 'Elements of the Nordic Practice: The Nordic Countries in Co-ordination' (2003) 72 *Nordic Journal of International Law* 521–535.

Spijkers, Otto, 'What's Running the World: Global Values, International Law and the United Nations' (2009–2010) 4 *Interdisciplinary Journal of Human Rights Law* 67–87.

Stacy, Helen, 'Criminalizing Culture', in Larry May and Zachary Hoskins (eds.), *International Criminal Law and Philosophy* (New York: Cambridge University Press, 2010), pp. 75–90.

Stockburger, Peter Z., 'Control and Capabilities Test: Toward a New Lex Specialis Governing State Responsibility for Third Party Cyber Incidents', in H. Roigas, R. Jakschis, L. Lindström and T. Minárik (eds.), *Defending the Core, 9th International Conference on Cyber Conflict* (Tallinn: NATO CCD COE Publications, 2017), pp. 149–162.

Strandberg, Hugo, *Escaping My Responsibility. Investigations into the Nature of Morality* (Frankfurt am Main: Peter Lang, 2009).

Stromseth, Jane, 'Justice on the Ground: Can International Criminal Courts Strengthen Domestic Rule of Law in Post-Conflict Societies?' (2009) 1 *Hague Journal on the Rule of Law* 89–97.

Strupp, Karl, *Das völkerrechtliche Delikt* (Stuttgart: W. Karlhammer, 1920).

Strupp, Karl, *Éléments du droit international public universel, européen et americain* (2nd ed., Paris: Les Éditions Internationales, 1930).

Suganami, Hidemi, *The Domestic Analogy and World Order Proposals* (Cambridge: Cambridge University Press, 1989).

Swart, Bert, 'Modes of International Criminal Liability', in Antonio Cassese (ed.), *The Oxford Companion to International Criminal Justice* (Oxford: Oxford University Press, 2009), pp. 82–93.

Székely, Alberto, '"General Principles" and "Planned Measures" Provisions in the International Law Commission's Draft Articles on the Non-Navigational Uses of International Watercourses: A Mexican Point of View' (1992) 3 *Colorado Journal of International Environmental Law & Policy* 93–101.

Tallgren, Immi, 'We Did It? The Vertigo of Law and Everyday Life at the Diplomatic Conference on the Establishment of an International Criminal Court' (1999) 12 *Leiden Journal of International Law* 683–707.

Tallgren, Immi, 'La Grande Illusion' (2002) 15 *Canadian Journal of Law and Jurisprudence* 297–316.

Tallgren, Immi, 'The Sense and Sensibility of International Criminal Law' (2002) 13 *European Journal of International Law* 561–595.

Tallgren, Immi, and Skouteris, Thomas, 'Editors' Introduction', in Immi Tallgren and Thomas Skouteris (eds.), *The New Histories of International Criminal Law: Retrials* (Oxford: Oxford University Press, 2019), pp. 1–11.

Talmon, Stefan, 'A Plurality of Responsible Actors: International Responsibility for Acts of the Coalition Provisional Authority in Iraq', in Phil Shiner and Andrew Williams (eds.), *The Iraqi War and International Law* (Oxford and Portland, OR: Hart Publishing, 2008), pp. 185–230.

Tams, Christian, 'Unity and Diversity in the Law of State Responsibility', in Andreas Zimmerman and Rainer Hoffmann (eds.), *Unity and Diversity in International Law. Proceedings of an International Symposium of the Kiel Walther Schücking Institute of International Law November 4–7, 2004* (Berlin: Duncker & Humblot, 2006), pp. 435–458.

Tams, Christian J., *Enforcing Obligations Erga Omnes in International Law* (Cambridge: Cambridge University Press, 2005).

Tams, Christian J., 'The Use of Force against Terrorists' (2009) 20 *European Journal of International Law* 359–397.

Tams, Christian J., 'Individual States as Guardians of Community Interests', in Ulrich Fastenrath, Rudolf Geiger, Daniel-Erasmus Khan et al. (eds.), *From Bilateralism to Community Interest: Essays in Honour of Judge Bruno Simma* (Oxford: Oxford University Press, 2011), pp. 379–405.

Tams, Christian J., 'Law-making in Complex Processes: The World Court and the Modern Law of State Responsibility', in Christine Chinkin and Freya Baetens (eds.), *Sovereignty, Statehood and State Responsibility: Essays in Honour of James Crawford* (Cambridge: Cambridge University Press, 2015), pp. 287–306.

Tams, Christian J., and Asteriti, Alessandra, 'Erga Omnes, Jus Cogens and Their Impact on the Law of Responsibility', in Malcolm Evans and Panos Koutrakos (eds.), *International Responsibility of the European Union: European and International Perspectives* (Oxford and Portland, OR: Hart Publishing, 2013), pp. 163–188.

Tasioulas, John, 'Customary International Law and the Quest for Global Justice', in Amanda Perreau-Saussine and James Bernard Murphy (eds.), *The Nature of Customary Law: Legal Historical and Philosophical Perspectives* (Cambridge: Cambridge University Press, 2007), pp. 307–335.

Templeton, Jessica, and Kohler, Pia, 'Implementation and Compliance under the Minamata Convention on Mercury' (2014) 23 *Review of European Community & International Environmental Law* 211–220.

Teubner, Günther, 'The Invisible Cupola: From Causal to Collective Attribution in Ecological Liability' (1994–1995) 16 *Cardozo Law Review* 429–464.

Thirlway, H. W. A, *International Customary Law and Codification* (Leiden: A.W Sijthoff, 1972).

Tietenberg, Thomas H., *Emissions Trading: An Exercise in Reforming Pollution Policy* (Washington, DC: Resources for the Future Inc., 1985).

Tiewul, S. Azadon, 'International Law and Nuclear Test Explosions on the High Seas' (1974–1975) 8 *Cornell International Law Journal* 45–70.

Togas, Marie-Louise, 'La responsabilité internationale d'État pour le fait d'entreprises militaires privées' (2008) 45 *Annuaire Canadien de droit international* 97–130.

Tomuschat, Christian, 'The Complementarity of International Treaty Law, Customary International Law, and Non-Contractual Lawmaking: Comment by Christian Tomuschat', in Rüdiger Wolfrum and Volken Röber (eds.), *Developments of International Law in Treaty Making* (Berlin: Springer, 2005), pp. 401–408.

Tomuschat, Christian, 'Global Warming and State Responsibility', in Holger Hestermeyer, Nele Matz-Lück, Anja Seibert-Fohr and Silja Vöneky (eds.), *Law of the Sea in Dialogue* (Heidelberg: Springer, 2011), pp. 3–30.

Tondini, Matteo, 'Coalitions of the Willing', in André Nollkaemper and Ilias Plakokefalos (eds.), *The Practice of Shared Responsibility in International Law* (Cambridge: Cambridge University Press, 2017), pp. 701–732.

Townsend, Gregory, 'State Responsibility for Acts of De Facto Agents' (1997) 14 *Arizona Journal of International and Comparative Law* 635–678.

Trachtman, Joel P., 'Reports of the Death of Treaty Are Premature, but Customary International Law May Have Outlived Its Usefulness' (2014) 108 *AJIL Unbound* 36–40.

Trapp, Kimberley, *State Responsibility for International Terrorism: Problems and Prospects* (Oxford: Oxford University Press, 2011).

Triffterer, Otto, 'The Preventive and Repressive Function of the International Criminal Court', in Mauro Politi and Giuseppe Nesi (eds.), *The Rome Statute of the International Criminal Court: A Challenge to Impunity* (Ashgate: Aldershot, 2001), pp. 137–175.

Ulfstein, Geir, 'Reflections on Institutional Design – Especially Treaty Bodies', in Jan Klabbers and Åsa Wallendahl (eds.), *Research Handbook on the Law of International Organizations* (Cheltenham: Edward Elgar Publishing Ltd, 2011), pp. 431–447.

Ulfstein, Geir, Marauhn Thilo, and Zimmerman, Andreas, 'Introduction', in Geir Ulfstein, Thilo Marauhn and Andreas Zimmerman (eds.), *Making Treaties Work: Human Rights, Environment and Arms Control* (Cambridge: Cambridge University Press, 2007), pp. 3–12.

van Aaken, Anne, 'Fragmentation of International Law: The Case of International Investment Law' (2006) XVII *Finnish Yearbook of International Law* 91–130.

van Aaken, Anne, 'Shared Responsibility in International Law: A Political Economy Analysis', in André Nollkaemper and Dov Jacobs (eds.), *Distribution of Responsibilities in International Law* (Cambridge: Cambridge University Press, 2015), pp. 153–191.

van der Wilt, Harmen, 'Corporate Criminal Responsibility for International Crimes: Exploring the Possibilities' (2013) 12 *Chinese Journal of International Law* 43–77.

van der Wilt, Harmen, 'Sreberenica: On Joint Criminal Enterprise, Aiding and Abetting and Command Responsibility' (2015) 62 *Netherlands International Law Review* 229–241.

van Sliedregt, Elies, *The Criminal Responsibility of Individuals for Violations of International Humanitarian Law* (The Hague: T.M.C. Asser Press, 2003).

van Sliedregt, Elies, 'Joint Criminal Enterprise as a Pathway to Convicting Individuals for Genocide' (2007) 5 *Journal of International Criminal Justice* 184–207.

Veitch, Scott, *Law and Irresponsibility. On the Legitimation of Human Suffering* (Oxon: Routledge-Cavendish, 2007).

Venzke, Ingo, 'Public Interests in the International Court of Justice – A Comparison between Nuclear Arms Race (2016) and South West Africa (1966)' (2017) 111 *AJIL Unbound* 68–74.

Vermeer-Künzli, Annemarieke, 'As If: The Legal Fiction in Diplomatic Protection' (2007) 18 *European Journal of International Law* 37–68.

Vermeer-Künzli, Annemarieke, 'A Matter of Interest: Diplomatic Protection and State Responsibility Erga Omnes' (2007) 56 *International and Comparative Law Quarterly* 553–581.

Villalpando, Santiago, 'Codification Light: A New Trend in the Codification of International Law at the United Nations' (2013) 8 *Anuário Brasileiro de Direito Internacional* 117–156.

Visscher, Charles, *La responsabilité des États* (Leiden, Lugduni Batavorum: Brill, 1924).

Voigt, Christina, 'State Responsibility for Climate Change Damages' (2008) 77 *Nordic Journal of International Law* 1–22.

von Jhering, Rudolf, *Das Schuldmoment im römischen Privatrecht: Eine Festchrift* (Giessen: E. Roth, 1867).

von Martens, Georg Friedrich, *Causes célèbres du droit des gens. Tome premier* (Leipzig and Ponthieu: F. A. Brockhaus, 1827).

Voyiakis, Emmanuel, 'International Law and the Objectivity of Value' (2009) 22 *Leiden Journal of International Law* 51–78.

Waibel, Michael, 'The Diplomatic Channel', in James Crawford, Alain Pellet and Simon Olleson (eds.), *The Law of International Responsibility* (Oxford: Oxford University Press, 2010), pp. 1085–1097.

Walker, Nigel, *Punishment, Danger and Stigma: The Morality of Criminal Justice* (Totowa: Barnes and Noble Books, 1980).

Wang, Hui, 'Transboundary Vessel-Source Marine Pollution – International Legal Framework and Its Application to China', in Michael Faure and Song Ying (eds.), *China and International Environmental Liability: Legal Remedies for Transboundary Pollution* (Cheltenham: Edward Elgar Publishing, 2008), pp. 64–106.

Wang, Hui, *Civil Liability for Marine Oil Pollution Damage: A Comparative and Economic Study of the International, US and Chinese Compensation Regimes* (Alphen aan den Rijn: Kluwer Law International, 2011).

Watts, Sir Arthur, 'The Art of Apology', in Maurizio Ragazzi (ed.), *International Responsibility Today: Essays in Memory of Oscar Schachter* (Leiden: Martinus Nijhoff Publishers, 2005), pp. 107–116.

Weil, Prosper, 'Towards Relative Normativity in International Law?' (1983) 77 *American Journal of International Law* 413–442.

Weiler, Joseph H. H., Cassese, Antonio, and Spinedi, Marina (eds.), *International Crimes of States: A Critical Analysis of the ILC's Draft Article 19 on State Responsibility* (Berlin and New York: de Gruyter, 1988).

Weiss Brown, Edith, 'The Rise or the Fall of International Law' (2000) 69 *Fordham Law Review* 345–372.

Werksman, Jacob, 'Compliance and Transition: Russia's Non-Compliance Tests the Ozone Regime' (1996) 56 *Zeitschrift für ausländisches öffentliches Recht und Völkerrecht* 750–773.

White, Nigel D., 'Responses of Political Organs to Crimes by States', in André Nollkaemper and Harmen van der Wilt (eds.), *System Criminality in International Law* (Cambridge: Cambridge University Press, 2009), pp. 314–337.

Willisch, Jan, *State Responsibility for Technological Damage in International Law* (Berlin: Duncker and Humblot, 1987).

Wippman, David, 'Atrocities, Deterrence, and the Limits of International Justice' (1999) 23 *Fordham International Law Journal* 473–488.

Wittich, Stephan, 'Punitive Damages', in James Crawford, Alain Pellet and Simon Olleson (eds.), *The Law of International Responsibility* (Oxford: Oxford University Press, 2010), pp. 667–675.

Wolff, Christian, *Jus Gentium Methodo Scientifica Pertractatum* (1764) (1st published 1750, trans. Joseph H. Drake, Oxford: Clarendon Press, 1934).

Wolfrum, Rüdiger, 'State Responsibility for Private Actors: An Old Problem of Renewed Relevance', in Maurizio Ragazzi (ed.), *International Responsibility Today: Essays in Memory of Oscar Schachter* (Leiden: Martinus Nijhoff Publishers, 2005), pp. 423–434.

Xue, Hanqin, *Transboundary Damage in International Law* (Cambridge: Cambridge University Press, 2003).

Yarwood, Lisa, *State Accountability under International Law: Holding States Accountable for a Breach of Jus Cogens Norms* (London and New York: Routledge, 2011).

Yihdego, Zeray, and Rieu-Clarke, Alistair, 'An Exploration of Fairness in International Law through the Blue Nile and GERD' (2016) 41 *Water International* 528–549.

Zemanek, Karl, 'Does the Prospect of Incurring Responsibility Improve the Observance of International Law', in Maurizio Ragazzi (ed.), *International Responsibility Today: Essays in Memory of Oscar Schachter* (Leiden: Martinus Nijhoff Publishers, 2005), pp. 125–134.

Zorzetto, Silvia, 'The Lex Specialis Principle and Its Uses in Legal Argumentation: An Analytical Inquire' (2012–2013), *Eunomia. Revista en Cultura de la Legalidad* 61–87.

# Index

www.ingramcontent.com/pod-product-compliance
Lightning Source LLC
LaVergne TN
LVHW011702200926
848484LV00004B/1044